Development and Growth
in the Mexican Economy

Development and Growth
in the Mexican Economy

A Historical Perspective

JUAN CARLOS MORENO-BRID

JAIME ROS

OXFORD
UNIVERSITY PRESS
2009

OXFORD
UNIVERSITY PRESS

Oxford University Press, Inc., publishes works that further
Oxford University's objective of excellence
in research, scholarship, and education.

Oxford   New York
Auckland   Cape Town   Dar es Salaam   Hong Kong   Karachi
Kuala Lumpur   Madrid   Melbourne   Mexico City   Nairobi
New Delhi   Shanghai   Taipei   Toronto

With offices in
Argentina   Austria   Brazil   Chile   Czech Republic   France   Greece
Guatemala   Hungary   Italy   Japan   Poland   Portugal   Singapore
South Korea   Switzerland   Thailand   Turkey   Ukraine   Vietnam

Published by Oxford University Press, Inc.
198 Madison Avenue, New York, New York 10016

www.oup.com

Oxford is a registered trademark of Oxford University Press.

Library of Congress Cataloging-in-Publication Data
Moreno-Brid, Juan Carlos.
Development and growth in the Mexican economy : a historical perspective /
Juan Carlos Moreno-Brid and Jaime Ros.
p. cm.
Includes bibliographical references and index.
ISBN 978-0-19-537116-1
1. Mexico—Economic conditions—19th century.
2. Mexico—Economic conditions—20th century.
I. Ros, Jaime. II. Title.
HC135.M728 2009
330.972—dc22   2008031944

The opinions here expressed are the authors' own responsibility. J. C. Moreno-Brid
states that these opinions may not necessarily coincide with those of the United Nations
Organization or of the Economic Commission for Latin America and the Caribbean.

1 3 5 7 9 8 6 4 2
Printed in the United States of America
on acid-free paper

To Leonora

—J.C.M.B.

To the memory of my parents

—J.R.

Preface

This book undertakes two tasks. First, it provides an overview of Mexico's economic development since independence. Second, it presents a reevaluation of Mexico's development policies during the state-led industrialization period from 1940 to 1982 and during the more recent market reform process, a reevaluation that is critical of the dominant trend in the economic literature and, indeed, revisionist. Both tasks are addressed with a common conceptual framework that compares the successive periods of stagnation and growth that have characterized Mexico's economic development since independence. The book's basic premise is that a historical approach may be helpful in illuminating current obstacles to economic development. It thus looks at Mexico's present development policies and problems from a historical perspective by reviewing long-term trends in the Mexican economy and examining in particular some past episodes of radical shifts in development strategy and in the role of markets and the state.

The book has its origins in a paper published in 1994 (Moreno-Brid and Ros, 1994) on Mexico's market reforms in a historical perspective. The paper was written in 1992 after the debt crisis and the lost decade of the 1980s were over and at a time when capital was flowing back to the Mexican economy, which was seen by many observers as a model for the rest of Latin America. Despite the fact that the worst was over, our paper expressed great skepticism about the long-term prospects for economic growth in Mexico. The reasons were that the market reforms undertaken by successive Mexican governments since 1983 were not addressing the fundamental obstacles to economic growth. Time was to prove us right. Soon after our paper was published, a severe financial crisis interrupted the moderate recovery of the early 1990s, causing the greatest decline in the level of output since the Great Depression of the 1930s, and again in the early 2000s the economy plunged into a new recession that caused a decrease in per capita income for three consecutive years. As a result, since 1990 the economy has grown at a slow pace and the performance of labor productivity growth has been even poorer. This mediocre performance has taken place in the midst of increased volatility in the level of economic activity. These developments led us to update the original paper and publish a new version in 2004, 10 years after the North American Free Trade Agreement (NAFTA) went into effect (Moreno-Brid and Ros, 2004). In the meantime, we initiated the more ambitious task of developing our arguments into a book that would provide a more detailed treatment of our theses on Mexico's economic history.

The book aims to answer the following questions: (1) How have the fundamental obstacles to Mexico's economic and social development been changing over time? (2) Which of these obstacles have had a structural nature (such as the high degree of income and wealth inequality or the fiscal weakness of the state) and which ones have had a short-term nature, such as those originating in temporary external shocks? (3) How have the perceptions (and misperceptions) of the constraints on growth changed in different key periods and how have they affected the design of development policy? (4) What lessons does historical experience give us about the current obstacles to economic development and to what extent current development policy will relax or not the constraints on long-term economic growth?

The book's value is not based on the use of historical primary sources. Its analysis is one of applied development economics written by economists rather than historians, with a scope that has no parallel in the existing literature on Mexico's economic development. Its contribution is to give an interpretation (from an unconventional analytical perspective) of the evolution of the Mexican economy over the past 2 centuries. For this we have relied heavily on the work of economic historians, in particular the recent and rapidly expanding literature on Mexico's economic history, and the available statistical information on the historical performance of the Mexican economy.[1]

---

1. Among the important and easily accessible sources of information on the historical performance of the Mexican economy the following stand out: INEGI's Banco de

The book also draws on the development economics literature, and in particular on alternative views of what drives development: the role of geography, institutions, state and markets, foreign trade, inequality in the distribution of income and wealth, external shocks, and political instability.

We are grateful to the following colleagues for thoughtful and constructive comments at different stages of this research project: Ernie Bartell, Ted Beatty, Robert Blecker, Victor Bulmer-Thomas, José Casar, Rolando Cordera, Victor Godínez, Carlos Guerrero de Lizardi, Carlos Ibarra, David Ibarra, Leonardo Lomelí, Julio López, Nora Lustig, José Luis Machinea, Carlos Marichal, Trinidad Martínez Tarragó, Kevin Middlebrook, José Antonio Ocampo, Carlo Panico, Esteban Pérez, Martín Puchet, Tania Rabasa, María Eugenia Romero Sotelo, Pablo Ruiz Nápoles, Carlos Tello, Samuel Valenzuela, and Jeffrey Williamson. Three anonymous referees also provided extremely useful comments. We are grateful to Elda Cervantes, Charles Cummings, Rubén Guerrero, and Jesús Santamaría for their valuable research assistance. We are also thankful to Catherine Rae, Liz Smith, Terry Vaughn, and their team at Oxford University Press for a superb job in turning a manuscript into a completed book and for continuous support throughout the process.

Información Económica (http://www.inegi.gob.mx/inegi), Banco de México (http://www. banxico.org.mx), the Asociación Mexicana de Historia Económica, (http://www.amhe.org. mx), and Oxford Latin American Economic History Database (http://oxlad.qeh.ox.ac.uk).

Contents

Development and Growth
in the Mexican Economy

1

Introduction

Aim and scope of the book

The economic history of independent Mexico appears as a succession of periods of stagnation or decline followed by periods of economic prosperity and transformation. The first period, from independence to about 1870, features five decades lost to economic development. This is the period during which, as Coatsworth (1978) has shown, Mexico's economic backwardness originates. From being a relatively prosperous region in the world economy at the end of the colonial period—with an income per capita of about 60% of that of the United States (see table 1.1)—by 1870 Mexico's gross domestic product (GDP) per capita had fallen by more than 10% with respect to its level five decades earlier (and probably much more with respect to its level on the eve of the independence wars). In the meantime, the gap with respect to the United States soared, with its income level falling to nearly one-quarter of the U.S. level, a gap that with minor ups and downs has remained since then (see table 1.1).

The causes of this economic decline are well known. The most important was probably the prolonged period of political instability rooted in a permanent conflict between liberals and conservatives. Half a century of civil and international wars, along with general social chaos and a lack of effective civil administration, destroyed the potentially beneficial effects of independence while curtailing the resources needed by the state and the private

3

Table 1.1 Mexico per capita GDP as a percentage of U.S. level, Latin America average, and world average

	U.S. level	Latin America average	World average
1820	60.4	109.8	113.9
1870	27.6	99.7	77.2
1910	34.1	115.9[a]	113.5[a]
1940	26.4	95.8	94.4
1970	28.7	108.3	115.6
1981	35.6	125.4	148.1
2003	24.6	123.4	109.5
2006	25.0	119.0	110.3

Source: Data for 1820–2003 based on Maddison (2006); data for 2006 estimated by the authors based on World Bank, World Development Indicators (WDI) (using per capita GDP in constant US$).
[a] 1913.

sector to reactivate the mining industry and improve transport infrastructure. This severely constrained the division of labor and regional specialization in a country where the lack of natural means of communication resulted in very high transport costs. In addition, and somewhat paradoxically, independence had some adverse effects on the mining sector—such as the loss of low-cost and guaranteed supplies of mercury from Spain—which partially counteracted the elimination of the fiscal burden, estimated to be much higher than that imposed by British colonialism on its North American colonies. The elimination of foreign trade restrictions also turned out to be a mixed blessing, as it accelerated the diversion of Mexico's foreign trade from Spain to the emerging industrializing powers of the North Atlantic, a trend that was highly adverse to the national manufacturing sector and thus to the main economic activity that could have compensated for the decline of the mining sector. Moreover, institutional modernization proceeded slowly in a regressive political and social order in a country with some of the largest economic and social disparities in the world, where a number of institutional arrangements tended to increase, rather than reduce, the gap between the private and social benefits of economic activity.

This first and prolonged period of decline was followed by one of sustained economic growth that begins with the restoration of the republic and accelerates during the *Porfiriato*, the 33-year period during which Porfirio Diaz governed Mexico as a dictator. Between 1870 and 1910, Mexico's income per capita grew at about 2.3% per year (Maddison, 2006), a rate greater than that of the then most economically advanced regions. Thus income per capita increased from less than 28% to more than 33% as a percentage of the U.S. level and from about 33% to 50% of Western European levels. Performance with respect to Spain was particularly remarkable: by 1910, income per capita was almost 90% of the Spanish level (compared to a little over 50% in 1870).

This rapid expansion, the beginning of modern economic growth in Mexico, proceeded as the old obstacles to economic development fell one after another: political instability ended following the establishment of a strong state; transport costs fell dramatically with the arrival of the railroads, allowing the emergence of an integrated national market with its positive effects on the division of labor and regional specialization; a process of institutional modernization in the areas of mining, banking, and commerce made the development of a banking system possible and attracted capital from abroad; and an embryonic industrial policy, based mainly on selective protection of domestic markets, together with the gradual depreciation of the real exchange rate, favored the emergence of a modern manufacturing industry. To these domestic changes one must add a favorable international economic environment, as the transportation revolution and the growing demand for raw materials in emerging industrial powers led to an export boom that effectively worked as an engine of growth.

The process of rapid economic growth during the *Porfiriato* came to an end with the 1910 revolution and the start of a second period in which the economy grew slowly on average and declined relative to the advanced regions of the world economy. In the 30 years between 1910 and 1940, per capita GDP grew on average at a rate of 0.5% per year (INEGI, 1999a; 0.3% according to Maddison, 2006). U.S. per capita GDP as a ratio of the Mexican level, which had fallen from 3.6 in 1870 to 2.9 in 1910, increased again to 3.8 in 1930 and remained constant until 1940. The process of retrogression is evident also with respect to the larger Latin American economies: Mexico's per capita GDP fell with respect to the levels prevailing in these economies with the exception of Argentina and Chile.

Economic stagnation during this period can be explained by internal political shocks, beginning with the revolution, and its sequel of several years of political instability, together with external economic shocks, including the Great Depression. It is interesting to note, however, that the disruptive effects of the revolution on economic activity appear to have been less than conventional wisdom suggests. In particular, the revolution did not prevent the continuity of the export boom of the *Porfiriato*, on top of which the first oil boom in Mexico's history took place. At the same time, the adverse effects of the Great Depression, exacerbated by the adoption of procyclical policies of balanced budgets and monetary contraction, were much greater than generally believed.

The legacy of the initial revolutionary period was the consolidation of a developmental state during the presidency of Lázaro Cárdenas (1934–1940), which opened the door to the next period, a phase of the fastest economic growth in Mexico's history. This period comprises the boom during World War II, the period from 1945 to 1955 of rapid growth with recurrent balance of payments crises, and the years of "stabilizing development" that combined macroeconomic stability with an acceleration of economic growth from 1956 to 1970. For the entire period, per capita GDP grew at a rate of 3.2% per year (INEGI, 1999a), the highest growth rate among the largest Latin American economies (with the exception of Brazil and Venezuela), and total GDP grew at a rate of 6.4%, with manufacturing as the engine of growth expanding at an annual rate of more than 8% (INEGI, 1999a). The gap with respect to the United States narrowed and per capita GDP increased from less than to greater than the world average (see table 1.1).

Economic and social transformations during this period were impressive. Society was transformed from an agrarian one into an urban, semi-industrial one in the midst of a demographic boom, the share of investment and manufacturing industries in total output soared, and the literacy rate and life expectancy jumped (see table A.3). What factors account for this outstanding performance? The short answer has to do with the prevailing development policies, geared towards the country's rapid industrialization. The long answer must explain why this development policy framework was more successful than in other countries with similar strategies and how, unlike what happened in many other Latin American countries, rapid growth was reconciled with relative macroeconomic stability. This answer includes, first, the impressive performance of agriculture up to the mid-1960s, associated in part with the land reform of the 1930s and the massive public irrigation projects and other infrastructure investments in the 1940s and 1950s. Second, the composition of public spending was heavily biased toward investments in economic development and made it possible to break the bottlenecks that naturally arise in any process of rapid growth. Third, Mexico's protectionism was successful in promoting industrialization, while at the same time, the size of the domestic market and the relatively low levels of effective protection maintained the costs of protection, both static and dynamic, at low levels. The large labor reserves, associated with the dualistic nature of the economy, also prevented the crowding out effects on labor employed in the export sectors of the economy, which in more mature economies (as in the Argentine one) exacerbated the antiexport bias of industrial protection.

The strong growth performance of the 1940–1970 period continued in the 1970s and up until 1981, although in the context of the external shocks and macroeconomic imbalances that led to growing external indebtedness, high inflation, and balance of payments crises in 1976–1977 and 1982. Preceded by this loss of macroeconomic stability during the 1970s, a new phase began in the early 1980s. Just as with the five lost decades of the 19th century and the initial revolutionary period between 1910 and 1940, these last 25 years appear in the historical context as a period of economic regress, with per capita GDP growing at an annual rate of only 0.6% (World Bank, World Development Indicators), similar to that recorded from 1910 to 1940. Since 1990, following the debt crisis, growth performance has been better, but still per capita GDP has expanded at a rate of only 1.6% per year amidst great volatility in the level of economic activity (World Bank, World Development Indicators). The growth of per capita income has not only fallen below the historical experience of the period before the debt crisis, it has also fallen short of the growth performance of most regions in the world economy, Latin America and the Caribbean included. By 2006, per capita GDP had fallen to one-quarter of the U.S. level, lower even than the percentage achieved in 1870 at the beginning of the process of modern economic growth (see table 1.1).

Unlike explanations that emphasize the slowdown of productivity growth, which in our view is a consequence rather than a cause of the slow rate of economic growth, or a sluggish rate of human capital formation, we believe that the direct cause of the slow growth process is the low rate of investment in physical capital that has characterized this period. In turn, the lower rate of capital accumulation is related to a number of factors. First, the sharp decrease in the rate of public investment, particularly in the area of infrastructure, a legacy of the fiscal adjustments in the face of the debt and oil crises of the 1980s, has contributed directly to a slower rate of capital formation in the public sector and possibly also, through crowding in effects, in the private sector. Second, a recurrent trend toward real exchange rate appreciation—which has resulted from the macroeconomic stabilization process of the 1990s and an exclusive focus on the part of the monetary authorities on the reduction of inflation—and the dismantling of all types of investment incentives, a casualty of the dismantling of industrial policy resulting from the structural reforms of the 1980s and 1990s, have caused a decrease in the profitability of private investment in the tradable goods sectors. Finally, the contraction of bank credit for productive activities, an outcome of the financial crisis of the mid-1990s that followed an ill-designed financial privatization and liberalization program, has prevented the realization of potentially profitable investment projects.

What features do the episodes of rapid growth have in common? In addition to political stability and a favorable international economic environment, we believe that there are three ingredients. The first is the establishment of a consensus on economic policy: the positivist consensus in the case of the *Porfiriato*, and the "developmentalist" consensus during the golden decades from World War II to 1970. Each of these consensuses appears in turn as a synthesis of previously opposed views. In the case of the *Porfiriato*, it was a synthesis of the market reforms and the institutional modernization supported by the liberals and the focus on industrialization emphasized by the conservatives. During the 30 years starting with World War II, and particularly during the period of stabilizing development, a consensus also emerged between the more orthodox views that underlined the need for macroeconomic stability and the priority for growth and industrialization advocated by those adopting more Keynesian and nationalistic views.

The periods of economic expansion feature also, and this is the second element, the presence of correct perceptions by the political and economic elites on the binding constraints on economic development. The regime of Porfirio Díaz, in addition to achieving political stability, focused on obstacles to economic development at the time such as high transport costs and the lack of financial capital. An example of these correct perceptions is the following succinct statement by Matías Romero, a minister of finance on four occasions under Benito Juárez and Porfirio Díaz: "This nation . . . has in its soil immense treasures of agricultural and mineral wealth, which now cannot be exploited due to the lack of capital and communications" (cited by Rosenzweig, 1965, translation by the authors). Similarly, the way out of the Great Depression in the 1930s, which will open the door to the second period of economic growth, can be attributed to a change in approach to the macroeconomic role of the state that, influenced by the Keynesian ideas of the time, was promoted by President Lázaro Cárdenas and his minister of finance, Eduardo Suárez.

Third, and this is what planted the seeds of their eventual demise, the periods of expansion featured a very unequal distribution of the benefits of economic growth, which in turn led to the loss of consensus in the subsequent periods of stagnation. Toward the end of the *Porfiriato*, in a society that was still predominantly agrarian, 835 families owned 95% of all the arable land while more than 70% of the population was illiterate and survived in conditions of meager subsistence. At the close of the stabilizing development period, the poorest 40% of the population earned less than 11% of total income, while the richest 10% appropriated four times that amount. The Gini concentration coefficient was among the highest in the world (more than 0.5) and the distribution of income had not improved compared to 1950 (see table A.7). Using a nutrition-based poverty line, almost one-quarter of the population lived in poverty (see table A.7).

In contrast, the periods of economic stagnation tend to feature political instability and adverse external economic shocks, together with misperceptions among the country's elites about the obstacles to development and the absence of consensus. Consider, first, the five lost decades of the 19th century. In addition to the lack of consensus among liberals and conservatives, neither one of the contending factions had a program fully adequate to the needs of the country's economic development. In fact, from a strict (and admittedly narrow) economic development perspective, some of the main elements of the liberal economic program—free trade, privatization of corporate and public property, and liberalization of the land market—were ill conceived. It is likely that the first of them, free trade, further stimulated the downfall of the local manufacturing industry. As a result of the second, the privatization of church property, the main, and for a long time the only, banking institution of the country was destroyed. The third, the liberalization of the land market, would further contribute to concentrate agrarian property and, over time, to the social explosion of 1910. At the same time, the conservative faction's views were not any better. While it is true that some of its members undertook a first and brief attempt at industrialization during the 1830s through trade protection and the creation of the first public bank to finance the expansion of the textile industry, the social and political forces that supported the conservatives tended to perpetuate the economic, social, and political disparities and the institutional backwardness that had had highly adverse effects on economic development since colonial times.

Similarly, the second period of stagnation begins with the breakdown of the positivist consensus and the political stability that characterized the *Porfiriato*. Later, when political stability was largely restored, the procyclical policies of balanced budgets and monetary contraction at times of recession, implemented between 1926 and 1932, exacerbated the negative effects on the Mexican economy of the Great Depression in the United States. This, together with the political shock of the revolution and its sequel, goes a long way toward explaining the slow rate of economic growth that, on average, characterized the second period of stagnation. What was required then were anticyclical policies that took the economy out of the recession, as would eventually be done during the Cárdenas administration and later at several points in the period 1940 to 1970.

The breakdown of the "stabilizing development consensus" together with misperceptions and severe external shocks also played a major role in the loss of macroeconomic stability in the 1970s and early 1980s and the transition to the third period of stagnation. The belief that development, especially social development, could be accelerated while sacrificing fiscal discipline, together with the end of the international golden age and the first oil price shock, which found Mexico as a net importer of oil, are some of the factors behind the reappearance of inflation in the 1970s and the 1976 crisis. Similarly, in the early 1980s, the incorrect diagnosis that the international interest rate shock of 1979–1980 (the Volker shock) was a temporary phenomenon while high and increasing oil prices were going to be a permanent feature of the world economy would play a major role in the 1982 debt crisis and the economic difficulties that characterized the lost decade.

What about the third period of stagnation, the present one? This period has witnessed a radical shift in the relationship between state and market, a result of a more open trade policy, liberalization of capital flows, deregulation of economic activity, and privatization of public enterprises. In the dominant perceptions among the country's elites, this change should have inaugurated a new period of rapid economic development as the obstacles to economic growth present in an economy that was overregulated by the state and excessively protected from external competition were brought down.

As we know, these expectations have not been fulfilled. Is it the case that, just as in previous periods of stagnation, the real obstacles to economic development are being misperceived? By reviewing the origins of the shift in the market-state balance and evaluating the results of the market reform process, this book argues that such seems to be the case. It argues, more precisely, that misperceptions about the causes of the slow growth of the economy since the early 1980s have prevented government policies from focusing on the real obstacles to high and sustained economic growth.

While so far this process of slow growth has not impeded a continued progress in health and educational indicators, and even a reduction in poverty rates in the recent past, there is no reason to take a complacent view of current economic and social performance. First, slow growth has been accompanied by a deterioration in the quality of jobs provided by the economy, that is, by a massive increase in underemployment in the informal sector. Moreover, as we shall argue, poverty reduction is due not so much to family remittances and conditional cash transfers, but to the demographic dividend. In fact, if poverty today is not rampant and the social situation is not explosive, this is due to a large extent to the near completion of the demographic transition—the demographic dividend—which so far has been, along with a large out-migration of labor, a main factor explaining the paradox of poverty reduction in the midst of slow growth. The effects of the demographic bonus will be largely over from now on, so high growth becomes more of an imperative than ever. In addition, the tasks of social policy are today far more formidable than in the past, as the present development pattern seems to be exacerbating economic and social disparities in a number of ways, leading to the impoverishment of large numbers of rural workers as the state has retreated from agriculture, as well as to the increasing wage inequality and rampant regional disparities that have accompanied the process of increasing international economic integration.

Overview

After this introduction, chapter 2 examines the five lost decades from the 1820s to the early 1870s, when Mexico's current economic underdevelopment originated, and puts this period in international perspective by comparing Mexico to other Latin American countries as well as to developed countries. This is preceded by a review of the characteristics of the economy of New Spain on the eve of independence and the disruptive effects of the wars of independence on economic activity. The chapter then focuses on the constraints to economic development resulting from political instability, the decline of mining activity, foreign competition, institutional backwardness, and the lack of transport infrastructure and financial capital. It also examines the economic programs of liberals and conservatives. A main argument is that a coalition that could forge a developmental state could not emerge: the politically liberal that could and were willing to carry out the country's institutional modernization were also antistatist in economic terms, while the only ones that favored an economic modernization through industrialization and an interventionist state were the politically conservative, who were strongly opposed to political and social modernization. In the absence of a developmental coalition, the major obstacles to economic development remained in place.

Chapter 3 examines the *Porfiriato* and the removal of some of the obstacles to economic growth starting in the early to mid-1870s: the achievement of political stability through the establishment of a strong state, the dramatic reduction of transport costs and the integration of the domestic market brought about by the expansion of the railway network, and the institutional modernization (including the abolition of tariffs on domestic trade and the modification of commercial and mining codes together with banking laws) that permitted the development of financial intermediaries and attracted foreign investment. The chapter then turns to the results of the change in development strategy. Economic growth and modernization were felt in many areas, primary exports boomed, and modern manufacturing production for the domestic market emerged. The other side of the coin were lagging and eventually declining real wages, the strengthening of the *peonage* and labor's links of dependence with the rural areas, high levels of market concentration in industry and banking, and an extreme concentration of land resulting from what amounted to an enclosure movement in which federal and peasant communal lands were redistributed to land development companies and rich individuals. In sum, modernization went together with a process of increasing inequalities in the distribution of income and wealth that proved to be the Achilles' heel of the regime.

Chapter 4 looks at economic performance from 1910 to 1940 and challenges the conventional hypotheses about the evolution of the economy during the revolution and the immediate postrevolutionary period. According to conventional views, the revolution had extremely disruptive economic consequences. At the same time, a generalized perception is that the Great Depression in the United States had, compared to its effects on other Latin American countries, relatively mild effects on the Mexican economy due to a relatively early and vigorous recovery starting in 1933 that was made possible by Mexico's export structure (its luck in the "commodity lottery"). Thus if Mexico had a relatively poor economic performance over the period 1910–1940, this was largely due to the adverse economic effects of the revolution and its sequel of political instability that more than offset the relatively mild consequences of the Great Depression. Our findings put these hypotheses upside down. We show, along with a number of authors in the recent literature on the subject, that the revolution did not prevent a fairly sustained economic expansion, except for a brief period during the hyperinflation of 1914–1916, and left the productive apparatus of the country largely intact. In fact, it was not an obstacle for a continuation of the export boom that started during the *Porfiriato* and for the extraordinary development of new exports such as oil. On the other hand, we conclude that the Great Depression was, in fact, particularly harmful in the case of Mexico compared to other Latin American countries. This was so, despite the recovery of exports and terms of trade early in the 1930s, because Mexico's recession started earlier (in 1926), and for this reason was more prolonged than elsewhere. In addition, the external shock of the Great Depression was among the worst in Latin America. Moreover, monetary and fiscal policies until 1932 were strongly procyclical. It was this, and not the economic consequences of revolution and political instability, that explains Mexico's comparatively poor economic growth performance over the period 1910–1940.

The 30 years that followed the consolidation of a developmental state under the presidency of Lázaro Cárdenas were, in contrast to the previous period, a phase of catching up with most of the rest of the world. Chapter 5 examines the postwar golden age of industrialization from 1940 to 1970 that made this process of catching up possible. It reviews the development policy framework that generated the rapid progress of the economy. This included trade policies that protected infant industries and toward the end of the period promoted the development of manufacturing exports, fiscal incentives oriented toward the creation of "new and necessary" industries, and industrial investment financing through the establishment of development banks. We then turn to analyze three subperiods: the war boom up to 1945, during which industrial expansion was driven by exports; the period of growth with a devaluation-inflation cycle from 1946 to 1955; and the gem of the golden age from 1956 to 1970, in which an acceleration of economic and industrial growth was reconciled with low inflation and balance of payments stability. The chapter also looks at the sources of productive capacity expansion, overall productivity growth, and factor accumulation, and challenges the conventional view that stresses the extensive nature of the pattern of growth (based more on factor accumulation than on productivity growth). The outstanding growth performance is also placed in an international comparative perspective. Here we assess the role of the impressive agricultural growth up to the mid-1960s, the large share of economic expenditures in the government budget, the low static costs of trade protection, and the geopolitical challenge of sharing a long border with an economic and military superpower. Finally, the shortcomings of the period and of the development strategy followed are highlighted: the persistency of inequality despite the progress achieved in reducing poverty, the failure of tax reforms that left Mexico with one of the lowest tax burdens in the world, the insufficient efforts at export promotion in industrial policy, and the inconsistent application of the infant industry protection argument.

Chapter 6 examines the period from 1970 to the early 1980s, marked by continued economic growth, but also by the reemergence of inflation and recurrent balance of payments crises in 1976 and 1982. The chapter begins by recounting the change in development strategy from stabilizing development to shared development under the Luis Echeverría administration (1970–1976) and how it achieved temporary success in improving real wages and income distribution, strengthening export competitiveness, and preserving economic growth. But in the face of the failure of the attempt at tax reform in 1972, the change was accompanied by the emergence of macroeconomic imbalances that eventually led in 1976 to abandonment of the peso-dollar exchange rate that had remained fixed for 22 years. Inflation at higher than foreign rates, in the context of a fixed nominal exchange rate, increasing fiscal deficits, and the end of the golden age in the international economy were the main components of the crisis. The 1976 crisis was, however, short lived, as the discovery and exploitation of massive oil reserves restored creditworthiness in international capital markets and triggered an oil boom from 1978 to 1981. However, as in the previous episode, the rapid growth process was accompanied by macroeconomic imbalances that were exacerbated in 1981 by the loss of control over public spending. Together with the dramatic change in the international environment—the sharp increase in foreign interest rates resulting from the Volker shock, the weakening of the oil market starting in 1981, and the eventual contraction of capital inflows—the result was the 1982 debt crisis. Finally, the chapter discusses three interpretations of the domestic causes of the 1976 and 1982 crises: the alleged exhaustion of import substitution industrialization, the role of populist pressures and macroeconomic populism during the Echeverría and Lopez Portillo administrations, and the existence of a sui generis political cycle by which public spending and fiscal deficits peak in the preelectoral year when the ruling party's internal competition for the presidential nomination reaches its climax. Our discussion challenges the first two interpretations and finds considerable support for the third one.

Chapter 7 looks at the years of adjustment to the debt crisis of 1982 and the oil price collapse of 1986, the resulting lost decade to economic development, and the radical transformation of the development policy framework starting in the mid-1980s. The adjustment processes are reviewed in a comparative perspective, arguing that the specificity of Mexico was a relatively minor internal transfer problem in the midst of a particularly severe external transfer one (as a result of being a large debtor). This is because, unlike what happened in Argentina or Brazil, devaluation acted as a mechanism of redistribution from the private to the public sector that facilitated the transfer of resources abroad in order to service the government's external debt. The chapter also describes how the adjustment problems conditioned the results of stabilization programs from the failed initial orthodox stabilization attempts to the more successful "heterodox shock" of late 1987. The analysis of the reform process examines trade liberalization from the initial relaxation of import controls in 1984 to the North American Free Trade Agreement (NAFTA) and beyond, the deregulation of foreign direct investment, and the opening of domestic financial markets to foreign capital. It also looks at the privatization of public enterprises—including the sale of many small and medium enterprises in a first stage and the sale of the telephone company and the domestic banking system, involving much larger assets, in a later stage—and the uses of privatization revenues. The watering down of industrial policy is also examined, including the elimination of production or credit subsidies, tax cuts, and trade protection schemes, as well as performance requirements on their beneficiaries, and the establishment of new programs, consistent with General Agreement on Tariffs and Trade/World Trade Organization (GATT/WTO) provisions, aimed at exploiting Mexico's static comparative advantages. The chapter also includes sections on competition policy and the deregulation of tertiary activities as well as reforms to the land tenure system and agricultural policy.

Chapter 8 evaluates the results of the shift in the market-state balance, the overall impact of the reform process on Mexico's quest for high and sustained, socially inclusive economic growth, and its limitations and strengths. It examines, first, the effects of privatization on economic efficiency and the productivity of investment and argues that the lack of an appropriate regulatory framework has resulted in an undesirable concentration of ownership in some of the privatized areas. The chapter then turns to the consequences of trade liberalization on the volume of trade flows and the pattern of trade specialization, as well as its static and dynamic effects on productivity in the tradable goods sectors. It also examines the results of the liberalization of the land market and the dismantling of agricultural support policies, arguing that while a market-oriented rural economy is certainly benefiting from the reforms, the overall performance of agriculture, and in particular peasant agriculture, has been very disappointing. The chapter also discusses the limitations of the financial liberalization process, arguing that the financial boom and bust cycle that culminated with the banking crisis of 1994–1995 was a consequence, at least in part, of an excessive reliance on financial deregulation and capital market liberalization. Finally, the chapter ends by pointing out the weakness of the contemporary Mexican state as revealed by the inefficiency of the fiscal adjustment process, its ineffectiveness in collecting taxes, its dependence on and vulnerability to oil incomes that are likely to decline in the near future, and its inability to carry out anticyclical macroeconomic policies.

Chapter 9 looks at social development. It describes the evolution of social policies during the structural reform process, from the elimination by the Miguel de la Madrid administration (1982–1988) of programs put in place during the oil bonanza to the strengthening of poverty alleviation programs that have accompanied the transition to democracy. It then evaluates the achievements and limitations of *Oportunidades*, the antipoverty program of the Vicente Fox administration (2000–2006) that was inherited from the Ernesto Zedillo government (1994–2000) with a different name—*Progresa*. The chapter then turns to recent trends in income distribution, focusing on increasing wage inequalities and regional disparities, and poverty, which paradoxically has been falling in the midst of slow growth after its sharp increase during the financial crisis and recession of 1995. A main argument is that the downward trend in the poverty rate cannot be fully explained by a firmer commitment of social policy to poverty alleviation goals. Our discussion suggests rather that the main factor explaining the puzzle of poverty reduction in the midst of slow growth is the completion of the demographic transition to low fertility rates and population growth rates that has taken place in recent decades, that is, the demographic dividend. This also suggests a warning: as the demographic transition is completed, the demographic bonus will disappear and further social progress will necessitate the resumption of rapid economic growth. The chapter concludes by arguing that the tasks of social policy are extremely demanding, especially if the growth imperative is not fully met. This is due to the legacy of increased inequality from the 1980s and the accumulated backlog of unmet social needs, the fact that in some ways the present development pattern is exacerbating economic and social disparities, and the dismantling of industrial policy which leaves in the hands of social policy the major development tasks of enhancing the present endowment of resources and changing the structure of comparative advantages of the economy.

Chapter 10 discusses the growth slowdown of the Mexican economy during the reform and post-reform periods. It addresses four possible factors behind the growth deceleration. First, the role of international trade integration, showing that the trade policy reforms of the 1980s and 1990s were in fact very successful in enhancing export growth and trade openness, but not in promoting a dynamic pattern of trade specialization. Second, the chapter discusses the productivity growth slowdown, which has been highlighted by numerous authors as the main factor responsible for the slow GDP growth, arguing that it should be seen as a consequence rather than a cause of the growth deceleration, as the evolution of productivity growth is closely associated with the expansion of underemployment in the tertiary sectors of the economy. Third, our discussion of the role of human capital formation suggests that educational and health indicators have been improving during the recent period, partly as a consequence of the demographic bonus, and cannot be held responsible for the decrease in output per worker that has taken place since the early 1980s. Rather than human capital constraining growth, it is the slow growth process that has prevented full use of the human capital reserves available to the economy. We then focus on the primary determinant of the growth slowdown, the low rate of physical capital accumulation. Our argument is that, together with the contraction of bank credit following the financial crisis of the mid-1990s, three main factors are constraining investment: the low level of public investment (particularly in the area of infrastructure), an appreciated real exchange rate for most of the period since 1988, and the dismantling of industrial policy during the reform period. The chapter concludes by arguing that the current agenda in policymaking circles—which emphasizes an insufficient fiscal reform, the restructuring of the energy sector, and the "flexibilization" of the labor market—largely misses the point by failing to fully address the binding constraints on economic growth.

Chapter 11 concludes by reviewing how the binding constraints on Mexico's economic development have been changing over time, distinguishing among those that have acted on the social returns to capital accumulation (such as a lack of infrastructure or human capital), on the private appropriability of those social returns (as a result of market and government failures or political instability), and on the cost and availability of financing for productive investments. It also discusses the lessons that the Mexican experience has for old and current debates in development economics, such as the role of geography and institutions, trade and trade openness, income inequality, and states and markets in development.

A statistical appendix presents historical series of economic and social indicators.

2

The "Origins of Backwardness": Obstacles to Economic Development in the 19th Century

Why has Mexico not joined the ranks of fully developed countries? Why has it lagged so much behind the United States? A popular explanation, present for example in an essay by Mexico's Nobel laureate poet and essayist Octavio Paz, identifies the root of this contrast between Mexico and the United States in their different colonial origins, stressing their contrasting national, cultural, and religious heritages. As he put it: "Ever since the seventeenth century, our history, a fragment of Spain's, has been an impassioned negation of the modernity being born: the Reformation, the Enlightenment, and all the rest" (Paz, 1985, p. 143). In his view, the United States benefited from being the product of the reformation and of the spirit of progress prevailing in the most prosperous countries in Europe. In contrast, Mexico's development has been hindered by the influence of the counterreformation and the reaction against modernization that marked Spain's political and cultural life.

This quote by Paz is an example of a common, but as we shall argue, partial interpretation that identifies the colonial heritage as the root of the Mexican economy's problems and failure to catch up with the United States. Certainly the centuries under Spanish colonialism determined Mexico's socioeconomic structure as well as its institutional development (Romero Sotelo and Jáuregui, 2003). But there are other elements that, in our view, are more relevant to understanding the contrasting dynamism of the two economies. Among them, the different factor endowments when they began their independent lives stand out. In particular, the availability of arable land and that of human capital were very dissimilar in the United States and Mexico. Geography was also very different, and unlike in the United States, led to very high domestic transport costs in Mexico. Similarly their links with colonial powers were also very different. These features significantly influenced the degree of integration of the domestic market, the evolution of productivity and production costs, and the development path.

In addition, the degree of inequality, social cohesion, and homogeneity of the population were different in the two countries. Colonial Mexico was a highly segregated society, split by ethnicity and skin color and characterized by sharp cultural and socioeconomic disparities. Of utmost importance is the fact that, in contrast to the U.S. experience, during a substantial part of the 19th century Mexico suffered violent episodes of war, civil unrest, and political instability. From its struggle for independence in 1810 to the various foreign interventions and invasions that it suffered, including the loss of a major portion of its territory to the United States, the century's prevalent political instability and violence was hardly a proper climate for investment, innovation, and economic growth.

Not surprisingly, it is in the 19th century when the development gap between the United States and Mexico rapidly widened.[1] According to Coatsworth (1990), although the Mexican economy of the 18th century was already growing at a slower pace than the U.S. economy, it is in the 19th century that one has to search for the "origins of backwardness" in Mexico. Indeed, in 1800 New Spain was a relatively prosperous region of the world, with a per capita gross domestic product (GDP) equivalent to between one-half and two-thirds of the U.S. level in estimates by Coatsworth (1990). However, in the next five decades it dramatically lagged behind the U.S. economy. Between 1800 and 1850 U.S. real per capita GDP averaged a 1.1% annual rate of expansion, the United Kingdom averaged 0.8%, and Brazil averaged 0.4%, while Mexico suffered an average contraction of 0.7% (Coatsworth, 1993). Coatsworth (1989) argued that if the Mexican economy had expanded *pari passu* with the U.S. economy from 1800 to 1860, by the early 1980s it would have been among the group of developed economies.

Mexico's economic decline in the 19th century is acutely evidenced in Maddison's (2006) data, according to which, while in 1820 Mexico's per capita GDP was 14% above the world's average, by 1870 it stood at 23% below

1. The consensus among historians is that during the 19th century not only Mexico but most of Latin America experienced a long-term economic decline relative to the United States. However, as we shall see, Mexico's decline was particularly acute.

the world's average (see table 1.1). Moreover, it was not until the end of the 1870s—or perhaps until the 1880s—that Mexico's real per capita GDP finally recovered to the level it had back in 1800 (Coatsworth and Tortella, 2002). In turn, Brazil's per capita GDP in 1820 and 1870 registered a deviation of less than 3% from the world's average. Chile experienced a fast expansion, going from 9% below the world average in 1820 to 49% above it by 1870. The United States was the country with perhaps the most dynamic performance during this period, with its per capita GDP going from a level 88% above the world's average to 182% above it by 1870. Thus, in these five decades, Mexico's per capita GDP went from being equivalent to 60% of the U.S. level to just 28% of the U.S. level. Since then the gap has oscillated between 25% and 36% (Maddison, 2006; see table 1.1). Why did the Mexican economy undergo such a prolonged period of stagnation in the 19th century? What were the key constraints binding its long-term growth after independence? This chapter addresses these questions.

The economy of New Spain on the eve of independence

According to Garner and Stefanou (1993), during the 18th century the population of New Spain expanded at an annual average rate of 0.7%–0.8%, and by the beginning of the 19th century it reached a total of between 5.5 and 6 million, with 75% of the population living in rural areas. The economy was closely organized around the extraction and exportation of precious metals, particularly silver, coming mostly from a few mining centers (*reales mineros*) in Pachuca (Real del Monte), Zacatecas, Guanajuato, and San Luis Potosí (Catorce).[2] Production of gold and other minerals (excluding quarries) was much less relevant (see Humboldt, 1822; Romero Sotelo, 1997). In the 18th century, New Spain's silver production grew at an annual average rate of 1.8%, higher than the 1.1% estimated by Crafts (1994) for British industry (Dobado and Marrero, 2006, referring to Lerdo de Tejada, 1853). At the end of that century, bullion represented close to 75% of Mexico's average annual exports, followed by cochineal (12%) and sugar (3%) (Brading, 1971, based on Lerdo

---

2. It is worth noting, however, that despite the importance of an export-oriented mining sector in the colonial economy, the role of foreign trade was still relatively small compared to the one it would have in the late 19th century (Coatsworth, 1990).

Table 2.1 Per capita GDP and by sector

	1800	1845	1860	1877
Per capita GDP at constant 1900 prices (index 1800 = 100)	100.0	78.4	70.9	85.0
Percent of GDP				
Agriculture[a]	44.4	48.1	42.1	42.2
Mining	8.2	6.2	9.7	10.4
Manufacturing	22.3	18.3	21.6	16.2
Construction	0.6	0.6	0.6	0.6
Transportation	2.5	2.5	2.5	2.5
Commerce	16.7	16.9	16.7	16.9
Government	4.2[b]	7.4	6.8	11.2
Other	1.1	—	—	—

Source: Based on Coatsworth (1990), tables V.4 and V.5.

[a] Includes livestock, forestry, and fishing.

[b] Does not include net fiscal remittances to the Spanish treasury. Total government revenues, including these remittances, amounted to 7.8% of colonial income.

de Tejada, 1853). By 1800, New Spain was by far the largest producer of silver in the world, with an output of almost two-thirds of the world's total (Dobado and Marrero, 2006, citing Schmitz, 1979).

Table 2.1 indicates that in 1800 mining represented 8.2% of the GDP of New Spain. However, Ibarra (1999) and Romano (1998) (cited by Dobado and Marrero, 2006) estimated that due to the prevalence of a large subsistence sector, the market-oriented sector represented between 30% and 50% of GDP. Thus mining had a much larger role in the market economy: between 16% and 27%.[3] As Dobado and Marrero (2006) state, the New Spain had most likely the biggest mining sector of any preindustrial economy. Most important, it was not an economic enclave. On the contrary, there is consensus that it played a key role in inducing economic expansion, though with important fluctuations (Ibarra, 2000; Blanco and Romero Sotelo, 2004). It certainly had significant and varied backward and forward linkages to other sectors, including agriculture and manufacturing—such as the textile and beverages industries—and services including finance, transportation, and retail. These linkages, mirroring

3. Dobado and Marrero (2006) give somewhat larger estimates for mining's share in New Spain's market economy: between 25% and 40%.

the concentration of mining centers, were especially strong in the central and northern regions (Dobado and Marrero, 2006). As Garner and Stefanou (1993) have argued, economic growth in New Spain during the 18th century would have been significantly slower without an expanding silver mining sector.

The state made a significant contribution to the development of silver production by establishing a sound institutional framework including the relatively liberal mining code of 1783. Selective granting of fiscal incentives and tax exemptions on certain silver and mining inputs resulted in low and decreasing fiscal pressure on this activity. In addition, specific legal bodies— the *Cuerpo de Minería* and the *Tribunal General*—served to safeguard mining interests and induce foreign investment. The existence of this institutional framework led Dobado and Marrero (2006) to define the model of preindustrial economic growth in Bourbon Mexico as "mining-led growth" and to conclude that "there was no predatory colonial state confiscating the results obtained by individuals from their productive efforts in New Spain's mining industry.... The picture of mining in New Spain around 1800 is far from being the extractive, unequal, and inefficient one assumed by some authors."

This assessment, however, cannot be extrapolated to the overall economic relation between Spain and its colony after the Bourbon reforms. The Spanish Bourbon administration carried out a remarkable overhaul of New Spain's tax structure. Indeed, in the 18th century, the taxes on Mexican silver fully paid for colonial military and administrative costs, and also served to finance the deficits of Spain itself. By a mix of coercion, increased efficiency, and political arrangements, Spain imposed a highly extractive tax regime in Bourbon Mexico. In per capita terms, the tax burden in colonial Mexico was perhaps 10 times heavier than in the Anglo-American colonies (Marichal, 2007). The amount of taxes transferred abroad was equivalent to 40% of the total taxes collected in the viceroyalty. In fact, by 1800 the population of New Spain was paying more taxes to the metropolis than Spaniards themselves (Prados de Escosura, 2004). In addition to this increased tax burden, and especially in the 1780s and 1790s, the viceregal administration complemented tax revenues with an additional extraction of revenues through loans, donations, and forced contributions. The church, as well as other rich and politically powerful colonial corporations, played a key role in the direct collection of such funds, as well as indirectly by inducing them to give donations or contributions to colonial authorities. During the last decades of the 18th century and the beginning of the 19th century, a massive amount of funds so extracted were exported to Spain and became a major restriction on Mexico's growth prospects at that time, and one of the reasons behind Mexico's economic decline during the wars of independence.

Excluding peasant production done with traditional methods for self-consumption, marketable agricultural output was produced in haciendas, hiring workers in debt peonage conditions,[4] as well as by rancheros and small and medium tenants (*arrendatarios*).[5] These were geared to serve the markets of mining centers and cities dispersed around the central and northern central regions of what is now Mexico, including the capital, Mexico City. The main agricultural products included corn, wheat, vegetables, fruits, and *pulque* (Solís, 2000). The agricultural sector, although by far the largest in New Spain's economy, did not have as much growth- and business-generating effects as mining (Garner and Stefanou, 1993). Moreover, it was subject to recurrent crises, and famines were not uncommon. The then most remembered major disaster occurred in 1784–1786, triggered by an August frost in the valley of Mexico, with acute impacts in terms of human losses, hunger, disease, and social tensions, especially among the rural population (MacLachlan and Rodríguez, 1980). By then, backwardness in the rural areas, evidenced in low productivity and the proliferation of in-kind remunerations, was pushing vast numbers of peasants to leave the countryside, augmenting the supply of unqualified, poorly trained labor in the cities (Garner and Stefanou, 1993).

Another major and extremely profitable economic activity was tobacco. Organized as a state monopoly since 1765, it employed thousands of workers, and up until the breakout of the independence war, it was shrewdly managed by the Bourbon administration. It actually became the second most important single industry, just behind silver production, and a major source of government revenue.

Colonial rules imposed severe restrictions on local manufacturing production. The few exceptions, strictly regulated, included goods to meet basic needs, such as ordinary fabrics and textiles (Garner and Stefanou, 1993). Investing in manufacturing activities that were seen to compete with Spanish

4. Although their formal labor relation was that of wage earners, in practice hacienda workers could not leave their jobs because of their massive indebtedness due to unpaid bills at the hacienda shop (*tienda de raya*) and cash advances received from the hacendados to pay poll taxes.

5. Brading (1971) states that in 1809 there were 4680 Indian villages, 6680 smaller ranchos, and 4945 haciendas, with a significant proportion of the latter being owned by the church.

production was simply banned. Not surprisingly, most of the manufacturing supply consisted of imports from Spain (oriented to satisfy the consumption patterns of high-income groups).[6] However, local industry gradually emerged under the protection provided by high transport costs and internal tariffs (*alcabalas*). Textile manufacturing was the most important, but not the only industrial activity benefiting from these conditions as well as from the interruption of maritime routes, and the consequent difficulties for the importation of textiles, provoked by European wars at the end of the 18th century (Cárdenas, 1985). Textile manufacturing was organized in *obrajes*, employing women and children as well as prisoners and slaves in hazardous working conditions with technologies similar to the ones in 18th-century pre-Industrial Revolution Europe.[7] A putting-out system coexisted along with the *obrajes* in the main urban centers, including Mexico City, Queretaro, Oaxaca, and Puebla, where half of the population depended on the production of textiles (Cárdenas, 1985; MacLachlan and Rodríguez, 1980). The sugar industry, another major manufacturing and exporting activity, developed in Morelos and Veracruz. By the early 19th century, small-scale manufacturing employed more workers and produced more output value than the mining sector (see table 2.1). As has been noted by several authors (see in particular Beato, 2004), the beginnings of industrialization in Mexico did not follow the British path characterized by the gradual transformation of handicraft textile production into mass production manufacturing establishments. Instead, the origins of the industrial capitalist class resided in the ranks of merchants and moneylenders.

By the middle to late 18th century, the discovery of new and rich silver deposits—La Valenciana in Guanajuato (1770) and Catorce in San Luis Potosí (1778)—together with the provision of cheap mercury, fiscal exemptions, and the introduction of explosives and other technological advances created a boom in silver production which then reached the peak levels of the colonial era (Brading, 1971) (see figure 2.1). Economic activities closely linked to the mining sector benefited directly from the boom. The expansion of silver exports also made available imported raw materials and capital goods for the new industries that were being developed in Europe as a consequence of the Industrial Revolution.

---

6. During 1802–1806, textiles represented on average 64% of imports; wine and hard liquor, 10%; cocoa from Caracas, 6%; paper, 5%; and iron and steel, 5% (Brading, 1971, based on Lerdo de Tejada, 1853).

7. On the *obrajes*, see Chávez Orozco (1938) and Salvucci (1987).

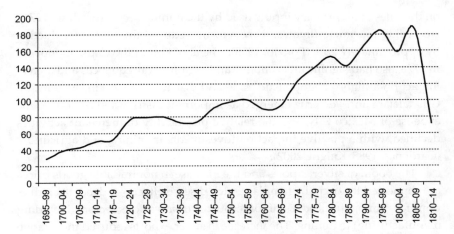

Figure 2.1 Production of precious metals, 1695–1814 (Index 1755–1759 = 100)
Source: Coatsworth (1986), based on Orozco y Berra (1857).

The duration of the mining boom and the role of the "economic liberalization" reforms of the Bourbon monarchs in the second half of the century are controversial. The conventional view—presented by, among others, Florescano and Gil Sánchez (1976) and Cárdenas (1985)—sees the Bourbon reforms as supportive of the economic expansion of the period and the mining boom as extending until the end of the colonial period in the early 19th century. Coatsworth (1989; see also Salvucci, 1997), in contrast, dates the beginning of economic decline and the end of the mining boom to the 1780s, well before the independence wars (1810–1821).[8] In this view, increasing costs as a result of inflation and falling market prices for silver output produced the decline in mining production (Coatsworth, 1989).

In any case, it seems clear that the reforms, the tax incentives to mining granted in the late 1760s, and the Free Trade Agreement of the late 1780s, which allowed freer trade between New Spain and Spain and allowed any port in Spain to establish trade with New Spain, significantly contributed to silver production and exports. The array of incentives to silver mining included the following: a reduction in the price of mercury by half (regulated by the government), exemption from the tithe for most mines, and elimination of taxes

---

8. Brading (1971), on the other hand, sees the boom of the 1770s as part of the continuous increase in silver production throughout the 18th century, only interrupted briefly during the 1760s.

on the sales of all primary inputs used by the mining sector (Brading, 1971). According to some estimates, these reforms reduced the cost of production by approximately 25% (Ponzio, 1998). The abolition of the Cadiz monopoly in 1778 also had significant economic and regional consequences and a great impact on a highly oligopolistic trade and distribution system. As a result, Guadalajara and Veracruz emerged as important distribution centers, at the expense of Mexico City, and the relative profitability of merchant activities declined, with a positive impact on investments in mining and agriculture (Cárdenas, 1985; Knight, 2002).

The boom of silver exports and the increase in nontradable goods prices are connected through the familiar Dutch disease effects.[9] Indeed, tax reductions for mining induced a shift of resources from various sectors (including manufacturing) to mining. The increase in silver exports reduced the relative price of silver in terms of imports—given Mexico's prominent position in the world silver market—thus increasing the domestic demand for it and further reinforcing the increase in silver production. The crowding out of nonmineral tradable goods sectors could have slowed down the rate of growth of the economy (if such sectors had a high potential for productivity growth and strong linkages with the rest of the domestic economy). However, Ponzio (1998) presents evidence concluding that there was no reduction in the rate of per capita GDP growth in the late colonial period (contrary to what has been claimed by other authors, starting with Coatsworth (1986).

During this period, the relationship between business and the state under the system of the Spanish Crown was one of pervasive law and regulation. Trade with any country other than Spain was illegal. Import and export licenses for trade with Spain could be obtained only through a board, sitting in Seville, controlled by Spanish merchants. Trade inside Mexico was controlled almost as rigorously as foreign trade. Local monopolies, trading privileges, and tax exemptions proliferated in every area of the colony. Production was controlled even more than trade. In principle, nothing fabricated in Spain could be produced in Mexico, and what was produced in Mexico was subject to strict regulations (see Coatsworth, 1982; Potash, 1953; Schaeffer, 1949).

---

9. The term *Dutch disease* was originally coined in 1977 by the *Economist* to refer to the experience of the Netherlands with the discovery and exploitation of North Sea gas and how this led to an increase in the price of local services and a weakening of investment and growth in the manufacturing sector and other exportable goods sectors. Ponzio (2006) states that the boom of silver production during the last three decades of the 18th century led to an increase in the relative price of nontradable goods such as maize, wheat, and sugar.

That is, economic life was organized by highly detailed and particularistic provisions in order to shape economic activity in colonial society and to grant and maintain a complex web of privileges and monopolies. These provisions included social and ethnic distinctions—among Europeans (*peninsulares* and *criollos*), castes (mixed races), and Indians—in the access to employment, residence, and fiscal treatment; corporate privileges; an extremely complex fiscal system; monopolies (such as the tobacco monopoly); and all kinds of regulations on production and trade (Coatsworth, 1982). The economic consequences of this organization were to reduce the geographic and occupational mobility of the labor force, distort the allocation of productive factors, and inhibit enterprise in new activities, thus reducing the allocative efficiency, productivity, and growth potential of the economy. At the same time, the state did not perform a number of functions much needed to increase the overall productivity of the economy, including improvements in the road and transport system and investment in human capital (Coatsworth, 1982).

Yet despite this adverse institutional framework, by the end of the 18th century New Spain was surely the most affluent Spanish colony in America, with an economy whose productivity may have been close to or even higher than that of Spain itself. Yields in the fertile wheat fields of the central highlands were, according to Brading (1978), as high as those of England. According to Humboldt (1822), miners earned higher wages in colonial Mexico than in Western Europe.[10] Output per capita in 1800 was close to two-thirds that of the United States (Coatsworth, 1998).[11] Moreover, its overall economic structure in terms of output was less agricultural, having an advanced mining industry and a significant manufacturing sector. The value of exports was similar to that of the United States, even though total output produced was about half (Coatsworth, 1978). A Mexican enlightenment made numerous contributions, described by Humboldt (1822) in his *Political Essay*, and the scientific community worked in impressive research centers and institutions of higher learning. Mexico City was the largest city in the Western Hemisphere, with a population of some 170,000 in 1810, larger than New York, Boston, and Philadelphia combined (Knight, 2002).

10. Around 1800 the average daily wage in terms of grams of silver for unskilled workers in the La Valenciana mine in Guanajuato was similar to that for workers in Amsterdam and London, and substantially higher than those in Leipzig, Milan, Beijing, Kyoto-Tokyo, and Canton (Dobado and Marrero, 2006, based on data from Allen et al., 2005, and Velasco, 1989).

11. Maddison (2006) estimates the gap in 1990 dollars to be 40% in 1820.

Several of the conditions for rapid capitalist development were in place. The relatively high share of manufacturing in total output in 1800 (22.3%; see table 2.1[12]) speaks to the presence of a critical mass of native entrepreneurs. The creation of a fully free labor force—that "most difficult and protracted process" by which the population's ties to the land are broken (Gerschenkron, 1952)—was still far from complete due to the prevalence of peonage in the rural economy. More precisely, in many regions outside central Mexico, haciendas in the rural economy strictly depended on the use of peonage; close to Mexico City, however, haciendas basically operated with temporary workers employed in a wage earning relationship (Katz, 1980). In any case, this process was at the time probably more advanced in Mexico than in many central and eastern European countries. The extent to which the existence of peonage constituted an obstacle to economic development is debatable, but it is worth noting that it did not prevent the process of modern economic growth from taking off during the *Porfiriato*.

Economic decline and political instability: the origins of backwardness

Between 1800 and approximately 1860—at the time when the United States and other now developed economies were industrializing and recording unprecedented rates of economic growth—Mexico's total production fell. Indeed, as Prados de Escosura (2004) has argued, the collapse of the economy in the first years of the independence struggle was only partly compensated by the subsequent recovery after the mid-1810s. The magnitude of the collapse or slowdown experienced during this period is disputed, but with population growing at an average annual rate of 0.6%–0.7%, there is consensus that per capita incomes did not grow and most likely had a sharp decline, by as much as 30% (Coatsworth, 1990; see table 2.1). The export sector did not recover its level of output per capita until the 1880s (Coatsworth, 1989). The economy reproduced on a smaller scale the colonial economy, with little structural change during the period (Coatsworth, 1989).

There is some debate concerning when the economic decline began. Ponzio (2006) presents evidence that suggests there was no reduction in the

---

12. The manufacturing employment share, according to INEGI (1985), was 10% in 1790.

growth rate of per capita GDP in the late colonial period. Other authors, starting with Coatsworth (1986), argue that by the end of the 18th century there were signs that New Spain's economic expansion was losing steam, as it progressively faced binding constraints. In this regard, Garner and Stefanou (1993) claim that the colony's economic dynamism had been based much more on the systematic addition of land, labor, and capital provided by the mining boom than on increases in productivity. They argue: "Toward the end of the eighteenth century... [economic] growth may have begun to sputter because those basic resources, especially capital, were more costly to add. Without fundamental changes in productivity levels, for which there is little direct evidence, the economy found itself stagnating." Moreover, as a consequence of the Bourbon reforms' drive to extract more resources from New Spain, credit had become acutely scarce, given that a substantial amount of funds that the church used for lending purposes had essentially been expropriated in the form of compulsory loans to be shifted to the metropolis.

In any case, whether or not this decline had already started in the final decades of the colonial period, everyone agrees that independence did nothing to prevent the contraction of the economy during the half century that followed it. Yet independence eliminated the fiscal burden on the gold and silver extracted from the colony, a substantial burden—estimated at nearly 10% of GDP in the late 1700s by Blanco and Romero Sotelo (2004). Whatever the exact burden, as Garner and Stefanou (1993) succinctly put it: "By the end of the eighteen century the main result of the Bourbon economic policy was the channeling of much of Mexico's wealth away from its own internal development and into state sponsored projects designed to shore up a faltering empire." Independence also abolished the trade monopoly, the cost of which has been estimated at 3% of GDP during the last two decades of the colonial period (Coatsworth, 1978). The total burden, fiscal and commercial, was thus much higher than the burden of British colonialism on its North American colonies, estimated by Thomas (1965, cited by Coatsworth, 1978) to be 0.3% of GNP. Why then did independence and the emergence of a national state not provide greater stimuli to economic development?

A most important reason is perhaps the prolonged period of violence and political instability that started with the independence wars. While independence eliminated the fiscal burden of Spanish colonialism, the independence wars had pervasive adverse effects on economic activity that partly offset the removal of this burden: the destruction of infrastructure in the haciendas of the central highlands, the flooding of mines, the interruption of the northern wool trade which paralyzed the *obrajes* of Queretaro and other textile centers, the hazardous conditions in which communications and trade took place (Cárdenas, 1985), and collapse of the tax system so that at the time of independence the only source of revenue left to the government came from the tobacco monopoly (Tenenbaum, 1986). Even this source of revenue had shrunk considerably as, during the insurgency years of 1810–1821, the tobacco monopoly had been devastated. On the one hand, the *villas* production was severely harmed by the violence and destruction in the rural areas. On the other hand, the monopoly's finances and productive capacity were depleted by the administration that decapitalized it in order to provide funds and secure loans to pay for the royalist armed forces.[13] Although the independent government later strengthened the tobacco monopoly, it did not recover its previous dynamism and its relevance as a major source of public revenue, and by the mid-1850s the tobacco monopoly was finally dissolved.

Moreover, the end of Spanish rule also brought some unexpected costs for the mining sector. Not only were the direct effects of the independence wars on mining production highly disruptive, they also involved the loss of low-cost and guaranteed supplies of mercury (essential for processing low-grade ores) that Spain had provided from its large state-owned mine at Almaden. As a result of this disruption, and the other mentioned factors, silver production fell to less than one-fifth of previous levels from 1812 to 1822.[14] According to some estimates, it did not recover its preindependence level until the 1870s, despite a plethora of tax incentives, the opening of the sector to foreign participation, and the availability of new technological developments (Cárdenas, 1985).

The depression of silver production had important consequences for the economy. First, it led to the contraction of all activities linked to the mining sector, including the haciendas and *obrajes* (Salvucci, 1987). Second, it caused a reduction in the volume of international trade, which in turn led to a decrease in fiscal revenues. Third, and most important, it caused a contraction in the means of payment available in the domestic economy (Cárdenas, 1985, 1997) as the monetary system of postindependence Mexico remained, for much of the century, identical to that during 300 years of colonial rule, one in which the determinants of the volume of circulating currency were the cycles of silver mining production rather than regulation by the government. The reduction in the means of payment aggravated the consequences of capital flight

---

13. For a study of the tobacco monopoly in New Spain, see Deans-Smith (1992).

14. Others estimate the decrease in mining production to be up to one-tenth of previous levels (Thomson, 1985, cited by Beatty, 2001).

brought about by the exodus of Spanish miners and merchants, and thus the general lack of financial capital that characterized this period up to the 1860s when the first commercial banks were founded. Capital flight has been estimated at between 8% and 32% of national income (Cárdenas, 1985).

In addition, as already pointed out, the Bourbon's efforts to extract surplus from New Spain had reduced the church's capacity to provide loanable funds without substituting other sources. Thus the credit rationing that had already begun to be felt in the late 18th century and in the first decade of the 1800s became even more acute. Indeed, political instability and the financial and fiscal weaknesses of the different governments were far from conducive to the creation of a solid banking system that economic recovery so badly needed. Indeed, the inability of postindependence governments to secure property rights had been felt in key sectors of the economy, including the banking sector, where in fact some banks had been expropriated. By the late 1870s the banking sector was extremely small, with only two chartered banks operating in the entire country: a British bank focusing on financing foreign trade and another associated with U.S. capital that operated in Chihuahua. It was not until the Porfirio Díaz regime when the banking sector finally began to consolidate based on the government's guarantee of oligopolistic or monopolistic privileges (Maurer and Haber, 2007).

Political instability continued for decades after independence. From 1821 to 1867, Mexico had 56 administrations (Ponzio, 2005), and in the 55 years between independence and the *Porfiriato*, the presidency changed hands 75 times as a result of the continuous struggle between the conservative and liberal factions (Haber, 1989). In contrast, the United States had 13 administrations in the 52 years between 1817 and 1869 (Ponzio, 2005). Between 1824 and 1867, the average term of a president in Mexico was 15 months, 7 months for both the ministers of war and justice, and less than 5 months for the ministers of finance and foreign relations (Ponzio, 2005). The generalized episodes of civil unrest and violence reduced the population, disrupted mining and agricultural production, and severely curtailed trade and communications, thus further fragmenting the linkages among different regions. In addition, the struggle for independence brought about a temporary dismantling of the monetary union.[15] A particularly disastrous consequence of the prolonged civil strife was the loss to the United States of half of Mexico's national terri-

---

15. In 1810, at the beginning of his armed struggle, Miguel Hidalgo proceeded to mint coins in Guanajuato. Although the colonial government soon confiscated his minting equipment, before the end of the decade similar coinage practices—legal or illegal—were evident in various regional entities in response to the scarcity of silver money. From that time, and

tory in the mid-19th century. Fifty years after the 1848 Treaty, which ended the U.S.–Mexico war, and also after the beginning of the California Gold Rush, the mineral output alone of the lost territories exceeded Mexico's total GNP (Coatsworth, 1978). The French occupation in the 1860s further contributed to conflict and instability.

All these effects were steps back in the creation of a domestic market. Continuity of economic policy for development became impossible, as fiscal revenues were severely curtailed during the independence war and after, thus adversely affecting public investment in roads, education, and social order. Indeed, from 1810 to 1812 tax collection was sharply reduced, in part because of the economic slowdown and the violence that disrupted trade and in part because of the elimination of certain taxes on the indigenous population (Blanco and Romero Sotelo, 2000). Moreover, the public funds that were collected were not invested in the colony, but were transferred to Spain or used to pay for military forces. In addition, in the early years of independence fiscal revenues again declined, partly due to policy decrees implemented in 1821 that cut the taxes levied on mining, trade, and agricultural production (Carmagnani, 1983). Econometric estimates by Ponzio (2005) conclude that between 50% and 100% of the reduction in economic growth during the first half century after independence was due to the increase in political instability and, moreover, between 50% and 88% of the increase in the growth rate after 1867 was due to the reduction in political instability.

The relationship between political instability and economic stagnation is perhaps best described as a vicious circle (Beatty, 2001). Violence and instability contributed in several ways to keep productive investment, and thus the economy's growth potential, at low levels and perpetuated a fragile fiscal system that limited the government's capacity to promote social and economic development. First, they created an uncertain and risky environment for fixed capital formation. Moreover, by weakening fiscal capacities and hindering modernization of the transport infrastructure, instability kept markets fundamentally restricted to the local area rather than expanding to regional or national horizons. This phenomenon constrained, from the demand side, investment in modern technologies. In addition, it diverted resources away from productive investment as governments, unable to collect taxes, resorted to borrowing from the *agiotistas* (moneylenders) who might otherwise have

---

for a number of decades, the state was unable to regain its firm and exclusive control of money coinage privileges (Romero Sotelo, 1997).

financed business investments.[16] At the same time, however, economic stagnation associated with weak fiscal capabilities fueled the conflict over limited resources, thus causing more instability.

Thus half a century of political, social, and international wars destroyed the potentially beneficial effects of independence on the economy, while at the same time curtailing the resources needed by the state to invest in human capital and infrastructure. Indeed, the diversion of resources into military expenditures implied that no efforts could be made to significantly invest in human capital in a country with very poor educational levels compared to the United States and the majority of European countries. Most important, it also prevented the improvement of transport infrastructure in a country where the lack of a river system suitable for transportation, its mountainous landscape, and the long distances between urban centers and the coast made its geography less favorable than that of the United States, Great Britain, or France, with major coastal cities, river systems, channels, and roads.[17] The resulting high transport costs had highly adverse effects on the division of labor, factor mobility, and regional specialization (Coatsworth, 1990).[18]

Railway construction was delayed by at least 20 years in Mexico with respect to South America. The first railway line—linking Mexico City to the seaport of Veracruz—was opened in 1873. In 1877, Mexico had a railway network of 570 km compared to 2388 km in Brazil, 2262 km in Argentina, 2030 km in Peru, and 1624 km in Chile (Cárdenas, 2003, citing Riguzzi, 1996). Why did it take so long for railways to arrive? Cárdenas (2003) argues that political instability, the associated fiscal crisis of the state, and the lack of financial capital played a major role due to the long-term nature of railway investments and the high cost of railway construction, which was exacerbated by Mexico's geography. Recall that the Veracruz–Mexico City line started at sea level but had to reach an altitude of 8333 ft before arriving at Mexico City, making it then one of the highest in the world.

16. The emergence of moneylenders was a response to three obstacles to the government's solvency and stability: the fact that the fiscal system as created in 1824 never generated enough revenue to cover expenses (as it was based on tariffs on trade that shrank with the contraction of foreign trade), the unwillingness of the wealthy to pay new taxes, and the refusal of foreign capitalists to lend after the default of 1827 (Tenenbaum, 1986).

17. By the 1870s, Mexico still had less than one-tenth the number of kilometers of road per 10,000 inhabitants than the United States (less than 5 km of road passable by four-wheel carts) (Beatty, 2001).

18. As a result, to cite just one example, machinery delivered to Mexico City was twice as expensive as in Veracruz, the port of entry (Cárdenas, 1985).

The deficiency of resources required to modernize the economy was aggravated by the lack of access to foreign credit. Mexico suspended payments on its foreign debt as early as 1828 and did not renew debt service for six decades, making the country an international pariah for foreign bankers during much of the 19th century (Marichal, 1989). Thus not only domestic but also foreign credit was severely restricted in these years.

The abolition of restrictions to foreign trade turned out to be a mixed blessing. While generally regarded by economic historians as beneficial for the Mexican economy, the end of nontariff trade restrictions accelerated the diversion of Mexican foreign trade away from Spain and toward the emerging industrializing powers in the North Atlantic, a trend that had very harmful effects on domestic manufacturing and therefore on the major activity that could have compensated for the decline of the mining sector. Exposure to U.S. and British competition, despite attempts at import prohibitions in the 1820s, led to the collapse of the wool textile industry at the turn of the century and to the prolonged decline of cotton textiles throughout part of the first half of the 19th century.[19] Trade opening toward the Atlantic economy and foreign competition—which in fact started in the period of *comercio libre* and *comercio neutral* introduced by the Bourbon reforms—also appears to have deepened regional fragmentation of local markets, and in particular the cleavage between a mining and agricultural north trading with the rest of the world and a manufacturing and agricultural south plunged into economic depression (Thomson, 1986). As argued by Salvucci (1987), successful protection, as that implemented during this period by the United States, would have required better enforcement and even higher tariffs. However, further increasing tariffs may perhaps have not been feasible. After all, tariff collections were actually not low and, on average between 1822 and 1832, represented 45% of total federal revenues (Salvucci, 1987). The Banco de Avío was established in 1830 to provide subsidies to manufacturing in response to the dilemma implied by tariff protection, but it became a casualty of the political turmoil of the 1830s. Ultimately the future of Mexican manufacturing at that time depended not so much on a return to stricter trade protection, but much more on the possibility of attracting new investment. Such investment was indispensable to expand, modernize, and make Mexico's manufacturing sector more efficient in order to enable it to compete successfully with the machine-produced textiles that were being fabricated in the more advanced economies.

---

19. British cotton exports to Mexico in the 1820s have been estimated at between 30% and 60% of Mexico's national production (Salvucci, 1987).

The persistence of financial backwardness until very late in the 19th century is striking compared not only to advanced economies in the United States and Europe, but also to other Latin American countries such as Argentina, Brazil, and Chile (Marichal, 1997). Financial underdevelopment was manifested in the absence of a banking system, the nonexistence of a formal stock market, the lack of modern financial legislation, and the volatile behavior of very high interest rates. Haber (1997; see also Marichal, 1997, and Maurer and Haber, 2007) argues that four factors prevented the early development of capital markets: the persistent defaulting on Mexican government debt, which prevented the development of a securities market; the political nature of enforcing property rights and contracts; the loose enforcement of financial reporting requirements; and the lack of modern commercial and incorporation legislation, which retarded the development of banks and joint-stock companies. The limitations of capital market development became in turn a serious obstacle to rapid industrial development.

In addition, little progress was made in other areas. The colony had some of the greatest social and regional disparities of any region in the world—the "country of inequality" as Humboldt observed[20]—where 18 families at the end of the 18th century were wealthier than any other family in the Western Hemisphere (MacLachlan and Rodríguez, 1980). It had been a caste society, in fact, where access to employment as well as geographical and occupational mobility were restricted on the basis of ethnic distinctions, and where a number of institutional arrangements tended to increase, rather than reduce, the gap between the private and social benefits of economic activity. This high degree of inequality tended to perpetuate backwardness by preventing the emergence of a middle-class market, reducing the productivity of the labor force due to malnutrition, illness, and lack of education, and producing higher risks of political and social upheaval leading to reduced investment.

To be sure, some changes did take place with independence. Ethnic distinctions in access to employment, justice, and fiscal treatment—which, among other things, had severely restricted capital and labor mobility—were formally abolished. Many corporate privileges, including most of the guilds, were eliminated, while corporate property rights were limited to the church and the Indian communities and town councils. The number of royal monopolies on the production and distribution of many commodities was reduced

---

20. "Mexico is the country of inequality. Nowhere does there exist such a fearful difference in the distribution of fortune, civilization, cultivation of the soil, and property" (Humboldt, 1822, p. 64).

and their activities regulated. Efforts were also made to modernize the judiciary and revise archaic judicial codes. The use of public force to collect the tithe ended in 1833 (Coatsworth, 1990). But many of these changes had little effect in a backward social and political order. The persistence of backwardness is in turn related to the nature of the foundational act of the postindependence state: the fact that having begun and been defeated as a popular insurrection[21]—feared by both the Spanish and Creole conservative elites—independence came eventually to Mexico through "a virtual *coup d'état* by the colony's Creole elite, carried out largely to separate Mexico from the liberalizing process under way in the mother country" (Coatsworth, 1978).[22]

This had several consequences. Institutional modernization was de facto, and sometimes de jure, slow. A new civil code was only produced in 1870—almost 50 years after independence—and even then nothing replaced the old commercial code. The colonial mining code remained almost intact until 1877. Modern banking and patent laws were nonexistent. In spite of constitutional dispositions, taxes and restrictions on domestic trade remained.[23]

The system of government preserved the arbitrary nature of political power in colonial times. Economic success or failure strictly depended on the relationship between enterprise and political authorities. As Coatsworth (1978, p. 94) put it:

> Every enterprise, urban or rural, [was forced] to operate in a highly
> politicized manner, using kinship networks, political influence, and
> family prestige to gain privileged access to subsidized credit, to aid
> various stratagems for recruiting labor, to collect debts or enforce
> contracts, to evade taxes or circumvent the courts, and to defend or
> assert titles to land.... The chief obstacle was the nature of the state
> itself, its operating principles, the basis for all its acts. Mexico's eco-
> nomic organization could not have been made more efficient with-

21. In contrast to other Latin American countries, independence in Mexico began as a radical, popular movement directed against *gachupines*, officials, and landlords. Knight (1992) traces this peculiarity back to the increase in rural protests during the economic expansion of the late 18th century combined with agricultural crises and political instability.

22. Behind the triumph of the army led by Agustín de Iturbide were conservative interests wanting to separate Mexico from a Spain controlled at the time by liberals.

23. Formally abolished by the 1857 Constitutional Assembly, domestic trade taxes (*alcabalas*) remained in effect well into the *Porfiriato*.

out a revolution in the relationship between the state and economic activity.

In sum, while economic activity had remained "state-centered," in the sense that every enterprise was forced to operate in a highly politicized manner, the state, compared to colonial times, had in fact been weakened and was unable to remove the obstacles to economic development resulting from the decline in mining activity, foreign competition, and the lack of transport infrastructure and financial capital. Economic and industrial stagnation followed as a consequence of a persistent lack of markets and their fragmentation.

The first signs of a moderate recovery appeared in the 1830s in mining and manufacturing. In textile manufacturing, the recovery was associated with the creation of the Banco de Avío in the 1830s, a protectionist stance in trade policy, and expansion of the money supply in the 1840s (Cárdenas, 1997).[24] In the 1820s, the government managed to temporarily attract some major new foreign investors to Mexico's mining sector. However, after a few decades of operation, they left the country, having failed to meet their expectations of a highly profitable business. Among the adverse factors that affected them were the political and social instability, the scarcity of a qualified labor force,[25] and the various governments' fiscal and financial ineptitudes (Romero Sotelo and Jáuregui, 2003). In addition, their reliance on modern machinery and techniques was far from a success, being plagued by difficulties in maintaining and repairing the equipment, and the problems posed by the lack of infrastructure and the resulting high transport costs. In any case, by 1850 no foreign capital remained in the industry, having been replaced by a new wave of local investors. These investors were pivotal to the mining industry's slow but persistent recovery that took place in the second half of the 19th century, helped by the discovery of new deposits, improvements in infrastructure—the railway system in particular—and the political and social stability of the *Porfiriato* (Cárdenas, 2003).

24. As documented in Sandoval (1976, cited by Cárdenas, 1997), the number of spindles increased by 34% between 1845 and 1865 and more than doubled between 1865 and 1879. The number of looms increased by nearly 70% between 1843 and 1854 and more than doubled between 1865 and 1879.

25. This explains the government's attempts to help reduce the scarcity of labor. These included the authorization to use incarcerated prisoners as workers in the mines and the granting of exemption of military recruitment to workers of the mining sector (Romero Sotelo and Jáuregui, 2003).

The signs of recovery notwithstanding, it was not until the late 1860s that the entire economy would start growing in a sustained way. A fundamental element behind the resumption of economic growth was the recovery of the mining sector. Indeed, after its drastic collapse during the years of the struggle for independence and its aftermath, many decades went by before mining activity gradually began to attract new investments. By the 1860s these investments, by local entrepreneurs, led to the discovery of new, rich deposits of precious metals and thus helped to boost mining activity once again. The recovery of silver mining, in particular, helped to put an end to the liquidity crisis and the credit crunch that had so adversely affected Mexican businesses for many years since independence. In addition, this mining boom and the expansion of local and international trade had a major impact in increasing tax revenues (Cárdenas, 2003).

Liberal misperceptions in the mid-19th century?

The list of obstacles to economic development in 19th-century Mexico is equally significant for what it excludes. Revisionism by economic historians suggests, indeed, that two of the traditional culprits, the land tenure system and the economic power of the church, were not in fact among the major causes of economic stagnation during this period.

The system of land tenure and agricultural production had been organized since the 17th century into large estates called haciendas. While highly inequitable and socially and macroeconomically inefficient, the hacienda system was far from a semifeudal organization, promoting waste and resource misallocation. Historical research has produced an image of the hacienda as one of a capitalistic and technologically dynamic undertaking with an economic rationality comparable to that of a modern agricultural enterprise. In this view, the hacienda largely exploited its comparative advantages— economies of scale and access to external credit and information on new technologies and distant markets (see, among others, Van Young, 1981, 1986, and García de León et al., 1988). A "division of labor" had, in fact, been established through time between the hacienda and other forms of agricultural production—small landowners, tenant farmers, or Indian villagers—by which each of them specialized in those products and crops where they enjoyed a competitive advantage: cattle, sheep, wool, food grains, *pulque*, sugar, and sisal on the haciendas, and fruits, tomatoes, chilies, silk, and small animals such as pigs and poultry among the small-scale producers and villages.

Similar revisionism applies to the church as an economic institution. By the middle of the 19th century, the church had become the country's single major landowner, owning about one-third of the arable land (López Cámara, 1967), and was the major financial institution. With respect to its first role, several studies suggest that church haciendas were at least as well managed as private haciendas. In any case, after independence most of these estates were rented to private farmers and *hacendados* so that their efficiency did not depend on church administration (see Bazant, 1977; Knowlton, 1985; Matute et al., 1995; Staples, 1976). On the other hand, the church appropriated the tithe (*diezmo*), a 10% tax on gross output (charged mainly on agricultural and livestock production). As with any other tax, the tithe reduced the profitability of agricultural production and probably discouraged it, even though some authors have doubts about this (see, in particular, Garcia Alba, 1974, and Coatsworth, 1978). The reason is that the effect of the tithe in pushing labor and capital out of private agriculture was probably very small because the church itself, and the Indian villages, produced a major portion of the country's farm products and livestock. The net effect on GDP was, in any case, probably positive, since differences in productivity between private agriculture and the rest of the economy suggest that nonagricultural activities were already more productive than agriculture.

More important, however, is the use to which church revenues were put. Far from financing wholly "unproductive" expenditures, the church invested a considerable portion of its revenues (including also private donations and net income from its various properties) in loans to private entrepreneurs, with no legal or practical restrictions to prevent recipients from investing in factories rather than haciendas or other activities. It did this by lending at below market interest rates—usually at a 6% rate on the security on real property. Because it dominated the mortgage-lending market, this probably had the effect, in turn, of bringing market interest rates down. In addition, given its close contacts with landowners, it likely let them run in arrears on their debt without foreclosure (Maddison, 1995). As Coatsworth (1978) put it, the church "performed like a modern development bank, charging taxpayers to subsidize the accumulation of private capital.... Indeed, the Church probably raised the rate of investment above what it would have been had the tithe revenues remained in private hands."

If this revisionism by economic historians is correct, then some of the main elements of the liberal economic program—free trade, the privatization of corporate and public property, and the liberalization of the land market— were largely misdirected from a strictly (and admittedly narrow) economic development perspective. The first (free trade) probably meant further stimulus to the decline of local manufacturing and to the "ruralization" of the labor force. The second, the privatization of corporate property, had the effect of destroying the major, and for a long time practically the only, banking institution in the economy. The third, the liberalization of the land market, was to contribute to further land concentration and eventually to the social explosion of 1910.

The conservative faction was, of course, no better. Although some of its members, Lucas Alamán (1792–1853)[26] in particular, pioneered the first, and short-lived, industrialization efforts in the 1830s—through industrial protection and the creation of the first public development bank (*Banco de Avío*) to finance the development of the textile industry—the social and political forces that supported them tended to perpetuate the very arbitrary nature of political power that had had such harmful effects on economic development since colonial times. As a result, a coalition that could forge a developmental state did not emerge, and in its absence some of the major obstacles to economic development remained in place. The liberals who were willing and able to carry out the country's political and social modernization were also antistatist in economic terms; while those that favored economic modernization through an interventionist state were the conservatives, who were strongly opposed to political and social modernization.

Mexico's decline in international perspective

While Latin America as a whole also fell behind during most of the 19th century, Mexico's decline was particularly deep. Brazil, Chile, and Venezuela, the other countries with available data, all registered a reduction of their per capita GDP relative to the United States, but were far from recording a collapse of the magnitude of the Mexican one and actually advanced relative to Mexico (see table 2.2). In fact, Mexico's economic retardation took place with respect to all regions in the world (see table 2.3).

---

26. Lucas Alamán was the first finance minister to implement trade protection measures for the development of Mexican manufactures. Another figure worth mentioning is Estevan de Antuñano, a Creole industrialist, whose many pamphlets best articulated the case for protectionism and industrialization. On Alamán and Antuñano, see Hale (1961) and Morales (1999).

Table 2.2   Per capita GDP as a percentage of U.S. level

	1820	1870
Mexico	**60.4**	**27.6**
Chile	55.2	52.8
Brazil	51.4	29.2
Venezuela	36.6	23.3

Source: Maddison (2006).
Per capita GDP in 1990 Geary-Khamis dollars.

Table 2.3   Mexico's per capita GDP as a percentage of per capita GDP

	1820	1870
USA	60.4	27.6
Western Europe	63.1	34.4
Eastern Europe	111.1	71.9
Latin America	109.8	99.7
Asia	130.6	121.2
Africa	180.7	134.8
World average	113.8	77.2

Source: Maddison (2006).
Per capita GDP in 1990 Geary-Khamis dollars.

The role of political instability in Mexico's decline can be illustrated with a comparison to Chile, the Latin American country among the four in table 2.2 with the smallest relative decline with respect to the United States. In contrast to Mexico, which was marked by continuous political instability until the dictatorship of Porfirio Díaz in 1877, Chile achieved political stability in the decade following independence with a modernizing conservative regime formalized in the 1833 Constitution.[27] The fortunes of these two countries could not be more different: while Mexico, as we have seen, plunged into economic decline for most of the century, Chile managed to prosper on the basis of its exports of copper and temperate agriculture products (wheat), as well

27. On the Chilean exception to the rule of political instability and the tradition of *caudillismo* in Hispanic America, see Valenzuela (2006).

Table 2.4   GDP and exports per capita
in Chile and Mexico

	1820	1870
Per capita GDP		
Chile	694	1290
Mexico	759	674
Per capita exports		
Chile	1.6[a]	14.2
Mexico	2.1[a]	2.3

Source: Maddison (2006) for per capita GDP;
Coatsworth (1998) for per capita exports
Per capita GDP in 1990 Geary-Khamis dollars.
Per capita exports are in current dollars.
[a] 1800.

as nitrates after the war of the Pacific.[28] Thus while Chile almost doubled its per capita GDP between 1820 and 1870, Mexico saw its own per capita income reduced by more than 10%. Chile's exports per capita, which in 1800 had been about 25% less than those of Mexico, were more than six times the Mexican level in 1870 (see table 2.4).

The comparison with Brazil, which had a peaceful transition to independence followed by relative political stability, also confirms the previous point. Starting from a lower per capita income than Mexico in 1820, Brazil moved ahead of Mexico by 1870 (table 2.2). The comparison also highlights the role of other obstacles, because political stability did not prevent Brazil from falling behind the United States and some European countries.[29] High transport costs and archaic economic institutions, as in the case of Mexico, remained in place

28. Causality, however, probably also ran the other way around from economic prosperity to political stability (just as in the case of Mexico, it also ran from economic stagnation to political instability). Furtado (1970), for example, gives the primary role to economic prosperity. He argues that the opportunities, determined by foreign demand conditions, were exceptional in the Chilean case. First, Chile had a mining economy based on copper, with nitrates replacing cooper after the War of the Pacific (1879–1883) and demand expanding during this period. Second, Chile produced a surplus of temperate agricultural commodities, notably wheat, which gave her distinct advantage in the Pacific zone at the time when gold was discovered in California and Australia.

29. Nor, incidentally, did the political stability provided by colonial rule in Cuba (until 1898) prevent this country from falling behind.

and prevented Brazil from catching up with the industrializing economies at the time (on the economic retardation of Brazil during the 19th century, see Leff, 1972).

The role of inequality, a feature that Mexico shares with the rest of Latin America, is highlighted by comparison with the United States. Engerman and Sokoloff (2002) emphasize how relative equality generated the conditions for growth in the former British colonies in North America. In the United States, together with high per capita income, equality in the distribution of income led to the formation of a middle-class market[30] that was essential to the development of industry (the mass production of standardized goods subject to economies of scale, "the American system of manufactures"). It was also favorable to technological innovation, as greater equality meant a general concern with extracting opportunities from innovation, and this led to a patent system most favorable to the common people. Greater equity also creates the possibility for broad-based local movements for free compulsory education that had political success, in contrast to relatively unequal societies where a disenfranchised majority could not effectively advocate widespread education. The favorable conditions present in the United States were absent in the case of Mexico, where, as already mentioned, the high degree of inequality inhibited growth by preventing the emergence of a middle-class market, reducing the productivity of the labor force, and contributing to political instability.

The strikingly different degrees of economic inequality and social cohesion in the United States and Mexico have their origins in different colonial experiences (and in the case of Mexico, its pre-Hispanic past) (see, among others, Beato, 2004). In Mexico, Spanish colonialism was based on an acute exploitation of vast masses of the indigenous population, forcing them to work in adverse human and economic conditions with the objective of transferring their surplus back to the metropolis. In the United States, such exploitation did not occur, as the indigenous population there was much smaller. The United States was a more egalitarian nation of immigrants with similar common beliefs.

Finally, it is worth noting that the role of inequality is complementary to that of other factors. This role cannot be fully separated from that of political instability—since this is one of the channels through which inequality has adverse effects on growth—nor from that of institutions, since such

---

30. To the extent that the poor spent a smaller share of their income on manufactures and the wealthy spent their income on nonstandardized goods.

institutions as the hacienda and debt peonage are precisely those that contribute most to inequality in wealth and human capital. On the other hand,
differences in the degree of inequality are unlikely to provide a complete
explanation for differential paths of development. Mexico was no less unequal
in the late 19th century when economic growth finally started. In fact, it may
have been more unequal, as a result of the liberal reforms in the mid- to late
19th century, than it was during the first part of the 19th century.

3

The *Porfiriato* and the Beginnings of Modern Economic Growth

While the consolidation of a developmental state in Mexico would take place well into the 20th century, the removal of some of the obstacles to economic development in the last decades of the previous century would open the door to a process of high and sustained economic growth. Such a process was made possible by, in particular, the emergence of a strong state, under the government of Porfirio Díaz, capable of ending social violence and achieving long-term political stability. In doing so, the Díaz regime was able to successfully stimulate and trigger a vast wave of foreign and domestic investments by discretionally and effectively protecting the economic interests and property rights of selected groups of businessmen and financial groups, and by implementing tax reform and debt rescheduling to strengthen fiscal revenues. This wave of investments transformed Mexico's economic structure by integrating its domestic market through the reduction of transport costs brought about by the arrival of railways.

In 1877, at the time when General Porfirio Díaz became Mexico's president for the first time, 42% of Mexico's gross domestic product (GDP) was generated by agriculture and only 16% by manufacturing (see table 3.1). More than 70% of the population of 9.5 million people lived in rural areas and more than 80% of those age 6 and older could not read or write (see table A.3). In the following years, a turnaround in Mexico's long-term economic decline took place. The main barriers to economic expansion were brought down by transformation of the international economic environment as well as by domestic

Table 3.1   Per capita GDP and sectoral composition of GDP

	1877	1895	1910
Per capita GDP at constant			
1900 prices (index 1800 = 100)	85.0	128.8	190.2
Percent of GDP			
Agriculture and livestock[a]	42.2	38.2	33.7
Agriculture	25.0	19.9	21.2
Livestock	13.6	18.0	12.2
Forestry	2.4	0.3	0.3
Fishing and hunting	1.2	n.s.	n.s.
Mining	10.4	6.3	8.4
Manufacturing	16.2	12.8	14.9
Construction	0.6	0.6	0.8
Transportation	2.5	3.3	2.7
Commerce	16.9	16.8	19.3
Government	11.2	8.9	7.2
Other	n.s.	13.1	12.9
Total	100.0	100.0	100.0

Source: Based on Coatsworth (1990), tables V.4 and V.5.

[a] Includes agriculture, livestock, forestry and fishing. According to Coatsworth (1990), his estimated figures for agriculture, reported here, include commercialized production as well as the estimated amount geared to self-consumption.

n.s. = not significant.

changes in Mexico's political and economic structure that took place during the Díaz dictatorship, a 33-year period of political stability (1877–1910), aptly named the *Porfiriato* by Mexican historians.

Order and progress

Historians' assessment of the *Porfiriato*'s significance for Mexico's social and economic development has changed markedly in recent decades. From being seen essentially as a period of dictatorship and harsh exploitation of peasants, it has come to be considered a key phase in Mexico's transition from a semi-feudal mode of production toward a capitalist one promoted by a strongly centralized state. It was the first period in Mexico's history as an independent nation when the country managed to build a strong state that, besides ending civil strife and guaranteeing a long period of political stability, created economic institutions that helped to remove key obstacles to its economic development (Tenorio and Gómez-Galvarriato, 2006). Most important, the Díaz administration secured sufficient financial and fiscal resources, thus giving the state room to maneuver to implement a strategy of sectoral incentives to promote the creation of infrastructure and industrialization. This strategy, combined with selective trade protection and a significant depreciation of the real exchange rate, served to foster a new and dynamic integration of the Mexican domestic economy in international markets.[1]

However, the rapid expansion and structural change in Mexico's economy was not accompanied by a more egalitarian distribution of income and wealth among the population. In fact, the society was characterized by sharp social cleavages and widespread poverty, especially in the rural areas. In addition, the state's arbitrary protection of the economic interests and property rights of certain business and banking groups led to the formation of highly profitable oligopolies/monopolies protected from market competition by high barriers to entry. The concentration of market power and land was fostered by the special privileges and concessions granted by the government. These concessions and privileges did stimulate the economic expansion of various industries, but tended to hinder the efficient allocation of investment and credit and thus constrained the economy below its growth potential. By the beginning of the 20th century, these factors, coupled with the increasing discontent of peasants, protests from the nascent workers' movement, and the disenchantment of some elite circles away from central Mexico—alienated from political or economic power—were becoming a lethal combination for the *Porfiriato*, and in 1910 they drew the closing curtain on it.

Melding a liberal political background with conservative economic goals, the *Porfiriato*'s ideology is summarized in the positivist lemma of "Order and Progress." This positivist ideology, which emerged fully in the country in the early 1890s, was promoted by the *científicos*, a group of highly educated managers, lawyers, and entrepreneurs in the government. They were led by José Yves Limantour and were trained in the positivist and liberal tradition that saw order as a precondition for economic progress. Indeed, order was seen as

---

1. For an in-depth analysis of Díaz's trade policy and its orientation to promote industrialization, see Kuntz Ficker (2007) and Márquez (2002).

a sine qua non for capital formation and the expansion of economic activity. More precisely, an end to the military and political struggles that had plagued Mexico since its independence was considered an essential precondition for business confidence and the recovery of private investment. Strengthening of the central government was efficiently pursued by a combination of the authoritarian use of force and alliances with relevant groups. An important element behind this strategy was also the selective enforcement or protection of the property rights of certain groups to thus secure their rents and economic privileges.

Another such precondition was securing a minimum of financial and fiscal revenues to ensure the state's ability to implement economic and social policies. Recall that the ensuing political instability and the economic slowdown after independence, lasting several decades, had wrecked public finances to such an extent that it was not possible to cover on a regular and adequate basis the salaries of civil servants and military personnel (Jáuregui, 2005).

A requirement for increasing the political power of the federal government during the *Porfiriato* was fiscal reform. This reform, actually launched in 1869 by Matías Romero, laid the basic groundwork for widening the tax base (Jáuregui, 2005). With this strengthened fiscal capacity and the practically complete control of the political structure, the Díaz regime provided nearly three decades of institutional stability, ending an era of violent insurrections. Moreover, in the absence of effective opposition, in all six presidential elections held between 1876 and 1910, Díaz received at least 75% of the vote.[2]

Progress meant transforming Mexico into an industrialized nation. To achieve this required addressing some of the traditional barriers to economic growth, such as the lack of integration of the domestic market and the lack of financial capital both for the state and for large-scale investment projects. The importance of these obstacles to economic development was well recognized at the time. In the words of Matías Romero: "This nation...has in its soil immense treasures of agricultural and mineral wealth, which now cannot be exploited due to the lack of capital and communications" (cited by Rosenzweig, 1965, translation by the authors).

2. Actually Díaz held the presidency from 1876 to 1880, and from 1884 until May 26, 1911, when he formally resigned and went into exile in France. During 1880–1884, though Manuel Gonzalez served as the formally elected president, the real political power remained in Díaz's hands.

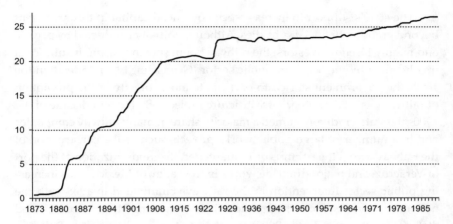

Figure 3.1 Expansion of the railway network during the *Porfiriato* and beyond
(Thousands of kilometers)
Source: INEGI (1999a).

Expansion of the railway network and integration of the domestic market

One of the *Porfiriato*'s major achievements was integration of the domestic market, rapidly pushed forward by expansion of the railway network. In 1877 Mexico had 570 km of railways constructed, and only one line was fully operational, the Mexico City–Veracruz line. By 1885, the network covered 6000 km, in 1890 it covered 10,000 km, in 1900 it covered 14,000 km, and in 1910 it covered close to 20,000 km (Kuntz Ficker, 1999; Rosenzweig, 1965).[3] By 1990 only some 6000 additional kilometers had been constructed, thus about 75% of the network had been built during the *Porfiriato* (see figure 3.1).

Such fast expansion of the railway network was made possible by the concessions and financial incentives awarded by the state to railway companies, mainly foreign ones. Subsidies granted on railway construction amounted to between 20% and 35% of the total cost (Calderón, 1965; Cárdenas, 1997). The subsidies granted to private companies were so large that, in general, they guaranteed that those companies would not incur any losses (Marichal, 1998).

3. By 1910, Mexico had 1 km of railway for every 100 sq. km of territory and 13 km for each 10,000 people (Rosenzweig, 1965).

The state's support to increase social overhead capital in this area went beyond granting financial subsidies. Although initially conducted by private and mainly foreign investors, the railway boom saw increasing institutional involvement by the Mexican public sector (Grunstein, 1999). Indeed, in the 1890s the government started to participate more directly in the promotion of railways as well as other infrastructure projects. By the first decade of the 1900s the state gradually gained a majority share in many railway companies and in a number of large public works projects such as the construction of the railway across the Isthmus of Tehuantepec, the modernization of the port of Veracruz, and major drainage works in the valley of Mexico. This increasing public sector intervention in the railways culminated in 1908 with the nationalization of some of the principal lines connecting Mexico to the United States (Marichal and Topik, 2003) and the creation of *Ferrocarriles Nacionales de México* (FNM), a public sector enterprise. In practice, FNM eliminated all competition in the railway system in the domestic market (Grunstein, 1999). The financial obligations entailed in this nationalization process led to an increase in Mexico's external debt (Marichal, 1998).

The railway network was mainly oriented from the center to the ports, essentially in the Gulf of Mexico, and toward the borders, mostly in the north, approximately along the routes of the mule trade that had prevailed for centuries (Rosenzweig, 1965). This pattern notwithstanding, Mexico's railway system served to meet the domestic market's demand as much, if not more, than transporting goods for export (Kuntz Ficker, 1999). The long railway lines did help boost foreign trade, but there were numerous short railways connecting local markets within regions and transporting inputs for construction, mining, metal, and other industries. In fact, the majority of the train freight was destined for the domestic market. For example, between 1898 and 1905, less than 2.5% of Mexico's total freight carried by train went to the United States (Kuntz Ficker, 1999).

As in other less developed countries, the most significant economic impacts of the creation of a railway system in Mexico were a reduction in transport costs and integration of the domestic market. According to Coatsworth's (1979) estimates, the railway boom brought an 80% reduction in freight costs per kilometer from 1878 to 1910. By this latter date, the average cost of transporting goods by train was 50% lower than for the alternative means of transportation then available (Kuntz Ficker, 1999). The impact was enormous, as Mexico's geography had required a rapid, modern transportation system at a national level. By reducing transport costs and interconnecting regions, expansion of the railway system gave a big push to the economy that lifted it from the stagnation trap in which it was mired. The trains' reliability, speed, and lower costs amplified enormously the size of the domestic market, increasing mobility and affecting the geographical redistribution of labor, and bringing down local and regional trade barriers while allowing for more intensified competition. These effects were reinforced by the significant increase in road travel safety that the Díaz regime achieved.

From 1861 to 1895 the internal market expanded threefold and had increased to 5 million people with sufficient purchasing power to acquire manufactured goods (Cárdenas, 1997; Haber, 1989). The boom also helped to integrate agricultural producers into the market economy and to integrate different regions. Simultaneously it contributed to the birth of new activities whose production scales and capital intensity made them unprofitable in the absence of a unified national market. The boom also benefited some old activities, such as mining, which would most likely have remained abandoned without the railway expansion, as neither the necessary capital inputs for its development nor the commercialization of mineral products would have occurred. In particular, without the railways, the exploitation of copper, zinc, and lead would have remained unprofitable due to the high transport costs (Cárdenas, 1997). This process allowed the exploitation of the rich northern mining zones in Sonora and Chihuahua, traditionally separated from the rest of the country by the lack of transportation. Another effect of railway expansion was the displacement of European countries by the United States as Mexico's main trading partner.

Besides providing cost reductions, railway systems tend to promote economic development by inducing innovations in the way trade and other activities are managed or carried out, as well as raising demand for domestic suppliers. In the case of Mexico at that time, however, the lack of backward linkages provided little impetus to local industrialization. Moreover, it may have even reinforced the comparative disadvantages in some manufacturing sectors. Indeed, although the demand from mining and railroad tracks led to the first steel plant in the country, most of its intermediate inputs and capital goods—from the simple ones like iron tools and rails to the more sophisticated ones like spare parts and locomotives—were imported. Moreover, the labor hired locally for the railway companies was generally low skilled and poorly paid, and supervisory and engineering personnel were hired from outside (Kuntz Ficker, 1999). Such a lack of domestic human capital restricted the spillover effects of the railway systems' administration processes on the managerial practices of other industries. In addition, reinvestment of profits was rather limited, as shown by the fact that by 1910, 57% of gross earnings were spent abroad (Coatsworth, 1979). Notwithstanding these limitations, there is consensus that the railway system made a fundamental contribution to Mexico's economic growth through its impact on integrating the regional networks of production and trade (Kuntz Ficker, 1999; Parlee, 1981).

Financial capital and foreign investment

During the *Porfiriato* the Mexican economy finally began to escape from the financial underdevelopment trap in which it had been stuck for most of the century. A crucial element for this process was the state-orchestrated merger in 1884 of the two largest banks to create the *Banco Nacional de México* (*Banamex*). *Banamex* was granted a privileged market position in Mexico's financial system, in particular by being exempted from the 5% tax that all other banks had to pay on the quantity of paper money they printed. In addition, it was allowed to have an outstanding ratio of money bills to reserves three times higher than the ratio allowed to other banks. In turn, *Banamex* gave Díaz sufficient resources to finance public spending and thus it allowed his regime to proceed at a slow pace in launching tax reform that would strengthen fiscal revenues in the long run. This room for maneuver was important, given that in the early years of his regime drastic tax reform was unviable and most likely risked political stability (Haber, 2006). The reforms were grounded on the legal changes put forward by Matías Romero. In particular, his introduction of stamp duties on various transactions led to a very significant increase in tax collections that—combined with changes in the tax codes on mining, oil, and commerce—brought about persistent increases in fiscal revenues and later produced balanced budgets and surpluses except in the last 3 years (Carmagnani, 1994; Haber, 2006) (see figure 3.2).

By modifying the commercial codes (1884, 1889), as well as the national banking law (1897), the government allowed a regulated increase in the number of banks, but maintained the highly concentrated nature of the banking sector. Indeed, 35 banks were created between 1864 and 1908, but by 1911 *Banamex* and *Banco de Londres y México* held more than 60% of the total assets of the domestic banking system (Haber, 2006). The concentration of the banking system, and the lack of effective regulations to oversee its practices, allowed for vast expansion of related lending (*auto-préstamos*), that is, long-term loans and credits to bank directors, their relatives, and their business groups. This practice was legal and well known, and was actually rooted in pre-*Porfiriato* times (Maurer, 2002). Most important, given Mexico's incipient financial

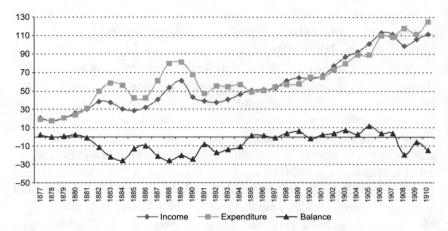

Figure 3.2 Public finances during the *Porfiriato*, 1877–1910 (Millions of pesos)
Source: Cardenas (2003), based on Carmagnani (1994).

development at that time, *auto-préstamos* reduced the transaction costs of channeling funds from savers to investors and thus provided vast financial resources to large, established, well-known firms and businessmen connected to the banking sector. However, given the legal barriers that constrained the creation of new banks under the *Porfiriato*, credit was severely restricted for small and medium firms, as well as for new firms whose management was not related to or closely associated with the banking elite (Haber, 1991, 2006).[4]

This lack of finance became a major obstacle for the expansion of new manufacturing activities and a force to increase its overall concentration. The acute duality of the credit market—with a few selected well-connected firms having unbounded access to bank loans and the vast majority of firms with no such access—took place even though the monetary means of payments expanded and brought about a drop in interest rates of from 10%–12% in about 1880 to 6%–8% in 1888 (Solís, 2000). The Bolsa, an embryo of a formal stock market, was created in 1895, and by the first decade of the 20th century the local press published regular quotations for an average of 80 mining companies, some 20 industrial firms, and 20 banks (Marichal, 1997). Note,

4. At the time, the creation of any new bank had to be formally approved by the federal government, Congress, and the Ministry of Finance. Most important, local and state governments did not have the legal power to authorize the creation of banks (Haber, 2006) and thus they could not break the highly oligopolistic position of *Banamex* and a few other large banks.

however, that by the end of the *Porfiriato* there was still no central bank that could act as a "lender of last resort" to guarantee the private sector's deposits and the solvency of the banking system.

Foreign investment in mining, the oil sector, and agroexports was a key element of the regime's development strategy, and was actively sought after through various incentives, including subsidies and tax exemptions (Haber, 2006; Solís, 2000). These inducements and profitable investment opportunities led to a vast inflow of foreign capital. After 1880, U.S. and European capital flowed in. This flow increased for the next 15 years and boomed in the first decade of the 1900s (King, 1970). From 1884 to 1911, foreign investment increased by more than 30 times. These investments were concentrated in railway construction, mining, and public debt, followed by public utilities (electricity), agriculture, and banking (Rosenzweig, 1965). In addition, an important category of investments was associated with immigrants and went into the development of industries serving the internal market. As described by Vernon (1963, p. 44): "Most of the major cotton textile plants that came into being during this period claimed a Frenchman as a major partner, usually a dominant one. The new large breweries of the period, such as those of Toluca, Monterrey, Guadalajara, and Orizaba, usually reported a German group among their founders. And in paper, cement, explosives, and steel, French, British, United States, or Spanish entrepreneurs were prominent." U.S. and British capital controlled most of the railways and the mining sector. German, French, and Spanish merchants dominated wholesale commerce and played a major role in the first banks.[5] By 1911, European capital represented 62% of total foreign capital and U.S. capital the remaining 38%, and Mexico represented more than 45% of total U.S. foreign investments (while being of secondary importance as a destination for European capital) (Cosío Villegas, 1965).

Institutional modernization and the international environment

More generally, state policies were geared to promote private investment and guarantee the best conditions for its operation. The legal framework for the

---

5. Marichal and Topik (2003) estimate foreign capital's share of total capital to possibly be greater than one-third. Navarrete (1963) states that during the *Porfiriato* more than half of new investments were foreign (cited by Paz Sánchez, 2000).

conduct of private business was soon transformed. In 1884 new legal codes for trade and mining were adopted to improve conditions for foreign investment. Regional tariffs on domestic trade (*alcabalas*) were finally abolished in 1896.[6] New patent laws were implemented with the purpose of strengthening intellectual property rights in order to build a better institutional framework capable of encouraging technology transfer and fostering domestic inventions. To what extent this reform in patent law was the key factor that caused the dramatic increases in technology transfer and patenting activity after 1890 (at annual rates of 17% between 1893 and 1910) is open to debate (see Beatty, 2001). An *Industrias Nuevas* program provided temporary tax and tariff exemptions to firms investing in new industrial activities (Beatty, 2001). Foreign trade policy was far from being exclusively export oriented. It combined focused high tariff protection, consistent with supporting import substitution in consumer goods industries, and declining *average* tariffs to enhance manufacturers' access to low-cost capital and intermediate goods (see Beatty, 2002; Kuntz Ficker, 2002, 2007; Márquez, 2002). In addition, it put in place a rationalization of import tariffs to ensure that the import tax rate on final goods was higher than on its inputs (Tenorio and Gómez-Galvarriato, 2006). The ratio of import duties to the value of imports was on the order of 46% in the 1870s and 1880s, falling to 21% in the 1900s (Beatty, 2002). In the early 1880s, government revenues from trade taxes represented more than 60% of total government revenue. The view that the *Porfiriato* gradually and successfully negotiated tariff policy with political actors in order to gear it (after 1893) to promote manufacturing runs against the previously held conventional view (i.e., Rosenzweig, in Cosío Villegas, 1965) that its aim was to provide tax revenues. In sum, an industrial policy partly based on selective trade protection and other policy instruments appears to have been gradually established to promote rapid industrialization.

Accompanying these policy changes was a more propitious external economic environment. By 1870 the second industrial revolution in the industrialized countries had spurred demand for minerals and other raw materials. Technological innovation in freight shipping and the expansion of railways in the United States drastically decreased the costs of international transportation. In addition, there was a notable flow of international investment to several less developed countries: between 1870 and 1900 this flow doubled the value of the outstanding capital stock held by foreign investors (Maddison,

---

6. The 1857 Constitution abolished the *alcabalas*, but the civil war and French intervention prevented application of the measure.

1989). Combined with the end of political instability, the new environment helped to restore Mexico's international creditworthiness. Having defaulted on its external debt on six different occasions between 1824 and 1880, as attempts to renegotiate and reinitiate debt payments were frustrated by recurrent fiscal crises associated with the outbreak of civil and international wars, in 1889 the Mexican government finally reached an agreement with foreign bankers on rescheduling Mexico's foreign debt. By the early 1890s, the country's access to international capital markets was restored. From then until 1911, Mexico's external debt increased fourfold, mostly to finance public works in infrastructure (Marichal, 1989).

Before discussing the results of the strategy and the new international environment, it is worth noting that the modernization of the institutional framework for industry, banking, and trade was absent in the legal framework of labor relations (Bortz and Haber, 2002). In practice, during the *Porfiriato*, no norms or legal rulings were put in place to modernize labor market regulations (de la Peña and Aguirre, 2006). This allowed for the simultaneous coexistence of quasi-feudal labor relations in some regions and activities with capitalist relations in other, more modern areas. The lack of progress on labor codes and regulations increased workers' fragility on matters regarding working hours, salaries, and social protection. Such limitations did not help to reduce the concentration of income.

Modernization with inequality

What was the overall development outcome of this strategy? Economic growth and modernization were felt in many areas, reversing several decades of decline, and from 1877 to 1910 Mexico's GDP increased by a multiple of 3.5 in real terms, achieving an annual average growth rate of 2.5% in per capita terms (Coatsworth, 1989). More recent estimates put this annual average growth figure somewhat lower, at 2.1% (Bortz and Haber, 2002) and 2.3% (Maddison, 2006, for the period 1870–1910). This relatively high rate of expansion would not be experienced again until after 1940, except for briefs periods of recovery after the revolution and the Great Depression. Overall, Mexico's growth performance from 1870 to 1910 was outstanding in the international context (see table 3.2). In Latin America, although it fell short of Argentina's golden age, it was superior to that of Uruguay and much better than that of Brazil. It also implied a process of catching up with respect to the advanced regions of the world economy. As a fraction of U.S. per capita GDP, Mexico's incomes per

Table 3.2 Mexico's per capita GDP as a percentage of per capita GDP

	1870	1890	1910
Brazil	94.5	127.3	220.3
Spain	55.8	62.3	89.4
Argentina	51.4	47.0	44.3
Western Europe[a]	32.3	38.3	50.1
Uruguay	30.9	47.1	54.0
United States	27.6	29.8	34.1

Source: Based on Maddison (2003).

GDP levels are in 1990 international Geary-Khamis dollars.

[a] 12 countries.

capita moved from less than 28% to 34%, and with respect to Western Europe, relative per capita GDP increased from about 32% to 50%. Performance compared to Spain's was particularly impressive. By 1910, Mexico's per capita GDP was nearly 90% of the Spanish level (compared to 56% in 1870).

Industrial and agricultural development together with increasing regional specialization modified the urban landscape. The main urban centers (locations with more than 20,000 inhabitants) expanded in number (from 22 to 29) from 1895 to 1910 and their urban populations grew at a rate of 2.5% per year, well above the average population growth (1.2%) (Rosenzweig, 1965).

As argued by Beatty (2001), economic growth in this period went through two distinct phases. In the first phase, which in fact starts before the *Porfiriato* in the late 1860s, the expansion was export led and characterized by the construction of railways and the recovery of silver mining and other traditional activities. Per capita GDP, according to Maddison (2006), grew in this period at an annual rate of 2.1% (1870–1895). Then from the early 1890s, still with a dynamic performance of exports, economic expansion accelerated and per capita GDP grew annually at 2.7% (Maddison, 2006, for the period 1895–1910).[7] This second phase is characterized by a diversification of investments and production into new activities both for export and inward-oriented manufacturing. Indicators of this diversification are the fact that manufacturing nearly doubled its rate of growth after 1893, the decrease in the share of consumer goods imports to just 43% of all imports in 1911 (compared to 75%

---

7. Coatsworth figures (see table 3.1) yield yearly growth rates of per capita GDP of 2.3% for 1877–1895 and 2.6% for 1895–1910.

in 1876), and the decline in silver's share of total exports to 20% in 1910 (compared to greater than 60% in the 1870s) (Beatty, 2001). While the first phase is driven by international economic conditions, the second is conditioned by domestic institutional reforms (in the areas of tariff policy, intellectual property, and fiscal incentives to industry). Each phase is also linked to different economic teams: the one led by Matías Romero during the first half of the *Porfiriato* with a liberal, free trade perspective, and the one associated with José Yves Limantour and the *científicos*, who advocated a greater role for industry protection and industrial policy (Beatty, 2001).[8] Moreover, as Beatty (2001) pointed out, this second phase is marked by a fundamental shift in the relation between Congress and the executive, who went from being active and critical to completely passive.

Foreign investment meant access to world markets, and between the 1890s and 1910 Mexico's foreign trade as a share of GDP increased by more than 10 percentage points, helping also to increase government funds, as taxes on foreign trade provided more than half of public revenues. Toward the end of the *Porfiriato*, foreign trade as a proportion of GDP reached more than 30%, compared to close to 10% before the 1870s (Coatsworth, 1990). The export sector became an engine of growth, as it had done previously in colonial times.[9] From 1877 to 1911, exports multiplied more than sixfold (and imports grew by nearly 3.5 times) (Rosenzweig, 1965). During this time the export basket became more diversified, as shown by the decline in the share of minerals and metals in total exports and the corresponding rise of agricultural goods (see table 3.3). Moreover, though not shown in the table, the export of the minerals and metals now included, besides silver, metals such as copper, lead, and zinc, whose demand from the industrial centers of the world economy was expanding rapidly. Agricultural exports now included coffee, livestock, garbanzo beans, and other products that were added to more traditional exports such as henequen and wood.[10]

---

8. But even Matías Romero, in the early 1890s, declared himself in favor of an "enlightened protectionism," defined as one that protects national industry without preventing the healthy competition of imported commodities (Paz Sánchez, 2000).

9. However, examining the evolution and composition of aggregate demand during 1877–1911, Catao (1998) argues that during the *Porfiriato*, the rapid expansion of the export sector had a rather small impact on the overall rate of expansion of the domestic economy, given the relatively small size as well as the lack of strong forward or backward linkages to the rest of the productive system.

10. Manufacturing exports lagged well behind minerals and precious metals, and by 1910–1911 represented only 1.3% of total exports (Paz Sánchez, 2000, citing *Estadísticas Económicas del Porfiriato* [El Colegio de México, 1960]).

Table 3.3 Composition of exports (percent of total exports)

Year	Metals and minerals[a]	Agriculture	Livestock	Other
1821–1824[b]	68.4	31.1	0.3	0.3
1825–1828	78.6	19.3	1.3	0.8
1856	91.7	6.8	1.1	0.3
1872–1873	80.0	12.5	6.4	1.1
1873–1874	76.1	15.8	7.3	0.8
1874–1875	74.3	16.0	8.0	1.8
1879–1880	72.2	19.1	5.7	3.0
1884–1885	74.0	19.5	5.8	0.6
1889–1890	64.8	29.4	4.3	1.5
1894–1895	68.1	26.1	4.2	1.6
1899–1900	60.7	30.7	6.4	2.1
1904–1905	59.4	32.7	4.3	3.6
1909–1910	61.0	29.2	7.6	2.1

Source: Authors' elaboration based on data presented in ITAM Estadísticas Históricas de México, electronic database (http://biblioteca.itam.mx/docs/ehm/), constructed in turn from Herrera (1977) for 1821–1875 and El Colegio de México (1960a and 1960b) for 1879–1910.

[a] Includes gold and silver.

[b] Only for the port of Veracruz.

The export boom appears to have been greatly helped by the depreciation of silver at the end of the 19th century, provoked by the adoption of the gold standard around 1870 in the advanced countries (Cárdenas and Manns, 1987) and the expansion of silver production in the United States and in Mexico after 1884 (Pletcher, 1958). The depreciation of silver amounted to a continuous real devaluation of the Mexican peso of 26% throughout the 1890s. Zabludovsky (1984) assesses the view, held by Rosenzweig (1965) and Nugent (1973), that devaluation promoted export-led growth and the purchasing power parity view of Limantour, Porfirio Díaz's minister of finance, according to which the silver depreciation was ultimately reflected in the price level. Zabludovsky's evaluation of the evidence supports the first view. The timing of the depreciation, concentrated in the 1890s (see figure 3.3[11] and Beatty, 2000, on the subject), suggests also that it may have been an important factor behind the economic diversification that takes place during the second

11. In this book, the exchange rate is defined as the price of foreign currency in terms of domestic currency and the real exchange rate as the ratio of foreign to domestic prices. An increase in the exchange rate means therefore a devaluation of the domestic currency.

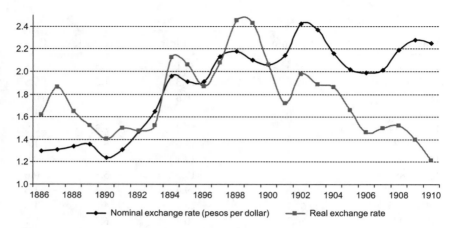

Figure 3.3 Nominal and real exchange rates during the *Porfiriato*
Source: Based on El Colegio de México (1960), *Estadísticas Económicas del Porfiriato*.

half of the *Porfiriato*. Empirical studies suggest that the real depreciation also gave a strong impulse to import substitution (Catao, 1991).

Underlying this modernization was Mexico's first wave of large-scale industrialization. Helped by trade protection and import substitution, new industrial activities (such as steel, cement, and dynamite) emerged on Mexico's economic landscape. In addition, other already existing manufacturing activities, like textiles, papermaking, and tobacco, were transformed and modernized (Haber, 1992). In fact, manufacturing output increased at an average rate of 3.6% per annum from 1877 to 1910 (Coatsworth, 1989; Cárdenas, 2003, puts this figure somewhat higher, 4.1% per year). As already mentioned, the expansion of manufacturing appears to have accelerated in the second half of the *Porfiriato*, during the diversification phase of the process of economic growth. Catao (1991) estimates that in the last decade of the 19th century import substitution accounted for more than 30% of the growth of manufacturing industries, especially the textile industry.

Manufacturing changed from being an artisan's activity, carried out in small handicraft firms, to a productive process done in large-scale plants using capital intensive techniques, frequently owned by monopolies or oligopolies protected by government regulations and concessions,[12] with

---

12. For example, dynamite was produced by a sole private monopoly, which benefited from import duty and tax exemptions (Haber et al., 2003b).

capital from foreign-born merchants and financial dealers (Haber, 1992). In fact, before 1890, the large-scale factory system had been present only in the cotton textile industry (Haber, 1989) and the production of cigarettes (Beatty, 2001). By 1900, factory production could be found in a wide array of industrial activities, including paper, beer, cement, and glass (Beatty, 2001). This phase of industrialization, as Haber points out, was accompanied by changes in business management methods and industrial organization. Joint-stock corporations increasingly replaced family-managed enterprises giving rise to large, vertically integrated firms in a diverse array of manufacturing activities.

The effects of manufacturing growth on employment and wages went in two different directions: a decline in employment in artisan production together with an expansion of employment in machine manufacturing production. From 1895 to 1900, the expansion of employment in machine manufacturing production outweighed the decline in artisan production, thus helping to push real wages in manufacturing and the manufacturing share in total employment. In contrast, from 1900 to 1910, the growth of machine manufacturing tended to displace artisans at a faster rate than labor was absorbed into the new plants. Such displacement, coupled with the rise in inflation at the end of the 1890s linked to frequent harvest crises, likely led to a decrease in the living standards of the average worker. Actually, the evolution of real minimum wages shows a considerable decrease starting in 1904–1905 (see figure 3.4). To what extent they correlate with the evolution of average wages is an open question.[13]

The size of the Mexican market was, nevertheless, rather small at the time for modern technologies. This favored high degrees of market concentration, as only oligopolies could survive. Market concentration was reinforced by the highly concentrated nature of the banking system, which, as explained earlier, severely restricted credit to businesses not related or associated with the banking elite. The selective granting of tax concessions and government permits to deter business entry also favored such concentration in various industries. Even then, dependence on foreign technology designed for bigger markets led to high operation costs and the insufficient exploitation of economies of scale (Reynolds, 1970). Collusion among producers probably inhibited efforts to innovate production methods and was often aimed at manipulating the

---

13. In fact, research based on wage information from a few big firms and on a more in-depth analysis of the evolution of domestic prices suggests that during 1907–1911 the average real wages of their workers fell only 18%, a smaller decline than that of minimum wages (see Gómez-Galvarriato, 1998).

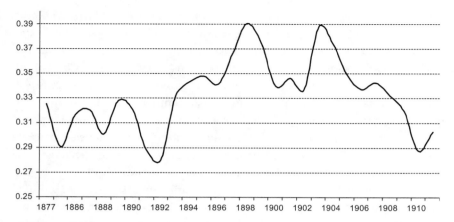

Figure 3.4 Real minimum wages during the *Porfiriato* (Minimum daily wage, 1900 pesos)
Source: Based on El Colegio de México (1960), *Estadísticas Económicas del Porfiriato*.

state and the market to reduce competition. These problems were aggravated by a scarcity of skilled workers and, more generally, by a predominantly rural labor force whose working practices were still very much alien to the proletariat. All these factors reduced labor productivity and, as a result, international competitiveness was weak: even though wages in Mexico were less than half that of workers in Britain or New England, costs of production in Mexico were 10%–20% higher (Haber, 1989).

Certainly such an aggregate picture is not valid for each industry or region. In particular, somewhat recent research on the cotton textile industry points to the opposite conclusion, showing that during the two last decades of the *Porfiriato* there was rapid expansion of its labor and total factor productivity (Razo and Haber, 1998). Similarly, Gómez-Galvarriato (1998) found evidence that productivity in the steel industry was comparable to that of its British competitors. This performance was most likely associated with investment and, to a certain extent, with the capacity to adapt technology and overcome the constraints imposed by the smaller size of the domestic market.[14]

14. Gómez-Galvarriato's (1998) research on large firms in selected sectors concludes that during the *Porfiriato*, Mexico's industrial sector was increasingly efficient and able to compete internationally, gradually overcoming the constraints brought about by the small size of its domestic market given the use of imported machinery and equipment designed for larger scales of production.

The *Porfiriato*'s impact was not restricted to mining, industry, and the banking system. Rural areas were also transformed in their social and economic structures. The Díaz administration pushed an accelerated redistribution of federal and communal land to private development companies and wealthy individuals.[15] As noted by Reynolds (1970, p. 136): "As a result, the government supported what amounted to an enclosure movement, in which federal land and peasant communal holdings, as well as other private properties with clouded titles, were redistributed to land development companies and to individuals successful in gaining favor with the administration." In this process, no attention was given to potential privatization revenues from the sale of federal land (part of it being the previously large landholdings of the church); rather, the aim was to extend private property in order to free idle resources, providing for their more efficient use. The expropriation and displacement of communal land was also stimulated by railway construction, as it led to an enormous increase in its market value (Katz, 2004).

Privatization promoted the concentration of land in large-scale properties (*latifundios*) for commercial cultivation. In fact, between 1878 and 1908 the Díaz government transferred 30 million hectares to the private sector, either selling them or giving them away as compensation payments to the *deslindadoras* (Holden, 1994, cited by Tenorio and Gómez-Galvarriato, 2006). Not surprisingly, by the early 1900s, 95% of all arable land was in the hands of 835 families (Manzanilla Schaffer, 1963). According to the 1910 census, most of the agricultural sector was made up of 850 proprietors who owned 8431 haciendas (Newell and Rubio, 1984, citing González Navarro, 1957). In fact by the end of the *Porfiriato*, 95% of all native Indian villages in Mexico (*aldeas comunales*) had lost their communal land (Katz, 1980). This massive expropriation led to massive emigration of peasants from their rural villages to become a new reserve labor force. This labor force eventually found some sort of employment, whether in the haciendas (in different and highly contrasting conditions that went from wage earning to debt peonage), in manufacturing, or in the service sector.

The expansion of agricultural output was concentrated in exportable raw materials, by far its most dynamic segment (Solís, 2000). At the same time, production of agricultural goods for domestic consumption tended to decline. As

---

15. In exchange for their services, the government would concede up to one-third of the built-up land to the land development companies (*companías deslindadoras*) (Paz Sánchez, 2000).

a result, from 1877 to 1907 total agricultural output grew at an annual average rate of only 0.7%, scarcely half the growth of the population (Solís, 2000).

By the early 1900s, this pattern of development started to show symptoms of exhaustion. From 1904, real wages began to decrease in a systematic and persistent way (see figure 3.4). A drought in 1907 reduced the output of food products and increased their prices. By 1911, the cumulative decline in average real wages was 26% relative to 1898. Miners were perhaps the only group whose wages did not decline in real terms, but, in contrast, the collapse was severe in agriculture (Hansen, 1971). Indeed, debt peonage kept rural workers in extreme poverty as landowners used their monopsonistic and monopolistic powers (the infamous *tienda de raya*) to push wages below subsistence levels. Hunger and poverty were common, especially in the rural areas. As noted by Haber (1989), the extent of poverty was such that the increase in the price of corn due to any bad harvest would reduce workers' consumption of manufactures by enough to provoke a crisis in the cotton garment industry. At the same time, the use of force to repress labor and suppress political opposition became more frequent. By 1910, the system's unequal distribution of benefits and access to power reached its limit. The increasing discontent in rural villages (caused by the deterioration in their living conditions and by the systematic expropriation of their land) combined with the resentment of the emerging middle classes (due to their exclusion from political decisions) and of the workers and peasants (due to their marginalization from the benefits of economic growth) were key elements that led to the development of a triumphant coalition under the banners of political democracy, agrarian reform, and labor rights.

Limits and downfall

What had gone wrong? Clearly, the *Porfiriato*'s primary contradiction was in its results: the growing imbalance between rapid economic growth on the one hand, and the slow pace of political and social progress on the other. Porfirio Díaz had set out to make of Mexico a modern industrial nation. But despite some progress on the educational front with the establishment of compulsory primary education in 1892 and the creation of the National University in 1910 (Paz Sánchez, 2000),[16] by 1910 only 22% of Mexicans age 10 years and

---

16. Public spending on education increased from 3.2% to 6.8% of total public spending between 1877–1878 and 1910–1911 and enrollment in primary school jumped from 142,000 to 658,000 from 1878 to 1907 (Paz Sánchez, 2000).

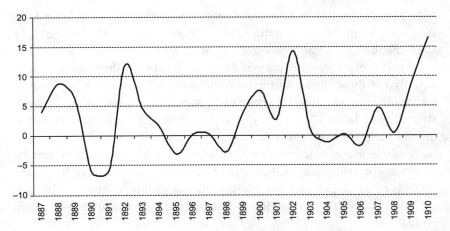

Figure 3.5 Inflation rate (annual rate of change in consumer prices), 1887–1910
Source: Based on Gómez Galvarriato and Mussachio (2000).

older could read and write (table A.3). Life expectancy at birth was probably
not much more than 30 years (table A.3) and some estimates even suggest
that average life expectancy fell between 1895 and 1910 (Rosenzweig, 1965).
Also, between 1895 and 1910 infant mortality increased from 160 to 216 per
1000 (Paz Sánchez, 2000, citing *Estadísticas Sociales del Porfiriato*). In the context
of ample labor reserves, which were augmented over time by the displacement of artisans by modern industrial undertakings and the natural increase
in population, modernization did little to improve the living conditions of the
poor, and the real minimum wage in 1911 had fallen to 7% below its level in
1877 (Rosenzweig, 1965).[17]

Moreover, as a result of the persistent depreciation of the exchange rate
that took place from the 1880s until the early 1900s, as well as droughts in the
last 3 years of the *Porfiriato*, inflation surged: while the price level increased at
an annual rate of 2.1% between 1894 and 1904, it increased by nearly 5% per
year between 1904 and 1910 (Gómez-Galvarriato and Mussachio, 2000) (see
figure 3.5). The last decade of the *Porfiriato* was marked by a slowdown in population growth and increased net emigration of Mexicans to the United States
which Reynolds (1970) has taken as evidence that, in that period, economic
conditions deteriorated for large segments of the population. With two-thirds

17. According to Bulnes (1952), the wage of a *peon de hacienda* measured in corn was
one-fourth of its level at the end of the colonial era.

of its population still living in rural areas and two-thirds of its labor force employed in agricultural activities in 1895 (Keesing, 1969), Mexico still had a fundamentally backward economy and, overall, a backward society.

There were also shortcomings in the design of the development strategy. Two of these turned out to be particularly relevant. First, rather than increasing labor mobility, the enclosure system implemented in the *Porfiriato* strengthened labor's links of dependency with the rural areas. Deprived of land plots, the great majority of the population was forced to work permanently as indebted labor in the haciendas. Thus, at the same time that the expansion of the railway system was creating a national market, huge contingents of the population did not have the possibility to enter it. This was reflected, as we have seen, in the very unequal development of agricultural production.

A second aspect concerns the sources of finance for development. The existing banking system had a dual nature that was incompatible with the financing needs of an economy undergoing a process of structural change. By 1897, no bank had legal authorization to give loans for a period longer than 1 year. By 1910, some banks were legally allowed to give such loans, but the great majority of them were provided for investments in real estate. Out of 47 banks in 1911, only 10 were legally allowed to lend for terms of more than 1 year (Haber, 1997). Moreover, bank credit was channeled to large, well-known firms whose managers were closely associated with or related to the banking elite. The remainder, and vast majority of firms, had practically no access to finance capital. Their growth potential was restricted by their own resources and capacity to reinvest profits. The relatively more available supply of short-term loans was, at most, suitable to fit purely commercial needs (Bortz and Haber, 2002). Besides foreign investors, Mexico's first wave of industrialization was mainly carried out by the merchant elite who financed it through reinvestment of their accumulated profits.[18] At the end of the *Porfiriato*, Mexico still faced the urgent need to create modern banking institutions capable of financing long-term investment needs of firms other than those associated with the banking elite. To achieve this, competition had to be allowed in order to change the highly concentrated nature of the banking sector.

Finally, what can be said about the role of the state in the *Porfiriato's* quest for development? According to the rhetoric of the *Porfiriato* elite, the role of the state, besides ensuring social peace and participating in infrastructure

---

18. For accounts of finance, banking, and industry during the *Porfiriato*, see Batiz and Canudas (1980) and Haber (1989).

projects, was to guarantee the best conditions for private investment, avoiding in principle direct intervention in the productive sphere. However, in practice, the *Porfiriato* state intervened in a conspicuous and significant way in various areas of economic activity. Indeed, banking was strictly regulated, trade policy was explicitly used to promote selected activities in manufacturing and agriculture, and the public sector persistently intervened to promote investment in the railway network.[19] However, it should be noted that during the *Porfiriato* between 6% and 10% of total public spending went to capital formation (Rosenzweig, 1965). Moreover, public investment probably never amounted to more than 5% of total investment. This was partly explained by a tradition of violence that diverted a large amount of government resources to the military.[20] In addition, government spending was constrained by the fiscal structure. Indeed, notwithstanding its successful reform to widen the potential base of taxpayers, it still failed to bring in sufficient public revenues to keep pace with the need for a social policy to meet the mounting social problems that accompanied the uneven distribution of the benefits of economic growth.[21] In 1910, total government expenditures at all levels were only 7.2% of GDP and federal expenditures were 4.4%, similar to the level of the colonial government in 1800. These are lower levels than those prevailing in Europe or even in Brazil, where the central government spent 13.4% of GDP (Coatsworth, 1985).

The achievement of political stability, the emergence of a more integrated national market, the creation of key economic institutions, and the use of various policy instruments to regulate or promote fundamental activities (banking and selected manufacturing) did break through some of the barriers of stagnation. However, the limited amount of public revenues, combined with the exclusion of vast contingents of the population from the benefits of the economic transformation, and the lack of competition in finance and other key markets ended up derailing the *Porfiriato*'s quest for economic development.

19. The contrast between the *Porfiriato* regime's liberal pronouncements and its various *dirigiste* actions in the economy has only rather recently been emphasized in the literature. This revisionist interpretation of the *Porfiriato* runs against its traditional perception as essentially a laissez-faire regime.

20. More than half of the lower ranking public employees were members of the armed forces and 38% of the 1888 federal budget was consumed by the armed forces. Compare this, for example, with Brazil's 18% share and the fact that in absolute numbers Mexico's soldiers and sailors were twice Brazil's military contingent (Marichal and Topik, 2003).

21. On this point, see Coatsworth (1990).

4

Revolution, the 1930s, and the Consolidation of a Developmental State

In 1910 the Pax Porfiriana drew to a dramatic close with the Mexican Revolution. Once more, the absence of social consensus—amidst widespread poverty and acute disparities in the distribution of income and wealth—became a fundamental obstacle for Mexico's development. The construction of a stable social pact would be fully achieved only three decades later. In the process, the economy was subject to political shocks (the armed struggle itself followed by a period of political instability) and economic turbulence (the crash from 1926 to 1932), but in this period the Mexican state would develop the policy instruments and institutions that eventually would permit a recovery of economic development at a faster pace than in the past.

Revolution and the emergence of a new social pact

The nearly two decades between the beginning of the revolution and the start of the Great Depression were a period of great political instability. The period witnessed the initial insurrection led by Francisco Madero against Porfirio Díaz (1910–1911), a reaction led by Victoriano Huerta in 1913, a counterreaction by the revolutionaries (1913–1914), and a civil war between revolutionary factions (1914–1917). While the scale of armed struggle diminished significantly afterward, political unrest continued for the next 10 years, marked by the killings of important figures such as Emiliano Zapata (1919), Venustiano

Carranza (1920), Pancho Villa (1923), and Álvaro Obregón (1928), military uprisings in 1923, 1927, and 1929, and a 3-year-long local civil war in center-west Mexico (1926–1929) over the anticlerical character of the new constitution (the war of the *Cristeros*).

The most violent stages of the Mexican Revolution ended with the adoption of a new constitution in 1917.[1] Taking the liberal constitution of 1857 as a starting point, the new constitution strengthened the executive by granting the president veto power and right to initiate legislation and issue personal decrees in special circumstances while, at the same time, preventing him from perpetuating himself in power through the provision of no reelection (the rallying cry of Madero against Díaz). It also restricted the role of foreigners both in politics (article 33) and in the economy.[2] More fundamental from an economic point of view, the 1917 Constitution redefined the legal framework for land property (article 27) and labor relations (article 123). Article 27 placed the nation over and above private property on matters regarding land, water, and subsoil resources. This article had two main aspects. First, it provided the juridical basis for an agrarian reform through the expropriation of large land holdings and its allocation to *ejidos*, a land tenure system combining collective ownership with private exploitation of the land ("Ownership of lands and waters...is vested originally in the Nation"). Second, it increased the scope for state intervention over mining and oil resources (thus repealing the Porfirian mining code of 1884) ("In the Nation is vested direct ownership of all minerals...such as...petroleum and all solid, liquid, or gaseous hydrocarbons"). Article 123 is also considered one of the most progressive labor legislations of the time, establishing the right to form trade unions, a system of minimum wages, 8-hour workdays within a 6-day workweek, and equal pay for equal work.

A fundamental move toward the consolidation of social peace and political stability was the creation of the *Partido Nacional Revolucionario* (PNR) in 1929.[3] Encompassing all relevant social forces of the Mexican Revolution,

1. Tello (2007) examines the Mexican economy's transformation since the revolution, showing how some of the major institutional changes starting with the 1917 Constitution are associated with marked shifts in social or political pacts and in the way the state perceives and exercises its role in promoting national development.

2. For example, by prohibiting the acquisition of any surface or subsurface rights to Mexican land, unless foreigners gave up their claim to protection by their home governments, as well as the acquisition of any rights in border and seaside areas.

3. For detailed accounts of the creation of the PNR and its role in long-term political stability, see Córdova (1972, 1973), Garay (2003), and Newell and Rubio (1984).

the PNR soon became a functional vehicle for political control and the only legitimate arena in which to settle political differences. Complete hegemony would be achieved during the presidency of Lazaro Cárdenas (1934–1940). Under the institutional framework established then, which remained in place for more than half a century, the ruling president was the most powerful political force, with no relevant opposition in presidential elections or in Congress. The official party—renamed *Partido de la Revolución Mexicana* (PRM) in 1938 and *Partido Revolucionario Institucional* (PRI) in 1946—was the central instrument of corporatist control through a mixture of cooptation, negotiation, and repression. This mixture proved most successful in retaining power control; until 1988, the PRI claimed ample-margin victories in all presidential elections and, with recent and increasing exceptions, in all state governor elections as well.

By 1940, the government party had formed solid alliances with labor through the *Confederación de Trabajadores Mexicanos* (CTM) and the *Federación de Sindicatos de Trabajadores al Servicio del Estado* (FSTSE), and controlled peasants' organizations through the *Confederación Nacional Campesina* (CNC). The private sector, although not formally included in the official party, was recognized and taken into account by the political system through a number of business organizations and chambers, such as the manufacturers' *Confederación de Cámaras Industriales* (CONCAMIN) and *Cámara Nacional de la Industria de la Transformación* (CANACINTRA) and the merchants' *Confederación de Cámaras Nacionales de Comercio* (CONCANACO). In addition, by the 1940s the military had been professionalized and divested of its political role. The age of persistent uprisings and revolts was over, and Mexico's particular form of institutionalized authoritarian control had begun.

Before turning to the analysis of the demographic and economic consequences of the revolution, it is worth noting that the Mexican Revolution was a unique event in Latin America in the early 20th century. Why was Mexico the first Latin American nation to undergo a social revolution in the 20th century? Why did oligarchic rule end with radical political mobilization and a peasant rebellion rather than through gradual and peaceful political and social reform?

We think that the key to the answer to these questions has to do with the economic roots of the peasant insurrection. As argued by Knight (1986, 1992), what is distinctive about Mexico is the nature of its process of agrarian commercialization. Like Argentina and Brazil, Mexico experienced a period of capitalist agricultural expansion that came about as a result of the rapid growth of the railway network and the emergence of new export opportunities. In Argentina and Brazil, this process did not lead to the dispossession of a large indigenous peasantry. In Argentina it involved the colonization of the pampas by a large immigrant population, while Brazil pushed its coffee frontier south by relying first on a large slave labor force and later on immigrant *colono* labor. In regions with an important native peasantry, such as the Brazilian northeast or the Peruvian and Bolivian highlands, the process of agrarian commercialization did not proceed at a sufficiently fast pace to threaten the disappearance of the traditional peasantry (in the Brazilian northeast, the sugar industry was actually in decline, while in Peru the cotton export boom took place along the coast, removed from the peasant heartland). As Knight puts it: "Porfirian Mexico experienced a process of 'Brazilian' or 'Argentine' agrarian commercialization which impinged upon a 'Peruvian' or 'Bolivian' peasantry. It was this combination, unique, certainly in terms of scale, in Latin America, which made possible Mexico's popular revolution and precocious agrarian reform" (Knight, 1992, p. 112). What was distinctive and what generated the peasant rebellion was "the close, antagonistic juxtaposition of commercial haciendas/ *ranchos* and a populous, established peasantry, typified by Morelos, much of the central plateau, and certain key regions of the remainder of Mexico" (Knight, 1986, p. 157).

The revolution and its aftermath: demographic consequences and economic changes

The revolution had a profound demographic influence. From 1910 to 1921, population fell by almost 1 million people from 15.2 to 14.3 million (INEGI, 1999a). In this decline, factors other than the casualties caused by the civil war had an impact, including migration to the United States, famine, and diseases such as the influenza epidemic in 1918–1919. According to recent (and comparatively high) estimates, the total demographic cost of the revolution was nearly 2.1 million (comparable to that of the Spanish Civil War), of which two-thirds are accounted for by excess deaths, one-fourth by lost births, and less than one-tenth by emigration (see McCaa, 2003, which also includes a review of previous studies).

The revolution also had great economic consequences. The monetary system was severely disrupted. The war effort on the part of the Huerta government[4] and the monetary emissions by the different revolutionary

---

4. The federal army of 50,000 troops under Madero grew to more than 200,000 under Huerta (Brown, 1993).

factions, starting in April 1913, led to an almost fivefold increase in the money stock from 1910 to 1915 (Cárdenas and Manns, 1987).[5] This was followed by a rapid depreciation of the exchange rate of the various monies, hyperinflation, and a distrust of paper money by the public.[6] Monetary chaos and intervention of the banks in 1916–1917 led to the collapse of the Porfirian banking system. Indeed, during the revolution banks were subject to many adverse pressures (Fujigaki, 2006). Huerta imposed on them the practice of forced lending, while the revolutionaries were hostile to banks, and eventually the government ordered the banks' intervention.

Production and investment were greatly affected in several areas.[7] In addition to bringing monetary chaos, the years of armed conflict disrupted the railway system and brought production in certain areas to a standstill. Agricultural activities were, in general, most severely affected, with the production of corn declining by about 40% from 1910 to 1920 (Vernon, 1963; see also Meyer, 2004). Manufacturing activity may have declined by about one-quarter during the same decade (INEGI, 1999a, based on Robles, 1960). Both consumer goods industries (textiles, beer, tobacco) and intermediate goods production (cement, steel) were adversely affected, with the effects on the latter being greater. Many intermediate goods industries were actually shut down because of the disruption of the transport and communications networks and the breakdown of the monetary system. Haber and Razo (2000) document the decline in manufacturing output and productivity and the collapse in investor confidence (as indicated by the evolution of a real, inflation-adjusted stock price index). The collapse of the established social and legal order, the breakdown of the national market and the domestic monetary system, and the uncertainty this brought about proved lethal for investment. Even though productive capacity was not physically destroyed, it deteriorated greatly as no investment or maintenance was undertaken except in a few areas.

Oil on the Gulf coast, on the other hand, as well as the production of henequen in Yucatan and a few manufacturing activities oriented to the production

---

5. For accounts of the hyperinflation, see also Kemmerer (1940) and Maurer (2002).

6. By April 1916 there were 21 different types of paper money in circulation (Cavazos Lerma, 1976).

7. The effects of the revolution on economic activity have been the subject of controversy. Womack (1978) is an early criticism of the conventional picture of disruption and decline. For a similar recent evaluation, see Meyer (2004). For a criticism of Womack's theses, see Paz Sánchez (2006).

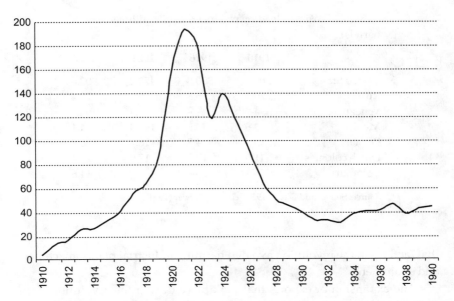

Figure 4.1 Oil production, 1910–1940 (Millions of barrels)
Source: INEGI (1999a).

of army supplies, actually expanded production. The first Mexican oil boom, carried out by British and American oil companies on the Gulf coast, reached a production peak in the early 1920s (see figure 4.1). While Mexico produced barely 1% of the world's oil in 1910 (Hall, 1995), by 1921 its share of world oil output had reached 25%, second only to the United States (Haber et al., 2003a). By 1921, Mexico was producing more than six times as much oil as Russia, the world's third largest producer (see table 4.1), and Mexican production accounted for more than 40% of the increase in the world's oil production between 1910 and 1921. By 1919, Mexico satisfied 14% of the vast American consumption of petroleum products (compared to a mere 1% in 1911), and more than 80% of Mexican oil was being exported to the United States (Brown, 1993). At about the same time, American companies produced 73% of the total oil generated in Mexico; the British, 21%; the Dutch, 4%; and Spanish-Mexican, 2% (U.S. Department of Commerce, cited by Brown, 1993). Of interest, the oil boom actually began in the midst of the armed struggle, with output climbing every year throughout the revolution from 3.6 million barrels at the beginning of the decade to more than 40 million in 1916 and more than 157 million in 1920 (see figure 4.1). Besides the attractive profit opportunities provided by recent oil discoveries, a major factor was probably

Table 4.1   World's leading producers of oil (millions of barrels)

	1910	1916	1921	1927
United States	209.6	300.8	472.2	903.8
Russia	70.3	65.8	29.0	72.4
Venezuela	—	—	1.4	64.4
Mexico	**3.6**	**40.5**	**193.4**	**64.1**
Persia	—	4.5	16.7	36.8
Dutch colonies	11.0	12.5	17.0	21.4
Colombia	—	—	—	14.6

Source: Sterret and Davis (1928), cited by Meyer (1991).

that factions in the revolution avoided harming industrial plants, machinery, and equipment.

The expansion of exports that took place during the revolution (from around 1915 to 1920) went beyond the oil boom, encompassing mineral products (silver, copper, and lead) and agricultural and animal products (henequen, *ixtle*, coffee, and livestock).[8] The reasons for continuity with the export expansion of the *Porfiriato*, interrupted only in 1913 and 1914, have to do with the location of some of the export activities in areas relatively unaffected by warfare and near the ocean (so that they were less dependent on the affected railway network). This is the case for oil and coffee on the Gulf coast and henequen in the Yucatan. It is worth noting that the growth of export revenues actually accelerated between 1915 and 1920 beyond the rates of growth recorded during the *Porfiriato*, with a good part of this acceleration being attributable to rising prices (Kuntz Ficker, 2004). The upward trend in exports continued until 1925, when the export age that began in the mid-1880s came to an end.

As soon as the most turbulent stages of the revolution were over, the economy began to recover. The recovery was preceded by the end of hyper-inflation. A return to the gold standard in 1916 provided the basis for rapid stabilization of prices. Two factors were behind the monetary stabilization. Cárdenas and Manns (1987), following Kemmerer (1940), argue that, as notes in circulation progressively lost the functions of money, a reversion of Gresham's law took place with notes ("bad money") being replaced by gold

8. On trade performance, see Kuntz Ficker (2004, 2007).

and silver ("good money"). The substitution of currencies occurred in a matter of a few days. As Kemmerer (1940, pp. 114–115) puts it:

> At this juncture there occurred a remarkable monetary phenomenon, one of the outstanding facts of recent monetary history. It was the sudden and unexpected return from hoards into active circulation of an enormous volume of gold and silver coin, driving out of circulation practically all the paper money and placing the country squarely back upon the gold standard—and all within the surprisingly short period of a few days.
>
> At the value of less than one centavo gold to the peso, the infalsificables proved to be too cheap to perform conveniently the functions of money and the public suddenly became disgusted with it. No one trusted it; no one wanted it. The Government itself had refused to accept it for most taxes.... In such an atmosphere the paper money quickly disappeared from circulation about the last week in November, and gold and silver money came back into general circulation almost as if by magic. The paper money died in its tracks and coins came out of hoards to perform the task of carrying out the country's monetary work.

Crucial in this process was a second factor (already alluded to by Kemmerer in the quote above): the decision by the Carranza government to collect taxes in gold and silver. This has been seen as acting as a "fiscal reform" that, as in a rational expectations and other interpretations, is always behind the abrupt end of high inflation (Cárdenas and Manns, 1987). In any case, the government's decision meant that notes would not function as a means of payment, thus acting as a monetary reform that stabilized prices in terms of the newly circulating coins. Paper money would not circulate again in large amounts until the end of 1931.

The economic recovery was stimulated by the resumption of mineral exports (silver, lead, zinc, and copper) and a world boom in henequen (Vernon, 1963) even though the total export amount began to decline after 1922 as the oil boom came to an end (see figure 4.2). Manufacturing activity began to grow in 1919, driven probably by the movement of capital and labor out of agriculture (Vernon, 1963), reaching by 1926 a level 44% higher than in 1910 (INEGI, 1999a). This rapid recovery was made possible by the fact that the manufacturing plants remained undamaged (Fondo de Cultura Económica, 1963). Revolutionaries viewed large firms and businesses as important sources of finance, both compulsory and voluntary. According

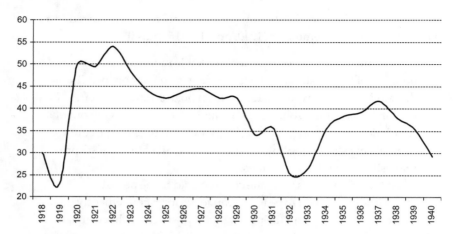

Figure 4.2 Export volume, 1918–1940 (Index 1970 = 100)
Source: Oxford Latin American Economics History Database (OxLAD).

to Cárdenas (1990), the two main reasons why the revolutionaries did not destroy manufacturing capital were, in the case of foreign-owned enterprises, the fear of retaliation by the United States, which supplied most of their weapons, and in the case of domestic firms, to protect a source of income that through confiscation could contribute to the revolution. Thus no large firms had been destroyed and neither the productive nor the organizational structure of manufacturing had been changed by the revolution. Its high concentration had perhaps even increased, and commanding oligopolistic positions were held by the same entrepreneurs as before (Haber, 1989). Nevertheless, the decrease in investment had reduced its productivity and competitiveness, intensifying the need for trade protection. In fact, in 1917, the First National Conference of Industrial Entrepreneurs—organized by the Ministry of Trade and Industry—agreed on the necessity of trade protection and the creation of a bank dedicated to financing industrial activities (Fondo de Cultura Económica, 1963).

The rapid recovery of the economy, and manufacturing in particular, after 1917, when the most violent phase of the revolution was over and monetary stability had been restored, may seem puzzling since political instability was going to last for another decade or so. This has led Haber and Razo (2000) to question the conventional analysis of the links between political instability and economic growth, which argues that an unstable political environment makes property rights less secure and government policies less certain, thus depressing growth. They tend to deny, based on the Mexican experience, that a necessary connection between political instability and the security of property rights exists and suggest that entrepreneurs may be less sensitive to institutional change than stated by the existing literature (Haber and Razo, 2000).

The revolution also brought with it important social transformations. Although there was little redistribution of land before the mid-1930s (see table 4.4), the peonage was considerably weakened and in some regions (center-south) disappeared altogether. With respect to industry, Bortz (2000) and Gómez-Galvarriato (2002) have documented the change in capital-labor relations in the textile industry during the revolution and its aftermath: the increase in union density and strength, the improvement in working conditions—including the reduction in the working shift from 12 to 8 hours—and the substantial increase in real wages from 1920 to 1929 (despite stagnating productivity levels) after the ups and downs during the armed phase of the revolution.[9]

Recession and depression from 1926 to 1932

The Mexican economy had its own crash from 1926 to 1932 which started earlier (and ended sooner) than in the United States and Western Europe (see figure 4.3). Balance of payments difficulties started in mid-1926 as a result of the U.S. recession and the reduction in mineral and oil exports (Cárdenas, 1994). The rate of investment (as a fraction of gross domestic product [GDP]) began falling in 1926 and between 1925 and 1932 declined from 12.1% to 4.5% (Oxford Latin American Economic History Database [OxLAD]). In 1932, GDP was 24% below its previous peak in 1926 (INEGI, 1999a). Over the same period, manufacturing production fell by almost 9% (INEGI, 1999a, based on Robles, 1960) and agricultural output fell by 14.8% (OxLAD). After stabilizing in the early 1920s following a deflation, prices started falling again in 1926, and by 1932, at the trough of the deflation, the price level had declined by 25% (see figure 4.4). Bank credit contracted from 342 million pesos in 1925 to 245 million in 1932, a 28% decline (Solís, 2000).

A first factor in these developments was the decline in oil exports driven by the decrease in production.[10] After its peak in 1921, over the next 11 years

---

9. Different waves of industrial strikes during the revolution that demanded wage increases and improvements in working conditions are described by Cárdenas (2003).

10. Given the lack of domestic linkages in oil production (except for the fiscal linkage), the end of the oil boom is unlikely to have had a major direct impact on the overall level of economic activity.

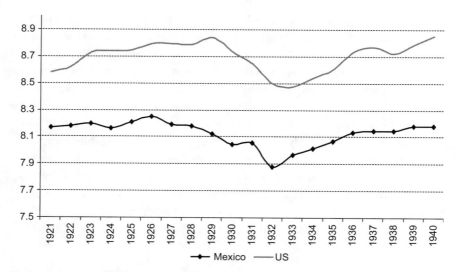

Figure 4.3 Per capita GDP in Mexico and the United States, 1921–1940 (Natural log of per capita GDP. Mexico's per capita GDP is at 1970 constant prices. U.S. per capita GDP is in 1990 international Geary-Khamis dollars.)
Source: INEGI (1999a) and Maddison (2006).

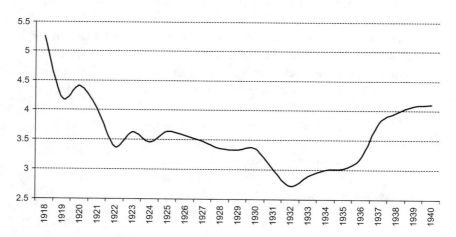

Figure 4.4 Wholesale price index in Mexico City, 1918–1940 (Annual averages; Index 1978 = 100)
Source: INEGI (1999a).

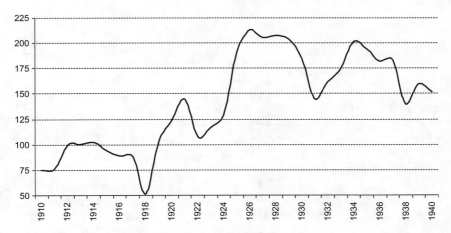

Figure 4.5 Terms of trade, 1910–1940 (Index 1970 = 100)
Source: Oxford Latin American Economics History Database (OxLAD).

oil production fell almost continuously and sharply, and in 1933 it was only 16% of what it had been in 1921 (see figure 4.1). The peak level of oil production would not be reached again until the mid-1970s (INEGI, 1999a). There is some debate about the causes of the decline, that is, whether it was due to geological or institutional reasons. The evidence seems to favor the hypothesis that Mexico simply ran out of oil deposits that could be exploited at a competitive cost (Haber et al., 2003a) but the controversy between the oil companies and the Mexican government over the property rights on subsoil resources (Article 27) and the attractiveness of oil discoveries in Venezuela must also have contributed to the oil companies shifting their operations out of Mexico.[11]

The impact of declining oil exports was aggravated by a reduction in the export revenues from silver and other metals (copper, lead, zinc) reflecting decreasing terms of trade (see figure 4.5). A collapse in internal expenditure followed, as fiscal revenues from oil production and exports represented at the beginning of the 1920s one-third of total government revenues (a share that fell to only 12% by 1927) and the government actively pursued a balanced budget (in fact, the federal government generated large fiscal surpluses from 1928 to 1931) (see figure 4.6). Fiscal tightening was concentrated in current

11. For an economic and political analysis of the oil industry and the oil controversy during this period, see Meyer (1968).

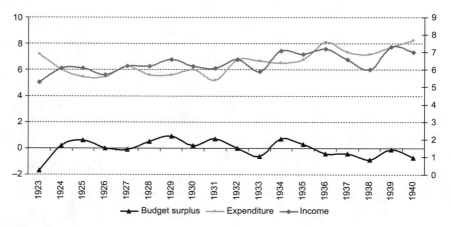

Figure 4.6 Federal government finance (percent of GDP)
Source: INEGI (1999a).

expenditures together with an increase in taxes. While public employees were being dismissed and wages of government workers lowered, public spending was maintained in refurbishing the railway and highway systems, two important capital-formation ventures. Whether intended or not, this pattern of response avoided further deterioration in the economy's productive potential and explains why consumer good industries suffered much more from the crash than intermediate goods industries (Haber, 1989).

Monetary policy was also procyclical, as the government actively sought to prevent a depreciation of the peso by minting less currency. Thus the minting of silver and gold coins fell from 29.4 and 30 million pesos, respectively, in 1926 to 1.3 and 26.9 million pesos, respectively, in 1928 (Cárdenas, 1982). This decreased the money stock and further depressed aggregate demand.

The economic difficulties that started in 1926 were suddenly aggravated by the impact of the Great Depression in the U.S. economy. The mechanisms and the initial policy response were similar to those of the period 1926–1929, but the external shock was far more devastating and the fiscal and monetary policies more draconian. The Depression was felt through a sharp decline in the volume of exports (40% during 1929–1932) and in the terms of trade (22% decline) (OxLAD) (see figures 4.2 and 4.5). The decline in the purchasing power of exports was the second most severe (after Chile) among 15 Latin American countries (Bulmer-Thomas, 2003). The decrease in exports had an initial direct impact on aggregate demand, which was moderated by the fact that, except for the fiscal link, oil and (to a lesser extent) mining did not have strong linkages with the rest of the economy, including backward, forward, and final demand linkages. With about 65% of total exports, these sectors employed only 3% of the nonrural labor force (Cárdenas, 1984).

More important, the depressive effects of the decrease in export revenues were transmitted to the rest of the economy through two mechanisms (see Cárdenas, 2000). The first was the classical price-specie-flow mechanism. The trade deficit generated by the decrease in export revenues triggered an outward flow of silver and gold that brought about a contraction of the money supply by 60.2% between 1929 and 1931 (Cárdenas, 1984), a decrease much larger than in the United States (26.5%) and, in fact, the steepest decline among a group of 12 Latin American countries (Bulmer-Thomas, 2003).[12] Coupled with the deflationary process brought about by the decline in aggregate demand (the wholesale price index fell by 19% during 1929–1932) (see figure 4.4), the nominal and real contraction of the means of payments brought in turn an increase in real interest rates and a decline of private spending (Cárdenas, 1984).

The second mechanism operated, as in the previous period, through the decrease in government revenues and expenditures, as 50% of fiscal revenues originated in foreign trade (Cárdenas, 1984). The collapse of the external sector reduced government revenues by 34% from 1929 to 1932 (INEGI, 1999a) despite efforts to increase tax collection. With no access to foreign credit (Mexico had fallen into debt default since the revolution) or domestic credit (given the public distrust of paper money and despite the existence of a central bank since 1925), the government, in a first stage, adopted a policy of curtailing expenditures in conjunction with the decrease in revenues. Thus government spending (particularly investment) declined 23% between 1929 and 1932 (INEGI, 1999a). This followed an 11% decline that had taken place between 1927 and 1929.

The overall result was a 21% decline in GDP from 1928 to 1932 (INEGI, 1999a) that was felt as a sharp reduction of industrial output, larger than in agriculture, and an increase in unemployment. A bad harvest in 1929, caused by unfavorable weather conditions, further aggravated the effects of the Great Depression on aggregate demand, as a majority of the population relied on agriculture for their livelihood (Cárdenas, 1984; Fitzgerald, 1984). The increase in unemployment was exacerbated by the deportation of more than 310,000 Mexican workers living in the United States between 1930 and 1933.

---

12. Bulmer-Thomas's data (based on the Statistical Yearbook of the League of Nations) refers only to commercial bank time and demand deposits.

These workers represented almost 6% of the labor force employed in 1930 (Carreras de Velasco, 1974).

Economic recovery and industry-led growth from 1933 to 1940

The crash came as a blow to the mild recovery of investment that had begun in the late 1910s. However, with hindsight, the crash brought about important positive changes in economic policy. As we have seen, from the mid-1920s through March 1932, the government had followed a very orthodox monetary and exchange rate policy, trying to keep a stable exchange rate for the silver peso by letting the money supply contract while officially remaining under the gold standard. Fiscal policy was equally procyclical, pursuing a balanced budget (and even budget surpluses) through a reduction of government employment, cuts in the salaries of government employees, and an increase in extraordinary taxes. However, after this initial phase of the Depression, Mexico became a reactive country (in the words of Díaz-Alejandro, 1984), abandoning orthodoxy in macroeconomic, trade, and debt policies. Monetary policy turned expansionary; under the action of the government the money supply increased by 31% in 1932 and 15% in 1933 while interest rates fell from 12% in 1931 to 8% in 1932 (Cárdenas, 1984). Eventually, in March 1932, the government let the peso float vis-à-vis the U.S. dollar, leading to a depreciation of the peso from 2.67 to 3.60 pesos per U.S. dollar at the end of 1933 when the exchange rate was again fixed. This implied a depreciation of 35% with respect to February 1932. Even with the nominal exchange rate fixed, the real exchange rate continued to depreciate (by almost 20%) between 1933 and 1935 because of U.S. inflation combined with price stability in Mexico (Cárdenas, 1984). The stimulus to the tradable goods sectors of the economy given by the sharp devaluation in 1932–1933 was reinforced in March 1938 by a new devaluation, so that from 1929 to 1939 the relative price of consumer goods imports (relative to domestic prices of similar goods) increased by more than 91% (Cárdenas, 2000). Such real depreciation of the exchange rate helped trigger a process of import substitution as demand for foreign goods shifted to local ones. Moreover, with Alberto J. Pani at the head of the Ministry of Finance, the government relaxed fiscal policy, and from 1931 to 1933 a fiscal surplus of 0.7% of GDP turned into a deficit of 0.6% (see figure 4.6).[13]

13. It is doubtful, however, that this change can be interpreted as a move toward an expansionary fiscal policy as Cárdenas (1984) asserts. Given the collapse of output, and thus

Table 4.2   Comparison of the Great Depression with the 1938 recession (percentages)

	1929–1932 depression[a]	1938 recession[b]
Exports	−29.5	−25.2
Terms of trade	−7.5[c]	−23.5
International reserves	−8.6[c]	−56.3
Money supply (M1)	−18.4[c]	10.8
Output (GDP)	−6.3	1.6
Industrial value added	−10.5	4.0

Source: Cárdenas (1982).

[a] 1929–1932 yearly average rate of change.

[b] 1937–1938 rate of change.

[c] These variables reached a bottom in 1931. The 1929–1931 figures are −15.8% for the terms of trade, −31.7% for reserves, and −25.4% for M1.

During the Cárdenas administration (1934–1940), with Eduardo Suárez as minister of finance, fiscal policy became clearly countercyclical and budget deficits were run to boost productive and social investment.[14] One example of countercyclical policy management was the reaction to the 1938 balance of payments crisis brought about by the U.S. recession of 1937 and capital flight in 1938, the year of oil industry nationalization. The fiscal deficit then reached 13% of public spending while the money supply increased by almost 11%. The peso was devalued from 3.6 pesos per dollar to 4.5 pesos in 1938 and 5.2 pesos in 1939 (averages for the year). Despite the fact that the external shock was similar in size to those of the years of the Great Depression, GDP increased by 1.6% (and industrial output increased by 4%) compared to annual reductions of 6.3% (and 10.5% for industrial output) from 1929 to 1932 (see table 4.2).

Trade and debt policies were also far from orthodox. The general level of specific tariffs increased throughout the 1930s. However, the implicit tariff fell after 1932 due to the increase in import prices (Cárdenas, 1987),[15] so that the stimulus to industrialization came largely from exchange rate depreciation, constituting a case of market-led import substitution. In the area of debt policy, Mexico remained in complete default of its external debt throughout the

---

of government revenues, in 1932 (a 15% decline in GDP), the structural budget balance, the appropriate indicator of the fiscal policy stance, must have changed little if at all.

14. For the opposite view that public expenditure could not be used as an instrument of demand management at the time, see Fitzgerald (1984).

15. Ad valorem rates fell from 29% on average for 1930–1934 to 22% in 1935–1939 as prices recovered (Villarreal, 1976).

1930s. This was to a large extent a continuation of developments during the 1910s and 1920s. Mexico defaulted on its external debt in 1914, as the government ran out of funds during the revolution, and then went through a series of debt renegotiations followed by defaults during the 1920s, from the renegotiation of 1922 between Adolfo de la Huerta and Thomas Lamont to the breakdown of the short-lived Montes de Oca–Lamont agreement signed in July 1930 (Marichal, 1989).[16]

The international context also eventually changed, bringing about a recovery in the terms of trade for Mexico's two main exports, oil and silver, at a faster pace than other commodity prices in the 1930s (Haber, 1989).[17] The increase in export revenues contributed to the reversal of the depressive cycle involving declining money stock, government revenues and expenditures, and total output. In this, Mexico was helped by a relatively diversified export structure—including foodstuffs, tropical fruits, and minerals besides oil and precious metals—that contrasts with the experiences of countries such as Chile and Colombia which depended almost completely on a single export good (copper and coffee, respectively) whose prices remained depressed throughout the 1930s (Cárdenas, 1984).

With the shift in the conduct of government policies and the extraordinary recovery in the terms of trade of silver and oil, Mexico resumed economic growth in 1933, and from 1932 to 1940 GDP grew at an annual rate of 5.6% (INEGI, 1999a). Under the stimulus of exchange rate protection, the first new round of investment since the *Porfiriato* began in manufacturing and concentrated in new textile activities.[18] Other stimuli to manufacturing investment came from the 86% shift in urban-rural relative prices between 1929 and 1940 and the likely decline in expected profit rates in agriculture as a result of the agrarian reform program (Cárdenas, 1984). A new group of industrialists, predominantly European Jews, Lebanese, and Syrians that arrived in Mexico in the 1920s escaping religious persecution, had a leading role in the process (Haber, 1989). Manufacturing became the most dynamic sector of the economy. Manufacturing production increased at an average annual rate of 8.1%

16. Adolfo de la Huerta and Luis Montes de Oca were the finance ministers at the time. Thomas Lamont was the head of the International Committee of Bankers on Mexico.

17. Out of the total increase in exports between 1932 and 1934, more than three-fourths was due to the recovery of gold, silver, and oil exports.

18. Total investment increased from 5% of GDP in 1925–1926 to almost 8% in 1939–1940 (Cárdenas, 2000). According to OxLAD, it increased from 4.5% of GDP in 1932 to 9.3% in 1940.

from 1932 to 1940 (INEGI, 1999a), increasing its share of GDP to more than 15% by the end of the period (see table 4.6). Within industry, intermediate goods sectors led the growth process under the effects of government spending in infrastructure. From 1929 to 1939, import substitution (stimulated by the changes in relative prices brought by devaluations and concentrated in consumer and intermediate goods) contributed almost 37% to industrial growth, with domestic demand contributing 56% (see table A.6). It is thus interesting to observe that contrary to what has often been asserted (see, for example, Villarreal, 1976; Hansen, 1971), import substitution industrialization did play an important role in the recovery from the Great Depression. In fact, the contribution of import substitution to industrial growth is comparable to that of Brazil, where it is generally considered to have been high during the 1930s (Cárdenas, 1984). For the economy as a whole and for the period 1929–1939, the contribution to the increase in GDP of the decrease in import coefficient appears to have been even greater than in Brazil and among the highest in a group of 12 Latin American countries (similar to Venezuela and Costa Rica and behind Argentina) (Bulmer-Thomas, 2003).

The consolidation of a developmental state under Cárdenas

Besides the role of external factors, the process of recovery and growth was made possible by the turnaround in macroeconomic policies that was part of a greater focus of government policies on economic development. Indeed, the depression convinced the government that rapid development would require a much more active economic role by the public sector. When Lázaro Cárdenas was named the official party's presidential candidate, he put forward a *Plan Sexenal* (1934–1940) in which, for the first time, the government explicitly presented a plan of actions for the next 6 years and committed itself to active development policies involving unprecedented investments in agriculture, industry, and infrastructure, as well as in social development.

The process of consolidation of political power after the revolution was accompanied by the creation of new institutions and an expansion in policy instruments available to the government. The Bank of Mexico was established in 1925 and began to operate as a central bank in the early 1930s in response to the Depression. By then, the Public Agricultural Credit Bank (1926) had been established, and the creation of other banks, such as the *Banco Nacional Hipotecario y de Obras Públicas* (1933), followed. In 1933, the Budget Ministry created the National Finance Entity, which was soon to become *Nacional Financiera* (NAFINSA), the first fully fledged development bank and the financial pivot for industrial and other long-term investment. During the Cárdenas presidency (1934–1940), the public sector expanded further with several development or financial entities. Nineteen state enterprises were established (Newel and Rubio, 1984). The *Banco Nacional de Crédito Ejidal* was created in 1935 to support the *ejido* sector and the *Banco Nacional de Comercio Exterior* was established in 1937 to support the export sector. The private banking system also expanded at a brisk pace. By the end of the 1930s there were seven public financial institutions (all created between 1925 and 1937) and 114 private banks (see table 4.3).

Agrarian reform began to be implemented on a massive scale, encompassing the north (the cotton growing Laguna region, the Mexicali Valley, and the restitution of land to the Yaqui and Mayo Indians in Sonora), the center (Michoacán), and the south (Yucatán). In the 20 years before Cárdenas took office, 11.6 million hectares of land had been distributed to peasants. During his 6-year term, Cárdenas distributed 18.8 million hectares (see table 4.4) benefiting more than 700,000 recipients (INEGI, 1999a). When he left office he had accounted for more than 60% of the land distribution program until then. Land reform was supported by credit from the *Banco Nacional de Crédito Ejidal* and programs of technical assistance in all phases of farming operations. Special importance was given to the development of collectivized *ejidos* in which the lands belonging to the village were owned and cultivated in common to take advantage of economies of scale. By 1940 *ejidos* of one sort or another represented about half of the cropland and half the rural population (while in 1930 they represented only 13% of aggregate Mexican cropland; Hansen, 1971), and the population on the haciendas had fallen from about 3 million in 1910 to 800,000 in 1940 (Vernon, 1963). This process of land reform laid the foundations of political stability in subsequent decades.

The oil industry was nationalized in 1938 after successive confrontations (to be repeated later in other oil-producing developing countries such as Venezuela, Iran, and Iraq) between the government and foreign companies concerning the distribution of oil rents and labor disputes. The confrontations between the government and the foreign oil companies had as a focal point the applicability of article 27 of the constitution, culminating in the Calles-Morrow accord of 1928 that preserved the companies' position. The labor disputes centered on a series of workers' claims for the Mexicanization of the workforce, the partial substitution of union members for "confidential" (non-union) workers, an increase in wages and social benefits, and the demand for a 40-hour workweek. The case was eventually taken to the Supreme Court,

Table 4.3   Financial institutions at the end of the 1930s

National[a]	Private[b]
Banking system institutions	
Banco de México (Central Bank) (1925)	Deposit banks (61)
Banco Nacional de Crédito Agrícola (National Agricultural Credit Bank) (1926)	Savings banks (6)[c]
Banco Nacional Hipotecario Urbano y de Obras Públicas (National Urban Mortgage and Public Works Bank) (1933)	Trust institutions (8)[c]
Nacional Financiera (1934)	Financial societies (29)[d]
Banco Nacional de Crédito Ejidal (National Ejido Credit bank) (1935)	
Banco Nacional de Comercio Exterior (National Foreign Commerce Bank) (1937)	Capitalization banks (8)
Banco Nacional Obrero de Fomento Industrial (National Worker's Bank for Industrial Promotion) (1937)[e]	Mortgage loan banks (2)
Other institutions	
Nacional Monte de Piedad (National Pawnshop) and Savings Institution (1775)[f]	Stock Exchange (1)
Dirección de Pensiones civiles (Governing Board of Civilian Pensions) (1925)[g]	General deposit warehouses (13)
Almacenes Nacionales de Depósito (National Deposit Warehouses) (1936)	Clearinghouse associations (5)
Unión Nacional de Productores de Azúcar (National Union of Sugar Producers) (1938)[h]	Credit unions (9)

Source: Brothers and Solís (1966).

[a] Figures in parentheses indicate the date institutions were originally established.

[b] Figures in parentheses indicate number of institutions operating in 1940. Branches and agencies are excluded.

[c] Includes departments of deposit banks.

[d] Officially classified as banking system institutions in 1941.

[e] Incorporated into the National Cooperative Promotion Bank when this institution was established in 1944.

[f] Nationalized in 1949.

[g] Replaced in 1959 by Institute of Security and Social Services for Public Employees.

[h] Nationalized in 1953.

which ruled against the oil companies. The intransigency of the companies triggered the expropriation of the industry. The railways were also nationalized (in 1937), completing a process started 30 years earlier during the *Porfiriato*.

Table 4.4   Land distribution since Carranza decree of 1915

Period	Land distributed per period	Cumulative
	(Millions of hectares)	
1915–1934	11.6	11.6
1935–1940	18.8	30.4
1941–1946	7.3	37.7
1947–1952	4.6	42.3
1953–1958	6.1	48.4
1959–1964	8.9	57.3
1965–1970	24.7	82.0
1971–1976	12.8	94.8
1977–1982	6.4	101.2
1983–1988	5.6	106.8
1989–1992[a]	0.6	107.4

Source: INEGI (1999a), based on Secretaría de la Reforma Agraria,
Dirección General de Información y Documentación Agraria.

[a] Up to February 21, 1992.

At the same time, during the Cárdenas administration, public expenditure per capita increased 41% over the average of the previous 6 years. It was also reoriented away from military and administrative spending, whose share of public spending fell from nearly 60% to around 44%, thus falling below 50% for the first time in Mexico's republican history (Wilkie, 1970). In turn, public social expenditures (such as spending on health and education) increased from 15% to 18% of the total and, most notably, economic expenditures (on, for example, infrastructure) went from 25% to nearly 38% of the total (see table 4.5). From 1930 to 1940 the roadway system increased sevenfold, covering more than 9900 km by 1940 (INEGI, 1999a). As a percentage of GNP, federal expenditures increased from 6.7% to 8.6%, while public sector capital investment expenditures rose from 2.6% to 4.3% (Wilkie, 1970).

In sum, the Cárdenas period saw the consolidation of a developmental state, in the sense of putting in place a state with the aim of raising social welfare and with sufficient autonomy and resources to pursue a coherent economic policy (Lal and Myint, 1996). The Cárdenas administration was also characterized by a prudent management of public finances, far from the populist experiments elsewhere in Latin America such as those of Juan Perón in Argentina and Getúlio Vargas in Brazil (see Cárdenas, 1993).

Table 4.5   Expenditure per capita in 1950 pesos

	Total	Economic	Social	Administrative
1929–1934	58.3	14.6	8.8	34.9
1935–1940	82.2	30.9	15.0	36.3
Composition (%)				
1929–1934	100.0	25.2	15.2	59.7
1935–1940	100.0	37.6	18.3	44.1

Source: Wilkie (1970), tables 2.1 and 2.2.

Overall performance (1910–1940)
and a comparative perspective

Overall, the economic and social performance in the 30-year period after the beginning of the revolution was characterized by the following trends. Despite a significant increase in manufacturing output (at an average yearly rate of 3.0%) (INEGI, 1999a, based on Robles, 1960), the expansion of total GDP and per capita GDP proceeded at a slow pace of around 1.3% and 0.5% per year, respectively (INEGI, 1999a). At the same time, significant changes took place in the structure of production, with manufacturing increasing its output share from around 11% in 1910 to 15% in 1940 (see table 4.6).

Even though the labor force remained predominantly rural by 1940,[19] increasing urbanization took place as the population of urban areas grew by 58% between 1910 and 1940, twice the pace of overall demographic change (INEGI, 1999a), and the population living in communities of less than 2500 persons fell from around 71% to about 65% (Wilkie, 1970) (see table A.3). Mexico City tripled in population, Monterrey more than doubled, and Guadalajara doubled (Vernon, 1963). Illiteracy (among the population age 10 and older) fell from about 78% to 58% (table A.3), a 20 percentage point decline, as a result in part of the sharp increase in rural schoolteachers (from practically nil in 1910 to close to 20,000 in 1940) (Vernon, 1963). The percentage of the population speaking only an Indian language fell by almost half, from 13% in 1910 to 7.4% in 1940 (Wilkie, 1970). Mortality rates fell from 32.9 per 1000 in 1910 to 23.5 per 1000 in 1940 (Collver, 1965, cited by Reynolds,

---

19. As can be seen in table A.5, about two-thirds of the economically active population was in the primary sector, most of which was composed of agricultural activities.

Table 4.6   Structure of GDP (percent)

	1910[a]	1926[a]	1940[a]
Agriculture[b]	24.0	19.7	19.4
Mining	4.9	9.3	6.4
Industry[c]	12.3	14.7	18.7
Manufacturing	10.7	11.6	15.4
Services	58.7	56.3	55.5
Total	100.0	100.0	100.0

Source: Table A.4.

[a] Based on 1960 prices.

[b] Includes livestock, forestry, and fishing.

[c] Includes manufacturing, construction, and electricity, gas, and water.

Table 4.7   Poverty and its components (percentages)

	1910	1921	1930	1940
Illiteracy[a]	76.9	71.2	66.6	58.0
Population speaking only an Indian language[b]	13.0	10.2	8.5	7.4
Population in communities under 2500	71.3	69.0	66.5	64.9
Poverty index (1940 = 100)	123.7	115.4	108.7	100.0

Source: Based on Wilkie (1970), tables 9-1, 9-2, 9-4, and 9-9.

Wilkie's poverty index is based on the unweighted average percent of the population reporting itself (1) illiterate, (2) speaking only Indian languages, (3) dwelling in communities of less than 2500 inhabitants.

[a] More than 6 years old.

[b] More than 5 years old.

1970) and life expectancy increased from 27.6 to 38.8 years (OxLAD). Wilkie's poverty index suggests that social deprivation fell at a rate of 0.7% per year during the 30-year period despite the slow progress in per capita GDP growth (see table 4.7).

Despite favorable social trends and the economic recovery after 1932, for Mexico this period was one of a slowdown in the rate of growth compared to the performance of the *Porfiriato* and of relative economic decline in the international context. The ratio of U.S. per capita GDP to Mexico's per capita GDP, which had steadily declined from 3.6 in 1870 to 2.9 in 1910, swelled again to 3.8 in 1930 and remained constant thereafter until 1940 (Maddison, 2003).

Table 4.8   Mexico's per capita GDP as a
percentage of per capita GDP

	1910	1926	1940
United States	34.1	30.2	26.4
Argentina	44.3	49.8	44.5
Uruguay	54.0	58.6	50.6
Chile	56.4	69.9	56.4
Colombia	145.8	148.6	97.7
Peru	173.7	156.5	81.8
Venezuela	191.2	80.1	45.8
Brazil	220.3	197.5	148.2

Source: Based on Maddison (2006).
GDP levels are in 1990 international Geary-Khamis
dollars.

The process of retrogression is also evident with respect to the major Latin American economies: Mexico's per capita GDP fell as a fraction of per capita GDP in each of Latin America's larger economies between 1910 and 1940 with the exception of Argentina and Chile (see table 4.8).

We have highlighted three factors behind the growth slowdown and relative decline: the breakdown of the "developmental consensus" under the *Porfiriato* and the period of political violence and instability that followed, the role of misperceptions in policymaking that were reflected in the adoption of procyclical fiscal and monetary policies in the early stages of the recession and depression from 1926 to 1932, and the strength of the external shock derived from the Great Depression in the United States. Of these three factors, we believe that the last two were probably the most decisive ones. The role of the first appears to have been exaggerated. While the revolution and its sequel certainly contribute to explain why the economy slowed down compared to the growth performance under the *Porfiriato*, it is less obvious that it explains why it declined relatively, at least in the Latin American context. As table 4.8 makes clear, the relative decline of the Mexican economy with respect to other large Latin American economies is a feature of the 1927–1940 period, when per capita GDP fell at a rate of 0.5% per year. For the years 1910–1926, Mexico's per capita GDP grew at a rate of 1.3% per year, and as a percentage of the average of the eight Latin American economies considered it remained

Table 4.9   GDP growth in eight Latin American countries
(percent annual growth rates)

	1926–1932	1932–1940	1926–1940
Venezuela	2.0	7.2	4.9
Colombia	3.9	4.5	4.3
Peru	−1.1	5.4	2.6
Brazil	2.2	4.7	3.6
Chile	−5.6	9.2	2.6
Argentina	0.4	3.8	2.4
Uruguay	1.0	3.1	2.2
Mexico	**−4.4**	**5.6**	**1.2**

Source: Based on Maddison (2006).
GDP levels are in 1990 international Geary-Khamis dollars.

practically unchanged (105.5% in 1926 compared to 108.5% in 1910). In fact, during this early period Mexico outperformed four countries (Argentina, Chile, Colombia, and Uruguay) out of the seven in the table.[20] What this suggests is that the relative decline of Mexico over the entire period from 1910 to 1940 must be attributed to the early recessionary trends after 1926, aggravated by procyclical macroeconomic policies, and the severity of the impact of the Great Depression in the United States documented in this chapter. Table 4.9 confirms this conclusion, showing that, among eight large Latin American countries and with the only exception of Chile, Mexico had the economy that suffered most from 1926 to 1932 and as a result had the worst growth performance from 1926 to 1940 despite the recovery from 1932 to 1940.

While this conclusion may seem surprising given all that has been written on the economic costs of the revolution,[21] it is consistent with the continuity up to 1926 of the export boom initiated during the *Porfiriato*, the fact that the revolution left the industrial plant largely undamaged, and the argument, put forward by a number of authors on whom we have relied here, that the negative effects of the revolution on economic activity were largely limited to its most violent phase (1914–1917), a phase that was followed by a rapid economic recovery.

20. It is worth noting also that Mexico's position relative to the average in 1926 is pulled down by Venezuela, which recorded an extraordinary oil boom in the latter part of the 1910–1926 period.

21. See, for example, Romero (1999).

5

The Golden Age of
Industrialization

In the process of achieving hegemony, the Mexican state became convinced that it should play an active role in investment and production if Mexico was to develop. By the late 1930s, it controlled fundamental resources and had increased the number of its policy instruments significantly. Whether it would succeed in transforming the economic recovery of the second half of the 1930s into a drive for growth on a permanent basis remained to be seen.

Not for long, however, as a complete overhaul of the economy and society was just beginning. For the next 30 years, Mexico's economy grew at a sustained annual pace of 6.4% in real terms and per capita gross domestic product (GDP) grew at a rate of 3.2% per year (INEGI, 1999a). Manufacturing was the engine of growth, with rates of growth of production of 8.2% per year (INEGI, 1999a) and, for most of the period, the dynamic domestic market was its major source of demand. The country was transformed from an agrarian society into an urban, semi-industrial one. The portion of the population living in urban areas soared from 35% to 58% at a time when the total population increased from 20 to 48 million people (table A.3) and the output share of manufacturing climbed from 15.4% to 23.3% (table 5.1).

The rate of investment soared from 8.6% to 20% of GDP and private investment as a fraction of GDP increased from less than 5% to more than 13% (table 5.2). Literacy rates nearly doubled, reaching 76% in 1970 (table A.3). The average number of years of schooling of the population (age 15 and older) increased from 2.6 to 3.4, and life expectancy at birth increased 22 years

Table 5.1   Structure of GDP (percent)

	1940	1945	1955	1970
Agriculture[a]	19.4	17.9	18.7	11.6
Mining	6.4	5.1	4.8	4.8
Manufacturing	15.4	15.9	17.5	23.3
Construction	2.5	3.4	3.7	4.6
Electricity	0.8	0.7	0.9	1.8
Services[b]	55.5	56.9	54.4	53.9

Source: INEGI (1985).
Based on 1960 constant prices.
[a] Includes livestock, forestry, and fishing.
[b] Includes residual.

Table 5.2   Fixed investment as a percent of GDP

	Private	Public	Total
1940	4.4	4.2	8.6
1945	6.1	6.0	12.1
1950	6.7	6.7	13.5
1955	10.1	4.7	14.8
1960	10.2	5.0	15.2
1965	10.3	6.0	16.4
1970	13.4	6.6	20.0

Source: INEGI (1999a).
Investment and GDP are measured at constant 1970
prices.

to about 61 years (table A.3). Infant mortality rates were nearly halved, falling
from 139 per 1000 to about 77 per 1000 (table A.3). In sum, during this truly
"*trente glorieuses*,"[1] the economy and society were radically transformed.

Trade, industrial, and financial policies

When Manuel Avila Camacho became president in December 1940, industrialization became a central goal of Mexico's economic policy. The industrialization drive came hand in hand with a deepening of trade protection

---

1. We follow here Albert Hirschman's (1986) use of the expression to refer to the period
1940–1970 rather than, as he does, to the period 1950–1980.

which became a key policy instrument in development strategy.[2] To be sure, at the time of the war, in 1943, Mexico and the United States signed a bilateral trade agreement committing both sides to freezing tariffs on various products (Cárdenas, 1994).[3] However, in 1944, the Mexican government announced a system of direct import controls with a view toward protecting domestic industries from foreign competition. Initially the system was justified officially as merely a defensive measure against dumping and to ensure effective use of accumulated foreign exchange reserves (King, 1970; Mosk, 1950). But by 1947, when the system of import controls actually started to be applied, protectionism had been officially adopted as a key government development policy instrument (Mosk, 1950). Also that year, specific tariffs were replaced with ad valorem tariffs in order to protect tariff revenues from inflation (Cárdenas, 1994). Through the 1950s trade protectionism enlarged its scope, eventually generalizing the imposition of license requirements to stimulate practically any new industry that substituted imports.

As import substitution was completed in most nondurable consumer goods and light intermediates by the early 1960s, industrial and trade policies focused on the local development of the durable consumer, heavy intermediate, and capital goods industries.[4] To do so, the protectionist regime relied largely and increasingly on import licenses—granted essentially on the criteria of availability of close domestic substitutes[5]—and tariff protection thus became less important than it had been previously.[6] Thus industrial protection

2. For a description of industrial policy in the early postwar period, see King (1970) and Mosk (1950).

3. Because specific tariffs were frozen and import prices increased, the implicit import tariffs fell from 17.1% in 1939 to 7.5% in 1945 (Cárdenas, 1994).

4. For a description of industrial policy during this period, see CEPAL-NAFINSA (1971), King (1970), Ros (1994c), Solís (1981), and Villarreal (1976).

5. King describes the procedure for granting import licenses as follows: "If the product is already produced in Mexico, and delivery dates are reasonably satisfactory and if local financial arrangements are not very inferior, then permission to import will not be granted. If there is no domestic substitute that seems to the committee close enough to the required article, then a licence will be recommended.... Price differences may be mentioned, particularly in an appeal against a decision, but it seems that in practice the domestic price has usually to be at least 100 percent higher than the imported price before price differences start to justify import licences, and on many items price differences are much higher and still licences are not given" (King, 1970, pp. 78–79; see also Izquierdo, 1964).

6. Even in the earlier period, tariff protection was rather limited. King (1970, p. 76) estimates the proportion of import duties to the value of imports as having varied between 8% and 13% during the period 1940 to 1964.

was maintained, and even increased, as the share of imports subject to licenses rose from 17.7% in 1956 to 68.3% in 1970 (Gil Diaz, 1984). This instrument was combined with a number of other policies to promote local industrial integration, including the establishment of domestic content requirements (DCRs) in the automobile industry (1962), the yearly publication of lists of industrial products with potential for import substitution, and "fabrication programs" in the heavy intermediates and capital goods sectors, comprising sector- or firm-specific fiscal incentives and import licenses. These programs were generally subject to an agreed schedule and a maximum domestic to import price differential. They included in some cases the meeting of export or foreign exchange targets. The number of these programs increased throughout the 1960s (and most of the 1970s), especially in the heavy intermediates and capital goods industries. They turned, in effect, into the major industrial policy instrument during the second and more difficult stage of import substitution industrialization.

The structure of protection was such that protection levels escalated significantly with the degree of manufacturing, especially among consumer durables, and did so increasingly over time both between the manufacturing and the primary sectors and within the industrial sector itself, where the relative position of nondurable consumer goods worsened and that of consumer durables improved. The main bias against primary activities was not suffered by agriculture—due to the offsetting influence of input subsidies and guaranteed prices on key staple crops[7]—except from the mid-1960s to the mid-1970s, when effective protection turned from positive to negative in this sector and apparently contributed to its economic slowdown. Rather, it was the mining and especially the oil sector that heavily subsidized the rest of the economy through low energy prices (table 5.3).

Export promotion policies, although certainly of lesser importance, were not completely absent in these 30 years, especially in the last decade of the period (see King, 1970; Ros, 1994c). The mid-1960s saw the establishment of the *maquiladora* or border industrialization program (1965), a special free trade and investment regime for export processing plants along the northern border region. This program allowed firms to import to Mexico raw materials free of tariffs provided that their entire production was reexported, and the United States charged import duties only on the amount of value added in Mexico.

7. Agricultural price supports were administered through *Compañía Nacional de Subsistencias Populares* (CONASUPO), a government agency created in 1961 to purchase agricultural goods and regulate their trading.

Table 5.3 Effective protection rates (percent)

	1960	1970
Agriculture	3.0	−1.4
Mining	−0.2	−12.3
Oil	−7.9	5.3
Manufacturing	46.6	36.9
Consumer goods	40.1	28.4
Light intermediates	42.7	15.1
Heavy intermediates	38.1	41.4
Consumer durables and capital goods	85.2	77.1
Average nominal protection (all tradables)	15.1	13.1

Source: Bueno (1971) for 1960; Ten Kate and Wallace (1980) for 1970.
Figures refer to implicit rates without exchange rate adjustment. Treatment of nontradables follows Balassa's modified method (value added of nontradables is assumed not to change).

Export financing was also extended over time. In 1960 banks and other financial institutions (*financieras*) were allowed to use part of their legal minimum reserves to supply export credit to manufacturing firms. In 1963 a Fund for the Exports of Manufactured Products (*Fondo para la exportación de productos manufacturados, Fomex*)—administered by the Bank of Mexico and financed by the revenues from import tariffs—was created to provide export credit at low interest rates to manufacturing exporters. At the same time, manufacturing exports were exempt from export duties. Export taxes as a proportion of exports fell from a high of 15.1% in 1955 (when such taxes were increased to reduce windfall profits from the 1954 devaluation) to less than 5% by 1966.

Government involvement in industrial investment financing was actively pursued through *Nacional Financiera*, which had an important role in financing investments in manufacturing industries facing wartime shortages (such as steel, cement, and other construction materials, and petroleum refining) (King, 1970). For example, in 1942 *Nacional Financiera* took a minority interest in *Altos Hornos de México*, which was to become Mexico's largest steel enterprise (Vernon, 1963). Later in the period there was a reduction of the state's promotion activity in the field of industrial financing and public enterprises—except for the nationalization of the electric industry in the early 1960s—both of which had been decisive in the earlier industrialization phase. These roles were increasingly taken over by domestic private banks in long-term financing and by direct foreign investment in the fastest growing manufacturing industries. Thus, following a trend started in the 1950s,

Nacional Financiera shifted its investment away from manufacturing industries and into infrastructure, which by 1965 represented two-thirds of its total accumulated investment (King, 1970).

Industrial policies also encompassed fiscal incentives, although their role was a relatively minor one and secondary to that of trade protection. These incentives were intended to diversify the industrial structure and stimulate capital formation in manufacturing. In 1941 a new law governing manufacturing industries was passed to provide tax concessions for 5 years to new industries and industries deemed necessary for the development of manufacturing.[8] The tax-free period was then lengthened by the 1946 law governing manufacturing development (*Ley de Fomento de Industrias de Transformación*) (Cárdenas, 1994). General fiscal incentives, provided in the framework of the 1955 law for the development of new and necessary industries, included tax rebates on corporate income and elimination of import duties on machinery, equipment, and raw materials (under the so-called Rule XIV). In exchange for these tax concessions, firms agreed to conditions regarding price and quality control as well as worker training. In 1961 a reform of the corporate income tax allowed the deduction of depreciation charges from taxable profits to foster the renewal of the fixed capital stock and the reinvestment of profits.

The shift in public spending priorities toward economic and social expenditures, initiated during the Cárdenas administration, continued and deepened. Economic expenditures rose to represent 55% of total public expenditure over the last 6 years of the period (up from 38% during the Cárdenas government), with particular emphasis given to these types of expenditures by the Miguel Alemán, Adolfo Ruiz Cortines, and Gustavo Díaz Ordaz administrations (table 5.4). Similarly, social spending increased to 32% toward the end of the period, up from 18% under Cárdenas (table 5.4). Public investment expanded systematically, increasing its share in GDP from 3% under Cárdenas to more than 6% under the Díaz Ordaz administration (table 5.5). Its composition reflected the priorities of the development strategy so that the allocation of investments to industrial development rose continuously throughout the period and reached a 40% share of total public investment, up from 7.4% under Cárdenas. Investments in the social sectors increased steadily and more than doubled their share in the total throughout

---

8. New industries referred to all those goods that were not produced within the country and necessary industries to those that supplied less than 80% of the internal market (Solís, 2000).

Table 5.4 Composition of federal budgetary expenditure (percentages)

	Total	Economic	Social	Administrative
1935–1940 (Cárdenas)	100	38	18	44
1941–1946 (Avila Camacho)	100	39	17	44
1947–1952 (Alemán Valdés)	100	52	13	35
1953–1958 (Ruiz Cortines)	100	53	14	33
1959–1964 (López Mateos)	100	39	19	42
1965–1970 (Díaz Ordaz)	100	55	32	13

Source: Wilkie (1970) and INEGI (1999a).

the period. Investments for agricultural development held their share in total public investment initially but then started declining toward the second half of the 1950s (table 5.5).

Mention should also be made of a number of actions taken at the beginning of the period to encourage the inflow of foreign capital and access to foreign credit. This included a final settlement, successfully negotiated by the Manuel Ávila Camacho government, with the expropriated American oil companies in which Mexico agreed to compensate them for the surface value and capital equipment but not for the oil in the ground (included in the oil companies' much higher estimates of their losses) (Marichal, 1989). It also included the renegotiation of external debt by which holders of Mexican bonds accepted a reduction of approximately 90% of the nominal value of the Mexican government securities. The Suárez-Lamont agreement of 1942, made possible by the intervention of the U.S. government seeking the strategic goal of hemispheric cooperation in a time of war, is considered the most favorable debt renegotiation of that era for a Latin American debtor country (Marichal, 1989; see also Bazant, 1968). A somewhat similar settlement was reached in 1946 with the shareholders of the National Railway Company of Mexico.

The long period of fast and sustained economic development that was nurtured by the policy framework described can be broken down into three phases: the war boom, the period of growth with inflation from 1946 to the mid-1950s, and the period from then until 1970 (the stabilizing development phase). Table 5.6 presents the main economic indicators for these three periods.

The war boom (1941–1945)

From 1940 to 1945 Mexico's GDP grew at an unprecedented average rate of 6% per year in real terms, and per capita GDP grew at a rate of 3.2%.

Table 5.5 Composition of federal public investment (percent)

	Total	Agriculture	Industry	T. and C.[a]	Social	Administration
1935–1940 (Cárdenas)	100 (3.0)	17.7	7.4	64.9	9.6	0.4
1941–1946 (Avila Camacho)	100 (3.9)	17.4	11.6	58.1	11.0	1.9
1947–1952 (Alemán Valdés)	100 (5.3)	19.9	23.1	42.1	13.7	1.2
1953–1958 (Ruiz Cortines)	100 (4.9)	13.9	34.5	34.4	14.4	2.9
1959–1964 (López Mateos)	100 (6.0)	10.6	37.5	24.9	24.2	2.8
1965–1970 (Díaz Ordaz)	100 (6.1)	11.0	40.1	21.8	25.2	1.9

Source: Based on INEGI (1999a).

Figures in parentheses refer to public investment as a percentage of GDP.

[a] Transport and communications.

Table 5.6 Macroeconomic performance

Annual averages	1941–1945	1946–1955	1956–1970
GDP growth rate[a]	6.0[b]	6.0[c]	6.7[d]
Inflation[e]	14.3[b]	9.3[c]	2.9[d]
Real exchange rate[f]	80.8	91.9	92.4
Real industrial wage[f]	81.7	90.3	174.0
Exports (% of GDP)[g]	6.4	5.5	4.8
Imports (% of GDP)[g]	8.7	11.3	7.6
Terms of trade[f]	84.9	95.5	63.7
Budget surplus[h]	−0.5	−0.1	0.0

Source: Oxford Latin American Economics History Database (OxLAD) (for terms of trade). Real exchange rate based on U.S. wholesale prices (U.S. Census Bureau, Statistical Abstract of the United States, 1971) and wholesale prices in Mexico City (INEGI, 1999a). The remainder, INEGI (1999a).

[a] Average annual growth rates.

[b] 1940–1945.

[c] 1945–1955.

[d] 1955–1970.

[e] Yearly average increase in the wholesale price index in Mexico City.

[f] Index 1940 = 100. Real wage refers to the end of the period. Real wages refers to average hourly wages in industrial districts deflated by the wholesale price index in Mexico City.

[g] Exports, imports, and GDP are measured at 1970 constant prices.

[h] Percent of GDP. Federal government.

Manufacturing was the engine of growth, with average rates of production expansion of 10.2% per year (INEGI, 1999a), while agriculture grew at 3.3% per year (OxLAD).

In this first stage during World War II, contrary to what has often been argued, the expansion of external demand, rather than import substitution, provided the most important boost to manufacturing activity.[9] As shown by Cárdenas (1994, 2000), Mexico's industrial expansion during these years, unlike that of many other Latin American countries, was led by exports (see table A.6), which grew rapidly despite a gradual real appreciation of the peso during the war (a consequence of a higher rate of inflation in Mexico than in the United States in the context of a fixed exchange rate) (table A.9). As a result, manufacturing exports increased their share in total exports sixfold, from around 7% to almost 40% in 1945, a share that would not be reached

9. For the conventional view which attributes industrial growth to import substitution during the war, see Cavazos (1976), Vernon (1963), Villarreal (1977).

again until the 1980s. The textile industry was the main beneficiary of the export boom. Textile products, which had represented less than 1% of exports in 1939, were up to 20% of exports by 1945 (Vernon, 1963). Textile plants went from a one-shift to a three-shift basis. Some stimulus came also from shortages of manufacturing goods in the domestic market. While imports as a whole expanded rapidly during the war, imports of textiles, chemicals, and vehicles lagged behind, generating internal shortages that presented opportunities for private entrepreneurs (Vernon, 1963). The stimuli to industry also included a rapid increase of public investment at rates of 14% per year, fueling a construction boom and contributing, together with the surge in private investment, to a very significant increase in the rate of investment (table 5.2). As already mentioned, agricultural development, with its share of public investment and public works, had a nearly threefold increase in the lands assisted by publicly financed irrigation systems. Large investments in transport and communications led to a doubling of the all-weather road network (Vernon, 1963).

The period saw the rise of a new group of industrialists that had begun under Cárdenas and is described by Mosk (1950) in his classic work on Mexico's industrial revolution. This new group consisted of owners of small manufacturing plants, using local capital and oriented toward the domestic market, with a nationalistic and fiercely protectionist outlook. The response to the business opportunities offered by the war boom in the industrial sector was strengthened by the inflow of refugees to Mexico in the early 1940s, in some cases with financial capital and in others with professional skills. In addition, it was pushed forward by the impact of the land reform program of the 1930s which limited the attractiveness of investment in agriculture. This is also the period in which the government began investing in manufacturing industries. This happened, in particular, through the manufacturing investments of *Nacional Financiera*.

The war boom brought with it inflationary pressures. The domestic price level (as measured by the wholesale price index in Mexico City) almost doubled from 1940 to 1945 (a rate of increase of more than 14% per year). This was the result of wartime shortages together with the monetary impact of trade surpluses[10] and capital inflows that led to a rapid increase in bank credit and aggregate demand despite the existence of rather austere, by Latin American

---

10. Note that in table 5.6 the share of exports and imports in GDP are expressed at constant 1970 prices. At current prices, exports in 1945 were more than one-third higher than imports and trade surpluses prevailed throughout the war.

standards of the time, fiscal and monetary policies (Cárdenas, 1994; Vernon, 1963) (see table A.9). Nominal wages lagged behind the price level and thus real wages fell by almost 20% between 1940 and 1945 (table 5.6). At the same time, shifts in the structure of employment from low-wage to higher wage occupations may have allowed real average earnings of wage earners to rise slightly (López Rosado and Noyola, 1951). In any case, the functional distribution of income deteriorated, with the wage share in GDP falling from 29.1% to 22.6% between 1940 and 1945.[11] The investment boom in the context of an elastic supply of labor from the agricultural sector and the lack of independent and strong labor unions help explain the drop in real wages and the wage share.

Growth with a devaluation-inflation cycle (1946–1955)

In the second stage, starting in 1946, the sustained momentum of industrial growth (at an annual rate of 6.3%) (INEGI, 1999a) was determined much more by domestic factors; industrialization, fostered by trade protection, was led more by import substitution and domestic demand than by exports (table A.6). In particular, import substitution in consumer products advanced rapidly during these years. In 1940 consumer and capital goods each accounted for 30% of total imports; by 1955 the consumer goods' share had been halved, while that of capital goods had jumped to 40%. This process of import substitution was stimulated by the increase in tariffs during the Miguel Alemán administration (1946–1952), which at the same time avoided placing heavy restrictions on capital goods and raw materials imports that local industry needed for continued expansion. It also benefited from the first postwar wave of foreign investment. This wave involved a new type of investor that was coming to produce manufactures for the domestic market and thus was different from the traditional buyer of railroad, utility, or government bonds or companies in search for raw materials for export.

Despite the emphasis on industrialization, agriculture as a whole recorded impressive growth. Success in agricultural development, in particular crop production, extended to the entire period from 1940 to 1965 when crop production grew at a rate of 5.7% per year and livestock production grew at

11. See Solís (2000), based on Ortiz Mena et al. (1953).

a rate of 3.7% (Yates, 1981). Three factors made possible this outstanding performance. First, an increase in harvest area (at a rate of 3.2% per year), which was partly located in rain-fed areas and partly in new areas opened to cultivation by massive investments in irrigation (the area under irrigation doubled between 1940 and 1960). Land reform also played a role here by bringing into cultivation previously idle land (Solís, 1981). Second, an increase in yields per hectare, made possible by the wider use of improved seeds, fertilizers, pesticides, and farm machinery. This rapid rate of technical change offset the effects on profitability of declining average real agricultural prices during the period. Third, and last in importance, changes in the composition of crops also made a contribution to the expansion of total production with the introduction of high-value crops, especially in the irrigated areas.

However, agriculture evinced a dual structure. A gap, which widened throughout the 1950s, developed between commercial private farms in the north and northwestern regions and the *ejidos* of the central and southern regions. The former were oriented much more toward export markets and were the main beneficiaries from public investments in irrigation and roads as well as from the technological advances of the Green Revolution. The latter continued to use traditional methods of cultivation and remained oriented toward the domestic market, with rapid population growth putting increasing pressure on the land. Nevertheless, each of the three types of landholders—large private farms, *ejidos*, and *minifundistas* (private plots of less than 5 hectares)—performed satisfactorily and substantially contributed to the record of rapid agricultural growth.

Overall, over this period (1940–1965), agriculture performed outstandingly in all the functions that it plays in economic development: (1) increased food production for a rapidly expanding urban population, providing it with increasing levels of food consumption; (2) the provision to the manufacturing sector of an increased production of raw materials and rapidly expanding foreign exchange earnings that were required to satisfy the import needs of industrialization; (3) a rapidly growing labor supply to satisfy at low wages the labor demands of the expanding industrial and service sectors; (4) savings to be used in infrastructure and industrial investment through the intermediation of the banking system and changing terms of trade between agriculture and industry;[12] and (5) an expanding market for industrial production

12. A study in the late 1960s found that the combined net transfer from agriculture to the rest of the economy through the fiscal system, the banking sector, and internal terms of trade amounted to 2% to 3% of total fixed investment over the previous 20 years and a

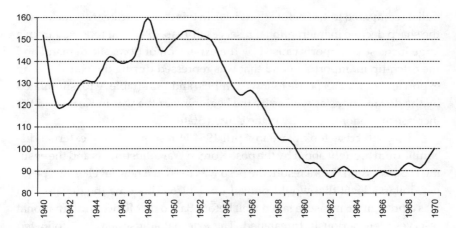

Figure 5.1 Terms of trade, 1940–1970 (Index 1970 = 100)
Source: Oxford Latin American Economics History Database (OxLAD).

constituted by a small, but growing rural middle class (Hansen, 1971). Perhaps most important is the contribution that rural Mexico made to political stability, and thus indirectly to the dynamic response of the private sector to the incentives provided by government policies.

The end of World War II witnessed the emergence of new and unforeseen macroeconomic problems. After several years of trade surpluses and rapid real exchange rate appreciation during the war (tables 5.6 and A.9), Mexico's foreign trade accounts began to register red figures with the decline in external demand after World War II and later with the decrease in terms of trade in the aftermath of the Korean War (table A.10 and figure 5.1). The strong expansion in economic activity led to higher imports, especially of capital and intermediate goods, over and above the availability of exports. The ensuing pressure on the foreign exchange market was at times worsened by short-term capital outflows, triggering periodic balance of payments crises. Devaluation and increased trade protection were the usual responses.

A first crisis occurred in July 1948 (with the abandonment of the central bank's intervention in the foreign exchange market after an almost 75% decline of international reserves compared to their level in December 1945), followed by an almost continuous depreciation of the peso until June 1949, when the float was abandoned and the peso was fixed again at 8.65 pesos per

---

considerably higher proportion of private investment in the industrial and services sector (Eckstein, 1966, cited by Hansen, 1971).

dollar (compared to 4.85 before the crisis). In this case the triggering factor was the sharp decline in international reserves in 1946–1947 that followed from a large increase in imports caused by the expansion of domestic demand and the catch-up in import demand that was repressed during the war. A strong export and output response followed in 1950 and 1951 (table A.10) stimulated by the devaluations as well as by the beginning of the war in Korea and the increase in economic activity in the United States.

A second crisis took place in April 1954 in response to the external disequilibrium brought about by the post-Korean War adjustments and the ensuing U.S. recession.[13] As a result, the peso was fixed at a new level of 12.5 pesos per dollar, a level that would prevail until 1976. This time the devaluation was a preventive measure taken well before Banco de Mexico's international reserves were seriously threatened. The external adjustment that followed in 1954–1955 was achieved, to an even greater extent than in 1948–1950, in the midst of a strong economic recovery—at a rate of 10% in 1954 and 8.5% in 1955—accompanied by significant export expansion and a moderate and transitory increase in inflation.

The differences between the 1954–1955 adjustment and subsequent currency crises in the 1970s, 1980s, and 1990s, when external adjustment was accompanied by the collapse of public and private investment, economic recession, and a sharp acceleration of inflation, are striking and can be explained by several factors (Lustig and Ros, 1987). First, the 1954 stabilization was not strictly an orthodox one. Indeed, devaluation was accompanied by expansionary fiscal policy, which led to a 14.3% increase in real public investment, most of which was directed toward industries which, at the time, had significant state participation and a high potential for import substitution.[14] Second, the contractionary effects of devaluation were probably much less important than later on: private dollar-denominated debt was nonexistent so that balance sheet effects of devaluation were largely absent, the share of wage earners (low savers) in income and consumption was small, and the trade deficit was very small at the time of devaluation (which, as mentioned above, had largely a preventive nature). Also, the expansionary effects of the devaluation were strong given that the potential for the replacement

---

13. Interestingly, Mexico's 1948 and 1954 balance of payments crises stimulated International Monetary Fund (IMF) thinking on, respectively, the absorption approach and the monetary approach to the balance of payments (see de Vries, 1987; Suárez Dávila, 2005).

14. Moreover, in February 1954 import tariffs were increased by 25% and from that point direct controls were used more intensely than in the past (Villarreal, 1976).

of competitive imports was large and the share of exports unresponsive to exchange rate adjustments (such as oil exports) was unimportant. Finally, the degree of wage indexation was small and considerably lower than in the 1980s (minimum wage settlements took place every 2 years) and thus the inertial component of inflation was very limited.

Inflation averaged 9.3% per year from 1945 to 1955 (as measured by the wholesale price index in Mexico City), fluctuating within a wide range. Inflation was fueled by the Korean War boom and later by the largely once-and-for-all effects of the 1954 devaluation on the price level. In addition, the new role of the state implied a restructuring and expansion of expenditures on its part, but no major equivalent reforms had been made on the revenue side of the fiscal accounts. The inflation tax substituted for this during most of this period.[15] Despite the inflationary pressures of the period, and unlike what happened during the war boom, real wages recorded a slow recovery at a pace of about 1% per year. As a result, the wage share in GDP rose between 1945 and 1955 from about 23% to nearly 27% (Solís, 2000).

Development with macroeconomic stability (1956–1970)

The period that followed, from 1956 to 1970, commonly known as "stabilizing development,"[16] is considered the golden age of Mexico's modern economic growth. During this era, real GDP growth accelerated to a rate of 6.7% per year, with an inflation rate of about 3% per year and a fixed exchange rate against the U.S. dollar that lasted for 22 years. Investment increased its share in GDP from 14.8% in 1955 to 20% in 1970 and the manufacturing output share went from 17.5% to 23.3% during the same period (tables 5.1 and 5.2). The increase in living standards and the emergence of a middle class is revealed in a number of indicators. Average real wages increased at a rate of 4.5% per year from 1955 to 1970 (table 5.6). From 1960 to 1970 the number of televisions increased from 17.5 to 58.5 per 1000, the number of telephones increased from

15. The role of monetary financing of the public deficit may, however, have been exaggerated (see Cárdenas, 1994).

16. Economists and economic historians sometimes refer to stabilizing development as the period from 1956 to 1970, which combined high growth and low inflation, and sometimes as the period from 1958 to 1970, during which Antonio Ortiz Mena was minister of finance.

14.1 to 29.6 per 1000, and the number of automobiles increased from 12.9 to 24.1 per 1000. Dwellings with gas or electricity increased from 18% of the total to 44% over the same period (Izquierdo, 1995). Different estimates show sharp declines in poverty between the mid-1950s and the late 1960s. For example, Székely (2005) estimates that the nutrition-based poverty rate fell from 64.3% in 1956 to 24.3% in 1968 (with a corresponding decrease in the number of poor from 20.7 to 11.6 million; see table A.7), while van Ginneken (1980) estimates a decrease from 45% in 1958 to 30% in 1969.

High economic growth rates prevailed with the exception of two brief slowdowns, one in 1959 and the other in 1961–1962 (the only years with growth rates less than 5%), possibly associated with private sector concerns regarding the impact of the Cuban revolution and the policies of the Adolfo López Mateos administration (1958–1964). To some analysts of the time, these pauses indicated that the "stagnationist" tendencies characteristic of peripheral development were finally surfacing. For others, they reflected the obstacles to continued growth exerted by what Vernon's (1963) influential book described as a dysfunctional system of public-private relationships, characterized by a too large degree of discretion and particularism in the application of government regulations. However, the almost immediate resumption of the historical growth rate removed those forebodings.

While development policy continued to be centered on industrialization, with the state as an important agent, price and balance of payments stability were added as major policy priorities, and thus high fiscal deficits and nominal exchange rate depreciation were avoided. Several factors made possible the transition to low inflation in the mid-1950s. These include, from the supply side, the outstanding performance of the agricultural sector, the weakness of wage indexation mechanisms (with biannual wage settlements that were a cushion against the propagation of inflationary pressures), and the "bottleneck-breaking" characteristic of public investment. Most important on the demand side were the financial reforms that solved the problem of government deficit financing through recourse to forced savings via the banking system reserve requirements. Indeed, through regulations on reserve requirements and portfolio allocations, the private banking system played an increasing role in the financing of the public sector deficit (Brothers and Solís, 1966; Hansen, 1971). Thus, while from 1950 to 1955 the central bank acquired more than 33% of the increase in the banking sector claims on the government, between 1956 and 1961 the holdings of the central bank fell both relatively and absolutely. At the same time, the share of private financial institutions in the banking system claims on the government sector rose from 23% to 63%.

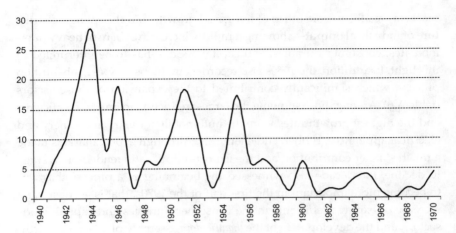

Figure 5.2 Inflation rate, 1940–1970 (Annual rate of increase in the wholesale price index of Mexico City)
Source: INEGI (1999a) based on data from Banco de Mexico.

Later, the problem of deficit financing was solved through the increasing use of external finance. The expansion of public expenditures was subject to considerations on the evolution of the monetary base. The strategy was thus consistent with the drive for development implemented since 1940, but reflected greater concern for the observance of macroeconomic balances.

Another important factor in the transition from the period of growth with inflation to stabilizing development was the relatively more stable external environment and the relative absence of domestic supply shocks. Positive shocks to exports, such as those during World War II and the Korean War, followed by sharp declines in external demand were absent after 1955, and the variability of the terms of trade fell significantly during the period of stabilizing development (figure 5.1). Similarly, negative agricultural supply shocks, which had been quite common during the period 1940–1956 (in 1940, 1943, 1945, 1952, and 1956), practically disappear afterward (Reynoso, 1989). In fact, Reynoso (1989) goes as far as to attribute between 85% and 90% of the improved performance in terms of growth and inflation to the reduction in external and other exogenous shocks, with the remaining 10% to 15% due to better policy management compared to the period of growth with inflation.

Fostered by this environment, manufacturing expanded at an annual rate of close to 9% (INEGI, 1999a) with the dynamic domestic market as its major source of demand. Indeed, Mexico followed a large-country pattern of industrialization (see Chenery et al., 1986), that is, the rapid expansion of domestic

markets was the major source of industrial growth, and the changing structure of industrial output—showing a rapidly increasing share of heavy intermediates, consumer durables, and capital goods—has to be interpreted in
this light. In addition, the 1960s also recorded an intense import-substitution
process, which significantly contributed to the expansion of those sectors
(table A.6). Among those showing the largest reduction in import coefficients
and the highest growth rates were the automobile industry, machinery and
electrical appliances, rubber, and chemicals. Although export markets made
a much smaller contribution and the export-output ratio tended on average
to decline, the decade also witnessed the beginning of a process that was
to become more important in the first half of the 1970s, that is, a substantial
increase of export coefficients in the consumer durables and capital goods
sectors, and the development of the *maquiladora* assembly plants in the northern border region. Transnational companies were prominent in the expansion
of the leading sectors, particularly in three of the four fastest growing industries (automobiles, nonelectrical machinery, and electrical appliances) and
were significant and increasing in the fourth one (chemicals). As noted earlier, the contribution of public enterprises became, in contrast, less important
compared to previous decades, even though they participated in some of the
fast-growing sectors as well as in the rapid development of the fertilizer and
heavy petrochemicals industries.

The pace of agricultural output growth slowed down and declined below
the growth of population in the last 5 years of the period (see figure 5.3).
Mexico turned from a cereal exporter to a cereal importer. A number of factors
contributed to this slowdown. As we have seen, the share of public investment
in agricultural development fell considerably starting in the second half of the
1950s (table 5.5). Prices of agricultural goods relative to manufacturing goods
faced an adverse trend. For example, in real terms between 1960 and 1971,
the prices of corn, beans, and wheat fell by 21.4%, 22.0%, and 41.5%, respectively. Agricultural credit, provided largely by the government, was scarce
and falling rapidly as a proportion of total credit.[17] Price and trade policies
also discriminated against agriculture, while land reform ran into diminish-
ing returns as newly distributed land was of poor quality and productivity.

After the revolution had largely destroyed the *Porfiriato*'s banking system and the Great Depression, together with inflation during the war boom
and immediate postwar period, had delayed development of the domestic
financial system, the period of stabilizing development was associated with

---

17. Agricultural credit as a proportion of total credit fell from 15% in 1960 to 9% in 1970
(Solís, 2000).

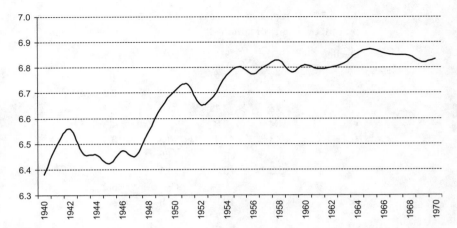

Figure 5.3 Agriculture per capita GDP, 1940–1970 (Natural log of agriculture per capita GDP; million 1970 pesos)
Source: Based on Oxford Latin American Economics History Database (OxLAD).

a resurgence of financial intermediation. This expansion was fostered by the fast growth of GDP, exchange rate stability, and positive real interest rates. Financial savings expanded at a rate of more than 17% per year between 1958 and 1969, a rate well above that of GDP at current prices, and as a result, the ratio of financial liabilities to GDP increased from 24.7% in 1958 to 42.6% in 1968 (Solís, 2000). Along with these changes, the structure of financial liabilities was modified, with a decline in the share of monetary liabilities and dollar-denominated deposits and an increase in nonmonetary liabilities such as bonds issued by financial institutions and time deposits, which recorded the fastest growth rates (Solís, 1981). The boom in financial intermediation and monetary stability became mutually reinforcing processes. The increase in the financial savings/GDP ratio, stimulated by monetary stability, made the financing of fiscal deficits more manageable, thus eliminating inflationary pressures from the demand side and reinforcing price stability.

Keeping in mind that the household surveys are not strictly comparable, the available evidence on income distribution suggests the following trends (table 5.7). First, after an initial reduction from 1950 to 1957, the share of the poorest 40% (on the order of 10% to 11%) stagnated from 1957 to 1968. Second, the share of the middle class (deciles 5 to 9) rose at the expense of the richest 10%.[18] This was the result of a rapid expansion of employment opportunities

---

18. The data on the Gini concentration coefficient show a slight increase from 0.52 to 0.54 between 1956 and 1968 (see table A.7).

Table 5.7 Personal income distribution (in percent by deciles of families)

Deciles	1950	1957	1963	1968
1	2.7	1.7	1.3	1
2	3.4	2.7	2.2	2.2
3	3.8	3.1	3.1	3.1
4	4.4	3.8	3.7	4.3
1–4	**14.3**	**11.3**	**10.3**	**10.6**
5	4.8	4.3	4.9	5.3
6	5.5	5.6	6.1	6
7	7	7.4	8	8.2
8	8.6	10	11.8	11.6
9	10.8	14.7	17	15.8
5–9	**36.7**	**42**	**47.8**	**46.9**
10	**49**	**46.7**	**41.9**	**42.4**

Source: For 1950 and 1957, Navarrete (1960). For 1963 and 1968, Solís (2000), based on Banco de México, Oficina de Estudios sobre Proyecciones Agrícolas y Encuestas sobre Ingreso y Gasto de las Familias en México.

for white-collar workers and professionals, whose share in the labor force[19] increased from 27% to 40% between 1950 and 1960 (having been around 15% in 1940) (Hansen, 1971). The rapid increase in real wages, the development of a middle class, and the relative expansion of the formal sector of the economy were also reflected in the functional distribution of income. Thus the wage share in GDP increased between 1955 and 1970 from around 27% to more than 35% (Solís, 2000).

Long-term productivity performance and the pattern of growth

We now look at the growth process from the perspective of sources of supply expansion, summarizing the available evidence on factor inputs and total factor productivity (TFP) growth. Estimates of long-term trends in TFP growth per year fall in the 2.0 to 2.6% range, thus "explaining" about 35% of the

---

19. This is the share of upper- and middle-class occupations (professionals, managers, technicians, office workers, small tradesmen, and artisans) according to Cline (1962).

Table 5.8 Growth of output, inputs, and total factor productivity (TFP) in various countries (percent annual growth rates)

Country	Years	Output	Capital	Labor	TFP
Mexico	**1950–75**[a]	**6.2**	**n.a**	**n.a**	**2.2**[b]
	1960–74[c]	**6.8**	**6.7**	**3.3**	**2.0**
	1960–75[d]	**6.4**	**6.2**	**2.4**	**2.6**
Developing					
Argentina	1960–74[c]	4.1	3.8	2.2	0.7
Brazil	1960–74[c]	7.3	7.5	3.3	1.6
Colombia	1960–74[c]	5.6	3.9	2.8	2.1
Latin America[e]	1960–74[c]	5.3	4.7	2.7	1.3
Turkey	1963–75[f]	6.4	6.8	1.0	2.1
Korea, Rep.	1960–73[g]	9.7	6.6	5.0	4.1
Developed[h]	1960–73[g]	5.7	6.3	0.8	2.7
US	1960–73[g]	4.3	4.0	2.2	1.3
Germany	1960–73[g]	5.4	7.0	–0.7	3.0
Japan	1960–73[g]	10.9	11.5	2.7	4.5

Source: Ros (1994a).

[a] Syrquin (1986).

[b] Derived from the rates of change of output per worker and the capital-labor ratio assuming a capital elasticity of 0.48.

[c] Elías (1978).

[d] Reynolds (1980).

[e] Average of six Latin American countries (excluding Mexico) (see Elías, 1978).

[f] Krueger and Tuncer (1980).

[g] Christensen et al. (1980).

[h] Average of eight developed countries (see Christensen et al., 1980).

increase in total output (table 5.8). This performance could suggest a rather extensive pattern of growth, largely based on a high rate of capital accumulation (on the order of 6.2% to 6.7% per year). This may well be the case when Mexico's record is compared to those of developed economies or to the South Korean experience (see table 5.8), where more than 40% of output expansion is attributable to TFP growth. But the growth pattern also appears to be significantly more intensive than the rest of Latin America (with a 25% contribution of TFP growth), and compares favorably with other fast-growing developing economies such as Brazil in terms of productivity performance.

The productivity performance of the manufacturing sector appears, however, to have been less satisfactory. Overall, the estimates suggest that for manufacturing as a whole (including large and small firms) and for the two decades since 1960, the Mexican industrial sector showed a slow rate of

Table 5.9   Growth of TFP and labor productivity in manufacturing (average annual growth rates)

Years	TFP	Labor productivity
1960–1980[a,b]	1.1	3.4/6.6[c]
1960–1973[a,b]	0.8	3.4/7.8[c]
1973–1980[a,b]	1.5	3.3/4.5[c]
1970–1980[d,e]	0.9	3.8
1950–1975[f]	2.0	3.0
1963–1981[g,h]	3.6	6.0

Source: Ros (1994a).

[a] Velasco (1985).

[b] Hernandez Laos and Velasco (1990).

[c] Value added per man-hour in manufacturing firms with more than 100 employees.

[d] Mean growth rates of 20 two-digit manufacturing industries.

[e] World Bank (1986).

[f] Syrquin (1986).

[g] Mean growth rate of 17 four-digit manufacturing industries.

[h] Samaniego (1984).

TFP growth (on the order of 1% per year), with divergent trends in productivity growth between small scale and large scale establishments, whose high productivity performance compares favorably with other developing and developed country experiences (Samaniego, 1984). These features—the slow TFP growth in manufacturing as a whole and the more satisfactory performance of large-scale manufacturing and the entire economy—suggest, taken together, that the main contribution of manufacturing expansion to aggregate productivity performance must have taken place through the reallocation effects of industrial growth rather than through rapid increases of factor productivity in manufacturing itself.[20] The overall positive impact of industrial growth qualifies again the notion of an extensive growth pattern. Given the initially very large labor surpluses in traditional agriculture and services and the very fast rate of demographic expansion during the period (on the order of 3.0% to 3.3% per year) (INEGI, 1999a)—which tended to moderate the

20. The importance of these reallocation effects in Mexico's development experience and productivity performance is examined and highlighted in Reynolds (1980) and Syrquin (1986). See also chapter 10.

overall productivity effects of resource reallocation toward manufacturing[21]—
it is hard to see how, given the actual rate of capital accumulation, the growth
pattern could have been much more intensive. The reason is that the slow
productivity growth in manufacturing can be largely attributed to the lack of
productivity increases in the small-scale sector, a feature which in turn reflects
a high rate of employment absorption from other sectors. There is thus a trade-
off between the reallocation effects of industrial growth and the productivity
increases within industry; a trade-off which was aggravated by the very fast
rates of population growth and could not be easily overcome except by means
of higher rates of capital accumulation.

Modernization with inequality revisited

To sum up, Mexico's industrial development during the golden age was nurtured in a rather typical import-substitution cum state-led industrialization
policy regime that provided, however, incentives to manufacturing exporters starting in the early 1960s and moderate levels of effective protection to
manufacturing with a limited, albeit increasing through time, dispersion of
protection rates across industries. The policy regime also included a number of sector-specific programs in infant industries which gave increasing
emphasis to export targets and price competitiveness. Manufacturing, especially its heavy intermediates, consumer durables, and capital goods sectors,
benefited from three main mechanisms of resource transfer: (1) high prices
for their products arising from protection of domestic industrial markets; (2)
lower input costs resulting from energy subsidies, export taxes, and licenses
on some agricultural raw materials and minerals; and (3) low prices for
imported capital goods as a consequence of appreciated real exchange rates
and high tariff exemptions on imports of machinery and equipment which
facilitated the financing of industrial investments.

The industrial response to these incentives was highly dynamic in terms
of output growth, and its resource allocation effects generated a rather good

21. We mean here the direct effects of resource reallocation toward higher productivity industries as well as the indirect effects on agriculture and services productivity levels
occurring as a result of the reduction of labor surpluses and the induced reorganization of
methods of production. The latter may be no less important than the former, as the postwar
development experience of developed countries clearly suggests (see Cripps and Tarling,
1973; Syrquin, 1986).

productivity performance in the economy as a whole. More generally, the macroeconomic performance from 1940 to 1970 was impressive. The strategy on which it was based tackled important obstacles on the road to Mexico's development. However, it ignored or underestimated the magnitude of other obstacles.

A first observation is that despite these improvements, the benefits of growth were far from being evenly distributed. Toward the end of the period (1968), the poorest 40% of the population accrued less than 11% of total income, while the richest 10% received nearly four times that amount (more than 42%) (see table 5.7). The Gini coefficient was very high, at around 0.54, and income distribution had not improved compared to 1950 (table A.7). In spite of sustained government efforts to provide social services to the population and several decades of continuous economic growth, most people were still poor (Székely, 2005). At the end of the 1970s, 10 years after the end of the golden age, out of a total population of 68 million, approximately 19 million people suffered from malnutrition, and infant mortality rates were still high compared with other countries with lower per capita incomes (50 per 1000 children born alive); about 45% of the population did not have access to free health care; 22.3% of dwellings had no services at all, while 50% had no access to water or sewage systems; and about 22 million persons age 14 years and older were either illiterate or had not finished primary school (Lustig and Ros, 1987). Regional disparities were also pronounced. Mexico City, Monterrey, and Guadalajara, with 25% of the total population, accounted for more than 60% of the manufacturing industry, while approximately 40% of the population lived in towns of less than 2500 inhabitants, depending on a low rural income (Solís, 2000). Thus despite the enormous economic and social progress made, poverty and inequality were still major problems to be solved.

The neglect of agriculture, which, as we have seen, faced serious difficulties in expanding production after 1965, became the source of important problems. Agricultural output grew from the mid-1940s to the mid-1960s at an impressive rate, under the stimuli of infrastructure investments and the expansion of cultivated area caused by large-scale irrigation projects and agrarian reform, but this source of growth was eventually exhausted and the sector's rate of growth in the second half of the 1960s fell below the pace of demographic expansion. As we have seen, among the factors behind this decline are the negative effective protection from the mid-1960s to mid-1970s, the adverse trend in the prices of agricultural goods relative to manufacturing goods, and the continuous decline of its share of public investment after the mid-1950s as well as in total credit. All these elements contributed to a contraction of agricultural exports and trade balance, an increase in rural poverty, and a loss of social cohesion that led to emergent social instability.

Trade protection proved a valuable instrument in promoting import substitution and growth in many sectors, and some industries, such as fertilizers and steel—with falling marginal costs driven by the vigorous expansion of the domestic market—even achieved international competitiveness (Solís, 1981). However, for most of the period there was no explicit policy aimed at strengthening over time the economy's export potential. After reaching a peak of 7.3% during World War II, the export share in output fell throughout the rest of the 1940s, 1950s, and 1960s, reaching a low of 3.6% in 1970 (see tables A.9, A.10, and A.11). Trade protection and progressive real appreciation of the exchange rate (table A.11) contributed to this erosion of the export share. Neither was it clear whether trade policy as it then stood would be able to complete the most difficult phase of import substitution involving high-technology capital goods. Indeed, by the end of the "stabilizing development" period, import substitution in the capital goods sector had yet to be accomplished. As the NAFINSA-ONUDI (1985) study found, Mexico's production of capital goods lagged considerably behind other semi-industrial economies: more than 90% of Mexico's market for machine tools was supplied from abroad, compared to only 20% in Brazil and 44% in Korea, countries which in addition exported 27% and 20%, respectively, of their local production of machine tools. Moreover, while based on the infant industry protection argument, protection was far from being consistently applied. Rather than being temporary, to allow for the initial development of new firms and industries, protection tended to become permanent. Indeed, despite the fact that, in principle, import licenses could only be granted for 3 to 5 years, once granted, they were never removed (Solís, 1981).

Finally, tax reforms were systematically aborted in 1961 and 1964, leaving the tax burden at 12.3% in 1970, compared with 10.3% in 1960 and an original target of close to 20% (Izquierdo, 1995). Mexico had, and continues to have, one of the lowest tax burdens in Latin America (Hansen, 1971; ECLAC, 2006a). Moreover, the few changes that took place in fiscal matters had regressive effects by increasing the tax burden on labor incomes and reducing it on property incomes (Solís, 1981).[22] The lack of fiscal reform, together with a de facto freeze on the prices of public sector goods and services (electricity, gasoline,

---

22. Revenue from labor income as a fraction of individual income tax increased from 58.1% in 1960 to 77.9% in 1966, while revenue from property income decreased from 40.5% of personal income tax to 10.7% over the same period (Solís, 1981).

railways), restricted social expenditures by the public sector at a time when rapid population growth generated a growing need for expanded programs in education and health. It also increased fiscal vulnerability by making public finances increasingly dependent on external debt.[23] So too did the balance of payments, which became more and more vulnerable to short-term capital flows, with their potentially destabilizing influence. As long as the golden age of world economic growth continued, misperceptions regarding the potential relevance of these issues for Mexico's development could and would remain. Unfortunately this golden age was coming to an end.

The previous list of problems is also significant for what it omits. For example, the stabilizing development strategy has been blamed for inadequate employment growth resulting from policies, including trade protection, that stimulated the use of capital-intensive technologies (see, among others, Clavijo and Valdivieso, 1983; Reynolds, 1970; and Solís, 1981). However, industrial employment growth was vigorous during the period and there is no clear-cut indication that underemployment increased (see Gregory, 1986). As table 5.10 shows, the proportion of the self-employed in the total labor force declined by about 14 percentage points from 1950 to 1970. Similarly, while the informal urban sector increased its share in the total labor force with the rapid process of urbanization, the combined share of the informal urban sector and traditional agriculture fell from 56.9% in 1950 to 43.1% in 1970 and the share of informal employment in the urban labor force declined from 37.4% to 34.9% over the same period. One of the striking features of the period is, in fact, the rapid expansion of wage employment and of the formal sector in the total labor force. It is worth noting that these trends differ somewhat from what happens in the rest of Latin America. For example, for Latin America as a whole, the share of the self-employed in the total labor force increases slightly between 1950 and 1970, and the increase in the share of wage employment is much less significant than in the Mexican case (see PREALC, 1982, table I–4).

Similarly, while Mexico was certainly a highly unequal society by the end of the period, as we stressed earlier, there is no compelling evidence that income distribution significantly deteriorated as has often been claimed (see, among others, Aspe and Beristain, 1984; Solís, 1981; and Villarreal, 1983). Nor

23. By 1970 the external public debt/GDP ratio reached 12% (compared to 1% in 1946) (INEGI, 1999a), and in 1968 amortization and interest payments on medium and long-term external public debt represented close to 30% of exports (Hansen, 1971). While these magnitudes did not yet imply a serious macroeconomic imbalance, they reflect the dynamic evolution of foreign indebtedness during the period.

Table 5.10 Composition of the labor force (percentages)

	1950	1960	1970
By type of employment			
Wage earners	51.1	63.3	63.4
Self-employed	37.4	31.2	23.2
Unpaid relatives	10.7	4.7	7.7
Employers	0.7	0.8	5.7
Total	100.0	100.0	100.0
By sector			
Urban formal sector	21.6	32.2	33.9
Urban informal sector[a]	12.9	13.5	18.2
Modern agriculture	20.4	25.4	21.9
Traditional agriculture	44.0	27.6	24.9
Mining	1.1	1.3	1.1
Total	100.0	100.0	100.0

Source: PREALC (1982).

[a] Includes domestic services.

is there convincing proof that the strategy was accompanied by a progressive lack of fiscal control (as argued by Camacho, 1977, and Solis, 1981; see Buffie, 1989) despite an inadequate tax burden and an increasing dependence of public finances on external debt.

The golden age in an international perspective

The period from 1940 to 1970 was truly a golden age. Although smaller than the rates recorded in the East Asian newly industrializing countries (NICs) from 1950 to 1970, the rate of expansion of the Mexican economy (measured by total GDP) was the fastest among the large Latin American countries and, perhaps more surprisingly, higher than that of the fast-growing economies in southern Europe (table 5.11). The rate of growth of its real per capita GDP was less outstanding, but one must take into account the very fast growth of population during the period, the fastest among the group of countries in table 5.11 (with the exception of Singapore). This demographic explosion caused population to grow at a faster pace than the labor force (which expanded at a rate of 2.7% per year) (INEGI, 1999a), leading to a sharp increase in the dependency ratio from 79% in 1940 to 83% in 1950, 92% in 1960, and 108% in 1970 (INEGI,

Table 5.11   Annual growth rates of GDP, per capita GDP, and population (1940–1970)

	GDP	Per capita GDP	Population
Latin America			
Mexico	**6.2**	**2.9**	**3.2**
Brazil	6.0	3.0	2.9
Colombia	4.6	1.6	2.9
Argentina	3.7	1.9	1.8
Chile	3.7	1.6	2.1
Southern Europe			
Portugal	4.7	4.2	0.5
Spain	4.7	3.8	0.9
Greece	4.1	3.5	0.6
Italy	4.1	3.5	0.6
East Asia			
Taiwan[a]	9.3	6.0	3.0
Hong Kong[a]	7.9	4.8	2.9
Singapore[a]	7.3	3.5	3.6
South Korea[a]	7.1	4.8	2.2

Source: Based on Maddison (2003).
GDP is in 1990 international Geary-Khamis dollars.
[a] 1950–1970.

Table 5.12   Mexico's per capita GDP as a percentage of GDP per capita

	1940	1970
United States	26.4	28.7
Argentina	44.5	59.2
Venezuela	45.8	40.5
Uruguay	50.6	83.3
Chile	56.8	81.6
Colombia	97.7	139.6
Peru	101.6	113.5
Brazil	148.2	141.3

Source: Based on Maddison (2003).
GDP is in 1990 international Geary-Khamis dollars.

1999a) (see table A.3). This rising dependency ratio acted as a negative demographic bonus that reduced per capita GDP growth below what it would otherwise have been. This is why, over the period 1950–1970, for which data on labor productivity growth is available, the growth of output per worker, at

4.1% per year, far outstripped the growth of per capita GDP (3.1%) as well as the growth of output per worker in the larger Latin American economies (Brazil included, with a growth rate of 3.3% per year) (GGDC, Total Economy Database 2006).

Clearly this was a period of catching up, with respect to the United States as well as to the larger Latin American economies. Unlike what happened in the previous 30-year period (see chapter 4), Mexico's per capita GDP increased as a fraction of U.S. per capita GDP as well as the per capita GDP of each of the larger Latin American economies with the exception of Brazil and oil-rich Venezuela (table 5.12). What reasons explain this comparatively fast pace of economic development?

A first set of reasons accounts for the comparative absence of foreign exchange constraints and domestic bottlenecks together with a stable macroeconomic framework. There is, first, the impressive performance of agriculture in the first part of the period, which contributed to reconcile the fast rate of GDP growth with balance of payments stability and the absence of domestic inflationary pressures. As noted by Hansen (1971), Mexico's rate of growth of agricultural production was outstanding during this period: it was twice the rate of Argentina and Chile and considerably faster than that of all other Latin American countries with the exception of Costa Rica. This allowed the agricultural sector to make a substantial contribution to overall development, not least by enhancing the capacity of the economy to generate foreign exchange. This fast pace of agricultural output growth was made possible, as we have seen, by several factors, including the land reforms of the 1930s together with considerable public investments in irrigation and other infrastructure, especially during the Miguel Alemán administration. Mexico's irrigation program, one of the largest in the world, reclaimed and irrigated more land than any other Latin American country (Hansen, 1971).

More generally, and this is the second factor, the structure of public expenditures was heavily biased toward developmental investments that made possible the removal of domestic bottlenecks. Federal expenditures on economic development rose almost continuously from 38% of the total budget in 1935–1940 to 55% in 1965–1970 (table 5.4), and from 1940 to 1970 the Mexican public sector accounted for between one-third and one-half of capital formation (table 5.2). This was made possible by squeezing defense and administrative expenditures. In contrast, of all the Latin American countries, only Costa Rica and Panama spent less than Mexico on defense (as a ratio of total government expenditure).

Third, together with rapid agricultural growth and economic development public spending, a diminished role of the central bank, from 1955 onward, in the financing of public sector deficits produced macroeconomic stability as epitomized by low inflation after 1955 and a stable exchange rate that lasted for 22 years. Such a stable macroeconomic framework, which contrasts with the experiences of Argentina, Brazil, and Chile, must have had an important feedback effect in the process of economic growth.

A second set of reasons has to do with the costs of protection. While protectionist policies effectively stimulated industrialization, the costs of protection, both static and dynamic,[24] were less burdensome than in other Latin American countries, and perhaps even than in some East Asian countries during this period. First, Mexico's protection rates were rather moderate when compared to most Latin American countries as well as other developing economies (see Balassa et al., 1971; Little et al., 1970; Ten Kate and Wallace, 1980). This feature has been attributed to the fact that, in spite of an extensive use of quantitative restrictions, a degree of domestic price discipline was enforced by the threat of smuggling and potential competition—given the long border with the U.S. economy—as well as by the role of price controls in manufacturing.

A second reason has to do with the relatively large domestic market. Mexico was the second most populated country in Latin America, with a population in 1970 similar to that of Italy and larger than the other southern European countries or the East Asian NICs. Despite the low level of income per capita and its unequal distribution, the size of the domestic market was sufficient for industrial sectors with high fixed costs (associated to their capital intensity) and, as a result, strong economies of scale to be established. It also attracted the foreign investment required to set up these capital- and technology-intensive industries. In other countries, as the opportunities for easy import substitution were exhausted, the pace of industrial development slowed down, and attempts to go into the "difficult phase" of import substitution would result in highly inefficient industrial sectors. All this is consistent with the rather low estimates of the static costs of Mexico's protectionist policies. Bergsman (1974) estimated the costs of protection in 1960 at 2.5% of GDP, with only 0.3 percentage points having an origin in resource misallocation effects (the rest, 2.2 percentage points, being attributed to "X-inefficiency" plus monopolistic rents).

Third, unlike Argentina's relatively mature economy and like Brazil's, Mexico had a dualistic, Lewis-type economy featuring a surplus of labor that

---

24. That is, the static effects of protection on the allocation of resources, technical efficiency, and market structure, and the dynamic effects on productivity growth performance.

generates a relatively elastic supply of labor to the modern sector of the economy.[25] This was important for the process of reallocation of labor. The expansion of the industrial sector meant that the process of industrialization caused labor to move from low-productivity to high-productivity sectors. These productivity gains were behind the rapid increases in per capita GDP. In contrast, in mature economies such as Argentina's, most sectors are modern and there is no large subsistence sector. Productivity levels are similar across sectors and, as a result, the economy could not benefit from the reallocation of labor from low- to high-productivity sectors. Rather, the expansion of the industrial sector caused labor to be taken away from the modern export sector. Because industrialization crowded out labor from the export sector, the antiexport bias was higher.

Finally, geopolitical reasons may have had a role to play. More than by encouraging exports to the largest market in the world or through the facilitation of the flow of technology, the presence of a great power (a superpower from the early postwar period) on its borders may have constituted an extraordinary challenge that triggered a dynamic response similar to that of Japan when it faced up to the West after the mid-19th century (Hansen, 1971).

25. Díaz-Alejandro (1988) has emphasized the nature of the domestic economy in the comparison of the growth performance of Argentina and Brazil.

6

The Loss of Macroeconomic
Stability, the Oil Boom,
and the Debt Crisis

The 1970s witnessed a transformation of the international economic environment and an attempt to change development strategy as Mexico's political leaders and policymakers became increasingly aware of the need to address the inequities that accompanied the process of economic growth and the obstacles to sustained economic development. A push for redistribution was seen as a way to relieve social tensions that became openly manifest in the student movement of 1968, which ended in bloody repression on the part of the Gustavo Díaz Ordaz government, and guerrilla activity, both rural and urban, throughout the 1960s and early 1970s. To the extent that the administrations of the 1970s were unable to successfully address these problems, new obstacles would arise, as the loss of macroeconomic stability became a casualty of this failure. Adverse exogenous shocks would further complicate Mexico's economic outlook in this period.

From shared development to two-digit
inflation and the 1976 currency crisis

The Luis Echeverría Álvarez administration, which took office in late 1970, had as a central point of its political platform the claim that the "stabilizing development" strategy of the period 1956–1970 had failed to address the fundamental problem of inequality. A new strategy of "shared development"

Table 6.1   Composition of federal public investment (percentages)

	Total	Agriculture	Industry	T and C[a]	Social	Other[b]
1965–1970	100	11.0	40.1	21.8	25.2	1.9
(Díaz Ordaz)	(6.1)					
1971–1976	100	15.6	40.1	21.7	18.8	3.8
(Echeverría)	(7.3)					
1977–1982	100	15.7	50.1	14.4	13.9	5.8
(López	(10.9)					
Portillo)						

Source: Based on INEGI (1999a).
Figures in parentheses refer to public investment as a percentage of GDP.
[a] Transport and communications.
[b] Includes administration, commerce and tourism, and "convenios de coordinación."

was thus proposed in which the benefits of economic growth would be more evenly distributed. At the same time, the strategy was meant to address the problems of sluggish agricultural development, tax reform, and lagging industrial competitiveness in export markets. Indeed, as originally conceived, "shared development" was going to achieve an improvement in the distribution of income by reorienting public investment and finance toward the agricultural sector, and reforming what was perceived to be a weak and inequitable tax system.

The allocation of public investment to agricultural development increased substantially to 15.6% of the total over the period 1971–1976 (compared to 11% under the Díaz Ordaz administration) (table 6.1). Other government initiatives in the agricultural sector included an increase in guaranteed prices for basic products (although complaints continued that they were not high enough to reflect increases in costs) and a rapid expansion of agricultural credit and extension services (see Yates, 1981), including the creation of the *Programa Integral de Desarrollo Rural* (PIDER), which, like its predecessor in the 1960s (the *Programa Coordinado de Inversiones Públicas en el Medio Rural*), was launched to give technical and financial support to rural communities in the design and execution of infrastructure projects.

Plans for tax reform included, most importantly, the accumulation of earnings from different sources for income tax purposes, an increased tax on interest from financial assets, a wealth tax, an increase in the highest personal income tax rate (from 35% to 42%) and the elimination of anonymity on different forms of holding wealth with a view to reduce tax evasion.[1] However, by 1972, private sector opposition (and, according to Solís, 1981, and Newell and Rubio, 1984, pressure from the central bank, which feared capital flight) had forced the government to abandon any ambitious plan of tax reform. Changes in this area were limited to the imposition of a 15% tax on the purchase of luxury goods and a small increase in the sales tax. Other government revenues lagged behind as real public sector prices continued to decline during 1970–1973 (Clavijo, 1980). Their correction in 1974 left them only 7% above their 1970 level.

Industrial policy diversified its objectives to give more emphasis to export promotion, the development of capital goods industries, regional decentralization of industrial activities, and foreign investment regulation (see in particular, CEPAL, 1979; Solís, 1980; and Secretaría de Patrimonio y Fomento Industrial, 1979). The new priorities were reflected in a number of policy reforms. Export promotion policies included the establishment of export subsidies (*Certificados de Devolución de Impuestos* [CEDIS]) in 1971, tariff rebates on imported inputs of exporting firms, the expansion of short-term credit provided by *Fondo para el Fomento de las Exportaciones de Productos Manufacturados* (FOMEX), the creation in 1972 of *Fondo de Equipamiento Industrial* (FONEI) for the financing of export-oriented investments, and the establishment of the *Instituto Mexicano de Comercio Exterior* (IMCE) in 1970 to strengthen export promotion efforts and facilitate access to international markets. The concern for promoting a domestic capital goods industry inspired the 1973 tariff reforms, which increased the level of protection for that industry and led to the replacement in 1975 of Rule XIV of the tariff legislation—which had traditionally provided subsidies on imported machinery and equipment—with subsidies on imported machinery for the production of new capital goods. Fiscal incentives were also revised and, through a unified framework (*Certificados de Promoción Fiscal* [CEPROFIS]), afforded preferential treatment to the production and purchase of domestic capital goods, as well as to small firms and regionally decentralized activities. The period also witnessed a reactivation of the role of development banks in industrial financing. The 1973 Law on Foreign Investment redefined the rules for the participation of foreign investors, including a general 49% restriction on foreign ownership.[2]

---

1. The plan was inspired by the failed 1964 tax package which was based on proposals, commissioned by the Mexican government, by Nicholas Kaldor, a Cambridge economist (for a detailed discussion of the 1964 and 1972 attempts at tax reform, see Solís, 1981).

2. In practice, the law applied to new foreign investment projects, since the regulatory agency established by the law—the National Committee for Foreign Investment

Table 6.2 Macroeconomic performance (annual averages for each period)

	1971–1976	1977	1978–1981	1982	1983
GDP growth rate (%)	6.0[a]	3.4	8.6[b]	−0.5	−5.3
Inflation (%)[c]	14.9[a]	20.7	23.5[b]	98.8	80.8
Nominal exchange rate[d]	13.0	22.7	23.3	57.2	150.3
Real exchange rate[e]	90.1	107.6	88.5	121.0	162.7
Real wage[f]	118.6	136.4	144.4	146.6	107.8
Wage share in GDP (%)	37.2	38.9	37.3	35.8	28.8
Composition of GDP (%)					
Private consumption	70.6	69.0	68.4	69.0	67.3
Public consumption	8.4	8.6	8.9	9.3	9.7
Fixed private investment	13.1	11.7	12.9	11.7	9.4
Fixed public investment	7.4	7.2	9.8	9.3	6.6
Change in inventories	2.5	3.5	3.9	0.5	1.0
Exports	8.0	8.8	9.1	10.2	12.1
Imports	9.8	8.8	13	10.1	6.2

Source: INEGI, Cuentas Nacionales de México; INEGI (1999a); Oxford Latin American Economics History Database (OxLAD) (for terms of trade); Council of Economic Advisors, Economic Report of the President 2007 (for U.S. consumer prices).

GDP and its components are at 1970 prices (INEGI, Cuentas Nacionales de México).

[a] 1970–1976.

[b] 1977–1981.

[c] End of year (December–December). Consumer price index.

[d] Pesos per dollar.

[e] Using the consumer price index in the United States and Mexico (Index 1970 = 100).

[f] Yearly average wage (whole economy) deflated by the consumer price index (INEGI, Cuentas Nacionales de México, and INEGI, 1999a) (Index 1970 = 100).

Temporarily the strategy did have success on a number of fronts. After an initial slowdown triggered by a significant decrease in public investment in 1971, in 1972 and 1973 gross domestic product (GDP) growth was greater than 8% per year and recorded an average rate of 6.0% over the period 1970–1976 (table 6.2). Private investment, after a slump in 1971, reacted positively to the recovery of public investment. Manufacturing exports responded to fiscal incentives and expanded at rates of around 14% to 15% in 1972 and 1973, well above the average rate of 5.4% per year in the 1960s (INEGI, Sistema de

---

(CNIE)—allowed companies fully owned by foreigners to maintain the capital structure in existence before the law became effective. The CNIE was also allowed to modify the 49% general rule, taking into account a number of criteria that included complementarity of investments with national capital and its effects on transfer of technology, balance of payments, and employment.

Cuentas Nacionales). Real wages increased by more than 40% between 1970 and 1976, and the wage share soared from 35.5% to 40.3% over the same period (table A.12). The evidence on personal income distribution, available for 1968 and 1977, shows a significant decline in the Gini coefficient from 0.54 to 0.49 (table A.7). Only in the agricultural sector did the strategy fail. The growth of agricultural production remained at about the same rate as that of the second half of the 1960s. This has been attributed to weather conditions, the slow start of agricultural development programs and their delayed impact, and the threat of land redistribution prompting larger farmers to switch toward more mechanized and lower value-added crops (Solís, 1981). The quasi-stagnation of agriculture is probably the explanation for the fact that the decline in the poverty rate probably slowed down during this period.[3]

Unfortunately, these achievements were accompanied by the emergence of severe macroeconomic imbalances. As changes in the level and structure of public revenue stalled, the burden of achieving a more equitable distribution of income was shifted to public expenditure. In 5 years its share of GDP increased by more than 10 percentage points (table A.13), growing at nearly 12% per year during the whole Echeverría administration, almost twice the rate of growth of the economy. The size of the public sector expanded rapidly—through both the increase in public expenditure and the rapidly expanding public enterprise sector[4]—even though by international standards it was not exceptionally large by the end of the administration.[5] To the extent that tax reform was not addressed, public revenues lagged behind despite an increased effort at tax collection which contributed to higher nonoil revenues (table A.13). Thus the primary fiscal deficit climbed from 0.5% of GDP to 6.4% between 1971 and 1975 (table A.13).[6] The financial deficit of the consolidated public sector soared from 2.5% to 10% of GDP (table A.13) and was covered through monetary expansion, increasing bank reserve requirements,

3. The available evidence shows in fact a slight increase in the poverty rate from 1968 to 1977 (see table A.7), but this increase is probably influenced by an abnormally high poverty rate in 1977 resulting from the balance of payments crisis and economic downturn of 1976–1977.

4. One hundred eight public enterprises were created in the period 1971–1976, many of which were small and included numerous funds and special trusts. In contrast, 83 public enterprises were created between 1952 and 1970 (Aspe and Beristain, 1984).

5. For example, in comparison to Italy or France, Mexico's public sector was still relatively small (Newell and Rubio, 1984).

6. The primary fiscal deficit is the difference between government spending (excluding interest payments) and government revenues.

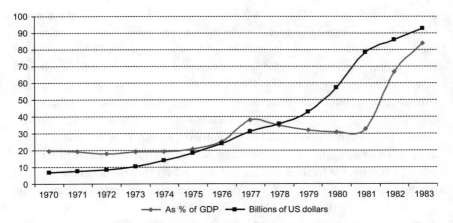

Figure 6.1 Total foreign debt, 1970–1983
Source: Oxford Latin American Economics History Database (OxLAD).

and external debt. Foreign debt, mostly public, jumped from US$7.5 billion in 1971 to US$24 billion in 1976 (figure 6.1). In practice, foreign debt substituted temporarily for the lack of tax reform. With an additional objective—income redistribution—and no fiscal reform, the policy strategy was left with fewer instruments than targets, thus generating an explosive growth in foreign public debt which acted for a while as the additional instrument (see Solís, 1977).

Inflation climbed to a two-digit rate in 1973 and was more than 20% in 1974. Inflation was fueled by the rapid expansion of public spending, the effects of the external oil shock in 1973, and also by negative agricultural supply shocks that turned the terms of trade in favor of agriculture. Moreover, by 1973 minimum wage settlements (and most likely other wage contracts) turned from biannual to annual, tending to reinforce the inflation momentum. A consequence of the resurgence of inflation was that the boom in financial intermediation of the stabilizing development period went into reverse. Indeed, the combination of increasing bank reserve requirements—as the fiscal deficit soared—and inflation forced banks to pay negative real interest rates on their deposits, resulting in financial disintermediation and a reduction of bank credit as a percentage of GDP (see Haber et al., 2008; Solís, 1981).

As domestic inflation accelerated above the foreign rate of inflation in the context of a fixed nominal exchange rate, the real exchange rate suffered a continuous and substantial appreciation (table A.12). Together with the expansion of the fiscal deficit and aggregate demand, this led to a sixfold increase in the trade deficit and to a more than fourfold increase in the current account deficit from 1972 to 1975 (table A.14). The deterioration of the international environment also had a role in these developments, as the collapse of the world's golden age took its toll on the Mexican economy. The first oil price shock found Mexico as a net importer of oil and, together with the decline in external demand, contributed to the increase in the external sector disequilibrium, while tightening the balance of payments constraints on growth. In fact, according to Zedillo (1986), external factors—terms of trade, foreign interest rates, and world recession shocks—explained two-thirds of the deterioration in the current account of the balance of payments between 1972 and 1975.

In addition, the business sector did not find fertile ground in the "shared development" rhetoric, and fixed private investment recorded a decrease as a fraction of GDP (table A.12). By 1975, the economy's expansion was being driven largely by public spending, with the shares in GDP of government consumption, and especially public investment, well above 1971 levels (table A.12). As the macroeconomic environment became highly unstable, and in particular the reemergence of inflation led to an appreciated and volatile exchange rate, it destroyed the incentives provided by industrial policy. Without a competitive exchange rate, the strategy failed to strengthen export competitiveness and import substitution in the capital goods sector. Manufacturing exports stagnated in 1974 and fell 15% in 1975 (INEGI, Sistema de Cuentas Nacionales) while the agricultural trade balance continued to decline. The limitations of capital goods manufacturing were evident, for example, in the fact that during 1974–1975 they accounted for less than 8% of manufacturing output, while at the same time they represented more than 50% of total imports. The share of imports in the domestic market started to climb as the investment process failed to diversify into new activities. Thus the contribution of import substitution to industrial growth declined sharply and even became negative (see table A.6). Starting in 1974, GDP growth gradually slowed down.

Eventually the situation worsened significantly as a result of capital flight driven by investors' anticipations of an unavoidable change in policy. Notwithstanding the increase in import controls and tariffs, balance of payments pressures forced the government to devalue the peso by nearly 100% in August 1976, thus abandoning the exchange rate parity that had remained fixed for more than 20 years. For the first time since the 1950s, the government turned to the International Monetary Fund (IMF) for financial assistance, and an extended fund facility was signed in late 1976. The contractionary effects of the devaluation—which led in particular to a decrease in real wages and private investment in 1977—together with the decline of public investment in 1976 and 1977 further slowed GDP growth, which fell to less than 4% in 1977.

The oil boom, 1978–1981

Despite the severity of the 1976 crisis, in a year or so the economy's prospects were fully turned around with the announcement of Mexico's vast oil
resources. Proven oil reserves increased from 6.3 billion barrels in November
1976 to 16 billion barrels by the end of 1977 and to 40 billion barrels a year later
(Székely, 1983). The trade deficit was under control again in 1977–1978, at levels below those in 1971–1972. The term profile of foreign debt was restruc-
tured and, for a while, new indebtedness did not grow in a noticeable way. An
ambitious industrialization plan, aimed at strengthening export competitiveness and deepening import substitution in capital goods, was launched on
the assumption of a sustained long-term increase in the price of oil. An agricultural program (*Sistema Alimentario Mexicano* [SAM]) strengthened support
policies for peasant agriculture, with the twin goals of stimulating food production, in order to reach self-sufficiency at the national level, and improving
the nutritional standards of the poor population.[7]

A major attempt at tax reform was also carried out in this period, and
these changes reduced some of the inequities of the Mexican tax system. An
adjustment for inflation was introduced in personal income taxation. A value-added tax and a new corporate income tax were established. The tax base
broadened as loopholes were closed and the entire administrative and com-
pliance process was simplified. The one to five minimum wage brackets went
from contributing 58% of labor income tax collections in 1978 to 28% in 1981,
whereas the contribution of the highest wage bracket (more than 15 minimum
wages) went from 8% to 25% of the total.[8]

Exploitation of the newly discovered oil resources in southern Mexico and
their sale on the international market would bring a swift and strong recovery.
Indeed, from 1978 to 1981 economic growth recovered strongly, leading to a
period of economic expansion at rates well above the historical norm. Led by
oil production (19.4% annual growth) and oil exports (52.7% annual growth),

---

7. Another poverty alleviation program, launched in 1977, was *Coordinación General
del Plan de Acción de Zonas Deprimidas y Grupos Marginados* (COPLAMAR), a special group
to work under direct supervision of the president's office with the responsibility of coordi-
nating all policy actions aimed at improving social conditions in marginalized communities.
Funds were given to federal entities that in turn used them to promote development at the
municipal level.

8. For a detailed description, see Gil Diaz (1987).

Table 6.3   GDP growth by sector (annual average growth rates in percent)

	1977	1977–1981	1982	1983
Agriculture[a]	7.7	4.2	−2.0	2.0
Oil and mining	6.8	15.9	8.7	−0.9
Manufacturing	2.9	8.0	−2.7	−7.8
Construction	−5.3	13.0	−7.1	−19.2
Electricity[b]	7.4	9.1	9.7	1.1
Commerce[c]	3.5	12.5	−0.9	−7.5
T and C[d]	4.5	10.9	9.3	−2.6
Financial services[e]	3.7	5.3	5.0	3.9
Other services	3.3	7.2	3.5	3.0
Total GDP	3.4	9.2	−0.6	−4.2

Source: INEGI, Banco de Información Económica.

GDP for the entire economy and by sector are at 1980 constant prices. GDP growth rates do not coincide with those in table 6.2 due to differences in the base year.

[a] Includes livestock, forestry, and fishing.
[b] Includes gas and water.
[c] Includes restaurants and hotels.
[d] Transport and communications.
[e] Includes insurance and real estate.

GDP expanded at about 9% per year, and real national income—benefiting from the favorable shift in the terms of trade provided by the oil price rise of 1979–1980—grew even faster (9%–10%) (Ros, 1987; see also table 6.3). In addition to the oil sector, transportation and construction, which benefited from an extraordinary investment boom, recorded double-digit growth rates. This time agriculture responded vigorously to the incentives provided by the government and its production expanded at nearly 5% per year from 1976 to 1981. Poverty rates resumed their decline, while personal income distribution improved. Thus, from 1977 to 1984 (the 2 years with available data), the nutrition-based poverty rate fell from 25% to 22.5% (and probably declined by even more before the 1982 crisis). The Gini coefficient saw a reduction from 49 to 42.5 (table A.7).

However, some signs were already worrying by the late 1970s. While the primary fiscal deficit remained subdued before 1981, it did so only in the context of a doubling of government oil revenues as a fraction of GDP (table A.13) and thus of a very fast expansion of government expenditures (public investment, in particular, grew at rates on the order of 13% per year from 1976 to 1980). The inflation rate had reached a plateau of about 18% and did not seem to decrease, contributing to a continuous real appreciation of the exchange

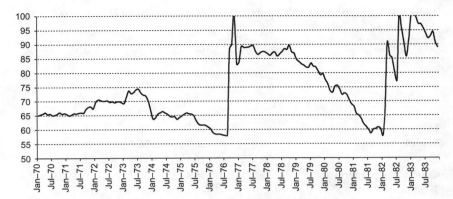

Figure 6.2 Multilateral real exchange rate, 1970–1983 (1990 = 100. Index estimated with consumer prices with respect to 111 countries.)
Source: Banco de México, Estadísticas.

rate (table A.12 and figure 6.2). Eventually inflation increased to more than 25% in 1980. Despite the extraordinary increase in oil exports there was a progressive imbalance in the balance of payments. The trade balance turned from a surplus of US$0.1 billion in 1977 to a deficit of US$2.6 billion in 1980, while the current account deficit climbed to a record level of US$7.2 billion in 1980, with rising interest payments on foreign debt having an increasing role. These increasing payment imbalances were financed through foreign debt, mainly public, which rose from US$31.2 billion in 1977 to US$57.4 billion in 1980 (see figure 6.1).

The pattern of growth presented some symptoms of Dutch disease that had their role in the increasing vulnerability and financial fragility of the economy. Although investment was very dynamic, its sectoral pattern was strongly biased in favor of the oil industry and the commerce and service sectors (table 6.4). With the exception of a moderate shift toward agriculture—which, as already mentioned, produced high returns in terms of agricultural output growth—public investment was strongly reoriented toward the oil industry, which absorbed nearly half of all public enterprise investment (compared with one-third in the period 1970–1977). Private investment, on the other hand, shifted radically toward services and against manufacturing, whose share declined from one-half in 1970–1977 to one-third in 1978–1980. It is not surprising then that in a boom period the growth of manufacturing output slowed below the overall rate of growth, declining from 10% in 1979 to about 6% in 1980 and 1981. Moreover, few investments were directed to the

Table 6.4   Composition of total public and private investment in 1970–1977 and during the oil boom (1978–1981)

	1970–1977	1978	1979	1980	1981
	Total investment				
Agriculture	7.3	8.4	7.5	7.2	n.a.
Mining	2.2	1.6	2.9	3.1	n.a.
Oil	11.2	20.7	18.4	19.0	n.a.
Manufacturing	38.0	20.7	24.7	25.6	n.a.
Electricity	8.1	10.1	9.5	9.8	n.a.
Commerce and services	33.3	38.4	36.9	35.3	n.a.
Total	100.0	100.0	100.0	100.0	
	Public investment (excluding central government)				
Agriculture	1.8	1.7	2.2	2.5	3.5
Mining	0.7	0.7	1.0	1.1	1.0
Oil	32.0	44.6	41.9	44.2	44.7
Manufacturing	14.2	9.8	14.3	11.6	15.2
Electricity	23.1	21.8	21.8	22.8	19.4
Commerce and services	28.2	21.4	18.8	17.8	16.2
Total	100.0	100.0	100.0	100.0	100.0
	Private nonresidential investment				
Agriculture	10.2	14.2	11.7	10.7	n.a.
Mining	3.0	2.3	4.4	4.6	n.a.
Oil	0.0	0.0	0.0	0.0	n.a.
Manufacturing	50.8	30.3	32.8	36.1	n.a.
Electricity	0.0	0.0	0.0	0.0	n.a.
Commerce and services	36.0	53.0	51.1	48.6	n.a.
Total	100.0	100.0	100.0	100.0	

Source: Santamaría (1985).
n.a. = not available.

manufacturing export sector, although two exceptions are worth noting: the motor vehicle industry—where a new generation of plants was being built with state-of-the-art technology, explicitly designed to compete in the world market—and the petrochemicals sector, where the public sector was investing heavily. Thus, in spite of the ambitious industrial and development plans, the oil boom was very far from creating conditions in which the industrial sectors could take a leading role once oil revenues could no longer fund expansion.

Doubling of the international oil price (figure 6.3) and an increase in foreign interest rates in 1979–1980 had, on balance, a favorable short-term effect.

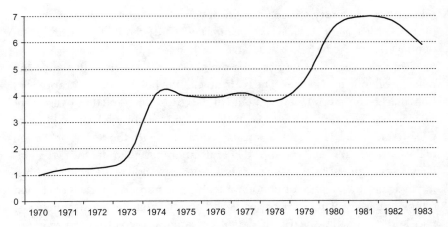

Figure 6.3 Real oil price, 1970–1983 (Index 1970 = 1.0. Oil price divided by U.S. producer price index.)
Source: Oxford Latin American Economics History Database (OxLAD).

Not only was oil export income twice what was originally projected, but, for the same reason, the rise in interest rates was accompanied by an almost unlimited availability of foreign loans. The oil bonanza turned Mexico into a preferred customer of international banks, and foreign loans were granted in amounts and with conditions notably more favorable than for the rest of the developing countries.[9]

With hindsight, the nature of this external shock was dramatically misinterpreted by the Mexican government (as well as by other economic agents). High and increasing real oil prices were taken to be a permanent feature of the international economy, while the increase in interest rates was interpreted as a temporary phenomenon. As an optimistic outlook continued to prevail during the first half of 1981, even though the U.S. recession had started weakening the international oil market and foreign interest rates had continued to rise (the U.S. prime rate reached a peak of 19% for 1981 as a whole), fiscal expansion was reinforced in 1981. This expansion was not only related to an error of diagnosis, but was stimulated by ready access to foreign finance and, as we shall discuss in greater detail later, by the particular phase in Mexico's political cycle: the fifth year of a 6-year presidential term when a rush occurred to carry out the government's plans and control over public expenditure was

9. Thus, from 1978 to 1981, while international bank loans to developing countries as a whole increased by 76%, in the case of Mexico (already a very large debtor in 1978) they rose by 146% (Frieden, 1984).

relaxed as the country entered a political period centered on the nomination of the next *Partido Revolucionario Institucional* (PRI) candidate for the presidential elections to be held a year later.

Thus the year 1981 witnessed a massive deterioration of the emerging macroeconomic imbalances. The real value of the peso (about 30% appreciation) reached a historic level by the end of 1981 (Ros, 1987) and the government financial deficit nearly doubled from 1980 to 1981, reaching a level of 14.1% of GDP (table A.13). The fiscal expansion, combined with the real appreciation of the exchange rate and the import liberalization started under the IMF stabilization program of 1976,[10] led to a massive deterioration of external accounts, in particular the balance of nonoil trade.[11] While nonoil exports had started falling in mid-1979, imports of goods had been growing at an extremely fast pace and increased by nearly 30% in 1981 (despite a reversal of the import liberalization program in the second half of the year). Thus the trade deficit doubled from 1980 to 1981, while the current account deficit reached a new record level of US$12.5 billion.

Foreign debt financed the external gap and jumped from US$57.4 billion to US$72.2 billion in 1 year (figure 6.1). At the same time, the debt structure became increasingly vulnerable. Short-term foreign public debt jumped from US$1.5 billion at the end of 1980 to US$10.8 billion a year later (Zedillo, 1986). By 1981, short-term loans accounted for more than half of net external indebtedness. The ratio of foreign debt interest payments to total exports rose from 27% in 1977–1978 to 37% in 1981–1982, although it is worth pointing out that this increase was fully explained by rising interest rates since the debt/export ratio shows a moderate decline over the same period (from 3.1 to 2.8). The financial fragility that developed over the period was also evident in the private sector. The boom in domestic demand and investment triggered the rapid growth of private indebtedness: the debt/capital ratio of large private firms rose from 0.9 in 1978 to 1.2 in 1981. More important was the change in composition of this debt: the share of dollar-denominated debt in the overall debt of large private firms rose from 30% in 1978 to 63%

---

10. Import liberalization included the progressive abandonment of import licenses and their replacement by tariffs and a general relaxation of controls over import licenses. Uncontrolled imports reached 40% of the total import bill by the first half of 1981.

11. There was much controversy over the relative weight of these three factors, particularly with respect to the role of import liberalization. See Eatwell and Singh (1981), Schatán (1981), and the papers by Bazdresch, Brailovsky, and Singh in Barker and Brailovsky (1982).

in 1981.[12] The upsurge in long-term foreign indebtedness by private firms in 1978–1980 can be explained by the optimistic expectations prevailing about the exchange rate at a time when the rule of monetary policy was to set domestic nominal interest rates equal to foreign interest rates plus the expected devaluation of the peso implied by the gap between the spot and forward exchange rates on the Chicago futures market. However, since the actual minidevaluations engineered by the central bank were not consistent with the (expected) devaluation implicit in its interest rate policy—the latter being much greater than the former—domestic interest rates remained well above ex post interest rates abroad (expressed in a common currency) for several years.

The government's optimistic expectations were shared by international banks, which redoubled their lending to Mexico. However, official expectations were not shared by everybody else: after borrowing heavily from abroad in 1979–1980, the Mexican private sector started an unprecedented speculative attack on the peso in the first half of 1981, and more than US$20 billion flew out of the country in a period of about 18 months. The magnitude of the capital flight was such that it absorbed as much as 54% of the increase in Mexico's total foreign debt (net of international reserves) in 1981 and 1982, generating growing political tension between the López Portillo government and the large private financial conglomerates.

Before turning to the denouement, it is worth asking where had the entire oil windfall gone? Gavin (1996) estimated that subsidies to the private sector were the main form in which the oil windfall was spent. This included domestic oil subsidies (about 70% of the oil windfall), by keeping *Petróleos Mexicanos* (PEMEX) domestic sales at prices well below world prices, budgetary transfers to sectors such as agriculture, and nonoil subsidies on publicly provided goods, such as electricity and transportation, that were channeled through the nonoil state enterprise sector. It is this pattern of public sector response that made possible the private investment boom. In addition to the rapid expansion of domestic demand, private firms benefited from the large domestic oil and nonoil government subsidies, as well as from an increasingly overvalued real exchange rate that reduced the relative price of imported capital goods, thus increasing the profitability of investments in nontradable goods sectors.

---

12. See López (1998) and the 1981 survey of large private firms by the *Oficina de Asesores del Presidente* based on a sample of 2200 firms.

The 1982 debt crisis

At the beginning of 1982 the international price of oil was still falling (figure 6.3), capital flight was at its peak, and nearly half the country's foreign debt was due for repayment or refinancing over the following 12 months. Although import controls were reimposed in mid-1981 and a 4% cut in the 1981 budget was introduced, a more radical shift in economic policies was now unavoidable.

In February, the government decided on a fiscal contraction plus a devaluation package, maintaining the free convertibility of the peso. This was the beginning of the recession and of a rapid acceleration of inflation (table 6.2). Thus, in 1982, for the first time since 1932, the level of economic activity fell, accelerating its decline throughout 1983. The decrease in aggregate demand was led by private investment, affected by the stagflation effects of devaluation and by the fiscal, especially public investment, contraction. Private investment was reduced, in particular, by the sharp increase in the price of imported capital goods and in the real value of firms' dollar liabilities resulting from the devaluation, together with the depression of the real market value of physical assets, determined to a large extent by the massive capital flight. The financial breakdown of Grupo Alfa, the country's largest industrial conglomerate, is the most representative and best-known example of the financial difficulties affecting, in early 1982, several large private firms with substantial dollar-denominated debts.

Although the trade balance became positive by the second quarter of 1982, the policy package was ineffective in stopping postdevaluation capital flight and the financial speculation that flourished in the absence of any kind of restriction on capital flows. Capital flight became by far the most important source of payment imbalances and, with foreign loans increasingly rationed, of the resulting decrease in foreign reserves at the central bank. In August 1982, when the official reserves were almost completely exhausted, the flow of international lending to Mexico was suddenly interrupted. Dramatic new devaluations followed, together with the adoption of a dual exchange rate regime, and the government suspended payments on its foreign debt, signaling the beginning of the international debt crisis. It was under these circumstances, further complicated by mounting political tensions between the government and the large financial conglomerates, that in his last annual presidential address to the nation (September 1, 1982), López Portillo dramatically announced the nationalization of the private banking system and the adoption of full exchange controls on capital flows (see del Angel-Mobarak et al., 2005; Espinosa and Cárdenas, 2008; Tello, 1984). It was too late, however, for the adoption of an exchange control regime: foreign reserves were exhausted and the international debt crisis had arrived.

What went wrong? The whole strategy had been based on (1) the premise of long-term foreign exchange and fiscal abundance from oil exports—and the 1979–1980 oil price hike appeared only to confirm expectations that the era of high real oil prices had come to stay; and (2) the notion that the external debt problem was over, given the low real interest rates that had so far prevailed. When the oil market started to crumble in 1981 and foreign interest rates drastically jumped upward, both of these shocks were taken to be transitory, and thus were to be dealt with by additional external finance. Indeed, the whole international economic environment that made the oil boom possible had been tragically misperceived (by the government, foreign banks, and international financial institutions alike). When this finally became clear, Mexico suddenly became a highly indebted country, that is, an overindebted borrower, given the new levels of interest rates and export revenues with which the old debt had to be serviced.

It is worth speculating on the issue of a possible alternative course of events. In mid-1981, two main alternatives to the prevailing inertia were put forward from different sides of the economic cabinet. The Ministry of Finance under David Ibarra (who remained in office until the devaluation of February 1982, when he was replaced by Jesús Silva Herzog) pressed for measures to rapidly correct the exchange rate and reduce the growth of public expenditure. In this view, the increasing trouble with the balance of payments, both in the current and in the capital accounts, was mainly attributable to the continuous real appreciation of the exchange rate and to the huge expansion of public spending. A second, and different, view put forward at the Ministry of Industry and by other close collaborators of López Portillo favored the adoption of direct controls on imports (as was done in June 1981) and on capital flows as the only effective policy response to the capital flight and to the external shocks coming from an increasingly unstable international economy. This position recognized the need for fiscal moderation—less emphatically than the former position—but for most of the period it opposed a maxidevaluation on the grounds that it would simply exacerbate inflation and could even accelerate capital flight.

The policy debates of the period focused increasingly on these two options, but no major shift occurred during 1981 to head off the worst of all possible worlds: a huge fiscal expansion plus free capital mobility plus real exchange rate appreciation.[13] The fiscal expansion of 1981 was, as we shall argue below, largely determined by the particular phase of Mexico's political cycle. But it was also a policy mistake in that it was based, as we have seen, on a misinterpretation of international developments and generated some of the incentives and the means for the massive capital flight. Given the extreme vulnerability of the Mexican economy at the time and, in particular, its external dependence on increasingly unstable oil and financial markets, we also tend to view the absence of any restrictions on capital flows as a major policy error of the period. With respect to the real appreciation, this was probably the unavoidable by-product of the oil boom and the 1981 fiscal expansion more than a policy mistake. However, when the growth of oil export revenues stopped, the real exchange rate became incompatible overnight with the simultaneous achievement of medium-term growth and a viable balance of payments. In other words, the sustainable real exchange rate in the medium term was suddenly and radically altered by the new prospects of stagnating or falling oil revenues. A gradual correction of the exchange rate, with a temporary increase in foreign finance during the transition, would probably have been the economically less costly and socially more efficient way to deal with the problem. This would have required, however, that foreign finance to Mexico behave countercyclically (with respect to the oil market), that is, exactly the opposite of its actual behavior. In practice, the pattern of external financing aggravated still more the extent of the real exchange rate adjustment.

Interpretations of the internal causes of the 1976 and 1982 crises

We now turn our discussion toward alternative interpretations of the 1976 and 1982 crises, or more precisely, their domestic determinants, having already highlighted the external factors that contributed to them. A first explanation attributes the crises to the model of industrialization followed by Mexico since the early 1940s. The argument runs as follows: The exhaustion of import substitution in the early 1970s caused a slowdown of growth and triggered political pressures to sustain growth through public spending, leading eventually to large fiscal deficits and a balance of payments crisis. In

13. On the policy debates of the period, see also Cordera and Tello (1981).

turn, the exhaustion of import substitution comes in two versions. In the first, slow growth is caused by industrial inefficiency created by high protectionism (see Golub, 1991, for a review of the literature, as well as Cárdenas, 1996, and Kaufman, 1979). In the second, the opportunities for replacing imports by domestic production progressively disappear, causing a slowdown of industrial expansion (see Boltvinik and Hernández Laos, 1981).

Schlefer (2008) has a convincing critique of the first version. First, he argues, there is no evidence that industrial inefficiency increased during the 1970s. As we saw in chapter 5 (table 5.10), total factor productivity in manufacturing grew 0.8% per year in 1960–1973 and then increased to 1.5% per year in 1973–1980. In the industrial sectors of the "difficult stage" of import substitution, total factor productivity (TFP) growth from 1973 to 1980 was particularly outstanding: it proceeded at 3.5% per year in the capital and durable goods sectors, faster than in the large advanced nations except Japan, and at 2.5% per year in chemicals and 3.2% in nonmetallic minerals, in both cases faster than in any large industrialized country, Japan included (Schlefer, 2008). Export performance during the 1970s and early 1980s, before any trade barriers were removed, also sheds doubts on the supposed creeping inefficiency of the industrialization model. As argued by Schlefer (2008), manufacturing exports grew on average 10% per year between the peak years of 1972 and 1984. Second, even if industrial inefficiency was causing a slowdown in economic growth, there is no evidence of a clear-cut relationship between the microeconomic distortions caused by protectionism and economic crises. Rodrik's (1999) study of developing countries shows that those countries with large microeconomic distortions caused by protectionism and subsidies did not suffer economic crises any more than those with small distortions, and also that countries that avoided the 1982 debt crisis actually had slightly larger distortions than those that suffered from it. He also compares two countries with relatively high protection, one with recurrent economic crises from the 1950s to the 1980s (Argentina) and the other with a record of outstanding macroeconomic stability during most of the 20th century and the only major Latin American country to escape the debt crisis in the 1980s (Colombia). The difference has to do of course with fiscal and monetary discipline, which is not systematically tied to underlying structural problems.

Regarding the second version, it is true that using a Chenery-like decomposition of the sources of industrial growth[14] into the expansion of domestic

14. See Chenery (1960).

demand, export growth, and import substitution, the contribution of import substitution is slightly negative in the 1970s after having been positive in the 1960s (see table A.6). But in this sense, import substitution had become exhausted in the mid-1960s when the import share in GDP reached a historic low (table A.11). Yet no recession or growth slowdown happened in the second half of the 1960s. There are, moreover, three additional problems with this version. One is that the measured contribution of import substitution is not independent of the expansion of domestic demand: the faster domestic demand grows, the more rapid is import growth, other things being equal. Given the very fast growth of domestic demand during the 1970s, it is not surprising that import coefficients tended to increase, making the measured contribution of import substitution negative. Another is that the model of industrialization followed in the 1970s was no longer one based exclusively on import substitution. As reviewed in this and the previous chapter, since the mid-1960s, with the Border Industrialization Program that established the *maquiladora* regime, and certainly since the early 1970s, with the establishment of export subsidies and the reorientation of fabrication programs to provide protection and duty-free access to inputs in exchange for export commitments or foreign exchange balances, Mexico's industrialization model was in a transition to an Asian-style "mixed model" combining protection of the domestic market with export promotion.[15] Finally, just as in the case of the links between protectionism, microeconomic distortions, and economic crises, there is no compelling logic tying the disappearance of import substitution opportunities to the appearance of economic crises. There is not even evidence of a slowdown of growth in the genesis of the 1976 and 1982 crises, with the exception of a mild slump in 1971 when, nevertheless, the economy recorded a very respectable (by today's standards) 3.8% growth.

A second explanation of the 1976 and 1982 crises focuses on populist economic policies. Were the 1976 and 1982 crises the outcome of macroeconomic populism? If one understands macroeconomic populism to mean macroeconomic policies of demand stimulation that fail to live within the constraints posed by the balance of payments and internal productive capacity leading

---

15. We follow here Cárdenas, Ocampo, and Thorp (2000) in calling this strategy a "mixed model," which is common to Mexico and other Latin American countries, although we differ from their appraisal that Mexico actually moved backward to a more traditional emphasis on import substitution in the later stages of state-led industrialization. On the role of export promotion in Latin America in the 1960s and 1970s, see also Bulmer-Thomas (2003).

Table 6.5   Public sector spending growth and budget deficits
(excludes debt service)

	Real spending growth (percent per year)	Budget deficit (percent of GDP)
Díaz Ordaz		
1966	3.0	0.3
1967	9.0	0.7
1968	7.0	0.2
1969	13.0	0.7
1970	1.0	−0.2
Echeverría		
1971	7.0	0.5
1972	21.0	1.8
1973	25.0	3.5
1974	10.0	3.3
1975	27.0	6.5
1976	0.0	4.2
López Portillo		
1977	−2.0	1.8
1978	12.0	1.6
1979	17.0	2.0
1980	21.0	2.4
1981	22.0	7.2
1982	−8.0	0.6

Source: Schlefer (2008, table 4-3).

to balance of payments crises and high inflation (Dornbusch and Edwards, 1991), then certainly populist policies were behind the crises. But such a definition of populism leaves unanswered the question of why the government lost fiscal and monetary discipline in the first place. Was the loss of economic stability the result of populist pressures on wages and public spending coming from labor unions and other social organizations (as may have been the case in classic cases of populism such as Juan Perón and Alan García)? The answer is not clear-cut. On the one hand, the loss of macroeconomic stability under the Echeverría administration certainly had to do with the failure to undertake a major fiscal reform in the midst of an attempt at redistribution that had its origin in the social tensions mentioned at the beginning of this chapter. On the other hand, as argued by Schlefer (2008), Mexico's political system at the time was largely immune to populist pressures, given the complete control of peasant, labor, and middle-class organizations by the dominant party and the absence of meaningful electoral competitions.[16] The resilience of the Mexican state to populist pressures at the time is also confirmed by the pattern of public spending, which is not conditioned by the need to obtain external political support. Indeed, rather than increasing during election years, public spending and fiscal deficits (excluding debt payments) actually declined in 1976 and 1982 (table 6.5). The traditional political business cycle argument does not fit Mexico. This is not surprising, given the absence at the time of significant electoral opposition.

Moreover, while there is evidence of an acceleration in the growth of public spending soon after Echeverría took office (see the rapid growth of spending in 1972 and 1973 in table 6.5), it is only in the fifth year of his administration that the budget deficit (excluding debt service) really gets out of control. Similarly, it is in the fifth year of the López Portillo administration, when the budget deficit jumps from 2.4% of GDP in 1980 to 7.2% in 1981 (table 6.5), that fiscal discipline is really abandoned, generating the conditions for the balance of payments crisis of 1982.

This pattern, which precedes in fact the Echeverría administration, suggests that behind the 1976 and 1982 crises there is more than the change in development strategy to give more emphasis to redistribution in the context of a failed tax reform. Indeed, as shown by Schlefer (2008), while there is no indication of a traditional electoral cycle in public spending, there is much evidence supporting a sui generis spending cycle in which public spending and fiscal deficits peak in the preelectoral year when the ruling party's internal competition for the presidential nomination reaches its climax. Table 6.5 illustrates the loss of control over public spending in the preelectoral years of 1969, 1975, and 1981, and the corresponding increases in the fiscal deficit (excluding debt service) as the main contenders in the preelectoral battles

16. It is true that there was a labor insurgency led by the Democratic Tendency of the electrical utility workers during the Echeverría presidency, but it was negligible compared to the 1958–1959 strike wave led by the railroad union, a powerful grassroots movement which was far from triggering a populist cycle. Moreover, it was largely prompted by the president himself, and receded when he abandoned it. In addition, the insurgency was not concerned (unlike the 1958–1959 movement) with wage demands, which could have triggered macroeconomic problems, but rather with union democratization.

within the PRI attempt to build support for their candidacies. It is perhaps in the macroeconomics of elite conflict within a dominant party state, rather that in the traditional interpretations of macroeconomic populism or in the exhaustion of the industrialization model, that we must search for the internal causes of the crises.

7

The Years of Adjustment, the Lost Decade, and the Reform Process

The Mexican economy was subject to two major external shocks during the 1980s. The first was the 1982 international debt crisis during which foreign debt service sharply increased and new external finance was drastically curtailed. In addition, given that the rise in U.S. interest rates led to a contraction in the pace of expansion of the U.S. economy and reduced its demand for imports, the adverse impact on the Mexican economy was exacerbated. The second was the 1986 oil price shock, which dramatically deteriorated the terms of trade of the Mexican economy and cut off a major part of the country's foreign exchange and fiscal revenues.[1] These shocks generated acute imbalances in Mexico's balance of payments and fiscal accounts, with a severe impact on the rate of inflation and the pace of economic expansion.

The strategies adopted to respond to these two shocks can be summarized as follows. In the wake of the 1982 debt crisis, after the adoption of imports and exchange controls and nationalization of the private banking system by the José López Portillo administration (discussed in the previous chapter), an orthodox, stabilization-first strategy was adopted by the Miguel de la Madrid administration, which took office in December 1982, with the aim of rapidly cutting the fiscal deficit and restoring price and balance of payments stability.

---

1. Between 1981 and 1986 Mexico's terms of trade, as measured by the average price of its exports relative to import prices, fell 46%. If the adverse impact of the rise in the interest rate on foreign debt is considered, they fell 57% (Banco de México, 1988).

This was to be followed by a structural adjustment process that would induce a gradual reallocation of resources toward the production of tradable goods within a stable and growth-oriented macroeconomic framework. The orthodox approach prevailed up until mid-1985. Its main results were to slash the trade and current account deficits, but the strategy failed to stabilize prices. With annual rates of inflation of consumer prices reaching three-digit levels in 1986, policy shifted in favor of increasingly radical market liberalization reforms and a different approach to stabilization. In late 1987, the government recognized the failure of its orthodox attempts at bringing down inflation and opted for a rather heterodox approach to stabilization by launching the Economic Solidarity Pact (the *Pacto*). The *Pacto* aimed at rapidly stopping inflation through a combination of wage and price controls, a nominal exchange rate freeze, and tight fiscal and monetary policy.[2] All this was accompanied by an acceleration of market liberalization reforms, especially in the areas of trade, industrial policy, and privatization. The *Pacto* proved to be a huge success in stabilizing inflation and in helping to reactivate the economy. However, it gradually led to an overvaluation of the real exchange rate that was drastically corrected in 1994–1995. But before analyzing its achievements and limitations, we must examine in more detail the whole macroeconomic adjustment process of the Mexican economy in the 1980s.

The years of adjustment and stabilization

The adjustment to the debt crisis

The size and speed of Mexico's external adjustment to the debt crisis was outstanding in the Latin American context. The turnaround of the trade balance was swift and massive—on the order of five percentage points of gross domestic product (GDP). Indeed, with the economy entering a deep and prolonged recession, its trade deficit of US$3.8 billion in 1981 turned into a surplus of US$7.1 billion over the next 12 months. In 1983 it doubled, to reach US$14.1 billion. The surplus in the current account of the balance of payments was somewhat less sizable, given the large interest payments on external debt. In the same period, other large debtors, like Brazil and Argentina, faced enormous difficulties in reducing their trade and current account deficits and were very far from obtaining surpluses.

2. Similar heterodox stabilization plans were then implemented in Argentina, Peru, and Brazil (see Alberro and Ibarra, 1987; Edwards, 1995).

Two features of this adjustment should be highlighted, as they help to explain its size and speed while at the same time revealing its long-term fragility. The first one refers to the role of oil revenues and can best be illustrated by a comparison with the Brazilian economy. To eliminate the deficit in its current account, Brazil had to then generate a surplus of US$20 billion in its nonoil trade balance to cover an oil import bill on the order of US$9 billion and to pay the interest on its external debt. Mexico, in contrast, with oil export revenues on the order of US$16 billion per year in 1983–1984—and through a drastic import compression—generated a massive trade surplus that more than compensated for the interest payments on external debt and achieved a surplus in the current account. Its nonoil trade balance was, at the same time, recording a deficit on the order of US$5–$6 billion.

The second feature is that the adjustment in Mexico's nonoil trade balance was achieved more through a decrease in domestic expenditure—and thus in imports—than through a dynamic response of nonoil exports. After several years of real exchange rate overvaluation, it was difficult to expect a strong expansion of nonoil exports in the short run. In any case, the fact is that Mexico's external adjustment was outstanding due to the brutal contraction of domestic spending (17% in real terms between 1981 and 1983) and, in particular, to the collapse of public and private fixed investment (40%). In the face of the enormous initial deficit in the private sector's trade balance and the low elasticity of overall export supply—the other side of the coin of the external surplus of the public sector and the dominance of oil in export revenues— the sharp exchange rate devaluation in 1982 was bound to operate essentially through the strong contractionary and redistributive impacts that it brought about on private spending.[3] Indeed, private expenditure fell by 15% in those same years and to this was added the sharp contraction of public investment (48%) that was the main mechanism of adjustment of the fiscal accounts. All

---

3. These include, in particular, the Hirschman and Díaz-Alejandro effects of a devaluation. The Hirschman effect refers to the redistribution of income caused by devaluation from residents to foreigners as a result of a trade deficit, or from foreigners to residents as a result of a trade surplus. In Mexico at that time, since the public sector had a foreign exchange surplus, it benefited from the devaluation, while the private sector had a trade deficit and was thus adversely affected by it. The Díaz-Alejandro effect refers to the redistribution from wages to profits caused by devaluation as wages lag behind the price increases brought about by the devaluation. See Krugman and Taylor (1978) on the subject. Note that in terms of assets, Mexico's private sector had probably a net creditor aggregate position because, as some estimates suggested, its total external debt may have been less than the total amount of its deposits abroad.

this is reflected in the severe contraction of imports, mainly intermediate and capital goods, whose contribution to the change in the nonoil trade balance was more than 70% (table 7.1). In just 2 years, the share of imports as a proportion of real GDP went down nearly 10 points.

From a medium and long-term perspective, Mexico's external adjustment in this period did not contribute much to build a solid platform for high and sustained export-led growth. As will be analyzed in this and the next chapter, local production did eventually reorient itself to sell much more in foreign markets. However, the renewed export drive became increasingly dependent on imported inputs and thus it did not build sufficient backward and forward linkages indispensable to pull the economy into a long-term path of high expansion. In fact, the moderate economic recovery in 1984–1985, and the real exchange rate appreciation that accompanied it, slashed the trade surpluses obtained in 1983–1984 and virtually sent the current account into a deficit.

Table 7.1   External and fiscal adjustments in three periods (changes during the period, first differences)

	1981–1984	1984–1987	1987–1991
Billions of US dollars			
Trade balance[a]	19.9	−3.5	−18.4
Oil exports	2.0	−8.0	−0.2
Nonoil trade balance	17.9	4.5	−18.2
Nonoil exports[b]	2.2	4.9	9.4
Imports	−12.7	1.0	25.3
Consumer goods	−2.0	−0.1	5.3
Intermediate goods	−5.7	1.0	14.4
Capital goods	−5.0	0.1	5.6
Nonfactor services[c] (net)	3.0	0.6	−2.3
Percent of nominal GDP			
Operational fiscal surplus	9.7	2.1	0.7
Public savings	4.2	0.7	0.0
External	2.3	−3.9	−0.8
Internal	1.9	4.6	0.8
Public investment	−5.5	−1.4	−0.7
Public consumption	−1.5	−0.7	−0.4
Internal disposable income	0.4	3.9	0.4

Source: Ros (1992), based on Banco de México, Indicadores Económicos.

[a] Includes nonfactor services.
[b] Includes *maquiladora* exports.
[c] Excludes *maquiladora* exports.

The same factors behind the external adjustment are reflected in the evolution of public finances. The operational balance of the public sector[4] turned from a deficit of 10% of GDP in 1981 to a modest surplus in 1984. This remarkable adjustment was the result of the collapse of public investment (5.5 percentage points of GDP) and the increase in external public savings (2.3 percentage points), that is, the difference between oil export revenues and interest payments on external public debt (table 7.1). In contrast, public disposable income of internal origin stagnated due to the fact that the increase in indirect taxes and in the rates of public utilities was offset by the decrease in direct tax collection—due to the reduction in the real value of taxes during periods of accelerated inflation, such as in 1982–1983[5]—and by the increase in real interest payments on domestic public debt.[6]

However, the increase of external public savings was to a large extent due to the effect of devaluations that raised the domestic currency value of the foreign exchange surplus of the public sector.[7] In contrast, other large debtors in Latin America saw exchange rate devaluations exacerbating their fiscal deficits, given that they augmented the domestic currency value of their external debt service. In contrast, Mexico's abundant foreign exchange government revenues, which comfortably exceeded its foreign interest payments on public debt, implied that the devaluations automatically had a positive impact on fiscal net revenue. Together with the decrease in public investment mentioned earlier, they led to the spectacular turnaround of the fiscal balance even though domestic public savings scarcely increased.[8]

4. The operational balance is the net outcome of public sector revenues minus expenditures, but with interest payments calculated in real terms, that is, excluding the amount of interest payments that merely compensate for the eroding effect of inflation over the value of debt holdings. As Blejer and Cheasty (1991) argue, in countries with high domestic rates of inflation, the operational deficit may be a better approximation of fiscal disequilibrium than the conventional measurement of the fiscal deficit.

5. In the fiscal policy literature, this is known as the Olivera–Tanzi effect and refers to the combined effects of inflation and lags in tax collection that result in a decrease in real tax revenues as inflation accelerates. For a detailed explanation see, for example, Tanzi (1977).

6. It is worth observing, however, that the exchange rate devaluations and the acceleration of inflation that followed had another positive fiscal effect by reducing the real value of domestic public debt. This meant that the real interest paid from then on was smaller than otherwise. See Ize and Ortiz (1987).

7. The other side of the coin was the contraction of private incomes and spending.

8. Their increase was mainly due to the reduction of real wages of public employees, also linked indirectly with devaluations.

The comfortable balance of payments position in 1983–1984 and, at the same time, the difficulties in reducing inflation merely through contractionary fiscal and monetary policies led to an increasing use of the exchange rate with counterinflation objectives. However, the persistent appreciation of the peso in real terms that it provoked—up through the first half of 1985—plus the moderate recovery of domestic demand led, in turn, to a rapid decline of the trade surplus and erosion of the operational fiscal balance. These difficulties were aggravated by a new wave of financial speculation, stimulated by the systematic failure in meeting inflation targets and increasing uncertainty in the international oil market. The result was a new foreign exchange crisis in July–August 1985, which was met with a peso devaluation (by 20% versus the U.S. dollar) and more fiscal austerity.

The collapse of the oil market, 1986–1987

The collapse in international oil prices in early 1986—which reduced oil export revenues by half—was met by strengthening fiscal adjustment measures and quickening the pace of exchange rate depreciation. The exchange rate reached an unprecedented level of real undervaluation in 1987, even higher than in 1983, and more than twice its level in 1981 (figure 7.1). In turn, the fiscal austerity measures turned the operational deficit, generated by this external shock, into a surplus of almost 2% of GDP in less than 12 months, even larger than in 1983, notwithstanding the considerable loss of oil revenues.

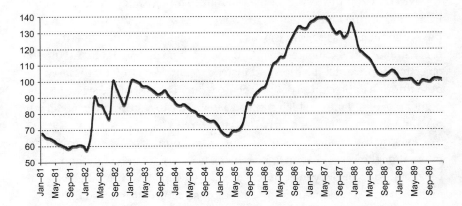

Figure 7.1 Multilateral real exchange rate, 1981–1989 (1990 = 100. Index estimated with consumer prices with respect to 111 countries.)
Source: Banco de México, Estadísticas.

Adjustment of the external and fiscal accounts during the oil crisis differed from the previous adjustment, 4 years earlier, to the debt crisis. Besides being smaller, the adjustment of the nonoil trade balance was much more efficient from an economic growth perspective. Indeed, the increase in nonoil exports (mainly manufactures)—stimulated by the exchange rate variation just described—explained practically the whole adjustment that took place between 1984 and 1987. The minor role played by imports in the trade balance adjustment is explained by their already very depressed levels as well as the smaller initial deficit in the private trade balance and the smaller external surplus of the public sector, which moderated the contractionary effects of devaluation.

Fiscal adjustment was also very different in this episode. The oil market crisis led to a decrease in external public savings of almost 4 percentage points of GDP which, added to the improvement by 2.1 percentage points in the operational surplus between 1984 and 1987, meant an internal fiscal adjustment of 6 percentage points of GDP. This adjustment took place, to a large extent, in 1986–1987, and relied much more on an increase in domestic public savings than on a decrease in public investment, as it had done before. The higher internal savings were achieved largely through an increase in public disposable income (rather than a decrease in public consumption) resulting from the decrease in real internal interest payments and in current expenditures in transfers and subsidies and the larger fiscal surplus of nonoil public enterprises (achieved through increases in real public sector prices and an additional reduction of real wages).

Not only did the results of the economic strategy adopted in 1986 differ from those of the adjustment to the debt crisis in 1982, but the hierarchy of the economic policy objectives was not the same. In fact, the severity of the fiscal and foreign exchange constraints now left no option but to sacrifice the objective of price stabilization and instead maintain a strongly undervalued peso through depreciation of the exchange rate. The cost of the strategy was a higher rate of inflation, which showed a tendency to continuously accelerate, reaching an annual rate of nearly 160% in 1987.

Eventually, as surpluses in the current account were reestablished and international reserves began to be replenished, a reduction of inflation again became the top priority in economic policy. The financial fragility created by high inflation contributed to this: the term structure of internal debt shortened progressively and, combined with the high nominal interest rates, made domestic debt policy increasingly vulnerable to shocks in the domestic financial markets. Two such shocks took place in the second half of 1987: large external debt amortization payments by private firms, and, in October, the collapse of the stock market followed by a new wave of speculation against the peso. With a new nominal devaluation of the peso in December, generalized wage demands, and the prospect of a further increase in the frequency of wage adjustments—which had moved from yearly to quarterly revisions since the inflation acceleration of 1982—hyperinflation became a real threat. Such concerns explain why policymakers tilted now in favor of a new effort at stabilization based on an alternative anti-inflation strategy: the *Pacto*.

The Economic Solidarity Pact and the achievement of stabilization

In December 1987, when de la Madrid's presidency entered its last year, the government, in coordination with unions and business organizations, launched a heterodox stabilization program. This program had as its main goal the rapid reduction of inflation through the deindexing of key prices in the economy—initially a freeze of wages, exchange rates, and public prices— additional measures of fiscal and monetary austerity, and acceleration of trade liberalization.

The *Pacto* was successful in bringing inflation under control by swiftly eliminating the so-called inertial component of inflation built in pricing and wage settlement mechanisms. Its end-of-year targets (1% to 2% monthly inflation) were met, in fact, a few months after its implementation. The annual inflation rate, which had reached 160% in 1987, fell to 20% in only 2 years (table 7.2). These achievements occurred in the context of a moderate recovery of private investment and economic activity. The success of the program, together with the foreign debt relief agreement in 1989 (Brady plan) and the turnaround in the capital account of the balance of payments—with Mexico once again having access to fresh funds from abroad—allowed the government to meet its exchange rate policy targets and even to reduce the daily rate of minidevaluations, which resulted, however, in a continuous real appreciation of the peso (see figure 7.1).

Trade performance dramatically changed during the stabilization and economic recovery brought about by the *Pacto* from 1988 onward. Exports became clearly dominated by manufactures and grew rapidly. But given the surge of imports, the overall trade balance soon and systematically began showing red figures. Stimulated by foreign debt restructuring, capital inflows acquired massive proportions and helped to finance a current account deficit in continuous expansion. The import boom was such that, despite the

Table 7.2 Macroeconomic performance

	1980	1981	1982	1983	1984	1985	1986	1987	1988	1989	1990
GDP growth rate (%)[a]	8.2	8.8	−0.6	−4.2	3.6	2.6	−3.8	1.7	1.2	3.5	4.5
Inflation rate (%)[b]	29.9	28.7	98.8	80.8	59.2	63.8	105.8	159.2	51.7	19.7	29.9
Real exchange rate[c]	100.0	92.1	136.4	154.1	135.8	136.2	176.8	178.0	143.6	135.8	129.2
Real wage[d]	100.0	101.5	92.5	78.6	72.1	71.0	64.0	60.8	53.6	49.4	43.4
Wage share (%)	36.0	37.5	35.2	29.4	28.7	28.7	28.5	26.8	26.0	25.5	25.0
Composition of GDP (%)											
Private consumption	65.1	64.2	63.0	62.3	62.1	62.7	63.3	62.4	68.3	70.3	71.2
Public consumption	10.0	10.2	10.5	11.2	11.5	11.2	11.9	11.6	11.4	11.2	11.0
Fixed private investment	14.1	14.5	12.4	10.0	10.5	11.4	10.6	11.2	11.7	11.8	12.8
Fixed public investment	10.7	12.0	9.8	6.6	6.6	6.5	5.7	4.9	3.9	4.0	4.2
Change in inventories	2.4	2.2	−0.3	0.1	0.0	0.4	−1.4	−0.7	2.5	1.8	1.7
Exports	10.7	11.0	13.5	16.0	16.3	15.2	16.2	17.6	13.8	14.1	14.1
Imports	13.0	14.0	8.8	6.1	6.9	7.5	6.8	7.0	11.7	13.2	15.0

Source: INEGI, Banco de Información Económica

[a] GDP is at constant 1980 prices.

[b] End of year (December–December). Consumer price index.

[c] Using consumer prices indices in the United States and Mexico (Index 1980 = 100).

[d] Average wage (entire economy) deflated by the consumer price index (Index 1980 = 100).

sustained dynamism of nonoil exports, the trade balance greatly deteriorated. By the early 1990s it was clear that the composition of imports had also been modified remarkably compared to 10 years earlier. While those of consumption and intermediate goods had rapidly risen (US$3 and US$9 billion, respectively, above their levels in 1981), purchases of capital goods were barely recovering their initial values in current dollars (table 7.1).

The upward trend in public revenues, which began in 1986, continued due to an expansion of the tax base, the renewed impulse of economic activity, improvements in fiscal administration, and the operation in reverse of the Olivera–Tanzi effect. This increase, together with the decrease in current spending, strengthened domestic public savings. However, the effect was fully offset by an equivalent erosion of external public savings linked to the decrease in the domestic currency value of the foreign exchange surplus of the public sector caused by the real appreciation of the peso that began in 1988 (table 7.1 and figure 7.1).

One implication of our analysis is that, contrary to the conventional view, the *Pacto* turned out to be a successful price stabilization program without further fiscal adjustment. This expression may in some ways appear as an exaggeration. It may be argued, indeed, that the huge primary surplus since 1987 contributed to the relaxation of credit rationing that the government had been facing and, to this extent, to the turnaround of the capital account. This in turn made viable the program's exchange rate policy, and thus its price and income policies, which successfully deindexed the economy's key prices. However, it is also true that without the *Pacto*'s price and income policies, the turnaround would not have occurred; and, as we shall see, there was no additional net fiscal adjustment (once the effects of the reduction of inflation are taken into account) after 1987. In our view, given Mexico's macroeconomic structure in those years, the price and income policies had a fundamental role in moving the economy from a high-inflation to a low-inflation equilibrium path.[9]

Indeed, during 1988–1991, the operational deficit of the public sector was higher by 2 percentage points of GDP than in 1987, essentially as a consequence of the higher real interest rates on domestic public debt. The primary fiscal surplus—the difference between government revenues and expenditures excluding interest payments—did improve, but by 1991 it was only 1.3

---

9. The recognition of multiple equilibria with different combinations of inflation and economic growth paths is an important element behind the rationale of heterodox stabilization programs.

percentage points of GDP higher than in 1987, a magnitude similar to that of the effects of 1987 inflation on tax collection, financial subsidies, and the composition of the public debt.[10] The decrease in the inflation tax during the stabilization process was therefore not compensated by an increase in the operational surplus. The expansionary effect of that reduction led to a deterioration of the current account and a sharp decline in international reserves (a loss of 3.4 percentage points of GDP). Such reserve losses threatened to compromise the exchange rate rules of the program. However, this pressure was eased given the turnaround of external savings from 1989 onward.

In our view, the crucial differences of the *Pacto* with respect to previous failed attempts at price stabilization were the use of income policy as a centerpiece, the availability of external finance, and an initially highly undervalued peso that made the inevitable exchange rate appreciation less damaging.

Mexico's adjustment in the Latin American context

Just as in Mexico, all the other large Latin American debtor countries faced external and fiscal disequilibria as a result of the external shocks of the 1980s. Closing these gaps involved two different problems. First, for the economy as a whole, and given the sharp decline in external financing, it implied generating a foreign exchange surplus large enough to compensate for the increased foreign debt service and the deterioration of the terms of trade. This is the external transfer problem. Its magnitude was determined by (1) the initial level of indebtedness, (2) the severity of the external financing contraction in the postcrisis period, (3) the significance of the terms of trade losses, (4) the degree of openness of the economy, and (5) the composition of exports and imports. The first two determined the size of the financial transfers abroad. The third determined the additional real resource transfers, while the characteristics of foreign trade, as given by the last two, affected the magnitude and effectiveness of the devaluation required to close the foreign exchange gap.

In order to tackle the external transfer problem, the government had to generate sufficient domestic savings because most of the debt was either public or guaranteed by the government and the decrease in the terms of

10. The sum of the three effects was 1.2 percentage points of GDP, the Olivera–Tanzi effect on tax collection (0.9 percentage points) being the most important one (Banco de México, 1989).

trade implied, in general, a loss of public sector revenues. This is the internal transfer problem that appeared as a fiscal adjustment challenge given the acute credit rationing faced by the public sector. It implied that in order to undertake the external transfer efficiently, that is, without relying on excessive contractions of domestic output and on the use of the inflation tax, the traditional measures of cutting down domestic expenditure combined with a devaluation were not sufficient. A noninflationary mobilization of the transfer required, in addition, a redistribution of income from the private to the public sector; that is, it specifically required an increase in public savings. In the literature on gap models, this requirement may be identified as the "third gap" or fiscal constraint.[11]

The severity of the internal transfer problem was partly determined by the magnitude of the external transfer one. The stronger the external shock, the larger the fiscal effort necessary to undertake a noninflationary mobilization of the transfer. Moreover, the exchange rate adjustments required to close the external gap had important fiscal implications which depended on the foreign exchange balance of the public sector, the currency composition of public debt, and the degree of indexation of domestic financial markets. This indexation determined the extent to which the increase in real terms in the foreign debt service was more or less offset by a reduction in the real value of domestic debt. The fiscal effort to be undertaken as a result of the external shock can be seen as an initial fiscal shock—at the exchange rate prevailing before devaluation—plus or minus the losses or gains of disposable public income associated with the devaluation and the changes in the real value of domestic debt.

On the other hand, together with the nature of the fiscal effects of devaluation, the inflationary implications of the fiscal and external shocks were affected by the degree of indexation of the tax system, by the pattern of price and wage determination, as well as by the state of local financial markets. A high degree of indexation of prices and wages and long fiscal lags tended to exacerbate the acceleration of inflation necessary to undertake a given real exchange rate adjustment. A low initial demand for domestic financial assets made the redistribution of savings to the public sector through bond finance and seigniorage more difficult.

Before looking at the implications of all this for the adjustment in Mexico, it is convenient to synthesize in a diagram the main forces which tended to generate a vicious circle of macroeconomic instability, low investment, and

11. The classic articles on the subject are Bacha (1984, 1990), and Taylor (1994).

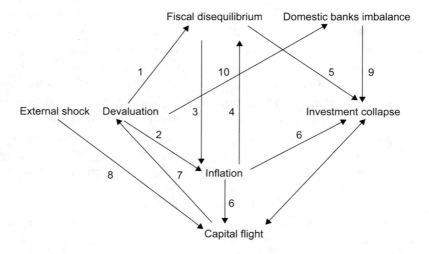

1) Fiscal effects of devaluation
2) Price and wage indexation
3) Monetization of fiscal deficit
4) Olivera–Tanzi effect
5) Fiscal constraints on public investment
6) Uncertainty and resource allocation effects
7) Higher burden on the current account
8) Default risk and fiscal rigidities
9) Credit rationing from domestic banks
10) Impact of devaluation on the banks' balance sheets

Figure 7.2 The vicious circle of instability and stagnation

stagnation of economic activity as a result of the interaction between the fiscal and external dimensions of the shocks of the 1980s (figure 7.2).

The vicious circle described in the diagram was put in motion, to a greater or lesser degree, in all of the adjustment processes of large Latin American debtor countries. It implied, as a common characteristic, a sharp reduction in the effectiveness of the traditional instruments of macroeconomic policy. Macroeconomic policy thus oscillated between the Scylla of a liquidity trap in the market for foreign assets and the Charybdis of a domestic debt trap in the local market for government bonds (see Ros, 1991b). However, although the vicious circle described and the resulting ineffectiveness of economic policy were present across Latin America, the size of the external and fiscal shocks— and the intensity with which they acted and interacted—were different from country to country.

In Mexico, at that time, the external transfer problem was particularly acute. As in the other debtor countries (with the exception of Chile), the financial transfers abroad were enormous, on the order of one-third of total exports on average during 1983–1989. In addition were the real resource transfers derived from the terms of trade losses following the oil price shock in 1986. Also worth noting is that in the period preceding this shock, the dominant presence of oil in total exports magnified the size and reduced the effectiveness of the devaluation required to close the external gap.

Given the size of the external shocks, aggravated by capital flight only comparable to those of Argentina and Venezuela in Latin America, Mexico's internal transfer problem appeared to be equally acute. There were, however, two attenuating factors. First, the fiscal effects of devaluation were positive in Mexico, and unlike in Brazil and Argentina, they reduced the internal transfer problem. Second, the initial conditions—a past of moderate inflation, relatively low degrees of indexation in the system of price and wage determination, and a large room for maneuver in wage policy—were far more favorable in the Mexican case than in economies with chronic inflation, a high degree of indexation, strong and independent trade unions, and relatively demonetized financial systems.[12]

In sum, the peculiarity of the Mexican adjustment experience was the combination of an acute external transfer problem—as in other large debtors, but exacerbated by the oil price collapse and the initial lack of response of exports to devaluation—with a relatively minor internal transfer problem. The solution of the latter was facilitated by the considerable foreign exchange surplus of the public sector, the moderate initial inflation, low initial degrees of wage/price indexation and demonetization, and the relative absence of a strict wage constraint like that prevailing in other Latin American countries.

Mexico's then peculiar situation was due to the fact that the initial current account deficit in the balance of payments had as its financial counterpart a deficit of the public sector and as a trade component a deficit of the private sector (with a foreign exchange surplus of the public sector). These features

12. For example, before the 1982 crisis wage adjustments in Mexico were once a year, in Brazil twice a year, and in Argentina the frequency was moving from quarterly to monthly. In Mexico, the coefficient of wage adjustment to past inflation in 1983 fell below 0.5 and remained below 1.0 from then on. Money balances in the first quarter of 1982 were equivalent to 10 percentage points of GDP, while in Brazil and Argentina they were 5.8 and 4.9 percentage points, respectively (Reisen and van Trotsenburg, 1988).

had profound implications for the fiscal adjustment and explain Mexico's better performance in bringing down inflation when compared with Brazil and
Argentina, the two other large debtors that faced an acute internal transfer
problem. The differences should not be underestimated. While the devaluations in 1982 explain almost the entire increase in public savings in Mexico,
in Argentina their fiscal effects determined an expansion of the fiscal deficit
of 5 percentage points of GDP, and in Brazil of 2 percentage points (Reisen
and van Trotsenburg, 1988). If we consider in addition the differences in the
degree of indexation and demonetization of the local financial system, it is not
necessary to go beyond the stabilizing effects (in one case) and destabilizing
impact (in the other) of exchange rate adjustments in order to account for the
enormous differences in the evolution of inflation.

However, these features magnified the external adjustment problem
and explain why, especially in the first stage, this adjustment was achieved
more through a reduction of absorption than through an elastic response of
the trade balance to devaluations. The initially dominating presence of oil in
exports reduced their overall elasticity. For that reason, as well as represent-
ing simultaneously fiscal and external income, oil revenues exacerbated the
devaluation's contractionary effects on private spending. In these conditions,
it is not surprising to find in Mexico (together with Venezuela, with similar
characteristics) one of the largest declines in investment in Latin America (see
table 7.3). This in turn explains why, despite a much lower inflation rate than
Brazil's or Argentina's, the growth performance of the Mexican economy was
not significantly better (and was in fact much worse than Brazil's from 1983
to 1989).

Table 7.3   Gross fixed investment as a percentage of GDP in
selected Latin American countries (annual averages)

	1979–1981	1982–1989
Colombia	16.6	17.5
Chile	17.8	17.1
Peru	24.8	22.7
Brazil	22.9	20.3
Latin America and Caribbean	23.2	19.3
Mexico	**24.9**	**18.9**
Venezuela	26.6	19.8

Source: World Bank, World Development Indicators. Data not available for
Argentina.

The lost decade

By the early 1990s the foreign exchange and fiscal gaps opened by the debt crisis and the oil shock had been closed. But the legacy of these external shocks and of the policies adopted to face them had been harsh, leading to an interruption of the growth process and a reduction of living standards. From 1982 to 1988 the average rate of expansion of real GDP was zero, falling in per capita terms more than 15%, and average inflation was nearly 90%. Total wage income declined an average of 8.1% per year between 1983 and 1988, with the sharpest declines—24.6% in 1983 and 10.7% in 1986—occurring during the 2 years of deepest economic crisis. Over the same period, government expenditures on education and health dropped by a cumulative 30.2% and 23.9%, respectively (Lustig, 1992), reflecting lower wages and public investment in the social sectors. While infant mortality continued to decline and the average number of years of schooling continued to increase (although at a slower rate than in the past), some social indicators deteriorated, reflecting a worsening of nutritional conditions and educational standards. For example, infant and preschool mortality associated with nutritional deficiencies increased from 1982 onward after years of steady decline. The decrease in the number of children registered for the first year of grammar school between 1981 and 1984 was larger than the population decline of the relevant age range. The crisis and its aftermath left Mexico with a relatively impoverished middle class, an increasing number of poor households, and probably with the poorest households being worse off than before. Indeed, during the 1980s the portion of the population living in conditions of poverty increased approximately 10 percentage points, reaching 48% by the end of the decade (Uthoff, 2007). According to other estimates, between 1984 and 1989, the extreme poverty rate increased from 13.9% to 17.1% and the moderate poverty rate increased from 28.5% to 32.6%. Inequality also jumped: the Gini concentration coefficient rose from 0.43 in 1984 to 0.47 in 1989 (see table A.7 and Lustig, 2008).

Moreover, the collapse of public and private investments in the wake of the debt crisis and the loss of foreign exchange and fiscal revenues after the 1986 oil shock—together with the stagnation of productive activity and the contraction of the population's real incomes—adversely affected the economy's growth potential by reducing the domestic savings rate and producing an aging of the capital stock and lower overall economic efficiency.[13]

13. For a detailed analysis, see Ros (1993).

This had adverse effects on international competitiveness, particularly serious within the context of the drastic trade liberalization then implemented. Moreover, these effects were particularly significant in the oil industry, as the government—since the early 1980s and up until today—stopped virtually all investment expenditure in it. Thus the economy emerged weaker, rather than stronger, after nearly 10 years of crisis and adjustment.

The reform process

In addition to the difficult processes of macroeconomic adjustment, the 1980s and early 1990s witnessed a complete overhaul of the development strategy. This overhaul was rooted in many policymakers' view that the 1982 debt crisis was the unavoidable consequence of the years of trade protectionism and heavy state intervention that had marked—and in their view distorted— Mexico's development during the postwar period.[14] Thus, as in other Latin American countries, but sooner and faster than in most of them, the government in Mexico undertook a far-reaching program of economic reforms covering different areas: trade and industrial policy, foreign investment and capital account liberalization, privatization of public enterprises, financial liberalization, and deregulation of domestic economic activities.

Trade policy reform

The first stage of trade policy reform began in early 1984 with a moderate liberalization of the import regime. Direct import controls, which had been fully reestablished in mid-1981, were relaxed (the value of imports subject to licenses fell from 100% to 83%), while the number and dispersion of tariffs was also decreased. The disappointing performance of nonoil exports during the first half of 1985, coupled with the failure in meeting inflation targets, led the government to accelerate the pace of import liberalization. As part of the devaluation cum fiscal adjustment package of July 1985, trade policy reform accelerated. The coverage of import licenses was reduced to 37.5%, with the liberalization of direct controls affecting mainly intermediate and capital goods as well as, more selectively, some consumer goods. At the same time,

---

14. Cordera and Cabrera (2007a) track the main ideological shifts that have accompanied the key changes in the form and extent of intervention of the state in the Mexican economy.

to compensate for the elimination of licenses, tariff rates were increased while their dispersion was reduced. By 1986, 90% of dutiable imports were subject to three rates (Zabludovsky, 1990).

A General Agreement on Tariffs and Trade (GATT) membership agreement was negotiated and signed in July 1986. Mexico pledged to continue the replacement of import controls with tariffs (which by then was well advanced), followed by tariff reductions, and a system to assess antidumping and countervailing duties was introduced. In addition to obtaining the advantages of GATT membership, the agreement was viewed by the administration as a means of strengthening the private sector's confidence in the government's long-term commitment to trade liberalization.

Trade liberalization was deepened again at the end of 1987, in the context of the *Pacto*. This time, import licenses were abolished for a large part of consumer manufactures and the tariff system was considerably simplified. Tariff dispersion was reduced to a range of 0% to 20%, with only five rates, while the average tariff fell to 10.4% (nonweighted average) and to 6.1% (import value-weighted tariff). Reform included abolishing all the remaining official prices on imports, which had traditionally constituted the basis for the payment of tariffs. The sectors that remained protected after these measures represented about 25% of the total tradable production, mainly agricultural products and a few manufacturing industries that were still under industrial promotion programs (especially the automobile industry).

Overall, from the beginning of trade liberalization in 1984–1985 to 1993, the year before the North America Free Trade Agreement (NAFTA) went into effect, import license coverage fell from 83.5% (1984) to 21.5%, the production-weighted average tariff declined from 23.5% (1985) to 12.5%, and the maximum tariff fell from 100% (1985) to 25% (table 7.4) (Tornell and Esquivel, 1997).

The culminating phase of Mexico's trade reform was NAFTA. When NAFTA negotiations started in 1990, Mexico was already one of the world's developing economies most open to foreign trade (OECD, 1992). The end of the main negotiations and the signing of the agreement by Canada, the United States, and Mexico came in late 1992, with U.S. congressional approval (by a slim majority in the House and a wide majority in the Senate) occurring in late 1993 after further negotiation of side agreements on labor and environmental standards. With NAFTA, which became effective in January 1994, the three parties committed themselves not only to the elimination of tariff and nontariff trade barriers to intraregional trade, but also to the loosening of restrictions on foreign investment over the next 10 years. For Mexico, in particular, it

Table 7.4 Import licenses and tariffs

	Import license coverage[a]	Tariff mean (unweighted)	Trade-weighted average tariff	Dispersion	Number of tariff rates
1982	100.0	27.0	16.4	24.8	16
1983	100.0	23.8	8.2	23.5	13
1984	83.5	23.3	8.6	22.5	10
1985	37.5[b]	25.5	13.3	18.8	10
1986	31.0[b]	22.6	13.1	14.1	11
1987	26.0[c]	10.0	5.6	6.9	5
1988	20.0[d]	10.4	6.1	7.1	5
1989[e]	n.a.	13.1	9.8	4.3	5

Source: Balassa (1985), de Mateo (1988), U.S. International Trade Commission (1990), Zabludovsky (1990).

[a] As percent of import value.
[b] June.
[c] May.
[d] April.
[e] To March 9, 1989.

entailed additional steps to deepen the unilateral trade liberalization process that it had started nearly 10 years before, but now in a quid pro quo fashion with the U.S. agreeing to open its domestic market to Mexican products. Nonetheless, Mexico did temporarily keep some trade restrictions in certain sectors (equivalent to close to 7% of the value of imports), with the promise of gradually phasing them out. These sectors included agriculture, particularly corn production (where it was feared that fast liberalization would lead to massive labor migration), oil refineries (due to sovereignty considerations), and the transportation equipment industry (where automobile enterprises had made investment decisions based on industrial programs that guaranteed protection in exchange for achieving trade balance-related performance targets).

The official rhetoric on NAFTA identified it as an ambitious step forward on the region's road toward integration. As stated in article 102 of the agreement, NAFTA's initial objectives were to

Eliminate barriers to trade in, and facilitate the cross-border movement of, goods and services between the territories of the Parties; promote conditions of fair competition in the free trade area; increase substantially investment opportunities in the territories of the Parties; provide adequate and effective protection and enforcement of intellectual property rights in each Party's territory; create effective procedures for the implementation and application of this Agreement, for its joint administration and for the resolution of disputes; and establish a framework for further trilateral, regional and multilateral cooperation to expand and enhance the benefits of this Agreement.

In our view, the Mexican government saw NAFTA as an instrument to achieve three immediate goals. First, the agreement was thought to have the potential to boost Mexico's trade with and foreign direct investment (FDI) flows from the United States and Canada. Second, it was assumed that NAFTA would induce local and foreign firms (both within and outside of the NAFTA region) to invest in the production of tradable goods in Mexico in order to exploit the country's potential as an export platform to the United States. The third and decisively political and economic objective of NAFTA was to guarantee the lock-in of Mexico's economic reform process. The belief was that ensuring the durability of market reforms and having privileged access to the North American market would step up the volume of foreign direct investment, which so far had not responded with the expected dynamism to the Brady agreement and the reform process, and would launch Mexico into a phase of high and sustained economic growth led by exports, which would rapidly raise productivity, employment, and living standards (for an analysis of the motivation of the Carlos Salinas de Gortari government in pursuing such a trade agreement, see Lustig, 1992). NAFTA formally institutionalized Mexico's trade liberalization strategy with a long-term perspective. Since it was put in place, Mexico has joined the Organization for Economic Cooperation and Development (OECD) and signed free trade agreements with numerous partners, including Chile, Costa Rica, Colombia, Venezuela, Bolivia, the European Union, and Japan.

Watering down industrial policy

Industrial policy reforms timidly started in the mid-1980s and then were strengthened during president Salinas's administration (1988–1994). The new measures eliminated production or credit subsidies, tax incentives, and trade protection schemes, as well as performance requirements (on export percentages or local content) on their beneficiaries. Reforms also inaugurated new programs, aimed at exploiting Mexico's static comparative advantages, fully complying with GATT/World Trade Organization (WTO) provisions. Open to all businesses, whether in manufacturing or services, the new programs aimed at putting forward a description of the economic activity in question and suggesting actions by the government and private entities to improve its performance (Ten Kate and Niels, 1996). A formal evaluation of these programs is not yet available but, in general, the magnitude of their resources—financial or otherwise—has been small. Thus most likely they were unable to significantly contribute solutions to the deeply rooted structural problems of Mexico's industry, inter alia technological gaps, weaknesses in the national innovation systems, lack of long-term financial resources, and insufficiency of investment to modernize local machinery and equipment. They certainly were inadequate to develop Mexico's potential as an export platform of manufactures over and above the assembling activities dependent on the tax-free entry of temporary imports to be reexported (Máttar et al., 2003). The persistent and significant appreciation of the Mexican peso in real terms that took place after the *Pacto* did not help.

A few months after the dramatic twin crises—in the balance of payments and in the domestic banking system—experienced in 1994–1995 (whose causes and effects are examined in later chapters), President Ernesto Zedillo (1994–2000) launched the Program for Industrial Policy and Foreign Trade (PROPICE) in May 1996, which implied a certain reorientation of industrial policies prevalent since 1985 (Ten Kate and Niels, 1996). The program's rationale was that trade liberalization had led to an excessive delinking of some productive chains in the Mexican manufacturing sector and claimed that sector-specific policies and incentives were required to increase domestic value-added. It explicitly excluded the notion of going back to trade protectionism or granting financial or tax subsidies to promote exports or investment. It identified the following as priority export industries: textiles, footwear, automobiles, electronics, appliances, steel, petrochemicals, and canned foodstuffs, and it marked the machine tools, plastic products, and electronic components industries as having major potential to become relevant indirect (i.e., suppliers of) exporters (Ten Kate and Niels, 1996). In practice, the program only granted a tax rebate on certain imported inputs and allowed for the accelerated phase-out of certain import tariffs. The initiatives launched, besides the *maquiladora* and drawback programs, included the *Programa de Importación Temporal para Producir Artículos de Exportación* (PITEX) and *Empresas Altamente Exportadoras* (ALTEX) program, programs favoring tax-free entry of temporary inputs from abroad to exporters. The *Sistema Mexicano de Promoción Externa* (SIMPEX) was later put in place to inform the business community of investment opportunities in Mexico and to provide local companies with marketing information. Some other programs were launched to offer consultancy to local companies to strengthen their possibilities for export.

The administration of President Vicente Fox (2000–2006) reaffirmed the notion that Mexico, though firmly inserted in a strategy of trade liberalization, had to implement sector-specific policies to stimulate investment and economic growth. The National Plan for Development (2001–2006) explicitly stated that, concerning the industrial sector, a key objective was to increase the generation of domestic value-added and strengthen the linkages among local productive chains. It argued that the state—at the national, regional, and local levels—has a leading role in promoting international competitiveness and declared as a key goal the implementation of specific sectoral programs to boost the international competitiveness of a number of industries (automobiles, electronics, software, aeronautical, textiles and garments, agriculture, *maquiladoras*, chemicals, leather and shoes, tourism, trade, and construction). By the end of the administration only four such programs had been formally completed and launched (in electronics, software, leather and shoes, and textiles). Contrary to the prevailing practice in the past two decades, these programs allow for more active involvement of the state and earmark public funds to provide financial support in preferential conditions. The minimal amount of programs' funds plus the long delay in putting them in place made it highly unlikely that they would have had a significant, positive impact.

In November 2006—less than a month from the end of the Fox presidency— a new program, *Fomento de la Industria Manufacturera, Maquiladora y de Servicios de Exportación* (IMMEX), was launched. This program simplifies the procedures for exporting firms to apply to the PITEX program and reduces the waiting period to receive the value-added tax (VAT) returns. Most important, it allows firms that export services to receive the same benefits that manufacturing exporters currently receive under PITEX. Obviously the IMMEX program is too new to be able to gauge its impact. Nevertheless, it is safe to conclude that, in practice, the Fox administration's key and perhaps only instrument of industrial policy was still the allowance of tax-free imported inputs to be reexported. Thus President Fox's announced change in the orientation of Mexican industrial policy, to move somewhat away from horizontal policies in order to implement sector-specific measures, was in practice more rhetoric than real. It remains to be seen what will be the approach of President Felipe Calderón (2006–2012) to industrial policy. At the time of writing, after 1½ years in office, his administration has not put forward any major modification in this policy area.

Liberalization of foreign investment and the opening of financial markets

The 1973 foreign investment law, as discussed in chapter 6, reserved certain economic activities to Mexican investment and introduced as a general rule a maximum limit of 49% on foreign ownership of companies. Even though it was not until 1993 that the 1973 law stopped being the reference framework regulating foreign participation in the economy, the governments of Presidents de la Madrid and Salinas gradually started interpreting the law less restrictively. The most far-reaching change within this process was the decree of May 1989 that abolished all administrative regulations and resolutions and presented a very liberal interpretation of the 1973 law (Lustig, 1992; Moreno-Brid et al., 2005; Peres, 1990). New regulations established automatic approval of full foreign participation in investment projects of less than US$100 million, as long as these projects fulfilled a series of conditions (such as generation of foreign exchange and regional development). The implicit goal of the new measures was to increase the share of foreign direct investment from 10% to 20% of the total investment level.

The law of 1993 incorporated the changes in regulations as well as NAFTA's enactment in matters of national dealings with foreign capital. The 49% limit disappeared as a general rule regulating participation of foreign investment and the number of sectors with restrictions to foreign ownership was considerably reduced. The activities with legal constraints on the extent of foreign participation included financial institutions, newspapers, fishing and harbors (all with 49%), and national air transportation and cooperatives (25% and 10%, respectively). The ones that remained strictly restricted to foreign investment included radio and television (except for cable TV), ground passenger transportation, tourism and cargo, credit unions and development banking, as well as distribution of gasoline and liquid gas. The sectors reserved exclusively to the state included oil and basic petrochemicals, electricity and nuclear energy, telegraph and mail, and radioactive minerals. Several post-1993 changes have allowed greater participation of foreign capital in some of these activities. In particular, in recent years FDI regulations were further relaxed to allow for foreign ownership of domestic banks.[15]

The liberalization and opening of local financial markets was initiated in 1988 with several measures that liberalized reserve requirements and interest rate ceilings, unified the free and controlled exchange rate, and elim-

---

15. For an analysis of the deregulation of FDI and its impact on Mexico's productive structure, see Ibarra (2005).

inated the exchange controls that had been adopted during the 1982 crisis. In 1989 and 1990, key measures to allow foreign investment in the domestic stock and money markets were adopted. The decree of May 1989 relaxed financial regulations in order to stimulate the entry of foreign investors into the Mexican stock market (SECOFI, 1993). In addition, in late 1990 restrictions on the purchase of fixed interest government bonds by foreigners were eliminated.

Privatization of public enterprises

Unlike in other countries, developed and developing, where the debate over privatization has been dominated by considerations of economic efficiency, this policy reform in Mexico was not initially based, at least in the official discourse, on the respective merits of public and private enterprises. The urge to privatize public firms was associated more with the need to ease the acute constraints on the financing of public investment and to reduce the administrative burden of the public sector. Its goal was to introduce greater selectivity in the participation of the state in the economy and, in particular, to concentrate it in areas where it has clear comparative advantages, that is, where the social rates of return are much higher than the private ones.

Mexico's privatization process went through two main stages. The first, 1983–1989, involved the sale, transfer, or liquidation of small and medium enterprises that had been acquired or created by the state, mostly in the 1960s and 1970s, without much economic or social justification. Their disappearance—beyond their numerical importance; in this period the number of public enterprises fell from 1155 to 310—did not have much effect on the economic weight of the public sector. Industrial firms represented about 40% of all public enterprises privatized in this first period; as a result the government stopped participating in approximately 22 industrial activities.[16] The bulk of the firms sold (84%) were acquired by the private sector and the remaining 16% were acquired by the social sector (cooperatives). Among the former, only 7% of buyers were foreign investors. Most private buyers were

16. See Gasca Zamora (1989). The more significant reductions in state participation within the manufacturing sector took place in food processing, including sugar, soft drinks and mineral water, seafood, and agro-industries of tropical products, as well as tobacco, textiles, the chemical industry, wood, and construction materials. The state also reduced its presence in the automobile industry and steel. The most significant events were the closing of *Fundidora Monterrey*—the oldest steel company in Latin America—in May 1986 and the sale of the government's share in *Renault de México* and other firms in the transport equipment and auto parts industries.

Table 7.5   Sources of privatization revenues, 1989–1992

	1989	1990	1991	1992	1989–1992	1989–1992
	Billions of U.S. dollars					% of total
Total	0.8	3.1	10.8	6.8	21.50	100.0
Banks	0.0	0.0	7.4	4.9	12.4	57.5
Telmex	0.0	2.1	2.8	1.4	6.3	29.1
Investors						
Foreign	0.0	0.0	2.4	1.2	3.6	16.7
National	0.0	2.1	0.4	0.2	2.7	12.4
Other	0.8	1.0	0.6	0.5	2.9	13.4

Source: Ros (1994), prepared based on SHCP (May 1993).

large consortia that produced the same goods as the enterprise being privatized, and thus this process served to consolidate their oligopolistic power in the domestic market. Other buyers were private suppliers or previous shareholders of the former public enterprise (Chong and López de Silanes, 1994a,b; Rogozinsky, 1996).

The second stage began in 1989 and peaked between late 1990 and mid-1992. Now the drive to privatize was marked by the government's belief that state intervention in the economy had been excessive and a source of distortions that undermined its growth potential and fueled inflation. This second stage included the sale of enterprises and banks with assets vastly more valuable than those of the first stage. As shown in table 7.5, in this phase privatization revenues amounted to some US$22 billion. The sale of *Teléfonos de México* (Telmex) to a group of national and foreign investors in 1990–1991—eventually concentrated in the group of Carlos Slim—and the sale of commercial banks to local financial groups in 1991–1992 constitute the bulk of such revenues. Telmex alone represented nearly 30%, while the sale of 18 banks contributed nearly 58%.[17] In 1991–1992, when the major privatizations took place, the revenues reached 3.3% of GDP. As shown in table 7.6, about one-third of such revenues was used to reduce the government's external debt and another third was used to reduce its debt with the central bank. The final

17. Two banks (*Banco Nacional de México* and *Banco de Comercio*) represented half of this subtotal. Other privatized firms (with a share of 13.4% in total revenues) include the airlines (*Mexicana de Aviación* and *AeroMéxico* in mid-1989) and *Compañia Minera de Cananea* and *Mexicana de Cobre*, the two major state producers of copper.

Table 7.6 Uses of privatization revenues, 1989–1992

	1989	1990	1991	1992	1989–1992	1991–1992
	Billions of U.S. dollars					%
Total	3.3	3.3	9.4	10.7	20.2	100.0
Financial deficit	1.4	0.1	4.0	0.3	4.3	21.3
Debt reduction	1.9	3.2	5.4	10.5	15.9	78.6
External	1.5	0.8	4.4	2.6	6.9	34.4
Central bank	1.9	0.2	5.5	0.7	6.2	30.7
Private sector	−1.5	2.2	−4.5	7.2	2.7	13.5
Residents	1.8	1.5	5.0	4.9	10.0	49.5
Nonresidents	−1.2	−2.7	−3.5	−8.8	−12.3	−61.1
Banks	−2.1	3.4	−6.0	11.0	5.1	25.1

Source: Ros (1994b), prepared based on Banco de México, Informe Anual (1991 and 1992, tables on balance of payments and sources of finance of the public sector deficit).

portion went either to decrease the government's internal debt with the private sector or to cover the financial deficit of the public sector.

The reform of the land tenure system and the overhaul of agricultural policies

Up until the debt crisis of 1982, state intervention in agriculture included price supports to staples producers, subsidies to agricultural inputs, credit and insurance, and government involvement in the commercialization and processing of grains, oils, and powdered milk, the production of fertilizers and improved seeds, and in granting consumption subsidies to the poor. After the 1982 debt crisis, the de la Madrid administration started to dismantle agricultural support policies by eliminating price supports for 5 of the 12 basic crops and reorganizing *Compañia Nacional de Subsistencias Populares* (CONASUPO), the state marketing board which bought staples from producers at guaranteed prices and sold them at low prices to processors and consumers, in order to reduce administrative costs.[18]

The Salinas government diagnosed the problems facing agriculture since its growth slowdown began in the mid-1960s as having their origin in

18. For an overview of the agricultural reform process since the early 1980s, see Yunez and Barceinas (2003).

excessive state intervention in the sector and in the inefficiency of the *ejidos*, which comprised in the early 1990s about half of Mexico's agricultural land, more than 75% of all agricultural producers, 70% of national maize production, and 80% of beans production (Davis, 2000; Johnson, 2001). With a view to increase land tenure security and, with it, productivity and investment in agriculture, the Salinas administration reformed the land tenure system and pushed for an overhaul of agricultural policies. In early 1992, a new agrarian law was enacted following the reform of article 27 of the constitution in late 1991. The law formally ended the process of land reform and allowed the privatization of *ejidos* by lifting restrictions on *ejido* land use. At the same time, import licenses were removed and tariffs were reduced in the context of the general overhaul of trade policy and the establishment of NAFTA, under which all tariffs were to be eliminated by 2008. Most important, price guarantees for basic crops (with the exception of maize and beans) were abolished in 1991 and support prices for maize and beans were eliminated in 1999. Official credit and credit subsidies were reduced with the elimination of Banrural, and fertilizer subsidies and technical assistance were reduced and redirected. Input and output markets were deregulated and CONASUPO began to be dismantled in 1991 and was abolished in 1999. Other state enterprises—in the production of fertilizers, seeds, and other inputs, and in the marketing of coffee, sugar, and tobacco—were eliminated or privatized.

Reform was accompanied by some compensatory measures. *Apoyos y Servicios a la Comercializacion Agropecuaria* (ASERCA) was created in 1991 to provide marketing support and services to producers. An income support program, *Procampo*, was established in 1993 with the goal of offseting the negative effects expected from the abolition of price guarantees and market support under NAFTA. *Alianza para el Campo* began operating in 1996, under the Zedillo government, with the goal of increasing agricultural productivity through small investment projects financed jointly by the government and producers. In 1997 *Procampo* reached more than 80% of all *ejidatarios*, but only 12% of *ejido* households participated in *Alianza* (Davis, 2000). In 2003 the Fox administration created the *Acuerdo Nacional para el Campo*, with the goal of defining policies for rural development, resulting in an increase in the benefits provided by *Procampo* to farmers (Yunez and Barceinas, 2003).

Deregulation and competition policies

Reforms in the regulatory framework involved changes in domestic competition policies, especially in the tertiary sector, where the barriers to entry and exit of firms, through permits and other legal constraints, had been important in the past.[19] Deregulation is based on the premise that excessive regulation is responsible, to a great extent, for inefficiency in resource use. In this view, it is essential to create a more competitive environment which leads to the modernization of financial services and to the reduction of transport, communications, and distribution costs so as to increase the international competitiveness of manufacturing and the economy as a whole. As part of this program, the government completed the revision of regulations affecting various economic activities.

The privatization of *Teléfonos de México*, described earlier, was the most important measure within a broader program of modernization of the telecommunications system. In a very few years, Mexico's telephone company went from being an example of an inefficient public sector monopoly to a top-level—quasi-monopolistic—enterprise capable of successfully competing and penetrating world markets. Most important, the privatization process guaranteed the new private telephone company—through special regulations—a dominant position in the domestic market for years after its transfer to the private sector. Such a privileged market position has played a key role in expanding and upgrading Mexico's telephone network and system, bringing their quality up to par with world competitors. However, at the same time, such a privileged and well-protected market position has allowed it to set its rates and fees well above those prevailing in developed or similar developing economies.[20]

Road transport—the most important mode of transportation for firms in Mexico—was characterized for a long time by legal barriers to entry (*concesiones de ruta*) and regulations on transactions that benefited the transport concessionaries. Reform in this area has been driven by the need to alleviate the perceived adverse consequences of such a highly oligopolistic structure (high transport costs among others). In July 1989, a new decree introduced radical deregulation of the sector through the liberalization of entry permits and the elimination of concessions. Moreover, in January 1990, price controls were eliminated, as was an overcharge of 15% for the transport of imported goods. The number of permits granted during the 8 months after the reform of 1989 more than tripled the number granted between 1986 and 1988, although

19. For an analysis of reforms in the domestic regulatory framework, see Lustig (2002) and Ros (1991a).

20. According to *Forbes*, in 2007 the owner and CEO of Telmex, Carlos Slim, was among the three richest men in the world.

a high percentage is explained by the legalization of companies that previously operated without a permit. It has been estimated also that following the reform—more precisely during 1987–94—tariffs for trucking services in real terms fell by 23% on average, and the general costs of distribution decreased 25% in real terms (World Bank, 1995).

Although the Mexican Constitution of 1917 explicitly prohibited monopolies, it was not until 1992 (i.e., 75 years later) that the Mexican Congress approved the *Ley Federal de Competencia Económica*, a federal law to regulate oligopolistic or monopolistic practices.[21] To implement such law the *Comisión Federal de Competencia* (CFC) was created as an independent regulating agency—although currently within the Ministry of the Economy—with the responsibility to investigate and sanction monopolistic practices, including potential implications of mergers and acquisitions.[22] The rationale behind it was that the extensive privatization processes, deregulation, and phasing out of the government's direct controls on price formation mechanisms made it necessary to have a federal agency that could monitor whether market mechanisms were being impaired by monopolistic practices.

In its 15 years of operation, the CFC has had to face many challenges, including in particular the lack of practice and expertise in this matter in the country. Key constraints on its performance are its budget and legal and technical expertise. In addition, a number of sectors, considered to be of strategic importance for national security, are excluded from its application (among others, the oil industry). In practice, despite the conspicuous monopolies or oligopolies that prevail in various sectors of the economy and the limitations on its budget, the CFC has nevertheless gained gradual and persistent recognition as an independent agency with apt technical and legal capacity. Another of its limitations has been the far from full efficiency and efficacy of the overall legal and judicial systems which results in a low likelihood of sanctions being enforced.

This chapter reviewed the macroeconomic stabilization polices put in place in Mexico from the outset of the 1982 balance of payments crisis—which inaugurated the international debt crisis in Latin America and pushed the region into its lost decade—up until the mid-1990s, just before the peso crisis in 1994–1995. Macroeconomic adjustment policies managed to correct the

---

21. For an in-depth analysis of the law, see Avalos (2006) and Levy (2000).
22. The CFC decisions are not subject to revision by the ministry, and the *Comisión* has the prerogative to present its own budget requests directly to Congress without any prior authorization from the ministry.

fiscal imbalances, in the sense of eliminating high and unsustainable deficits, but relied excessively on downsizing public investment, while failing dramatically to strengthen nonoil tax revenues. Such a reduction in public investment had major adverse consequences on the infrastructure of the economy and, most worrying, has severely undermined the capacity and competitiveness of Mexico's oil industry throughout the different phases of the production process: exploration, extraction, shipping, and refining, including the petrochemical industry. We also reviewed the structural reforms, meant to shift Mexico's traditional strategy away from trade protection and state-led industrialization, that have been firmly and rapidly put in place since the mid-1980s. Trade reform was launched, initially with the unilateral and drastic opening of the domestic market to imported goods, and further deepened with a negotiated trilateral agreement with the United States and Canada. Trade liberalization, incorrectly as we shall see, was seen as a necessary and sufficient condition for export-led growth. In this process, fundamental instruments of industrial policy were dismantled. Privatization essentially meant downsizing the public sector in order to obtain extraordinary fiscal revenues and not so much with a clear view on the impact that such divestitures would have on the competitive conditions, efficiency, and growth potential of key markets. What was the overall impact of these reforms on Mexico's quest for high and sustained, socially inclusive economic growth? What were their limitations and strengths? These key questions are explored in the next chapters.

8

The Shift in the Market-State Balance and the Quest for Export-Led Growth

Following the reform process described in the previous chapter, a "great transformation" has been taking place, if we may appropriate Karl Polanyi's expression for events of a different scale. Trade and financial liberalization and the implementation of the North American Free Trade Agreement (NAFTA) have strengthened the close ties of the Mexican economy with that of the United States, both in terms of capital flows and trade in goods and services. Reform in the rules and regulations on foreign investment opened the door to a surge of capital flows and led to a greater presence of foreign capital in the domestic economy through new investments and acquisitions of local firms, particularly of privatized public enterprises. In this process the state closed or privatized a vast number of its public enterprises; in particular, most state banks were turned over to private hands. Privatization revenues, together with debt relief (granted under the 1989 Brady plan) and fiscal adjustment, allowed the government to reduce its external debt as a proportion of gross domestic product (GDP) to low levels by international standards (see figure 8.1). At the same time, in various rural regions typically characterized by communal property, a much more market-oriented economy began to emerge as a result of far-reaching changes in the legal regulations concerning the land tenure system, the government's price support policies, and the privatization or elimination of key government agencies—including the state marketing board and the rural development bank. These changes, plus the adoption of a different perspective on subsidies to stimulate agricultural

176

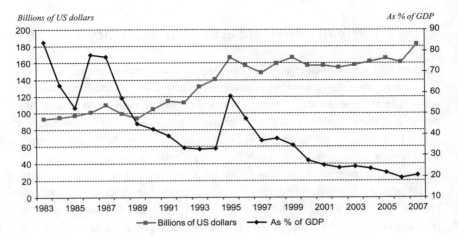

Figure 8.1 Total external debt, 1983–2007
Source: Oxford Latin American Economics History Database (OxLAD) and Banco de México (Informe Anual, several issues)

production and the introduction of social programs targeted to alleviate poverty, transformed Mexico's rural economy. In sum, Mexico's drastic reform process gave a larger role to the private sector in the allocation of resources and greater scope to market forces and international competition, all this with the goal of entering a phase of strong export-led economic expansion.

What has been the outcome of these reforms? Has the Mexican economy shown signs of entering or being on the brink of entering a path of long-term, socially inclusive development? Has it been able to remove some of the crucial binding constraints on its economic growth? Is the Mexican economy closing its gap vis-à-vis the United States and other developed economies? Have the economic and social conditions of the poor population significantly improved? These are fundamental questions that we address in this and following chapters.

Some policy reforms—for example, the creation of a federal entity to promote competition—were long overdue. In such cases, their effects have been beneficial on both efficiency and equity grounds, and most likely their benefits have largely exceeded the costs they may have had. However, these reforms have not been the most radical ones, nor those from which the greatest benefits were a priori to be expected. In this chapter we focus on the most important reforms—privatizations, trade and financial liberalization, as well as the overhaul of industrial and agricultural policies—offering an evaluation of their effects.

Privatization and economic efficiency

The case for greater selectivity in state participation in the economy and for its disengagement in a number of productive activities was mainly based, as we saw in the previous chapter, on macroeconomic grounds. As it was then presented, the argument that the government was severely rationed in credit markets and faced pressing social needs was combined with the assumption that the private sector's ample financial resources abroad were ready to be invested in previously state-dominated activities that do not have a high social priority. Free from the tight fiscal and credit constraints to which the government was subject, private and overall investment were expected to increase significantly. There is also, of course, the traditional microeconomic case based on the notion that greater participation of the private sector will bring about microeconomic efficiency gains and improvements in the overall efficiency of investment. If the latter is an increasing function of the share of private investment in overall investment, then part, if not all, of the decrease in the rate of accumulation in the 1980s could be compensated by the shift in the composition of investment.

The macroeconomic case for privatization was extremely powerful, given the macroeconomic constraints that prevailed in the 1980s. However, privatizations appear to have had a minor impact, if any, on the long-term growth potential of the economy beyond the promise (which so far remains largely just that) of a considerable expansion in human capital investments that the huge privatization revenues could make possible. Indeed, as we shall see in greater detail in chapter 10, the expected boom in private investment has failed to materialize. While public investment fell by 6.6 percentage points of GDP from 1979–1981 to 2004–2007, private investment increased by only 1.7 percentage points of GDP over the same period, with the result that overall fixed investment is, in the middle of the present decade, some 4.9 percentage points below its level during the oil boom (see table 10.11 in chapter 10). Thus the shift in the private/public composition of investment came about as a result of a decline in the rate of public investment, and not so much an increase in private investment.

Moreover, there is no evidence that the large shift in the private/public composition of total investment has brought about an increase in investment efficiency. In fact, the evidence points to the contrary. Rather than increasing, the productivity of capital has declined at a rate of about 0.8% per year since

1980 (see table 10.6 in chapter 10). This decline in the efficiency of investment should not be surprising. First, because the efficiency of aggregate investment not only depends on its private/public sector composition, but also on the rate of investment itself. It is precisely the pace of capital accumulation that, to a great extent, determines its overall efficiency as it modernizes the vintage composition of the capital stock and changes its structure (residential construction/machinery and equipment, net investment/depreciation). Thus, with the aging of the capital stock and with the shift in the composition of the capital stock from nonresidential to residential investment (see table A.15 and Hofman, 2000), both of which resulted from the decrease in the rate of investment after the debt crisis, an increase in the capital-output ratio was to be expected.

Second, as we have seen, the increase in the share of the private sector in total investment since the early 1980s was largely due to the collapse of public investment. In these conditions, the efficiency losses resulting from the absolute decrease in the overall rate of investment were likely to outweigh any efficiency gains brought about by the shift in its composition. In addition, the relationship between the efficiency and the composition of overall investment is surely more complex than generally assumed. It is likely to have the shape of an inverted U curve, with low efficiency levels being consistent with both too high and too low shares of public investment. This is so because public investment itself affects positively the productivity of private investment, as much of the public capital literature suggests (see, in particular, Aschauer, 2000), and thus at low levels of public investment further reductions can bring about losses rather than gains in overall efficiency. Given the sharp contraction of public investments during the 1980s, the question arises as to whether the economy moved to the wrong side of the Laffer-type curve in which further reductions in public investment bring about losses in overall efficiency. In such circumstances, an increase in public investment in areas with high social returns and high positive externalities for the profitability of private investment, such as public infrastructure, may be the best way of addressing the problem of investment efficiency.

What about the traditional microeconomic efficiency gains from privatizations? Some of the expected effects have materialized (see Chong and López de Silanes, 2005). Profitability has tended to increase in the newly privatized enterprises and this is largely related to efficiency gains (measured by reductions in unit costs and increases in the sales-to-capital ratio). The productivity of employees, measured by sales per employee, dramatically increased as a result, in part, of equally dramatic reductions in employment of both blue-collar and white-collar workers. Privatized firms tended to catch up with private firms and even surpass them, most remarkably in the ratio of net income to sales, so that the bulk of the improved firm performance does not seem to be attributable to macroeconomic factors.

In a number of other ways, however, privatizations left a lot to be desired. First, in the case of banks, the purchases were in some cases ultimately financed by credits extended by the banks themselves to the new owners, who had no previous experience in banking. These limitations soon proved to be of monumental relevance when the newly privatized banking system collapsed in 1994–1995 and had to be rescued by the government to protect savings accounts and keep the financial intermediation system working. Eventually most of the privatized domestic banking system was sold to foreign international banks, with outstanding results in terms of profitability but severe shortcomings in the extension and allocation of credit. A second major failure was the road privatization program. The moral hazard incentives created by the program led concession holders to inflate construction costs, paying scant attention to quality, and to charge excessively high tolls that limited access to travelers (see Rogozinsky and Tovar, 1998; World Bank, 2003). The situation deteriorated with the devaluation of 1994, as higher interest rates pushed many concession holders to the brink of bankruptcy, eventually leading to their rescue by the government. Third, some privatizations were simply not lasting, and the state had to absorb the firms once again. Besides some of the road concessions, the airlines and the sugar industry are cases in point, as the new owners proved unable to operate them in an efficient and profitable way, leading to further rounds of nationalization and privatization.

Moreover, the lack of an appropriate regulatory framework before the privatization process started has resulted in a high concentration of wealth and ownership in some of the privatized activities. The bulk of the purchases and shares went to established industrial or financial groups, so that while the stated objective of privatization was higher efficiency, in practice, several privatized sectors turned into private oligopolistic markets. Telmex, the privatized telephone company, is a quasi-monopoly in the telecommunications market. The banking sector continues to be highly concentrated and features oligopolistic practices. Privatization in one of the areas consolidated control of almost all of chloric acid production. The sale of the two largest copper companies to one owner resulted in more than 90% of copper production falling under the control of one company.

Trade liberalization, industrial policy reform, and the quest for (nonoil) export-led growth

The export boom and the transformation of the export structure

Trade liberalization and NAFTA have profoundly transformed the insertion of Mexico into global markets. The growth of exports since the early 1980s has been very fast (greater than 8% per year) and has accelerated since NAFTA took effect, increasing from a rate of 5.8% per year in the period 1982–1993 to 11.1% in 1993–2006 (table 8.1), with nonoil exports increasing even faster. Although clearly inferior to the rates of China and South Korea, the export growth rate in the second period is remarkable in the international context: similar to that of Turkey and clearly greater than that of Argentina, Brazil, Chile, Malaysia, and Thailand.

Exports (and imports) grew to such an extent that their combined total as a proportion of GDP has increased from 27% on average in the period 1982–1984 to more than 60% in 2004–2006. Although it does not reach the levels of some East Asian countries, this conventional measure of trade openness is well above that of Argentina or Brazil, and not far from that of Chile, a smaller economy, and for that reason, prone to being more open (table 8.2).

Besides the role of trade liberalization and NAFTA in eliminating the antiexport bias of protection, the export boom was helped by two other factors.

Table 8.1 Export growth for Mexico and selected developing countries (average annual rate in percent)

	1982–1993	1993–2006
China	6.9	18.7
South Korea	10.9	14.2
Turkey	7.0[a]	11.5
Mexico	**5.8**	**11.1**
Malaysia	12.3	8.9
Argentina	3.7	8.3
Thailand	14.5	7.8
Chile	8.4	7.5
Brazil	8.0	7.1

Source: World Bank, World Development Indicators.

[a] 1987–1993.

Table 8.2   Share of international trade for Mexico and selected developing countries in GDP (percent)

	1982–1984	2004–2006
Malaysia	107.0	216.4
Thailand	47.7	143.0
South Korea	67.7	83.7
Chile	45.3	74.0
China	22.0	68.9
Turkey	30.3	63.0
Mexico	**27.0**	**62.6**
Argentina	14.3	43.9
Brazil	19.0	27.4

Source: World Bank, World Development Indicators.

The first was the collapse of Mexico's domestic market in the 1980s and then again in 1995 (when real GDP fell 6%), which forced firms to export in order to compensate for the decline in domestic sales. The second was the acute depreciation of the real exchange rate of the peso vis-à-vis the U.S. dollar in response to the 1982 debt crisis and the oil price shock in 1986, and again in 1995 (45% in real terms) in response to the foreign exchange crisis.[1] This real depreciation, however, has gradually but systematically eroded since then and has practically been eliminated relative to its level in 1994.[2]

Trade liberalization and NAFTA have also radically affected the pattern of trade specialization. From being an oil exporting economy in the early 1980s, in just a few years Mexico became a relevant player in the world markets of manufactures and its export mix was radically transformed. In fact, between 1985, when trade liberalization was beginning, and 1994, when NAFTA came into effect, Mexico ranked fifth in the world among the countries with the largest increase in their share in world exports of manufactures (see table 8.3). With NAFTA in operation, from 1994 to 2004 (the most recent

---

1. Blecker (2003) and Pacheco-López (2005) conclude that NAFTA had no significant impact on Mexican exports, after controlling for the effect of real exchange rate movements. However, Lederman et al. (2003) argue the opposite.

2. Comparing consumer price indices measured in a common currency indicates that the peso appreciated in real terms 30% between 1995 and 2006. The ratio of the price deflators of tradables (manufactures) vis-à-vis nontradables (services) suggests a real exchange appreciation of about 15% during this same period.

Table 8.3 Changes in participation of manufacturing exports in the world market (top 20 countries)

	1985	1994	Variation 1985–1994	Rank		1994	2004	Variation 1994–2004
	(A)	**(B)**	**(B – A)**			**(C)**	**(D)**	**(D – C)**
China	1.42	5.86	4.45	**1**	China	5.86	12.27	6.41
Malaysia	0.55	1.73	1.18	**2**	**Mexico**	**1.71**	**2.80**	**1.09**
Singapore	0.88	1.88	1.00	**3**	Philippines	0.43	0.93	0.50
Thailand	0.30	1.07	0.77	**4**	Czech Republic	0.31	0.74	0.42
Mexico	**1.01**	**1.71**	**0.70**	**5**	Hungary	0.23	0.65	0.42
United States	12.82	13.36	0.55	**6**	Malaysia	1.73	2.13	0.39
Indonesia	0.19	0.67	0.48	**7**	Turkey	0.41	0.77	0.37
Spain	1.49	1.79	0.30	**8**	Poland	0.40	0.75	0.35
Poland	0.18	0.40	0.22	**9**	Thailand	1.07	1.31	0.25
India	0.47	0.67	0.20	**10**	Slovakia	0.10	0.31	0.22
Turkey	0.22	0.41	0.19	**11**	Vietnam	0.08	0.29	0.21
Philippines	0.31	0.43	0.12	**12**	Romania	0.15	0.32	0.17
Hungary	0.15	0.23	0.09	**13**	United Arab Emirates	0.10	0.21	0.11
Vietnam	0.00	0.08	0.08	**14**	Costa Rica	0.05	0.15	0.10
Australia	0.35	0.43	0.08	**15**	Israel	0.41	0.49	0.08
Portugal	0.44	0.51	0.07	**16**	Ukraine	0.09	0.17	0.07
Pakistan	0.14	0.20	0.06	**17**	Bangladesh	0.10	0.17	0.07
Dominican Republic	0.06	0.11	0.05	**18**	Cambodia	0.00	0.05	0.05
Israel	0.36	0.41	0.05	**19**	Estonia	0.02	0.06	0.04
Morocco	0.05	0.10	0.05	**20**	Bulgaria	0.07	0.11	0.04

Source: Authors' calculations based on ECLAC (2006b).
Manufactures covers items 6, 7, and 8 of the CAN classification.

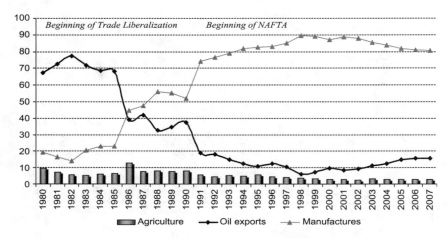

Figure 8.2 Composition of total exports, 1980–2007 (percentages)
Source: Based on INEGI, Banco de Información Económica.

year for which such comparative data are available at the time of writing) Mexico had climbed to second place, just behind China.

This impressive success in penetrating the world markets of manufactures is mirrored in a change in the composition of Mexican exports. As figure 8.2 shows, from the mid-1980s onward the share of manufactures in total exports has been climbing steadily and substantially. By the end of the 1980s it was more than 50%, and in 2007—even though the price of crude oil has soared in the last few years—it was about 80%. In turn, agricultural products continued their long-term decline in the export mix.

It is worth noting that this pattern of international integration is similar to that of other countries in Central America and the Caribbean and differs from the South American case. The southern countries have integrated as geographically diversified exporters of primary goods and natural resource intensive manufactures (minerals in the case of several Andean countries or agricultural products in the case of *Mercado Común del Sur* (Mercosur) economies, with Brazil being a case of a diversified exporter) (see table 8.4).

The export drive has been accompanied by increased technological sophistication of the manufactured goods Mexico sells abroad. Table 8.5 presents the structure of Mexican exports and their share in the Organization for Economic Cooperation and Development's (OECD's) total imports from 1985 to 2004, distinguishing three groups: (1) exports directly based on natural resources (agriculture, energy, textile fibers, minerals and metals),

Table 8.4 Export structure (2003) (percentage of total exports)

	Agriculture and processed foods[a]	Minerals and oil	Manufactures[b]
Mexico and Central America	8.0	10.0	82.0
MERCOSUR and Chile	35.4	10.3	54.3
Andean Community	15.4	53.3	31.3
Latin America	18.8	16.7	64.5

Source: CEPAL, Anuario Estadístico 2004.

[a] Includes beverages and tobacco.

[b] Excludes foodstuffs, beverages, and tobacco.

Table 8.5 Selected indicators of Mexican exports to the OECD

Mexico	1985	1990	1994	2000	2004
Market share	1.8	1.5	2.0	3.5	3.2
Natural resources	3.1	2.1	2.0	2.6	2.7
Agriculture[a]	1.3	1.3	1.4	2.0	2.0
Energy[b]	4.6	3.3	2.9	3.3	3.5
Textile fibers, minerals, and metals[c]	1.9	1.5	1.6	1.5	1.5
Manufactures	1.2	1.4	2.2	4.1	3.3
Based on natural resources[d]	1.2	1.0	1.0	1.2	1.0
Not based on natural resources[e]	1.1	1.3	2.1	3.8	3.4
Others[f]	1.6	2.5	2.7	4.0	3.5
Structure of exports	100.0	100.0	100.0	100.0	100.0
Natural resources	58.6	33.6	21.4	14.4	18.4
Agriculture[a]	9.7	10.3	8.2	5.3	5.8
Energy[b]	45.9	21.0	11.8	8.5	12.1
Textile fibers, minerals, and metals[c]	3.0	2.3	1.4	0.6	0.6
Manufactures	39.1	62.5	74.9	81.7	77.7
Based on natural resources[d]	3.4	3.4	2.5	1.6	1.3
Not based on natural resources[e]	35.8	59.1	72.4	80.1	74.5
Others[f]	2.3	3.9	3.7	3.9	3.9

Source: Authors' elaboration based on ECLAC (2006b).

[a] Sections 0, 1, and 4; Chapters 21, 22, 23, 24, 25, and 29.

[b] Section 3.

[c] Chapters 26, 27, and 28.

[d] Chapters 61, 63, and 68; groups 661, 662, 663, 667, and 671.

[e] Sections 5, 6 (less chapters included in[d]), 7, and 8.

[f] Section 9.

Table 8.6   High technology exports in Mexico and selected
developing countries (percentage of total manufacturing exports)

	1990	1997	2006
Malaysia	38.2	49	53.8
Korea	17.8	26.4	32.0
China	6.1[a]	12.7	30.3
Thailand	20.7	30.7	27.3
Mexico	**8.3**	**17.5**	**18.9**
Brazil	7.1	7.3	12.1
Argentina	7.1[a]	4.5	6.8
Chile	4.6	3.3	6.5

Source: World Bank, World Development Indicators.
[a] 1992.

(2) manufactures, and (3) other exports. In turn, manufactured goods are classified in two groups, those that make intensive use of natural resources and those that tend to use more other resources.[3] The second part of the table shows the composition of Mexico's total exports in terms of the same categories. Note the rapid penetration of the OECD market of manufactures *not based on natural resources*, raising their share from 1.1% in 1985 to 2.1% in 1994 and 3.4% in 2004. In 1985 these manufactures accounted for 36% of Mexico's total exports, by 1994 the share was 72.4%, and by 2004 it stood at 74.5%.

Moreover, the share of high technology exports in total manufacturing exports has been increasing over time and reached close to 20% by 2006. Although lower than that of China, Malaysia, South Korea, and Thailand, this share is well above that of Brazil, Argentina, and Chile (table 8.6). A significant share of medium and high technology intensive exports has also been found in many other studies for the Mexican case (see, among others, Moreno-Brid et al., 2005; ECLAC, 2005).[4]

Export dynamism placed Mexico among the most successful competitors in many branches of the U.S. market of manufactures, although in recent years it has been considerably lagging behind China. *Maquiladoras* were a key

---

3. Table 8.6 does not give any information on the technological content of the actual processes adopted to manufacture export goods. In particular, all *maquiladoras* exports are registered as "not based on natural resources."

4. However, as will be discussed in chapter 10, one can have reservations about the way the technological content of exports from developing countries is measured.

driving force behind this export drive: their share of total exports increased from 15% in 1980 (Kose et al., 2004) to about 37% in 1991 and 45% in 2006 (INEGI, Banco de Información Económica). Other important actors behind this boom have been the foreign firms already well established in Mexico, as well as some that arrived as part of the vast inflow of foreign direct investment (FDI) triggered by trade liberalization, NAFTA, and privatization. Actually FDI grew from about 2% of GDP in the early 1990s to reach a peak of 4% in 2001, but has declined since then. The manufacturing industry absorbed 53% of all FDI inflows to Mexico from 1994 to 2004 and was heavily concentrated in three subsectors: metal products (48%), chemical products (16%), and food, beverages, and tobacco (18%) (Moreno-Brid et al., 2007).

More generally, Mexico's export drive has been highly concentrated. According to some authors, the bulk of manufacturing exports was generated by no more than 300 firms, a majority of them linked to transnational corporations (see Dussel, 2003; Máttar et al., 2003). A few industries—motor engines and auto parts, automobiles, and computers and other electronic equipment—accounted for approximately 60% of total exports of manufactures in 1994–2006. Thus, along with the export boom, a dual structure in Mexico's manufacturing sector has been taking shape. A few very large firms, whose oligopolistic power in the domestic market and links with transnational corporations and access to foreign capital help them to successfully become relevant players in export markets, coexist with a vast number of medium and small firms without access to bank credit and technology that struggle to survive the intensified pressure from their external competitors.

The import surge and the disintegration of domestic linkages

Notwithstanding the export boom, Mexico has systematically recorded trade deficits—except during severe recessions—as the *maquiladoras* and oil industry surpluses have been more than counterbalanced by the deficit in other activities (see figure 8.3). The reason is that besides the export boom, trade liberalization brought about a massive surge of imports.

After decades of trade protection, opening the domestic market to foreign competition was expected to cause an intense, but temporary, flow of imports. However, purchases of imported goods have kept growing at a brisk pace, especially in periods of expansion of the domestic economy (see table 8.7). As a share of GDP, they went from 10% in 1982 to about 38% in 2000 and 45% in 2006. Their intense and persistent penetration of the domestic

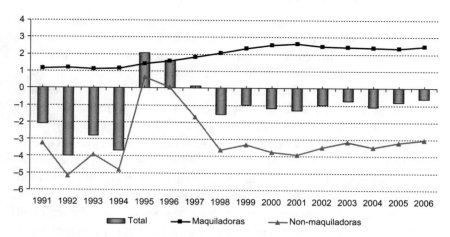

Figure 8.3 Trade balance (% GDP), 1991–2006
Source: Moreno-Brid et al. (2007)

Table 8.7 Macroeconomic performance

Annual averages	1991–1994	1995	1996–2000	2001–2007
GDP growth rate (%)[a]	3.5[b]	−6.2	5.5[c]	2.4[d]
Inflation rate (%)[e]	11.4[b]	52.0	16.5[c]	4.3[d]
Real exchange rate[f]	81.6	117.1	89.5	70.5
Real wage[g]	90.8	76.6	70.0	68.4
Wage share in GDP (%)	32.7	31.0	30.4	31.9
Composition of GDP (%)				
Private consumption	71.8	69.5	68.1	72.0
Public consumption	11.0	11.4	10.5	9.3
Fixed private investment	14.3	11.0	15.1	16.8
Fixed public investment	4.2	3.6	3.1	3.7
Change in inventories	2.2	0.8	2.6	1.6
Exports	15.0	23.9	29.3	37.0
Imports	18.5	20.2	28.6	40.3

Source: INEGI, Banco de Información Económica; Banco de México, Estadísticas.
[a] GDP is at 1980 constant prices.
[b] 1990–1994.
[c] 1995–2000.
[d] 2000–2007.
[e] End of year (December–December). Consumer price index.
[f] Using consumer prices indices in U.S. and Mexico. Index 1980 = 100.
[g] Average wage (whole economy) deflated by consumer price index (Index 1980 = 100).

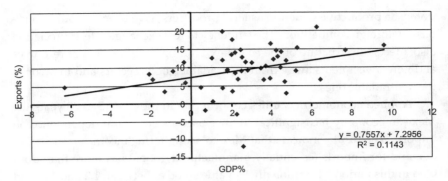

Figure 8.4 Manufacturing industries: real value added and exports, 1988–2004 (Annual average rates of growth, excluding *maquiladoras*)
Source: Moreno-Brid et al. (2007).

market has weakened the "pulling" power of the export sector relative to the rest of the economy. Indeed, the evolution of real value added in manufacturing activities—even excluding *maquiladoras*—tends to be weakly associated with the evolution of its exports. As figure 8.4 shows, during the period 1988–2004 there was no significant correlation between the growth rate of exports and that of value added across manufacturing industries.

The lack of a significant correlation between the growth rate of exports and that of value added, which is behind the fact that exports have not served as a strong engine of growth of the manufacturing sector, is largely due to the fact that Mexico's manufactured exports have become heavily dependent on imports, with rather reduced local content and weak linkages with domestic suppliers. This is true of *maquiladoras*,[5] but also for a substantial proportion of other firms that export manufactures. In fact, about 70% of Mexico's exports of manufactures are produced through assembling processes of imported inputs that enter the country under the preferential tax schemes PITEX and ALTEX (see chapter 7). Most important, such tax facilities entail approximately 30% lower input costs for manufacturing firms that rely on foreign suppliers— entering through a program of temporary imports—relative to a similar firm that relies instead on locally produced inputs (Dussel, 2000b, 2003). Another key element behind the surge of imports is an appreciated real exchange rate that has contributed to the breakdown of internal linkages in Mexico's

5. According to some estimates, on average no more than 5% of *maquiladoras* intermediate inputs are locally supplied (Dussel, 2000a).

domestic productive structure as local producers have been put out of business by foreign competition. The tendency to real exchange rate appreciation also affects the structure of the economy, shifting the allocation of resources and new investments away from the tradable goods sectors and in favor of the nontradable ones.

Applied econometric studies confirm that in the past 15 to 20 years the Mexican economy has significantly increased its structural dependence on imports. The results indicate that Mexico's long-term "income elasticity" of demand for imports (essentially manufactured goods) has more than doubled in this period.[6] Traditionally its value stood at between 1.2 and 1.5, and it has risen to levels close to 3.0. Thus if Mexico's real income is to grow at an annual average long-term rate of say 5%, its imports in real terms will tend to expand at a rate of 15%. To keep the trade deficit in check, and avoid it bulging as a proportion of income, Mexican exports must then expand at least 15% per year. If the terms of trade move in an adverse way, the required expansion of exports would have to be larger. Such fast growth of exports seems unlikely to be sustained in the long run. Recall that during 1988–1999, when the U.S. economy grew rapidly, Mexican exports increased at an annual average rate of 10%.

The upward shift in the long-run income elasticity of imports may not, however, be a long-term phenomenon. Most likely, the elasticity will abate somewhat as some once-and-for-all effects of trade liberalization on the demand for foreign goods and services wear off. But if it remains at or near current high levels,[7] the external sector will be a major constraint in Mexico's development path and a source of recurrent balance of payments problems.

Figure 8.5 illustrates how trade liberalization and macroeconomic reforms have failed to launch Mexico on a path of strong export-led growth. It shows that, for the Mexican economy as a whole, the relation between trade performance and economic growth has in fact deteriorated (except for a short period in 1995–2000 when the real exchange rate was relatively undervalued). The trade-off curve relating growth and the trade balance has shifted inward in recent times so that today, in order to achieve a given rate of growth, the economy tends to generate a larger trade deficit than in the past. Thus the

6. The "income elasticity" of imports refers to the increase—in percentage points—that imports will register for every 1% increase in income with both measured at constant prices.

7. The data for 2006 show an annualized increase of 15.5% in imports, while real GDP expanded 4.8%.

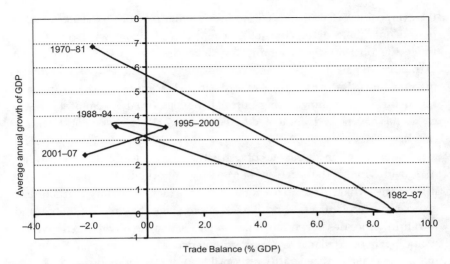

Figure 8.5 Trade balance and real GDP growth, 1970–2007
Source: Based on INEGI, Banco de Información Económica.

balance of payments constraint on the economy's long-term growth has
tended to become more binding over time.[8]

The efficiency and productivity gains from trade reform

The smoothness of the microeconomic processes of resource reallocation is a
striking feature of the Mexican transition toward a liberalized trade regime.
Applying the United Nations Industrial Development Organization's
(UNIDO's) index of structural variation, a measure (varying between zero
and one) of the degree of structural change, it has been found that the change
in the composition of manufactured exports between 1988 and 2003 was
equivalent to 32% of their total volume. If *maquiladoras* are excluded, the index
is lower, 27.6%.[9] The same methodology suggests a much smaller change in

8. The literature on balance of payments constrained growth can be traced back to the
seminal contributions of Harrod, and further developed in the Latin American structuralist
tradition by Raul Prebisch in ECLAC and by Thirlwall and collaborators including—for the
Mexican case—Guerrero de Lizardi (2006), López and Cruz (2000), Loria and Fuji (1997),
Moreno-Brid (2001), Ocegueda (2000), and Pacheco-López (2003). See also McCombie and
Thirlwall (1994) .

9. For the construction of the index, see UNIDO (1998). The application for the Mexican
case can be found in Moreno-Brid (1999).

the composition of value added in Mexico's manufacturing industry in this period: only 13.2% of total output! One may conclude that, with some exceptions, the post-reform economic transformation has to a certain extent extrapolated past trends in the composition of value added within the manufacturing industry. In other words, there is scant evidence of a massive restructuring of manufacturing output. The lack of labor reallocation processes has also been documented by Feliciano (2001), Hanson and Harrison (1999), and Revenga (1997).

The explanation for this lack of restructuring is unclear, but it probably has to do with some of the successes of Mexico's import-substitution experience in the past—which led to an irreversible change in the economy's structure of comparative advantages—and the advanced stage that intra-industry (and intrafirm) processes of specialization and trade had already reached by 1980, including, in particular, those in capital-intensive, large-scale manufacturing industries that have been partly responsible for the export boom.

In any case, the lack of significant processes of resource reallocation within the industrial sector has important implications for the assessment of the efficiency gains from trade reform. Indeed, the counterpart of this smoothness and of the lack of reversal in the direction of structural change in manufacturing is that the classic allocative efficiency gains expected from trade liberalization cannot possibly be very important. For those expecting a large, painful, but greatly beneficial reallocation of resources in favor of traditional exportable goods, the experience with trade liberalization to date should have been, in fact, greatly disappointing.

What can be said now about the dynamic effects of trade liberalization on productivity performance? As can be seen in table 8.8, labor productivity growth in manufacturing, the main tradable goods sector, slowed down in the period 1981–1994, undoubtedly as a result of the adverse demand shocks associated with the debt crisis and oil price shock of the 1980s. Since 1994, it has almost recovered its past trend increase over the period 1970–1981, despite a much lower rate of output growth (roughly half that of the period 1970–1981). This implies that for each percentage increase in output, productivity now increases at a faster rate than in the past, suggesting that, indeed, the increasing openness of the Mexican manufacturing sector has had a positive effect on the rate of labor productivity growth. A cautionary note, however, is that the effects of trade liberalization are difficult to disentangle from those of some privatizations and recurrent episodes of real exchange rate appreciation (through the competitive pressures generated by appreciation on import competing and exporting firms). For example, in the basic metals

Table 8.8 Output, employment, and productivity growth in manufacturing (annual growth rates in percent)

	Output			Employment			Labor productivity		
	1970–1981	1981–1994	1994–2004	1970–1981	1981–1994	1994–2004	1970–1981	1981–1994	1994–2004
Food processing[a]	4.8	2.6	3.0	3.0	1.2	0.3	1.8	1.4	2.7
Textiles, apparel, and leather	4.8	-0.4	1.1	2.6	-1.5	0.9	2.2	1.1	0.2
Lumber, wood, and furniture	5.8	-0.1	0.2	3.9	-2.4	-1.0	1.9	2.3	1.2
Paper	5.8	2.6	1.4	2.8	0.5	-0.8	3.0	2.1	2.2
Chemicals	8.9	2.7	2.4	4.0	0.9	-0.4	4.9	1.8	2.8
Stone, clay, and glass	5.5	2.3	1.8	2.7	0.8	-1.7	2.8	1.5	3.5
Basic metals	6.8	1.5	4.4	4.9	-6.2	-0.3	1.9	7.7	4.7
Machinery and equipment[b]	8.3	1.8	4.8	5.2	-0.2	2.0	3.1	2.0	2.8
Total manufacturing	6.1	2.0	3.1	3.6	0.1	0.8	2.5	1.9	2.3

Source: Based on INEGI, Cuentas Nacionales de México.
Growth rates are calculated as the change in the logarithm divided by the number of years. The choice of periods is such that the initial and final years are roughly in the same phase of the economic cycle.
[a] Includes beverages and tobacco.
[b] Includes fabricated metals.

sector, the fast rate of productivity growth both in 1981–1994 and 1994–2004 is strongly associated with the shedding of labor, probably partly determined by a government program that included the shutdown and privatization of many public enterprises in a sector where the latter had traditionally shown a relatively high share of the industry's output.

The contribution of trade liberalization to productivity growth appears to have been positive in sectors producing capital goods and transport equipment, where productivity growth has almost recovered past trends despite a lower rate of output growth and where trade liberalization has probably facilitated a greater degree of intra-industry (and intrafirm) specialization in foreign trade, as suggested by the rapid and simultaneous expansion of both exports and imports in some of these industries. In some sectors producing intermediate inputs, such as the cement and glass industries, productivity performance has been outstanding, well ahead of the historical norm. In this sector, just as in the chemical industry, the failure of output growth to maintain even the slow growth rates of the period 1981–1994 has meant, however, that the recovery of productivity growth has taken place in the midst of a very significant reduction of employment in the most recent period. In some light manufacturing industries—such as food processing—greater foreign competition has shaken out less efficient local producers or forced them to modernize, as shown by the fact that the recovery of productivity growth has taken place here in the midst of a relatively slow rate of output growth partly explained by an intense import penetration in these industries. The benefits of import penetration, in terms of productivity performance, become more doubtful when we look at other sectors—such as the textile and wood industries, with the slowest rates of output and productivity growth in the manufacturing sector—which show a rapid displacement of local producers resulting from increased exposure to foreign competition. In these cases, the result of the slowdown of output growth generated by import penetration has been a worsening of productivity performance whether compared to historical trends or to the period 1981–1994.

To the extent that the productivity gains that have occurred were based on the elimination or displacement of local producers, their short-term social impact may have been adverse. Whether in the medium term such impact becomes positive depends on the degree to which the thus redundant labor successfully makes the transition to be gainfully employed in dynamic, high-productivity sectors. So far, as we shall see in the next chapter, this has not happened, as investment has failed to respond in a commensurate way.[10] This is the reason why the productivity gains in manufacturing have failed to accelerate the rate of productivity growth in the economy as a whole. In fact, output per worker in the economy as a whole is, in the middle of the present decade, below its level in 1980, as the increase in labor productivity in manufacturing has been offset by a large productivity decline in the services sectors of the economy. As we shall see later, the failure of the economy to grow at a fast rate, the consequence of a low rate of capital accumulation, is behind the massive increase in underemployment in the tertiary sectors of the economy and the resulting decline in output per worker in these sectors.

In the face of the sluggish growth of aggregate productivity and the absence of a significant restructuring of manufacturing, the key tradable goods sector, it is not surprising that Mexico's international competitiveness is lagging behind (for survey data on the subject, see the annual reports produced by the World Economic Forum).

The paradoxical increase in wage inequality

A paradoxical development during the period of economic reform has been a rising wage premium on skilled labor that has resulted in increased wage inequality (see, for example, Chiquiar, 2008; Esquivel and Rodríguez-López, 2003).[11] The paradox arises from the fact that, in a country with an abundance of unskilled labor, conventional trade theory leads us to expect exactly the opposite result. Indeed, according to this theory, the relatively abundant factor (unskilled labor in Mexico) should have gained from trade liberalization relative to the scarce factors (including skilled labor): the induced shift in relative prices in favor of unskilled intensive goods increases the demand for labor in industries intensive in unskilled labor, thus causing the wages of unskilled labor to increase relative to those of skilled labor.[12] The consequence of the increase in international trade is then a greater equality in the distribution of wage incomes rather than the increased inequality observed in Mexico after trade liberalization.

10. Note too that contrary to the support policies in place in the United States, Mexico has not implemented any program to ease such transition or to compensate displaced workers for the potentially adverse effects of NAFTA.

11. This increase has been reversed in recent years, but wage inequality remains higher than in the prereform period.

12. This is known in the literature as the Stolper-Samuelson theorem.

Several explanations link this increase in the skill premium to the effects of trade liberalization. There is, in fact, no dearth of such explanations. Hanson and Harrison (1999) discuss the possibility that before trade liberalization the structure of protection in Mexico may have favored industries intensive in unskilled labor so that trade reform could then conceivably have shifted relative prices in the "wrong" direction. Another line of explanation, also consistent with the logic of the Stolper-Samuelson theorem, is that, even though relatively abundant in unskilled labor relative to the United States, Mexico may have a relative abundance of skilled labor with respect to the rest of the world given, in particular, the emergence in world trade over the past two decades of China, India, and other low-wage competitors in unskilled labor-intensive industries (Londoño and Székely, 1997). Larudee (1998) highlights that Mexico, despite its abundance of unskilled labor, may not have a comparative advantage in many activities intensive in unskilled labor for reasons related to technological differences (backwardness in unskilled labor-intensive industries) and factor intensity reversals.[13] Feenstra and Hanson (1997) focus on the effects of "outsourcing," stimulated by trade liberalization and removal of capital controls, whereby products shifted to Mexico (and other developing countries) are characterized by a relatively high skill intensity from the perspective of the developing country, but at the same time are relatively unskilled labor intensive from a developed country perspective. The result is an increase in the average skill intensity of production that raises the skill premium in both developed and developing countries. Cañonero and Werner (2002) and Cragg and Epelbaum (1996) suggest that trade liberalization operated through decreases in the relative prices of imported capital goods. This stimulated the adoption of more capital-intensive techniques and, given the complementarity between skilled labor and physical capital, a skill-biased shift in the demand for labor. Ros (2001a) emphasizes the effects of import competition and real exchange rate appreciation on profitability and employment in the tradable goods sectors and the adjustment of firms to the profitability squeeze by reducing the employment of unskilled labor, the variable factor in the short run.

Other explanations emphasize the role of skill-biased technological progress. Esquivel and Rodríguez-López (2003) argue that trade liberalization operated along Stolper-Samuelson lines in the direction of increasing the

13. This could be the case of agriculture, which is intensive in unskilled labor in Mexico and relatively capital intensive in the United States, so that the United States may have a comparative advantage in agriculture despite Mexico's abundance in unskilled labor.

relative incomes of unskilled workers, but its effect was offset by the unequalizing influence of skill-biased technological progress (see also Chiquiar, 2008, on the consistency of the evolution of regional wage differentials and the Stolper-Samuelson theorem).

Despite these differences of opinion about the relative contributions of trade liberalization and technological change to the increase in the skill premium, it is now generally agreed that even if skill-biased technological change were to be considered the most important influence, this technological change was itself an endogenous response to the competitive pressures associated with greater international integration, which was thus indirectly responsible for the increase in the skill premium and wage inequality. As noted by Esquivel and Rodríguez-López (2003), the effects of technological change and trade liberalization cannot be clearly separated, since the adoption of new technologies and productivity improvements are frequently the result of external competitive pressures associated with trade liberalization.

A deepening agricultural dualism

While foreign trade as a proportion of agricultural production rapidly expanded after NAFTA took effect—increasing from an average of 23% in 1990–1993 to almost 40% in 1994–2001 (Yunez, 2002)—the overall expansion of agricultural production, at a rate of 1.9% per year from 1991–1993 to 2003–2006,[14] has been disappointing.[15] On average, rural incomes have grown at a very slow pace (0.7% per year in 1992–2004) and only a small fraction (35%) of this increase is due to productive activities (the bulk of it being explained by public and private transfers) (Inter-American Development Bank, 2006). Moreover, there has been a clearly differentiated behavior between the commercial sector and the *ejido* sector. The former, producing exportable goods (such as fruits and vegetables), benefited from and responded positively to the reforms—exports in constant dollars grew by almost 50% in 1994–2003 compared to 1989–1993 (Inter-American Development Bank, 2006)—while the latter has not: imports grew by 53% over the same period, affecting this sector which largely produces importable goods (basic grains and beans). This is reflected in the evolution of the harvested areas of different crops

14. See Presidencia de la República (2006).
15. On the evolution of the agricultural sector under NAFTA, see Puyana and Romero (2005) and Rosenweig (2005).

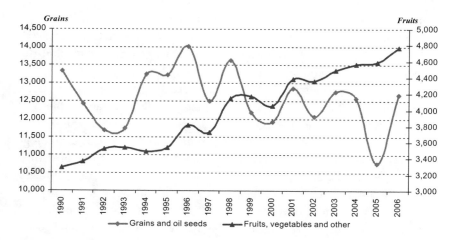

Figure 8.6 Harvested area: basic grains and oil seeds, and fruits and vegetables (Thousands of hectares)
Source: Secretaría de la Presidencia (2006) based on Secretaria de Agricultura.

(see figure 8.6). Rather than shifting into high-value crops, the *ejidatarios'* risk-averse response to the agricultural reforms has been to stay in maize and fodder while accumulating livestock and, at the same time, diversifying into wage and own account off-farm activities as well as migrating to the United States (Davis, 2000). By the beginning of the present decade almost half of the sector's income came from nonfarm sources, including remittances, and more than 60% of all *ejido* households had some family member working off farm.[16] Within the importable goods sector there has also been a differentiated response of land productivity after NAFTA went into effect. While yields have increased significantly in irrigated areas, they have stagnated in rain-fed areas where subsistence farmers are located (Yunez and Taylor, 2006).

Some of the expected benefits from the reform process have materialized. Foreign investment flowed into the agro-industrial sector, although not into primary agricultural production, tripling since the beginning of NAFTA (Inter-American Development Bank, 2006). Other expected benefits have not occurred. In fact, the slow growth of agricultural output and the persistence of rural poverty seem to be related to the reforms themselves (see Giugale et al., 2001). The downward trend in real agricultural prices throughout the 1990s and until 2003–2004 (see figure 8.7) is largely explained by the evolution

16. See Davis (2000) and Giugale et al. (2001).

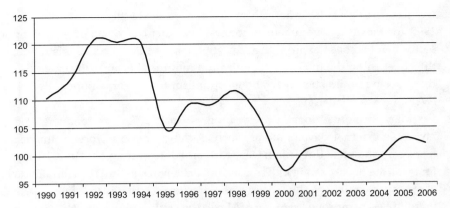

Figure 8.7 Real agricultural prices (Agricultural sector prices divided by the producer price index.)
Source: Secretaría de la Presidencia (2006), based on INEGI.

of international prices, but was probably also strengthened by the removal of trade protection (and exchange rate overvaluation in the early part of the 1990s and since 2000). The elimination of extension programs and technical assistance has affected a large proportion of small producers. The retreat of the state from distribution was followed by the domination of marketing channels by oligopolistic intermediaries that depress the prices obtained by producers, affecting particularly the poorest areas. In the absence of competitive markets and without proper consideration to the large regional diversity and income heterogeneity of the Mexican countryside, liberalization did not yield the expected benefits.

Financial liberalization, the capital surge, and the 1994–1995 peso crisis

If the efficiency and productivity effects of market reforms have been unable to make up for the loss of growth potential during the 1980s, what about their effects on external capital inflows and the prospects for increasing the rate of investment by these means? Would the shift in the market-state balance bring about a permanently higher flow of external savings, significantly greater than historical rates that would allow an increase in the rate of investment? Such was the optimistic outlook of many observers who, in the early 1990s, believed that Mexico, a model reformer and successful emerging market, would turn into a Latin American economic miracle. Recall too that in August 1990, the Mexican government announced its plan to reprivatize the banking sector that had been expropriated during the López Portillo administration, thus deepening the financial liberalization reform. This announcement further boosted optimistic expectations, optimism that became rampant when NAFTA was signed in 1993.

Market reforms, together with progress in NAFTA's negotiations and favorable external developments, such as the decrease in foreign interest rates, contributed in three main ways to a capital surge from 1990 to 1993. The first was the liberalization of domestic financial markets and the elimination of exchange controls.[17] The second was a drastic reduction in the country risk premium—an improved ranking of Mexico by credit rating agencies—which resulted from the debt relief agreement and the repayment of foreign debt financed by the large privatization revenues of 1991–1992. The third, which interacted with the reduction of country risk, was the real appreciation of the peso and the very high interest rates that prevailed in the initial stages of the disinflation program of late 1987.

The size and composition of capital inflows, heavily biased toward short-term portfolio investments, had three consequences on the economy. First, the continuous appreciation of the real exchange rate that was taking place in the midst of radical trade liberalization produced a profit squeeze in the tradable goods sectors of the economy, with negative consequences on investment (Ros, 2001a). Second, as a result of the difficulties in intermediating massive capital inflows, an allocation of resources biased toward consumption rather than investment (Trigueros, 1998) reinforced a decline in the private savings rate. Third, increasing financial fragility, which resulted from the concentration of the inflows in highly liquid assets and the excessive expansion of domestic credit for consumption, accompanied a progressive deterioration of the banking system balance sheets (Trigueros, 1998). Financial fragility was also the result of the new bankers' lack of experience, which soon became evident. Indeed, the average rate of return in the banking sector fell from its average of 50% in 1987 to 12% in 1994, at the same time that the proportion of nonperforming loans steadily increased. With banks progressively borrowing more in the foreign capital markets to lend domestically, their vulnerability to exchange rate movements was exacerbated.

---

17. Ros (1994b) studied the determinants of capital inflows and found that the opening of the bond market was the main determinant of the "change in asset preferences" during this period.

These trends should have been a legitimate concern for economic policy. Yet they were misperceived, as had happened before in the events leading to the 1982 debt crisis. By 1993, the current account deficit reached levels on the order of 6% to 7% of GDP, and by early 1994 the capital surge was over. Thus throughout 1994, the massive current account deficit was financed through the depletion of international reserves. Clearly there was an incorrect diagnosis by the government of the causes of the macroeconomic disequilibria, as it was considered that the pressure on the reserves was temporary and would be corrected without the need for a depreciation of the exchange rate. Thus no significant depreciation of the exchange rate was implemented on the grounds that it would rekindle inflation and would give "alarming signs to the market," augmenting capital flight and triggering a balance of payments crisis. In any case, such policy was gradually perceived as nonsustainable by investors in Mexico's capital and money markets. In the course of the year, the Bank of Mexico allowed increases in the interest rates on *Certificados de la Tesorería de la Federación* (CETES) (Treasury bills) and *Tesobonos* (government bonds indexed to the dollar), and increased the guarantees on the rates of return on government paper denominated in foreign currency. Nevertheless, the foreign exchange reserves continued to be depleted, ultimately forcing the perception that macroeconomic policy was unsustainable, and triggering a massive speculative attack and a major devaluation of the peso in December 1994 (see table 8.7 and figure 8.8). At the end of 1994, scarcely a year after NAFTA took effect, the Mexican economy was in the midst of a financial crisis and on the

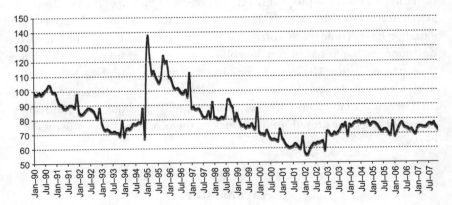

Figure 8.8 Multilateral real exchange rate, 1990–2007 (1990 = 100. Index estimated with consumer prices with respect to 111 countries.)
Source: Banco de México, Estadísticas.

brink of its worst recession since the Great Depression of the 1930s. Moreover, the country had been experiencing instability and political violence through-out 1994, a year of presidential elections, starting with the armed revolt of the Zapatistas launched on January 1 (the same day that NAFTA took effect).

The boom-and-bust cycle that culminated with the banking crisis of 1994–1995 was a consequence, at least in part, of an excessive reliance on financial deregulation and capital market liberalization (Clavijo and Boltvinik, 2000; Lustig, 2002; OECD, 2002). The leftover from that cycle was a bankrupt bank-ing system whose bailout through the *Fondo Bancario de Protección al Ahorro* (FOBAPROA), including the bailout of huge and highly questionable loans, added some 20 percentage points of GDP to the public debt and left those households and firms, mostly small and medium enterprises with no access to foreign finance, virtually without access to bank credit. Indeed, the current balance sheet of commercial banks—now subsidiaries of foreign financial institutions—shows that loans, which used to make up more than 80% of its assets, now represent less than 12%. As documented in greater detail in chap-ter 10, there has been a sharp decline in bank lending for productive activities. Paradoxically, this has happened in the midst of a mortgage and consumer credit boom. In any case, the progressive and acute weakening of the financial intermediation functions of the banking system for business purposes hap-pened at the same time that the oligopolistic profits they generate, mainly due to user fees, are a major proportion of the total profits of the foreign financial corporations that own them.

It is ironic that the banking sector returned to a situation of acute credit rationing for business purposes, a characteristic of the era of financial repres-sion that preceded the financial liberalization of the late 1980s. Moreover, this situation has become more worrisome given the constraints that the reform of development banks has put on their ability to directly grant credit to the non-bank private sector. The lack of credit has become a major obstacle to invest-ment (especially by small and medium-size firms) and has also reinforced the dual structure of the productive sector. In chapter 10, we look at this and other causes of the poor growth performance of the economy in the post-reform period.

A weak state

The other side of the market reform process reviewed in this and the previous chapter is the retreat of the state and its restructuring. By shrinking in size, the

Table 8.9 Tax revenues in developed and developing countries (percentage of GDP, circa 2004)

European Union (15)[a]	40.6
Canada[a]	33.5
Australia[a]	31.2
Japan[a]	26.4
Brazil[b]	25.8
United States[a]	25.5
South Korea[a]	24.6
Uruguay[b]	24.4
Colombia[b]	17.3
Chile[b]	17.2
Argentina[b]	16.6
Dominican Republic[b]	15.3
Peru[b]	14.9
Venezuela[b]	11.7
Mexico	**11.4b/19.0c**

Source: OECD (2004b, 2007), ILPES, Estadisticas sobre finanzas públicas (online).

[a] Total tax revenues.

[b] Central government tax revenues.

[c] Total tax revenues, including royalties and fees paid by PEMEX.

chances improve that it will be able to do a better job in its priority tasks, or so the argument goes. However, while the state is smaller, it is not necessarily more effective.[18] The tax burden continues today to be extremely low by international standards. At 11% to 12% of GDP in the mid-2000s, tax revenues are well below those of OECD countries, and even below those of Latin American countries with similar income per capita (see table 8.9). The main problems are that the tax base is narrow, reflecting numerous tax exemptions and special regimes, and there is a high level of informality (OECD, 2007).

Moreover the capacity of the state to collect taxes appears to have been declining in recent years. As shown in figure 8.9, the nonoil revenues of the federal government were down to 9.8% of GDP in 2005, after having reached a peak in 2002. Meanwhile, the share of oil income in total government

18. Ibarra (2005) gives an account of how the reform process reduced excessively the state's margin of maneuver and economic policy instruments without paying sufficient attention to the deficiencies and weaknesses of the regulatory and institutional setting in certain key markets.

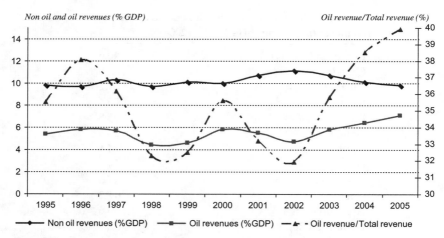

Figure 8.9 Composition of federal government revenues
Source: Presidencia de la República (2008).

revenue has been increasing, reaching 42% in 2005. Thus, besides constraining much needed public investment, the low tax burden implies that the fiscal accounts continue to be highly vulnerable to changes in volatile oil revenues. Together with the volatility of external capital flows and the reorientation of monetary policy from growth to purely price stabilization objectives, this vulnerability to oil revenues is the source of a major macroeconomic problem: the fact that it contributes to procyclical macroeconomic policies that exacerbate the negative effects of shocks on economic activity with deleterious effects on long-term growth.

Some second-generation reforms,[19] such as fiscal responsibility legislation, have further contributed to the procyclical character of macroeconomic policy. As is well known, keeping a fiscal deficit constant throughout the business cycle exacerbates the cycle. Yet this is exactly the principle that has been inspiring fiscal policy management for several administrations and which has been institutionalized by the fiscal responsibility legislation passed in 2006. The most frequent explanation to justify the adoption of a fiscal policy that turns out to be procyclical makes reference to the problems of credibility generated by governments that in the past were characterized by their "fiscal

19. In the literature, the first-generation reforms included trade opening, financial liberalization, privatization, and other policy reforms described in chapter 7 (see Williamson, 1990).

excesses." As discussed in Casar and Ros (2004), in the case of Mexico this argument seems an exaggeration after four 6-year administrations in which the principal banner of economic policy has been the achievement of "healthy public finances." Moreover, even if the diagnosis of a lack of credibility was true, the response should be to establish credibility rather than to continue with a practice that contributes to deepening recessions. One can think, for example, of institutional arrangements—such as a multiyear fiscal rule with a ceiling to public indebtedness as a proportion of GDP—that guarantee the stability of public finance over the medium term without eliminating the room for maneuver for fiscal policy in the short run. The growth benefits of a countercyclical fiscal policy should not be underestimated, as suggested by recent research (Aghion, Barro, and Marinescu, 2006; Aghion and Marinescu, 2006) and its successful application in, for example, Chile.

Nor is the state necessarily more efficient. Mexico's fiscal adjustment did not encourage a greater internal efficiency of the public sector, despite, or perhaps because of, its massive character. Especially before 1985, fiscal adjustment was, by and large, achieved through deep cuts in public investment and the real salaries of public employees, hardly a useful means to improve the efficiency of the state and its bureaucracy. Moreover, the retreat of the state has gone well beyond areas where the private sector has a comparative advantage. In fact, as we shall see in chapter 10, public infrastructure investment has been a major victim of fiscal adjustment. It is also clear that, despite some positive recent trends in social spending, state disengagement has not primarily served its main stated purpose: the rapid expansion of social infrastructure. The main contribution of privatization revenues was to reduce public debt (see chapter 7) and to support (very effectively, no doubt) stabilization efforts by temporarily compensating for the decrease in the inflation tax and strengthening the capital account of the balance of payments through the financial assets that the private sector had to bring back home to purchase the public enterprises on sale.

9

Social Policy, Poverty, and Inequality

As in the rest of Latin America, economic reforms in Mexico were accompanied by a shift in both the goals and instruments of social policies. Traditionally social policies in Mexico have been centered on gearing public expenditure and subsidies to expand the supply of health, education, and other basic services with the ambitious—though far from being achieved—goal of guaranteeing social access for wage earners and eventually universal access (as the share of wage earners in the population increased). With the market-oriented reforms, these policies were gradually reoriented to subsidizing demand, with an emphasis on focusing social spending on a targeted segment of the poor population. Also, social spending began to rely more on the provision of conditional cash transfers in order to alleviate poverty, increase the human capital of the poor, and ameliorate their long-term employment and economic prospects. The results so far of this shift in social policies apparently have been positive: despite the growth slowdown since the early 1980s, Mexico has continued to see an improvement in some social indicators and has also recorded a reduction in its poverty rate in recent years. This chapter describes the social policies adopted since the 1980s and the trends in poverty and inequality and addresses the question of whether the increase in social spending, a dividend from the transition to democracy, can help explain the paradox of poverty alleviation in the midst of slow growth.

The increase in social spending and the rise of targeted antipoverty programs

After the cancellation of social programs put in place during the oil bonanza[1] and drastic cuts in public social spending throughout the severe external and fiscal crises faced by the Miguel de la Madrid administration, social policy became a key part of the president's political strategy during the Carlos Salinas administration. A national antipoverty program, *Pronasol*, was established, offering funds for public works, with assistance being conditioned on the beneficiary communities' active participation and cooperation in carrying out different tasks in building them. With this program, marked by rather discretionary and highly publicized fiscal allocations of public spending on the poor, President Salinas, even more than his predecessors, exploited the political assets of the welfare budget. The government attempted to legitimize its revolutionary credentials through this antipoverty program, with the strategy becoming one component of the political machinery exercised through the budget.

The transition to democracy since the late 1990s has been combined with an increase in social spending and poverty alleviation programs.[2] Table 9.1 shows selected indicators of Mexico's public expenditures on social development and poverty alleviation for the Salinas, Ernesto Zedillo, and Vicente Fox administrations. Social spending rose as a share of gross domestic product (GDP) from 1988–1994 to 2000–2006, going from an average of 7.1% to 10.1%.[3] This increase in social spending has not been concentrated only in the programs earmarked for poverty alleviation. These expenditures have risen from an average of 0.8% of GDP in the Salinas administration to an average of 1.4% in the Fox *Sexenio*.

On the poverty alleviation front, in 1997 the Zedillo administration launched *Progresa*, a scheme that combined cash transfers to poor households

---

1. The two social programs that were put in place during the oil boom were *Coordinación General del Plan de Acción de Zonas Deprimidas y Grupos Marginados* (COPLAMAR), launched in 1977, and the *Sistema Alimentario Mexicano*, started in 1980. See chapter 6.

2. For an analysis of social policy in this period, see Cordera and Cabrera (2007b).

3. The increase in social spending from the early 1990s to 2003 was slightly higher than in Latin America as a whole. However, despite this increase, social spending as a proportion of GDP in Mexico is currently below the Latin American average and also below that of the other medium and large economies in the region (see Moreno-Brid and Pardinas, 2007).

Table 9.1   Public expenditure on social development (percentage of GDP)

	1988–1994	1995–2000	2001–2006
Public expenditure on social development	7.1	8.9	10.1
Public expenditure on poverty alleviation	0.8	1.1	1.4

Source: Cabrera (2007) and Giugale et al. (2001).

in rural areas on the conditions that their children attend local schools and the family undergoes regular checkups at regional health clinics. These cash transfers are given to the woman, independent of whether she is the head of the household.

When President Fox took office in December 2000, he adopted *Progresa*, changing its name to *Oportunidades*. The program retained the multidimensional approach developed under the Zedillo administration of targeted subsidies combined with obligatory school attendance and medical clinic visits. Like *Progresa*, *Oportunidades* represents an effort to implement a long-term antipoverty strategy, independent of the political party that controls the government. At the same time, the Fox administration introduced some changes. It widened the program's coverage to include urban areas and also to subsidize three more years of education, thus covering elementary, junior high, and high school (12 years of education). A third change was the creation of the subprogram *Jóvenes con Oportunidades*, committed to opening a savings account for the beneficiary family's youngsters enrolled and performing satisfactorily in the last 3 years of high school. The funds may be used only after graduation, hopefully to help the family meet university costs or to open a small business. The number of beneficiaries of *Oportunidades* jumped from 2.5 million families in 2000 to 5 million since 2004, with 68.8% of the beneficiaries located in rural areas, 17.2% in semi-urban regions, and 14% in urban centers. By 2006, the beneficiary households were receiving an average transfer of US$45 per month. The program also provided nutritional supplements for pregnant and breast-feeding mothers, as well as for children under the age of 5.

Independent evaluations have systematically confirmed the positive and significant impact of *Oportunidades* in improving the nutrition, health, and education of its beneficiaries (see, among others, Behrman et al., 2002; de Janvry and Sadoulet, 2002, 2006). In 2006, Mexico's National Institute of Public Health prepared an independent evaluation of the program whose major findings are summarized in Table 9.2.

Table 9.2 Evaluation of *Oportunidades*, 2006

Area	Achievements
Education	Reduced failure rates and dropout rates in general, and improved the likelihood of students (especially female ones) continuing their education cycles: from elementary to high school and from high school to college.
	Improved educational achievement and greater disposition from parents to promote continuous schooling for their children and the fulfillment of their school obligations.
	Effects usually larger on girls than on boys.
Health	Reduced mortality rates in mothers and children. Municipalities incorporated to the program had, on average, lower rates (11% and 2%, respectively) than other municipalities.
	Large increase in the use of public outpatient health services for all ages and reduction in the use of private services, thus generating savings in this area for beneficiaries.
Nutrition	Reduction in the proportion of anemia and an increase in the height and weight of children in their early years.
	Children 24 to 71 months of age in the beneficiary communities grew on average somewhat more than the control group, and the high proportion of low weight was reduced by 12.4%.
	The incidence of anemia was reduced in rural children of 2 and 3 years. The motor abilities of girls and boys from 3 to 6 years of age increased by 10% and 15%, respectively.
	Improvement in the diet of beneficiary households, allowing them to buy products of animal origin, and provision of nutritional supplements for a large proportion of children.

Source: Cruz et al. (2006).

Other recent social policy initiatives include the *Ley de Desarrollo Social* (LDS), unanimously approved by the Mexican Congress in November 2003. This is a federal law with the ambitious goal of guaranteeing the Mexican population's access to social development. Perhaps its most important characteristics are that it established that annual public expenditure on social development measured at constant prices must not be reduced, either in absolute or in per capita terms, from one fiscal year to another (article 20) and that the government budget should program an increase in social expenditure so that it does not decrease as a proportion of GDP. These provisions aim at establishing a lower limit to social expenditures while at the same time trying to insulate it from political pressures or the impact of adverse economic shocks.

In addition, to enhance the legitimacy and efficiency of social expenditure policies, the law also created the *Consejo Nacional de Evaluación de la Política Social* (CONEVAL). This council operates as part of the Ministry of Social Development, with the responsibility of putting forward a methodology to measure poverty as well as identifying criteria that will allow the evaluation of social policies.[4] The LDS also gave birth to the Inter-Secretarial Commission for Social Development (*Comisión Intersecretarial de Desarrollo Social*) to coordinate the government's actions aimed at poverty alleviation and putting forward the budget proposals for the amount of public expenditure that should be allocated to social improvement. As part of this effort, the Fox administration made the commitment to implement a disclosure of the government's methodology for measuring poverty and a Technical Committee for Poverty Measurement was established with the participation of renowned economists and experts. This committee put forward three consistent and complementary measures of poverty based on a combination of indicators of basic needs and income: (1) nutritional poverty, the most extreme level, covering people who live in households whose income is not enough to cover basic nutritional needs; (2) poverty in access to basic services, which includes all the people classified under nutritional poverty plus those who lack access to basic health and education services; (3) poverty in overall resources, which encompasses the population living under nutritional and access poverty, while also covering individuals whose incomes are insufficient to meet their clothing, shoes, housing, and public transportation needs.

Regarding the approach of the Felipe Calderón government (2006–2012) to social development and poverty alleviation, after a year and a half in office, and the approval of his first budget, there is no sign of a radical policy change regarding *Oportunidades*. In addition, an emphasis on the need to evaluate social policies has been present in his rhetoric, and CONEVAL has gained more political and media presence. Moreover, in April 2007 the Secretary of Social Development of the new government announced the launching of a

---

4. The introduction of a systematic and compulsory evaluation mechanism in the design and implementation of social policies, if and when correctly implemented, would be a major contribution to begin to fill a crucial and long-standing institutional gap in Mexico's public administration practices. Indeed, although Mexico has decades of relevant experience in implementing social policies, the assessment of their impact has been the exception and not the norm. There has been no accurate measurement of the actual benefits and costs of the initiatives that the government has undertaken to alleviate poverty or to improve the population's social and economic welfare.

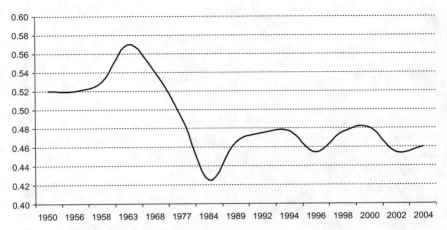

Figure 9.1 Inequality in the distribution of income, 1950–2004 (Measured by Gini coefficient)
Source: Székely (2005).

new program, the *Programa de Apoyo Productivo*, to help poor families engage in income-generating activities or businesses (*La Jornada*, April 11, 2007). The details of it are yet to be defined, but in any case, the budget so far announced is, in our view, rather low to have a national impact. The other new program of the current administration is the *Programa para la Generación del Primer Empleo*, launched on March 1, 2007, which grants subsidies to induce firms to expand formal employment of youngsters. The subsidies are equivalent to the corresponding social security contribution of the firm associated with the new jobs thus created. According to the Ministry of Labor, the program was expected to create 300,000 jobs in its first 12 months of operation. This estimate proved to be overly optimistic (Pedrero, 2007).

Trends in inequality and poverty

As discussed in previous chapters, during the 1950s and up to the early 1960s, the distribution of income became more unequal (see figure 9.1). Since then and until the mid-1980s, inequality declined. For the next 15 years, coinciding with the implementation of economic reforms, the Gini coefficient again followed an upward trend with minor fluctuations and by 2004 it stood at

212   DEVELOPMENT AND GROWTH IN THE MEXICAN ECONOMY

Table 9.3 Mexico: Economic and social indicators of the southeast (circa 2000)
(percentages)

	Southeast	Rest of the country
Share of total population	23.0	77.0
Share of GDP	14.0	86.0
Share of manufacturing	6.9	93.1
Rural population[a]	43.5	19.9
Poverty index[b]	36.0	17.6
Dwellings without water	32.8	15.4
Dwellings without electricity	15.2	7.2
Literacy	80.8	91.7
Population not speaking Spanish[c]	2.7	0.2

Source: Dávila et al. (2002).

The southeast comprises the states of Campeche, Chiapas, Guerrero, Oaxaca, Quintana Roo, Tabasco, Veracruz, and Yucatan.

[a] Population living in localities of less than 2500 people.

[b] Foster-Greer-Thorbecke index.

[c] Population between 15 and 49 years old.

0.46. This figure is above the minimum reached in 1984, and also above the world's average (0.40).[5] A major cause of persistent inequality in the distribution of personal incomes has been a substantial increase of the wage premium on skilled labor with a resulting relative decline in unskilled labor incomes. This development, as discussed in chapter 8, appears to be related to greater international integration, whether as a result of skill-biased technological change or of the direct effects of trade liberalization.

As in other developing countries, in Mexico the concentration of wealth is probably much higher than the concentration of income, although there are no reliable data to confirm this hypothesis. In addition, income disparities among the population are also reflected regionally. Southern states are in general much poorer than those in the north. The economic and social backwardness of the southeast relative to the rest of the country is illustrated in table 9.3.

5. Other sources suggest a similar pattern. Lustig (2002) shows that income inequality measured by the Gini concentration coefficient increased quite sharply from 1984 to 1989 (about 4 percentage points) and then fell from 1989 to 1994 (although remaining slightly above its 1984 level). Then from 1994 to 2000, OECD (2002) estimates show a slight increase in income inequality (the Gini increases from 0.477 to 0.481). From 2000 to 2004, Székely (2005), the source for figure 9.1, estimates a decline in the Gini coefficient (from 0.48 to 0.46), but inequality remains higher than in 1984.

In addition, there is considerable intrastate inequality, with acute differences in income and socioeconomic indicators within the same state, frequently associated with the rural-urban divide. Such differences are mirrored to some extent in the indicators of access to basic services, health, schooling, and in general the indicators of human development (UNDP, 2004).

Regional inequalities have been on the rise. As documented by Esquivel (1999) for the period 1940–1985 and by Chiquiar (2005), Dussel (2000a), and Godínez (2000) for 1970–1985, general regional trends had pointed toward a deconcentration of economic activity (away from the main industrial centers in the metropolitan areas of Mexico City, Nuevo León, and Jalisco) and convergence of income levels, with the poorest states growing faster than the richest ones (see figure 9.2). This process of convergence was interrupted in the mid-1980s (Chiquiar, 2005; Esquivel and Messmacher, 2002; Sánchez-Reaza and Rodríguez-Pose, 2002). Since then, a process of divergence has taken place—with the richest states growing faster than the poorest ones (see figure 9.3)—especially as the northern states linked to export activities and benefiting from stronger investment performance have been rapidly increasing their share in national income. In contrast, the relatively poor south (with the exception of Quintana Roo, which benefited from the expansion of tourism) has been lagging behind. These regional trends are clearly linked to the economy's structural changes, such as lagging cereal agriculture, expanding export sectors of agro-industrial products, fruits, and vegetables, and the

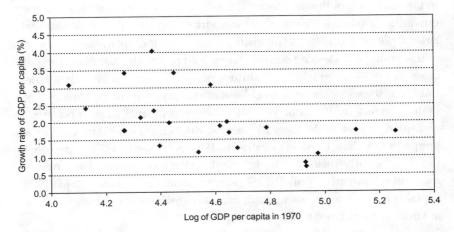

Figure 9.2 Mexican states: growth rate of per capita GDP (1970–1985) and (log of) per capita GDP in 1970
Source: Based on data from Chiquiar (2005).

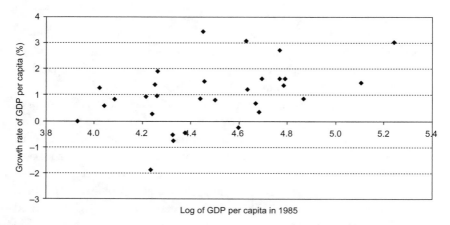

Figure 9.3 Mexican states: growth rate of per capita GDP (1985–2001) and (log of) per capita GDP in 1985
Source: Based on data from Chiquiar (2005).

rapidly growing export-oriented manufacturing activities in the northern and central areas.

The persistence of inequality and insufficient growth rates have prevented, except for the very recent period, a sustained reduction in the poverty rate and have led to an increase in the number of poor. The long-term decline in poverty rates observed before the 1980s (see figure 9.4) was interrupted in the aftermath of the international debt crisis in the mid-1980s. From then onward, until the mid-1990s, there was virtually no progress in the struggle against poverty. This is not surprising, given that for quite a number of years in this period the Mexican economy remained practically stagnant. The peso crisis in 1995—when real GDP shrunk nearly 7%—had a brutally adverse impact on the socioeconomic conditions of a large portion of the Mexican population. In fact, by 1996, one year after the crisis, the incidence of poverty as measured by each of the three distinct indicators put forward by CONEVAL jumped more than 15 points relative to 1994, reaching levels comparable to those of the early 1960s. The more recent period has witnessed an improvement on the poverty front. The ministry of social development (SEDESOL) explains these changes as the result of an expansion of social programs such as *Oportunidades*, among other factors.[6]

6. These other factors include a slight improvement in real incomes, greater macroeconomic stability, and an increase in family remittances (i.e., money orders sent home by Mexican workers in the United States). In 2006, the money sent as family remittances

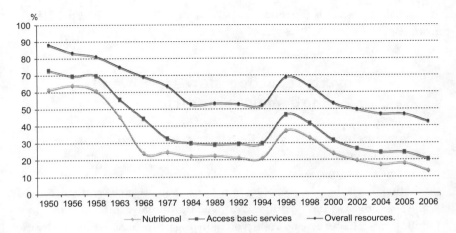

Figure 9.4 Poverty rate, 1950–2004 (The three graphs presented refer, from bottom to top, to nutritional poverty, poverty in access to basic services and poverty in overall resources.)
Source: Székely (2005) and CONEVAL (2007).

Table 9.4   Mexico: Health and educational indicators

	1980–1985	2000–2005
Life expectancy at birth (years)	67.7	73.4
Infant mortality rate[a]	47.0	28.2
	1985	2004
Gross enrollment ratios (%)		
Primary level	117.6	109.2
Secondary level	56.5	79.7
Tertiary level	15.9	23.4

Source: CELADE (1998), and World Bank, Education Statistics.
[a] Per 1000 births.

Meanwhile, health and educational indicators have continued to improve from the early 1980s to the present. As shown in table 9.4, between 1980–1985 and 2000–2005, life expectancy increased more than 5 years and infant mortality decreased by almost half. Gross enrollment ratios—except for the primary enrollment ratio, which was already greater than 100% in the 1980s—have

from abroad exceeded US$23 billion, most of it destined for the low-income groups of the population.

increased substantially (by more than 40% at the secondary and tertiary levels from 1985 to 2004).

Poverty reduction, slow growth, and the demographic dividend

Are the recent downward trend in the poverty rate and the continued improvement in social indicators a result of economic growth combined with a firmer commitment of social policy to poverty alleviation goals? There are reasons to doubt that this is the whole explanation. Growth has been very sluggish, and while *Oportunidades* has no doubt improved the human capital of many poor families, as we have seen, its impact on reducing poverty, as evidenced by the low rates of "graduation" of poor families among its beneficiaries, is far from adequate. Indeed, the most recent verification process—undertaken every 3 years to assess whether the families being protected by the program still meet its requirements—took place in 2006 and concluded that 20,000 families had graduated, so to speak, from *Oportunidades*.[7] In other words, they had stopped living under conditions of extreme poverty and now had incomes high enough to satisfy their food, health, and education needs. This represents barely 0.4% of the 5 million families covered by *Oportunidades*.

This discussion suggests that other factors must be at work in the reduction of poverty rates. Our argument is that, together with the role of international migration and foreign remittances, the main factor explaining the puzzle of poverty reduction in the midst of slow growth is the completion of the demographic transition to low fertility rates and population growth rates that has taken place in recent decades, that is, the demographic dividend (see, in particular, Ros, 2008). The data on the demographic transition are worth recalling. Having reached a peak of more than 3% per year, population growth started a sharp deceleration in the mid-1970s. Since then the demographic structure has been undergoing dramatic change, with an increasing participation of working-age groups in the population, which has kept a high-growth momentum in the expansion of the labor force. Declines in fertility rates and in the dependency ratio contribute to an increase in the participation of women in the labor market, further raising the participation ratio (table 9.5).

---

7. Figures given in an interview by the coordinator of *Oportunidades* (see Rea, 2007).

Table 9.5 The demographic transition in Mexico

	1965–1970	1975–1980	1985–1990	1995–2000	2005–2010
Total fertility rate	6.8	5.3	3.6	2.8	2.5
Population growth rate	3.2	2.7	2	1.6	1.4

	1970	1980	1990	2000	2005
Population under 15 years[a]	46.5	45.1	38.6	33.1	30.8
Dependency ratio[b]	103	95.8	74	61	56.4
Participation ratio (%)[c]	n.a.	30.4	35.5	40.3	41

Source: CELADE (1998), Boletín Demográfico n. 69. América Latina y el Caribe: Estimaciones y Proyecciones de Población. 1950–2050; World Bank, World Development Indicators (for participation ratio).

n.a. = not available.

[a] As a percentage of the total population.

[b] ([population age 0–14 + population age 65 and over]/population age 15–64) * 100.

[c] Labor force divided by population.

How can the demographic transition explain the puzzle of slow growth with social progress? We stress the following mechanisms. First, the decrease in the dependency ratio and the resulting increase in the activity rate produce the traditional demographic dividend, that is, they imply that the increase in income per capita has been higher than what it otherwise would have been. In fact, as we shall see in chapter 10, practically the whole increase in income per capita since 1990 is explained by the increase in the activity rate (given the near stagnation of output per worker). In other words, the increase in household incomes has been largely the result of an increase in the number of employed workers per household rather than an increase in the income per employee (see López de Acevedo, 2007). Second, the sharp reduction in the growth rate of the number of children allows for an inertial increase, resulting from past investments in education, in enrollments and teacher-student ratios at the primary and secondary levels. Third, the change in the age structure of the population has a positive composition effect on the poverty rate given that the incidence of poverty is higher among children than for the population as a whole. Fourth, completion of the demographic transition probably partly explains the expansion in social spending itself: with the aging of the population, the increased demand for secondary and higher education has forced an expansion of public spending in education while at the same time putting pressure on the spending on health.

In the model estimated in Ros (2008), the poverty rate is dependent on the level of GDP per worker, the Gini concentration coefficient, social spending as a percentage of GDP, and an indicator of the age structure of the population. The results presented there, following two different empirical estimations, are striking. They suggest that among the four factors contributing to reduction of the poverty rate between 1990 and 2006—the increase in GDP per worker, the reduction in inequality, the increase in social spending, and the demographic dividend—the main contribution comes from the demographic dividend (measured by the decrease in the dependency ratio), which explains between 45% and 60.8% of the reduction in the poverty rate (table 9.6). This conclusion also applies to the average of 12 Latin American countries, but not to the case of Chile, where the demographic transition was already well advanced at the beginning of the period and growth has been the major contributor to the reduction in poverty.

Another important aspect in the reduction of poverty refers to the increasing emigration of Mexicans to the United States. The annual flow of permanent migrants increased from about 250,000 in the 1980s to about 300,000 in the first half of the 1990s, and close to 400,000 in the early years of the first decade of the 21st century (OECD, 2004a). This represents one of the highest migration rates in the world. As a result, in the early years of this decade there

Table 9.6 Percentage contributions to the reduction in the poverty rate

	Method A			Method B		
	Mexico	Latin America[a]	Chile	Mexico	Latin America[a]	Chile
Growth[b]	18.6	26.4	77.7	12	17.4	69.2
Inequality[c]	20.6	2.4	9.2	24	2.8	14.9
Social spending[d]	0	0	0	19	26.4	2.6
Demographic change[e]	60.8	71.2	13	45	53.5	13.2

Source: Ros (2008).
Method A ordinary least squares estimates; Method B fixed effects estimates.
[a] Average of 12 countries.
[b] Measured by the increase in GDP per worker.
[c] Measured by the decrease in the Gini coefficient.
[d] Measured by the increase in social spending as a percentage of GDP.
[e] Measured by the decrease in the dependency ratio.

were 8.5 million Mexicans residing in the United States, which amounts to almost 9% of the Mexican population and 30% of the foreign population in the United States. Mexican workers in the United States represented then 13% of the total Mexican labor force. One can estimate that today there are more than 10 million Mexicans living in the United States.

Migration has a dual economic role. First, it plays a crucial role as an escape valve in the adjustment of the labor market. To absorb the growth of the labor force, the economy must create some 1.3 million new jobs each year. In fact, out of this total the economy has been able to create some 400,000 formal jobs. Some 400,000 to 500,000 workers emigrate to the United States, and the rest, some 400,000 to 500,000, enter the informal sector.[8] Without this escape valve, the unemployment rate would not have remained at the low levels of the recent past (around 3%) and underemployment, and thus poverty, would have been higher. The second economic role of migration, which also contributes to the reduction of poverty, refers to the growing importance of family remittances. Remittances quadrupled between 1990 and the early 2000s, and today are well over US$20 billion per year, the highest in the world after India. Although compared to other countries of out-migration (Central American countries, Portugal, and Turkey), remittances as a percentage of GDP are relatively small, nevertheless in 2002 they represented 90% of oil revenues, 145% of revenues from tourism, and 72% of the net inflows of foreign direct investment (OECD, 2004a).

This discussion has implications for the present and future of social progress in Mexico. For the present, it suggests that had the demographic dividend and international migration been absent, poverty would probably have been rampant. For the future, the demographic transition is now largely over: the fertility rate, at around 2.5, is near the 2.1 replacement level and is not expected to fall below replacement levels in the future, while the dependency ratio will not fall more than a few percentage points and will eventually start rising toward 2025 as the elderly represent an increasing portion of the population. Thus, from now on, the effects of the demographic dividend on poverty and social indicators will largely disappear. Moreover, the current slowdown in the U.S. economy will put additional pressure on Mexican social policy as the flows of migrants and family remittances will decrease. The resumption of high economic growth, in the context of redistributive

8. This calculation exaggerates the role of migration, since not all the 400,000 to 500,000 migrants are workers.

policies, becomes an imperative if Mexico is to continue to record a substantial reduction in poverty rates.

The difficult tasks of social policy

If the growth imperative is not fully met, the tasks of social policy become extremely demanding, and perhaps impossible to achieve. This is true for several reasons. There is, first, the legacy of increased inequality from the 1980s and the accumulated backlog of unmet social needs. As we have seen in this chapter, income inequality remains higher than at its low point in 1984, and the persistence of inequality, together with insufficient growth rates, has prevented a sustained reduction in the poverty rate, except in the very recent past, and has led to an increase in the number of poor.

Second, as discussed here and in chapter 8, there are a number of ways in which the present development pattern, as has happened in the past, is exacerbating economic and social disparities. The state's retreat from agriculture and reform of the land tenure system may have brought private capital and prosperity to some rural areas, but they have also inadvertently impoverished large masses of rural workers in a similar way that agricultural modernization under the *Porfiriato* did on purpose and on a much more massive scale. The benefits of greater integration with the international economy, and with the U.S. economy in particular, are also being very unevenly distributed within the country. Wage inequality has increased as a result of a higher wage premium on skilled labor that has accompanied greater international integration. Regional inequalities are also increasing, in a reversion of earlier trends. Just as in the late 18th century, when the "opening of North Atlantic trade" exacerbated the "fragmentation of regional markets," there is today a tendency toward a deepening of regional disparities, especially between a prosperous north increasingly integrated with the U.S. economy and a poor and backward south plunged into agricultural stagnation.

Finally, and no less fundamentally, by abandoning, without effective replacement, the trade and industrial policy instruments that have worked successfully in the past, the current development strategy encourages exploitation of present rather than potential comparative advantages. The basic task of development policy—the task of changing and enhancing the present endowment of resources and, over time, shifting the pattern of comparative advantages toward higher value-added, technology-intensive activities—falls now fully, in the absence of industrial policy, upon social policies. A proportionate response to this challenge could actually make things better than otherwise (i.e., than, say, under an active industrial policy with little social policy), but our point is that the challenge itself is immense and the response remains to be seen. A less than proportionate response could lead to freezing the present stage of development—of getting stuck in the relatively unskilled and low-pay tasks of the production processes of capital-intensive industries. This is a far from desirable prospect for a country that needs to rapidly increase the living standards of its more than 100 million people.

10

Why Has Post-reform Growth Been Disappointing?

The expectations of the advocates of market reforms were that the change in the structure of economic incentives, the introduction of market competition, and a stable macroeconomic policy framework would result in high and sustained growth. In particular, the benefits of greater integration with the U.S. economy, exploiting a unique geographical position, were expected to trigger a process of convergence in incomes per capita similar to that which took place in countries such as Spain, Ireland, Greece, and Portugal after their entry into the European common market. Reality has been different, as we shall see in this chapter. Not only did Mexico face a severe macroeconomic crisis in 1995, as discussed in chapter 8, but its rate of economic growth has been mediocre while divergence, rather than convergence, with respect to the United States has taken place. This chapter examines the growth performance of the Mexican economy over the past two and a half decades and reviews the roles of trade, the productivity slowdown, human capital accumulation, and physical capital investments in accounting for the poor growth record.

Mexico's development gap

In 1980, Mexico was an upper middle-income country with a gross domestic product (GDP) per capita that was well over 40% of the average of the high-income Organization for Economic Cooperation and Development (OECD)

Table 10.1   Mexico's development gap in 1980 and 2005

	1980		2005	
	Mexico	OECD	Mexico	OECD
GDP per capita[a]	47	100	34	100
Participation ratio (%)[b]	31	46	41	50
Output per worker[c]	69	100	41	100
Agriculture[d]	49	100	23	100
Industry[d]	74	100	40	100
Services[d]	88	100	49	100
Employment shares (%)[e]				
Agriculture	28	9	15	3
Industry	29	34	26	25
Services	44	58	58	72
Output shares (%)[e]				
Agriculture	9	4	4	2
Industry	34	37	26	26
Services	57	59	70	73

OECD = High-income countries.

[a] Purchasing Power Parity estimates in 2005 international dollars, OECD = 100. World Bank, World Development Indicators.

[b] Labor force divided by population. World Bank, World Development Indicators.

[c] Estimated as the ratio of per capita GDP to the participation ratio (OECD = 100).

[d] Estimated as the average output per worker multiplied by the sector's output share and divided by the sector's employment share (OECD = 100).

[e] For Mexico 1980, Ros (2000) (employment shares based on ILO Yearbook of Labour Statistics and World Bank, World Development Report). For rest of Mexico 1980, Mexico 2005, and OECD, World Bank, World Development Indicators.

countries (see table 10.1). The difference in income per capita separating Mexico from the high-income countries in table 10.1—its development gap—can be decomposed as the sum of three components:[1] (1) differences in the labor force participation ratio—the ratio of labor force to population—largely attributable to differences in the population's age structure and women's participation rates; (2) differences in occupational structure arising from the fact that the employment share of low productivity sectors is typically larger in developing countries than in developed countries; (3) differences in output per worker in individual sectors (leaving aside differences in occupational structure) or the productivity gap *stricto sensu*.

1. See Ros (2000b) for a formal analysis.

Table 10.2   The components of Mexico's development gap

	1980	2005
Percentage points due to differences in:		
Participation ratios	42.8	11.5
Occupational structures	21.6	7.4
Output per worker by sector	35.6	81.2

Source: Authors' calculations based on table 10.1.

Table 10.2 shows the results of this decomposition exercise. In 1980, nearly two-thirds of Mexico's development gap was attributable to differences related to demographic and occupational structures. This was largely due to Mexico's high dependency ratio (more than 40% of the gap was related to differences in participation ratios), a legacy of very high rates of population growth in the past. Still significant, although probably less than in earlier decades, was the difference in occupational structure: about 21% of the gap, largely due to the still high employment share of low productivity agriculture. This is what leaves just over one-third to be accounted for by a "pure productivity component," arising largely in agriculture and industry productivity differences.

These results can be looked at as follows. With OECD participation ratios and occupational structures, Mexico's per capita GDP would have been almost twice its level in 1980, and therefore about 80% of the level of high-income OECD countries (a smaller development gap than that separating Spain from the high-income OECD countries). In other words, had the Mexican economy absorbed the rapidly growing labor force since 1980 while simply maintaining 1980 levels of output per worker and changing its occupational structure along past trends, it would have largely become a high-income country as its demographic and occupational structures and women's participation ratio in the labor market converged to those of a typical OECD country.

Had output per worker continued to grow at the rate of the period 1950–1981, this transition to high income levels would have been accomplished during the last 2½ decades. With the increase in the labor participation ratio since 1981 (1.2% per year) and the growth of output per worker from 1950 to 1981 (3.2% per year), per capita income would have reached by 2005 about 80% of today's level in the high-income OECD countries (and would have been 25% above the 1980

Table 10.3   Growth of per capita GDP and GDP per worker

	1940–1981	1981–2006	1990–2006
Growth rate of per capita GDP	3.2	0.6	1.6
Growth rate of GDP per worker	3.2[a]	−0.5	0.7

Source: Based on INEGI (1999a), World Bank, World Development Indicators, and Groningen Growth and Development Center, Total Economy Database.
[a] 1950–1981.

level in these countries).[2] The reason, of course, is that per capita GDP growth would have accelerated from 3.2% (in the period 1940–1981) to about 4.4% per year, thus multiplying per capita income by almost 3 times over 25 years.

This process of convergence did not happen. Instead, over the past two and a half decades the pace of Mexico's economic growth suffered a severe slowdown compared to the historical record of the previous 40 years. Between 1981 and 2006, Mexico's per capita GDP has grown at an average rate of only 0.6% per year (table 10.3), which is similar to that of the period 1910 to 1940 and compares very unfavorably with the historical record of 3.2% per year over the period 1940 to 1981. This poor performance is partly due to the decline in per capita income from 1982 to 1989, a period characterized by highly adverse external shocks, acute macroeconomic instability, and a continuous transfer of resources abroad (to cover the foreign debt service) in the context of severe external credit rationing. But even leaving aside this period, economic growth has been wanting: from 1990 to 2006, per capita GDP has expanded at an annual rate of 1.6% (table 10.3), and this in the context of great volatility in the level of economic activity.

Even such meager recent growth has to be attributed to the rapid increase in the labor force participation ratio, as GDP per worker has in fact fallen over the period 1981 to 2006 and has increased at a very slow pace since 1990 (see table 10.3). The growth slowdown is thus particularly serious to the extent that it implies wasting the "demographic dividend" associated with the transition toward low rates of population growth in the context of still very dynamic growth of the working age population.[3] Indeed, while in other historical experiences this demographic transition is associated with an acceleration in

2. This calculation uses the identity by which the growth rate of per capita GDP is equal to the sum of the growth rates of GDP per worker and the participation ratio.
3. As shown in table 9.5, as a result of this transition, the dependency ratio fell from 95.8% to 56.4% between 1980 and 2005.

Table 10.4   Mexico's per capita GDP as a ratio of per capita GDP

	1981	1990	2006
East Asia and Pacific	12.1	6.6	2.8
South Asia	11.1	7.7	5.3
Sub-Saharan Africa	6.0	6.0	6.8
Middle East and North Africa	2.3	2.0	1.9
World	1.7	1.4	1.3
Latin America and Caribbean	1.4	1.4	1.4
Europe and Central Asia[a]	n.a.	1.1	1.2
High income OECD	0.5	0.4	0.3

Source: Based on World Bank, World Development Indicators.
Per capita GDP is in 2005 international dollars (Purchasing Power Parity).
[a] Developing countries.

the growth of per capita income, what one observes in the Mexican case is an increasing underemployment of the labor force and a deceleration in the growth of per capita income.

The rate of growth of per capita GDP has not only fallen below the historical experience in the pre-debt crisis period, but as can be seen in table 10.4, by 2006 Mexico's per capita income had fallen to about one-third of the level in high-income OECD countries, despite the fact that there had been a process of convergence in labor force participation ratios and occupational structures. The relative decline of the Mexican economy has taken place also with respect to the major developing country groupings, with the exception of sub-Saharan Africa and the transition economies of Europe and Central Asia. This includes middle-income and poor countries, oil exporters and oil importers, economic reformers and nonreformers. Moreover, this relative decline is not an exclusive feature of the lost decade of the 1980s since it has continued (albeit at a generally slower pace) in the period since 1990 (see table 10.4).

Trade expansion without export-led growth

In reviewing the causes of the slow growth of the Mexican economy we must first discard a lack of international trade integration and export growth.[4] The

---

4. For an explanation of the slow growth rate of Latin American economies that emphasizes the still low degree of trade openness of the region (especially in comparison to East Asia), see de Gregorio (2005).

premises on which the trade liberalization process launched in the mid-1980s was expected to improve the growth performance of the economy were the following. First, exports, and foreign trade more generally, would be stimulated by trade liberalization as it removed the antiexport bias of protection and opened up domestic markets to foreign competition. Second, the expansion of international trade would act as an engine of growth by improving the allocation of resources and the dynamic efficiency of the economy as competition in domestic and world markets would force producers to adopt best practice techniques and thus accelerate the rate of technological progress, improve overall productivity, and strengthen international competitiveness.

As we saw in chapter 8, the first of these assumptions turned out to be correct. There is little doubt that trade liberalization, by eliminating the antiexport bias of protection, has greatly stimulated the growth of nonoil exports. Yet the second premise turned out to be wrong. Clearly international trade has not acted as a sufficiently strong engine of growth capable of leading to a substantial improvement in the growth performance of the economy. There has been rapid export growth, but no rapid export-led growth.

Why has this rapid export expansion failed to generate broad-based growth? In answering this question one must first look at what technological benefits firms derive from exporting and the associated issue of the causality between exports and productivity performance. The evidence from micro-econometric analyses of the relationship between exports and firm productivity performance using plant-level data sets suggests that causality seems to run from productivity to exports rather than the other way around as generally believed. In other words, efficient firms seem to self-select into export markets rather than deriving technological benefits from exporting.[5]

Second, the most careful studies of the relationship between trade liberalization and growth across countries do not find a clear-cut relationship between the two (see Rodríguez and Rodrik, 2001). Ultimately, the reason, we think, is that freer trade may contribute to growth or not depending on the structure of static comparative advantages that an economy has at a point in time and the dynamic potential of this structure. Recent models of endogenous growth have formalized old ideas on infant industry protection, showing that whether trade promotes growth or not depends on whether the forces of comparative advantage push the economy to allocate more resources to sectors

---

5. See Aw et al. (2000), Bernard and Jensen (1995, 1998), and Clerides et al. (1998). Note that the earlier literature on cross-country regressions of the relationship between exports and growth reached inconclusive results. For a survey of this literature, see Edwards (1993).

with increasing returns to scale and knowledge externalities or whether they prevent the development of such activities (see Feenstra, 1990; Grossman and Helpman, 1991; Matsuyama, 1992; Rodríguez and Rodrik, 2001). In other words, freer trade may promote more or less dynamic patterns of specialization depending on the present factor endowment of the economy.

At first glance, the nature of Mexican exports should have generated faster economic growth. Indeed, Hausmann et al. (2005a) show that the level of technological sophistication of a country's exports relative to its per capita income is a good predictor of a country's subsequent growth, and it is clear from their findings that Mexico has a relatively high level of sophistication of its export basket, higher certainly than other Latin American economies with similar or even higher levels of per capita income (Chile and Argentina, for example). Mexico acquired a comparative advantage in manufacturing during the import substitution industrialization (ISI) period, unlike many South American countries that maintained a comparative advantage largely in primary goods. As a result, Mexico has integrated into the international economy as an exporter of not only oil, but also of manufactures, both labor intensive (garment and assembly of electronic products) and of medium and high-technological intensity (automobiles, metal mechanic industries). Thus, as we saw in chapter 8, the share of manufactures in total exports climbed from less than 20% in the early 1980s to nearly 80% today at the expense of the share of oil exports, which fell from more than 66% of the total in the early 1980s to less than 20% today (see figure 8.2). This transformation is remarkable in the international context. Today, the manufacturing exports' share in total exports is higher in Mexico than in several Latin American and East Asian countries (table 10.5). Moreover, as discussed in chapter 8, the share of high-technology exports in total manufacturing exports has been increasing over time and stands at about 20% today.

However, the evidence put forward in chapter 8 raises serious doubts about the ability of the current industrial structure to generate high, self-sustained growth. The counterpart of the processes of intrafirm and intraindustry trade specialization[6] is that many, if not most, exporting sectors and firms, while dynamic, either do not have adequate domestic linkages or have

---

6. Within manufacturing, the most dynamic component both before and after NAFTA is associated with intraindustry and intrafirm trade, including, in particular, the *maquiladora* industry. The share of intraindustry trade (closely associated with the *maquiladora* industry) in the manufacturing sector increased from 62.5% in 1988–1991 to 73.4% in 1996–2000 (OECD, 2002).

Table 10.5 Composition of merchandise exports (in percent of total)

	Argentina	Brazil	Chile	Indonesia	Korea	Malaysia	Mexico	Thailand
Manufactures								
1980	23.2	37.2	9.1	2.3	89.6	18.8	11.9	25.0
1993	31.9	58.9	16.5	53.1	93.1	69.7	74.6	71.1
2006	32.0	50.8	11.1	44.7	89.5	73.7	76.0	76.0
Agriculture[a]								
1980	71.2	50.3	24.9	21.7	8.8	46.0	14.7	57.1
1993	57.4	28.4	38.3	15.0	3.8	18.1	8.5	25.8
2006	46.4	28.7	20.5	18.1	1.6	9.7	5.8	16.6
Minerals and oil[b]								
1980	5.7	11.2	65.4	75.8	1.3	34.9	73.3	13.9
1993	10.7	12.3	43.3	31.9	3.0	11.5	16.5	1.6
2006	20.2	18.5	66.4	37.2	8.5	15.1	17.9	6.2

Source: World Bank, World Development Indicators.

[a] Food and agricultural raw material exports.

[b] Ore, metals, and fuel exports.

seen their weakening in the past decades. The consequences have been negative for the trade balance and the growth effects of exports. Moreover, the
fragility of Mexico's pattern of industrial production and trade specialization
goes beyond the lack of domestic linkages in export-oriented activities and the
dependence of export demand on U.S. economic activity. Indeed, the increasing dominance of the import-intensive industries, the *maquiladoras*, in export
activities is a motive for concern for another reason. As the United Nations
Conference on Trade and Development's (UNCTAD's) report (2002) points
out, the statistics that show a significant share of manufacturing exports with
medium or high-technology intensity in developing countries may be mis-
leading. Most of the technology in these manufactures is in fact incorporated in
the components produced in technologically advanced countries while developing countries are merely involved in the assembly of these components,
a process characterized by low technological sophistication, the use of low-
skilled labor, little value added, and low and stagnant labor productivity. This
is certainly the case of most segments of the *maquiladora* industry, which, as
we have seen, have vastly increased their importance in Mexico's manufacturing exports and employment. Given that these industries tend to be characterized by a low potential for productivity growth, the counterpart of their high
capacity of employment absorption, the persistency of an appreciated real
exchange rate in the recent past has led to a decrease in profit margins in these
activities as wages in Mexico measured in U.S. dollars have tended to increase.
This, together with increasing competition from China and the slowdown in
the U.S. economy in the early 2000s, put a brake on the expansion of productive capacity and output in the *maquiladora* sector and led to a sharp decline in
employment starting in the third quarter of 2000 from which the industry has
yet to recover (see figure 10.1). With no productivity growth, the *maquiladoras*
constitute a sector that can only expand on the basis of low wages. Given the
tendency of wages to increase in other sectors along with productivity gains,
the maintenance of the *maquiladoras'* capacity to attract resources from the rest
of the economy would require a continuous undervaluation of the currency.

This is probably the major reason, along with the disintegration of
backward and forward linkages that has accompanied the very fast growth
of imports since trade was liberalized, why the pattern of specialization in
Mexico has not been particularly dynamic. In some sense, the Mexican economy is trapped by the loss of comparative advantages in labor-intensive
manufacturing to countries with lower labor costs and by the inability thus
far to acquire comparative advantages in more human capital and technology-intensive goods that are produced by countries with high per capita
incomes.

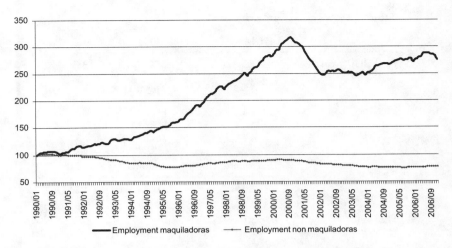

Figure 10.1 Employment in the *maquiladora* and non-*maquiladora* industries, 1990–2006 (Indices January 1990 = 100. Employment in non-*maquiladoras* is based on the Monthly Industrial Survey [Encuesta Industrial Mensual]).
Source: INEGI, Banco de Información Económica.

Is productivity performance the culprit for the growth slowdown?

In accounting exercises that decompose the rate of GDP growth into the contributions of factor accumulation and total factor productivity (TFP) growth, it is customary to attribute Mexico's growth slowdown since the early 1980s to a weak growth performance of TFP.[7] A recent exercise (Faal, 2005) finds, for example, that about two-thirds of the decline in the rate of GDP growth (a reduction of 3.9 percentage points comparing 1980–2003 to 1960–1979) is explained by lower TFP growth, which in fact *declined* at a rate of 0.5% per year from 1980 to 2003 (see table 10.6). These findings are consistent with those of other similar decomposition exercises (see Bergoeing et al., 2002; Bosworth, 1998; Santaella, 1998; World Bank, 2000). In this view of the growth process, the weakness of productivity growth is in turn often attributed, without any

---

7. More generally, TFP growth is often seen as a major "source of growth" in growth accounting exercises (see, e.g., Easterly and Levine, 2001). It has also become almost commonplace to attribute the income gap separating developed and underdeveloped countries primarily to differences in productivity, that is, to differences in the efficiency with which the available factors are used in production (rather than to, say, the endowment of factors of production) (see Hall and Jones, 1999; Helpman, 2004; Klenow and Rodriguez-Clare, 1997; and, in the Mexican context, Bazdresch and Mayer, 2006).

Table 10.6   Sources of growth

	1960–1979	1980–2003	1996–2003
Real GDP growth	6.5	2.6	3.5
	Factor growth rates (in percent)		
Capital	6.1	3.4	3.8
Labor	3.6	3.0	2.4
TFP	2.1	−0.5	0.7
	Factor contributions (in percentage points)		
Capital	2.0	1.1	1.2
Labor	2.4	2.0	1.6
TFP	2.1	−0.5	0.7

Source: Faal (2005).

evidence being provided, to the incompleteness of market reforms or the lack of a second generation of structural reforms (in the areas of energy, the labor market, or the judicial system).

The growth decomposition exercises on which these claims are based are flawed in several ways, but it is not our purpose here to address this subject (see Cripps and Tarling, 1973; Felipe and McCombie, 2006; Kaldor, 1966; Lavoie, 1992). We want, however, to illustrate what is wrong with these claims in the Mexican case by using a different decomposition exercise.

Consider a sectoral decomposition exercise of labor productivity growth, a variant of a shift-share analysis. The analytical framework is discussed in Ros (1995) and shows the absolute change in labor productivity for the economy as a whole in a given period divided into four components:[8]

1. The change due to the increase in productivity in agriculture (weighted by the initial agricultural employment share).
2. The change due to the increase in productivity in industry (weighted by the initial industrial employment share).
3. The change due to the increase in productivity in services (weighted by the initial employment share of services).

---

8. The decomposition is an approximation that assumes, as it is almost the case, that the productivity differential between industry and services is so small that it can be neglected.

Table 10.7 Sources of labor productivity growth in the Mexican economy (percentage points)

	1950–1981	1981–2005	1994–2005
Contributions from			
Agriculture	0.8	0.1	0.2
Industry	0.7	0	0.4
Services	1.2	−0.7	0.2
Labor reallocation	2.7	0.3	0.4
Total	5.4	−0.2	1.1
Annual productivity growth rates			
Agriculture	2.9	1.2	2.7
Industry	2.3	0	1.1
Manufacturing	2.4	0.6	1.9
Services	1.6	−1.2	0.3
Total	3.2	−0.2	1.1

Source: Based on employment data and data on value added at 1993 constant prices from Timmer and de Vries (2007).

4. The change due to the reallocation of labor from agriculture, with relatively low productivity, to industry and services with higher productivity levels (weighted by the end of period productivity differential between industry and services, on one hand, and agriculture, on the other).

Table 10.7 shows the results of the exercise for 1950–1981, 1981–2005, and 1994–2005, together with the annual growth rates of productivity in each of the three sectors and the whole economy. To facilitate comparison between periods, the total increase, as well as each of the four sources, is presented as an average annual percentage increase over the productivity level in the initial year (i.e., as the absolute contribution divided by the overall productivity in the initial year and by the number of years within each period). Each component can thus be seen as an average growth rate, the sum of which adds up to the average percentage increase in productivity in the whole economy.[9]

As shown in the table, in the period 1950–1981 the four sources of growth made a positive contribution to overall productivity growth. Particularly

9. The latter is not, however, the compound rate of growth of productivity (also shown in table 10.7) since it is estimated as a percentage of the initial productivity level (and thus will only coincide with the growth rate for 1-year periods).

significant was the effect of labor reallocation (which explains half of the increase in overall productivity) derived from the strong expansion of the employment shares of industry and services and the high productivity differential between, on the one hand, industry and services, and on the other hand, agriculture.

The productivity growth slowdown in the period 1981–2005 (by 5.6 percentage points) is largely due to the decrease in productivity in the services sector. Indeed, this reduction operated on the growth of overall productivity through two mechanisms. First, through the decrease in the direct contribution of services (by almost 2 percentage points) to the increase in overall productivity, a reduction that is much greater than that of agriculture or industry during this period. This decrease in the direct contribution of services is the result of an absolute reduction of productivity in this sector (at an annual rate of 1.2%), the only sector that records an absolute decrease in productivity. In addition, the decrease in services productivity made an indirect contribution to the productivity slowdown by sharply reducing the productivity differential with agriculture (in contrast, the productivity differential between industry and agriculture remained relatively stable). This is what explains to a large extent the substantial reduction of the labor reallocation effect (which, as we have seen before, weights the increase in the labor force in industry and services by the productivity differential with agriculture in the final year of the period).[10]

Thus what appears to have happened is simply that as the economy was unable to absorb the new entrants to the labor force into the high-productivity sectors, the expanding labor force found its way into the low-productivity activities of the services sectors where, in addition, a decline in hours worked (per worker) could have taken place. This simultaneously increased the employment share of services and reduced the average output per worker in this sector.[11] In other words, what explains the strong productivity slowdown is a massive increase in underemployment in the tertiary sectors of the economy that is also reflected in the well-documented decline in the share of wage and salary employment in the total labor force and in the increase in the size

10. The dominant role of the services sector in the decline of productivity growth after 1982 has been documented in other studies (see Bosworth, 1998; Escaith, 2006).

11. See also table 10.1. This phenomenon would probably reveal itself more clearly had we been able to adjust productivity for hours worked or had we been able to disaggregate the services sector at a high level. In that case, the decomposition exercise would probably show that the decrease in output per worker in the services sector is the result of an increasing employment share of the low-productivity activities of the services sector and of a decline in hours worked.

of the informal sector, largely made up of low-productivity activities in the services sectors (see Bosworth, 1998; OECD, 2003).

The message of the exercise is that the deterioration in the productivity growth performance of the Mexican economy since 1980 has to be seen as an endogenous consequence of the sluggish economic expansion. It was the slow growth of the economy that explains the disappointing productivity performance. Who really believes that the collapse of productivity in the services sectors of the economy is the cause, rather than a consequence, of the slow growth of the economy since 1982?[12]

Human capital formation and the growth slowdown

Is a slow process of human capital formation responsible for the growth slowdown? Has human capital accumulation been a binding constraint on the growth process? There are, we think, three reasons why the answers to these questions are negative. First, during the decades of slow growth, Mexico has in fact continued to record rapid improvements in educational and health indicators. As shown in table 10.8, enrollment rates have continued to climb at the secondary and tertiary levels of education and student:teacher ratios, helped by the demographic transition and the reduction in dependency ratios, have been falling since 1980, plummeting in the case of primary education. Illiteracy has continued to decrease, while average school attainment increased from 4.6 years in 1980 to 8.1 years in 2005. The annual growth rate of average years of schooling increased from 1.4% in 1940–1980 to 2.3% in 1980–2005 (see table A.3). Nor is there any evidence that educational indicators are lagging behind the rest of the world (as is the case with per capita GDP). As a percentage of the world average, the secondary enrollment rate increased

---

12. The cross-country evidence also points to the endogeneity of TFP growth. This evidence shows a strong and positive relationship across countries between the output share of investment in machinery and equipment and the rate of TFP growth, as well as a positive relationship between TFP growth and the rate of capital deepening (see, e.g., de Long and Summers, 1991). If TFP growth is an autonomous process of disembodied changes in technical efficiency, why should it be positively correlated with the rate of capital accumulation minus the growth of the labor force? And if TFP growth reflects the role of labor force reallocation, embodied technical progress, increasing returns to scale, and learning by doing, then of course it cannot be viewed as a separate factor, independent from capital accumulation, in the determination of economic growth.

Table 10.8   Educational indicators

Year	Gross enrollment rates (%)			Students/Teachers			Years of schooling	Illiteracy rate (%)
	Primary	Secondary	Tertiary	Primary	Secondary	Tertiary		
1950	53	3	2	n.a.	n.a.	n.a.	n.a.	35
1960	92[a]	17[a]	3	50	11.8	7.3	n.a.	35
1970	106	23	5	47.7	16.3	10.8	3.4	26
1980	120	49	14	39.1	18	12.7	4.6	17
1990	114	53	15	30.5	17.9	9.4	6.6	13
2000	113	75	21	26.7[b]	17.4[b]	9.7[b]	7.3[c]	8.8

Source: Enrollment rates: Reimers (2006), based on different sources. Students/Teachers: Santaella (1998) for 1960 and 1970; INEGI (2006) for 1980–2002. Average years of schooling (population 15 years and older): table A.3. Illiteracy rate: Reimers (2006), based on different sources.

n.a. = not available.
[a] 1965.
[b] 2002.
[c] 8.1 in 2005.

between 1993 and 2003 from 100% to 122%, while in higher education the enrollment rate remained constant at 92% (Presidencia de la República, 2006). In 2005, 16% of all Mexicans age 24 to 35 years possessed a university degree and Mexico had surpassed most of Latin America in terms of the fraction of its citizens who were university graduates (see Haber et al., 2008). Similarly, as we saw in chapter 9 (table 9.4), life expectancy has continued to increase, from 67.7 years in 1980–1985 to 73.4 in 2000–2005. If the growth slowdown is to be attributed to the lack of human capital formation, how are we to explain that a more educated and healthier labor force produces less output per worker today than in 1980?

Second, there are also unequivocal signs that slow growth has been constraining the use of human capital in production rather than vice versa. Indeed, there are two worrying trends in the Mexican labor markets. One is that the percentage of young people employed in the low-productivity occupations of the informal sector increased between 1989 and 2002 for the groups with relatively high educational level (10 to 12 years of schooling and 13 and more years of schooling), with an increase of almost 40% in the case of the second group (see table 10.9).[13] In addition, youth unemployment rates have also increased for the groups with higher educational levels, more than doubling in the case

13. We are grateful to Jurgen Weller for providing the data for tables 10.9 and 10.10.

Table 10.9   Percentage of young people (15–29 years old) by educational level in low productivity occupations[a]

Years of schooling	1989	2002
0–3	41.2	38.9
4–7	31.2	36.9
7–9	18.1	30.6
10–12	15.2	21.5
13 or more	6.8	9.3

Source: Based on INEGI (1999b).

[a] Includes nonprofessional self-employed, nonremunerated family workers, and domestic service.

Table 10.10   Unemployment rates of young people (15–29 years old) by educational level

Years of schooling	1989	2002
0–3	2.3	2.2
4–6	5.4	5.3
7–9	7.1	5.2
10–12	4.4	5.7
13 or more	4.5	9.5

Source: Based on INEGI (2003).

of young people with 13 and more years of education (see table 10.10). In fact, these groups are the only ones for which the unemployment rate increased. Both of these trends suggest that the best trained young people are not finding jobs appropriate to their qualifications.

Third, if human capital formation has not been faster, this should be partly attributed to the growth slowdown itself. A comparison between Mexico and South Korea illustrates this point (see Birdsall et al., 1995). In 1970, public expenditure on basic education per eligible child was only slightly higher in Korea than in Mexico. Two decades later, it was only 25% of the Korean level, secondary enrollment rates were half of the Korean levels, and the gap in tertiary enrollment rates had grown even larger (39% versus 15%). Public expenditure policy does not explain this divergence: in fact, in the mid-1970s, after an expansion during the first half of that decade, expenditure in basic education as percentage of GDP reached temporarily higher levels in Mexico than in Korea. The explanation for these increasing gaps is the fact that Korea's

GDP grew at an annual rate of 9.6% compared to Mexico's 3.5%. This difference in growth rates meant that, with the same percentage of GDP invested in education, the resources that Korea was able to invest in this sector expanded at a vastly higher rate.[14]

All this does not mean that all is well with Mexico's educational system. A major shortcoming is that the quality of primary education is on average very low, particularly in poor rural areas. The test for 2003 of the OECD Program for International Student Assessment (PISA), taken by more than a quarter of a million students in 41 countries, ranked Mexico in 38th place for the average of the three sections of the test (mathematics, reading, science and problem solving) (see OECD, 2003). In mathematics, Mexico was placed in last position with 375 points, way below the top performers, Korea and Finland (550 points). Moreover, the results of the test showed that only one-third of the group of 15-year-old students who participated had adequate basic skills in mathematics. A second major problem is that attrition rates are very high at the secondary level. As a result, in 2003 only 25% of the Mexican population age 25 to 34 years had graduated from high school. This rate is very low compared not only with the rates prevailing in developed countries, but also with those of other large countries of Latin America (Haber et al., 2008).

Low investment, slow growth

What then? The crucial factor in the slowdown of Mexico's rate of economic expansion appears to have been simply weak investment performance. As shown in table 10.6, the rate of capital accumulation fell from 6.1% per year to 3.8% per year between 1960–1979 and 1996–2003 (being only 3.4% for the entire period 1980–2003). The failure of capital formation to grow at a fast pace—after the years of decline during the debt crisis—has reduced the expansion of employment in high productivity sectors and the modernization of productive capacity while simultaneously restricting the growth of aggregate demand.

This poor performance is evident in the evolution of the fixed investment:GDP ratio (see figure 10.2). During the 1970s and early 1980s this ratio oscillated with the business cycle between 18% and 26.4%, rapidly

---

14. The demographic transition that began earlier in Korea than in Mexico also played a role. This explains why, during these two decades, the number of school-age children increased by 60% in Mexico while decreasing by 2% in Korea.

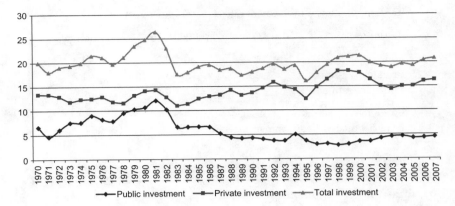

Figure 10.2 Fixed investment as a fraction of GDP (percent) (Investment and GDP are at current prices.)
Source: INEGI, Banco de Información Economica.

increasing toward the end of the period and reaching a historical peak in 1981 in the context of the high rates of economic growth associated with the oil boom. With the debt crisis, the investment rate decreased drastically in 1982–1983, reaching a value of 17.6% in 1983, some 9 percentage points below its value at the 1981 peak. It then hovered around 17% to 19% thereafter during the lost decade of the 1980s and the early 1990s. With the 1995 crisis and recession it dropped by more than 3 percentage points, to reach a low of 16.1%. In spite of its subsequent expansion, by 2004–2007 it stood at 20%, still well below its 1980–1981 levels. What are the causes of the disappointing performance of investment?

The failure of investment rates to recover their pre-debt crisis levels should not be attributed to a sluggishness of foreign direct investment (FDI). Despite a somewhat lethargic performance since 2002 (when FDI started decreasing as a percentage of GDP), the assumption that market-oriented reforms, FDI deregulation and privatization in particular, and NAFTA would significantly increase FDI has been validated by events as already discussed in chapter 8. Indeed, the inflow of FDI increased from about US$12 billion in 1991–1993 to more than US$46 billion in 2003–2005 (INEGI, Banco de Información Económica) while its amount soared as a proportion of total fixed investment from 6.7% in 1991–1993 to 11.8% in 2002–2004 (World Bank, World Development Indicators). The record is outstanding in the international context. According to Palma (2005), in the 1990s Mexico's manufacturing sector

Table 10.11   Fixed investment rates (as a proportion of GDP)

	1979–1981	2004–2007	Difference
Total	24.9	20.0	−4.9
Private investment	13.9	15.6	1.7
Public investment	11.0	4.4	−6.6

Source: INEGI, Cuentas Nacionales de México.
Investment and GDP are at current prices.

alone attracted twice as much FDI as the manufacturing sectors of Brazil, Argentina, and Chile combined.

The proximate determinant of the decline in the investment rate is the retreat of public investment. As shown in table 10.11 (see also figure 10.2), while total fixed investment fell by 4.9 percentage points of GDP between 1979–1981 and 2004–2007,[15] public investment actually fell by more (collapsing by 6.6 percentage points). Whether there are crowding-out or crowding-in effects of public investment on private investment is subject to controversy (for opposing views see Lachler and Aschauer, 1998, which finds a partial crowding-out effect, and Ramirez, 2004, which finds an important crowding-in effect). There is, however, consensus on the fact that, even if crowding-out effects exist, these are at worst partial, that is, an increase in public investment increases total investment rather than displacing fully an equal amount of private investment. It follows that the decline in public investment is partly responsible for the decrease in the overall investment rate and may even have had an adverse effect on private investment (if crowding-in effects predominate).

The decrease in public investment has partly to do with privatizations, but also with the type of fiscal adjustment followed after the debt crisis, as discussed in chapter 7. As shown by Giugale et al. (2001), there is a close correlation since 1980 between fiscal deficit reductions and the decrease in public investment (the correlation coefficient between the two is 0.82 between 1980 and 1997). Infrastructure investment, which has the largest potential to affect productivity growth and private investment, has suffered in this contraction. By the early 2000s, Mexico was last among the large Latin American economies

15. The decline in nonresidential investment (machinery and equipment and nonresidential construction) appears to have been greater, as residential construction increased its share in total investment (see chapter 8 and Moguillansky and Bielschowsky, 2001).

in infrastructure investment as a fraction of GDP, and this applied to both public and private investment (Calderón and Servén, 2004). The decrease in infrastructure investment occurs in road construction, water provision, and electricity. Only in the case of telecommunications was there a recovery of investment in the 1990s. However, even in this case, Mexico today is lagging behind other Latin American countries such as Chile and Brazil, which were behind Mexico in 1980.

The appreciation of the real exchange rate in 1988–1994 and later in the period since 2000 further conspired against investment in manufacturing and more generally in tradable goods sectors. While real exchange rate appreciation can encourage fixed investment in developing countries by lowering the relative prices of imported machinery and equipment, it also shifts relative prices in favor of nontradable goods sectors, reducing the profitability of the tradable goods sectors and inhibiting capital accumulation in these activities. There is ample evidence (Ibarra, 2006) that the overall effect on investment profitability is adverse and very significant in the Mexican case. Table 10.12, which shows the composition of FDI in alternative periods of undervaluation and overvaluation, reveals the connection between investment in manufacturing and the real exchange rate. As can be seen from the table, the periods of currency depreciation and undervaluation (1982–1990 and 1995–1999) were associated with a composition of FDI heavily biased toward the industrial sector (the overwhelming fraction of this investment being in manufacturing). In contrast, the periods of overvaluation (1991–1994 and 2000–2007) featured a composition of investment biased against manufacturing and in favor of nontradable goods sectors (commerce and services).

A third factor constraining the investment rate has to do with the reforms themselves, which had the explicit goal of eliminating all types of industrial policy incentives, including measures to promote domestic investment, both aggregate and in specific sectors. No attempt was made to orient domestic

Table 10.12 Composition of foreign direct investment in periods of undervaluation and overvaluation of the real exchange rate

Sector/Period	1982–1990	1991–1994	1995–1999	2000–2007
Primary	1.6	1.6	1.3	1.7
Industrial	61.0	41.5	62.5	48.1
Commerce and services	37.5	57.0	36.3	50.2
Real exchange rate	100.5	81.7	93.8	70.5

Source: Based on INEGI, Banco de Información Económica.

spending to investment as opposed to consumption expenditure. The elimination of sectoral incentives had an especially strong adverse impact on manufacturing investment, given that manufacturing had traditionally been the most favored sector under the previous development model based on import substitution and state-led industrialization. The adverse effects reduced manufacturing's relative rate of return, which in turn curbed investment.

The lack of bank finance for productive activities is an additional factor that has been constraining investment in recent years. As Banco de México's figures show, commercial banks' lending to the nonfinancial private sector has dramatically declined since 1995. For example, at the end of 1995 the outstanding balance was equivalent to 49.7% of GDP and at the end of 2000 it stood at 20% of GDP. Although it has somewhat recovered since then, at the end of 2007 it was 25% of GDP. If we focus on domestic lending from development and commercial banks to private enterprises—that is, excluding consumer and housing loans to the personal sector—the collapse of financial intermediation is even more dramatic. While at the end of 1995 the outstanding balance was equivalent to 35% of GDP, at the end of 2000 it had fallen to 21.2%, and at the end of 2007 it was even lower (18% of GDP). These ratios are well below those of typical OECD countries and stand at one of the lowest levels in the whole of Latin America. In fact, the size of Mexico's banking system as a percentage of GDP was smaller in 2005 than those of Nicaragua, Honduras, and Guatemala (Haber et al., 2008). Thus Mexico's privatized commercial banking system, especially after the 1994–1995 financial crisis, has been unable to provide sufficient credit for productive purposes, so that with the exception of the few large conglomerates that have close ties with the international capital markets, the large majority of Mexican enterprises—especially the small and medium ones—have faced acute bank credit rationing and have had to rely on their suppliers for financing (see Haber, 2005). Moreover, credit rationing has become worse over time. For example, while 29% of small firms obtained capital from banks in 1998, in 2005 only 18% did. This pattern of significant declines in the use of banks was similar for medium and large firms (see Haber et al., 2008).

In sum, our argument is that the proximate determinant of Mexico's slow growth since the early 1980s is a reduced investment rate, and four factors are constraining investment: the low level of public investment (particularly in the area of infrastructure), an appreciated real exchange rate for most of the period since 1990, the dismantling of industrial policy during the reform period, and the lack of bank finance. The first factor contributes directly to a slower rate of capital formation in the public sector, and possibly also in the private sector. The second and third have affected private investment profitability, particularly in the manufacturing sector, with deleterious effects on the process of economic development. The fourth has prevented the realization of potentially profitable investment projects.[16]

Liberal misperceptions at the turn of the century?

With macroeconomic stability (narrowly defined in terms of low inflation and small budget deficits) having been achieved, the currently dominant view in both government and international financial institutions alike attributes the growth and employment problems to a supposed incompleteness of liberalizing reforms. In a "permanent escape into the future," this orientation recommends further market reform in the face of any difficulty arising in economic performance. Thus structural reforms in the fiscal area, the energy sector, and the labor market in particular are seen as the major development tasks and the key necessary conditions to resume high and sustained growth. To this, a wider list of so-called second-generation reforms is often added, ranging from the educational and health systems to the judicial system and the rule of law (see, e.g., Werner et al., 2006).

We believe that the dominant agenda among policymakers largely misses the point. With regard to fiscal reform, this is certainly part of the necessary effort to mobilize resources for the increase in public investment and social expenditures as well as to reduce the dependence of government resources on oil revenues. However, the Vicente Fox administration largely focused, unsuccessfully, on increasing the value-added tax base by eliminating tax exemptions on foodstuffs and medications, aiming at increasing tax revenues by only about 2 percentage points of GDP. The tax reform proposed by the Felipe Calderón administration, approved by the Chamber of Deputies in September 2007, aims to raise revenues by 2.5% to 3% of GDP. Central features of the reform are an increase in corporate taxes (a 16.5% charge on corporate income after deductions including, among others, investments) and

---

16. It is worth pointing out that our emphasis on the investment rate is quite consistent with the empirical literature on economic growth, where in cross sections of countries the investment rate is found to be the most systematic and statistically significant determinant of growth (Levine and Renelt, 1992; see also de Long and Summers, 1991, for the role of investment in machinery and equipment).

an attempt to increase tax collection in the informal sector by establishing a 2% tax on cash bank deposits exceeding a cumulative total of 25,000 pesos per month. While more ambitious than the failed fiscal reform of the Fox administration, this recent tax reform falls short of what is needed, as the expected future decline in oil production and revenues may be enough to practically negate its effects. To make a significant difference in the state's dependence on oil revenues and its capacity to invest in infrastructure projects, as well as in the area of social spending, will require an increase in the tax burden of about 8 percentage points of GDP (see Casar and Ros, 2004).

With respect to reform of the energy sector, recent initiatives have focused on the oil industry. At the time of writing, there is a heated debate on the future of PEMEX and the Calderón administration's proposals to partially privatize segments of the oil industry. It is clear that the country's medium-term growth prospects depend on the urgent reform of PEMEX, for unless considerable investment in exploration occurs soon, Mexico's oil reserves, extraction, and exports will decline sharply in the next 10 years.

In our view, reform should focus on the following aspects. The first is the appropriation and use of oil rents. How are they used? How much of these rents is PEMEX allowed to use for investment purposes? As is well known, the enormous gap between the costs of oil extraction and its sale price generates massive profits for oil companies. PEMEX is no exception. In 2007 its average cost of extracting a barrel of oil was about US$4 to US$5 in the face of a sales price greater than US$80. These oil rents have been systematically captured by the state and, to a smaller, but not insignificant extent, by the ruling party and PEMEX's trade union. In the past 10 years PEMEX has contributed 40% of total revenues (8% of GDP). In 2007 it recorded US$584 million in before-tax profits but paid US$583 million in taxes (Ibarra, 2008). These practices have transformed PEMEX into a tax collecting agency, dramatically reducing PEMEX's ability to invest in expanding or maintaining its productive capacity, its exploration activities, and its proven reserves, as well as undermining its capacity to become a key dynamic player in the international petroleum and petrochemical products market. Moreover, its capacities for technological innovation have been drastically eroded, by decreasing the fiscal, financial, and human resources allocated to the *Instituto Mexicano del Petróleo* (PEMEX's technological research institute).

A second aspect refers to the room to maneuver of PEMEX's board of directors. As it currently stands, PEMEX's management functions are severely bounded. Its chief executive officer (CEO) and governing board of directors lack the independence to make or implement key decisions regarding investment projects, pricing mechanisms, employment plans, and labor relations. All of these aspects need to be revised. In particular, its pricing strategy of subsidizing gasoline for car transportation may help to keep inflation temporarily under control, but runs against the need to develop a more fuel efficient and environmentally sound industrial and transport structures.

A third aspect is the role ahead for PEMEX regarding insertion in the world economy and its linkages with the rest of Mexico's industrial sectors. Indeed, since the 1982 debt crisis, Mexico has opted to accompany its quest for an export-led strategy with a path of specialization of PEMEX as merely an exporter of crude oil. Policymakers explicitly made the decision to abandon any plans to develop PEMEX as a major player in the petrochemical industry. Perhaps this decision may have appeared to be soundly based decades ago, given Mexico's then tight credit rationing in the international capital markets and in a context where the prices of oil and gasoline were on a downward trend. But this is not so today. The medium-term outlook of the international petroleum and gasoline markets points in a different direction. Developing the national petrochemical industry will enhance PEMEX's capacity to generate value added, to build stronger forward and backward linkages with the local industrial sectors, and, much more important, it will strengthen Mexico's long-term economic growth prospects.

In sum, the status quo in PEMEX and the oil industry cannot continue, as it means the state is failing to adequately fulfill its dual role as a principal and as an agent in matters regarding oil reserves and industrial capacities. Indeed, the strategy adopted in the past two decades has brought about a systematic decline in PEMEX, and thus Mexico's oil reserves, as well as a systematic failure to augment or even maintain the physical, financial, and human capital of its oil and petrochemical industry. The state's regulatory abilities are also wanting, having failed to put in place sound pricing and investment strategies and promote an industrial structure that accurately reflects the relative scarcity of oil and gasoline, not to mention to reduce Mexico's fiscal dependence on oil revenues.

With regard to competitiveness and employment problems, the dominant orientation sees the institutional rigidity of the labor market as the most important obstacle and advocates "flexibilization" as the main policy instrument to resolve these problems. In this respect, a few points should be made. First, the international experience shows that there is a multiplicity of institutional arrangements in the labor market compatible with the achievement of a high level of economic development, so that it is far from clear why a reform in a given direction is indispensable to the achievement of high rates of economic growth. Second, a clear relationship between labor market flex-ibility and job creation has not been shown, let alone a relationship between flexibility and productivity and growth (see, e.g., Chor and Freeman, 2005). Third, losses of competitiveness associated with currency appreciation have not been offset in the development experience by reductions in labor costs. Moreover, and more important from a normative point of view, even if pro-cesses of this kind are viable, they would surely be long and painful stories and promote a social structure that is even more unequal and unfair than the one we currently find in Mexico. These opinions should not be interpreted as a defense of existing labor legislation—which in many ways is obsolete and inefficient—but rather as a criticism of the prevailing idea that the "cause" of employment performance is located in the rigidity of labor market institu-tions and that, consequently, flexibilization is the most important policy ori-entation in this regard, if not the only one (for further discussion, see Frenkel and Ros, 2004; Bensusán, 2006).

In the area of other second-generation reforms, progress in the solution to such problems as lagging educational and health systems or the functioning of the judiciary and the enforcement of the rule of law is equivalent, in fact, to achieving an advanced stage of development in a two-way relationship of causality. In this relationship, the impact of economic development on the solution to these problems is likely to be much greater than the effect that solv-ing them will have on economic development. In other words, it is difficult, if not impossible, to achieve, say, Swedish standards of health, education, and public services when one has a per capita income that is three times lower. This does not mean that one cannot, and that one should not, make progress in these areas. It simply points to the fact that its definitive solution requires as a necessary condition, although possibly not sufficient, to solve the problem of economic growth (see Casar and Ros, 2004; Rodrik, 2004).

The dominant agenda also misses the point because, as discussed previ-ously, the most binding constraints on growth are today derived from the low level of public investment, the dismantling of industrial policy, the lack of bank finance and an appreciated real exchange rate. These are then the areas in which growth-oriented reform efforts should concentrate.

Removing the constraints on public investment leads directly to the ques-tion of fiscal reform, already discussed, and mobilization of the fiscal space given by the low levels of public debt. A priority area for investing increased resources is the development of the poor south. A "New Deal" that creates the conditions to take advantage of the productive potential of the south, and to allow it to reach the medium development level of the rest of the country, would generate by itself a considerable additional impulse to the growth process, in addition to the reduction of regional inequalities. This requires eliminating and reverting the bias against these regions that most policies in public capital and development incentives have shown so far. Infrastructure investment in these regions and the introduction of positive discrimination in their favor would open up new areas of investment and new markets, thus liberating a growth potential that would contribute, for a considerable period, to a higher rate of growth in the economy as a whole (see Dávila et al., 2002).

The second area of reform concerns industrial policy in order to create the conditions for a rapid process of structural change. If Mexico is to succeed in its thus far failed quest to achieve high and sustained economic growth, there is urgent need to rethink key elements of its overall strategy and industrial policies. Mexico's economy is at a crossroads. It cannot further base its international insertion on low wages and labor-intensive *maquiladoras*, but, at the same time, it has not yet successfully entered the international markets based on high value-added processes and products. The transition toward a new pattern of trade specialization based on activities with higher technological intensity and greater human capital intensity will require the reform or abandonment of existing policies and the undertaking of new tasks. The first category includes, in particular, reconsideration of the incentives currently in place to induce the tax-free entry of imported inputs for export purposes. In place of these incentives, priority should be given to the integration of productive chains that allow taking advantage of the competitiveness of certain activities in order to strengthen the competitiveness of other activities upstream or downstream, while at the same time enhancing the capacity of the export sector to generate growth in the rest of the economy. If special programs to promote the development of selected industrial sectors are implemented, they should be supported by sufficient financial and human resources as required by the daunting magnitude of the challenge. In this regard, the institutional framework should be tailored to guarantee, as best as possible, that all subsidies are granted in a temporary, transparent, accountable, and goal-oriented way.

There are also several new areas in which public action is indispensable. This includes the development of long-term capital markets, technology policies focused on innovation and the development of new sectors, investments in training and the acquisition of new abilities, and direct support to strategic sectors (i.e., those that generate strong positive externalities on other sectors). The task is, in short, to design policies that creatively address market failures in the factor markets, coordination problems among producers, and information externalities in new activities, all of which generate less than socially optimal rates of investment in activities that are decisive for the successful transition toward a new pattern of specialization and development (see Hausmann and Rodrik, 2006; Ros, 2001b; Shapiro, 2008; and, for a skeptical viewpoint, Pack and Saggi, 2006).

Another area of reform relates to financial intermediation. As argued earlier, lack of credit to private firms, in particular to producers of tradable goods or to start-up enterprises, is a major constraint on investment and, thus, on the economy's growth potential. The downsizing and weakening of development banks (NAFINSA and Bancomext) brought about by the reform process made bank lending to firms more scarce. The acquisition of the largest banks by foreign ones in the late 1990s failed to solve this problem. In fact, although the foreign banks established in Mexico are highly profitable, their activities concentrate much more on consumer lending and financial commissions than on lending to private businesses. In fact, Mexico's ratio of banking lending to private businesses is among the lowest in Latin America. Such a situation implies that while large firms may have access to international credit markets, the vast majority of small and medium enterprises are severely credit rationed. Clearly, without a strong financial intermediation system, the Mexican economy will remain stuck in a path of low growth.

Part of the solution lies in strengthening the rule of law. Indeed, as some analysts have argued, the weakness of Mexico's contract enforcement rules, in case of default, makes the banks' repossession of collateral much more difficult in the case of loans to small and medium firms than to private consumers (see Tornell, Westermann, and Martinez, 2003). The reinforcement of the legal and judiciary power is certainly a must, not only regarding financial transactions but also regarding the full administration of justice.

However, by itself, this will be insufficient to solve the credit crunch and correct the acute fragilities and limitations of the financial system, such as the high segmentation and shallowness of the banking system, the lack of capital markets, and the scarcity of long-term finance, particularly for start-up innovative firms. To correct such structural limitations, we consider that the following additional measures are needed. The first is restoring the role of development banks to grant long-term credit mainly for innovative firms and for the production of tradable goods and services. Contrary to conventional views, we believe that, given Mexico's far from fully developed financial system, the lending activities of such banks are complementary to those of the private banking system. Moreover, if correctly monitored and managed, they may promote financial deepening by strengthening long-term capital markets.

The second is putting in place regulations to effectively cap the commissions being charged by banks on banking transactions, like payment of services, checking facilities, and cash disposal (ATMs), thus creating incentives for the banks to allocate a greater proportion of their activity to lending to firms. The third is to facilitate the entry of small banks, if possible with regional specialization. The increased competition may help break the oligopolistic power of the large banks and reduce interest rates and commissions, as well as increase credit access to small and medium firms. This should be accompanied by a strengthening of the regulatory bodies to ensure a prudent regulation of the financial system.

Establishing a competitive real exchange rate calls for the reform of monetary policy. In this respect, if one accepts that price stability is consistent with multiple configurations of real wages, interest rates, and exchange rates, and that some of them are more favorable than others to economic growth, it follows that, without violating the constitutional mandate that requires the central bank to pursue price stability, monetary policy should seek such stability within the set of configurations favorable to growth. Moreover, given that the configurations of relative prices that inhibit growth have often proven to be unsustainable, prudence dictates seeking price stability only within a context that is favorable to growth. This requires systematically avoiding exchange rate overvaluation, especially in times of recession; to avoid, that is, the implementation of a procyclical monetary policy such as the one followed in the early 2000s. This would involve the flexibilization of the currently very strict inflation targeting framework[17] and its combination with real exchange rate targeting. More precisely, the central bank could promote a competitive exchange rate by establishing a sliding floor to the exchange rate in order to prevent excessive appreciation (see Galindo and Ros, 2008). This would imply managing interest rates or intervening in the foreign exchange market at times when the exchange rate hits the floor but allowing the exchange rate to float freely otherwise. Thus, under this alternative, the central bank does not target a particular real exchange rate, but only establishes a floor on its value.

The orthodox objection to such a proposal is that by defending the floor the central bank loses control of the money supply, and this could imply

17. The evidence suggests that the central bank has adopted a strict inflation-targeting regime, focused exclusively on inflation targets, rather than a flexible framework that takes into account the output gap in the design of monetary policy (for a review of the evidence, see Esquivel, 2008).

giving up the achievement of the inflation target (for more discussion, see Frenkel and Rapetti, 2004). The problem arises at times of excess supply of foreign currency as a result, in particular, of massive capital inflows. It is worth noting, however, that speculative capital inflows will tend to be deterred to the extent that the central bank clearly signals that it will prevent the appreciation of the domestic currency, thus stabilizing exchange rate expectations. If necessary, however, the central bank, as in other Latin American experiences, can impose capital account regulations on short-term capital flows in order to recover control over the money supply.[18]

Perhaps the divide over policy recommendations can be better understood if we express it in more technical terms. As such, it becomes clear that its deep roots date back to the origins of macroeconomics as a discipline, to Keynes's analysis of the causes and remedies of the Great Depression's unemployment and the debate Keynes sustained with his contemporaries. The dominant orientation we are criticizing asserts that there is only one equilibrium price configuration in every economy that yields full employment (or better, unemployment at its natural rate) in the labor market and a natural rate of growth. This view disregards the importance of the precise trajectory followed by the economy in the past and its influence over the present, the so-called hysteresis phenomenon, which implies that the current macroeconomic configuration may be heavily determined by the past.

In this regard, consider Mexico's economic situation at two points in time: the second half of the 1980s and the first half of the first decade of the 21st century. During most of the first period, the international interest rate was high, the economy was financially rationed and made significant transfers abroad, absorption was lower than output, and inflation was out of control. In the second period, the international interest rate was lower, the economy had access to international financial markets and received transfers from abroad, absorption was greater than output, and macroeconomic stability had been restored. However, employment and growth performance in the second period was hardly better than in the first,[19] even though there seems to be no doubt that there was a positive shock between the two.

18. When the increase in foreign currency is associated with massive inflows of family remittances or great improvements in the terms of trade, the challenge of avoiding a persistent real exchange rate appreciation may be more complex but is still manageable with appropriate interest rate management and intervention in the foreign exchange market.

19. GDP growth was 1.8% per year in 2000–2005 and 1.7% per year in 1985–1990 (World Bank, World Development Indicators).

The paradox we reach from the idea of a unique equilibrium configuration highlights the inadequacy of the dominant perspective. The alternative implies considering the possibility of multiple equilibrium configurations depending, among other circumstances, on the factors imposed by the external context and economic policies. Some configurations are more favorable to employment and growth. Others imply that the economy is being driven to low-growth and low-employment traps. The observed changes between 1985–1990 and 2000–2005 do not appear to be paradoxical from this perspective. The conjunction of real currency appreciation and the specific implementation of adjustment and liberalization policies drove the Mexican economy to low-investment and low-growth macroeconomic configurations. We believe that, just as a century and a half ago, the real obstacles to economic development are being misperceived in today's dominant orientation in economic policy.

11

Conclusions

An old tradition in development economics views the rate of growth of an economy as the outcome of constraints acting on economic development. These binding constraints vary over time and across countries. They may act through the supply side of the process of capital accumulation, such as the savings and foreign exchange constraints of two-gap models, or they may act through the demand side of the process of capital accumulation, such as the fiscal and investment constraints of three-gap models.[1] This approach differs quite radically from conventional neoclassical growth theory, which attempts to identify universal determinants of economic growth while focusing exclusively on the supply side of the economy.

Hausmann et al. (2005b) recently revived this tradition and extended the approach. In this view, capital accumulation may face three types of constraints resulting from inadequate social returns to investment, poor private appropriability of the social returns, or a high cost or lack of availability of finance for domestic investment. In the first case, low social returns may in turn be due to poor geography or an insufficient supply of complementary factors of production (such as physical infrastructure and human capital). In the second case, a large wedge between social and private returns may be associated with government failures (such as high taxation, corruption, or poor property rights and contract enforcement) or market failures (arising

---

1. For a review of gap models, see Ros (1994b).

252

from information or coordination externalities). In the third case, the high cost or lack of availability of finance for domestic investment may be due to poor access to international finance or to insufficient local finance (associated with low domestic savings or poor financial intermediation).

Hausmann et al.'s (2005b) work is an important contribution to understanding why some economies remain stuck, for a long time, on paths of slow expansion. They identify fundamental elements that may impede the start of growth spurts, be it poor investment prospects or a lack of funds/financial capital. However, their analytical framework is insufficient to comprehend the unfortunately rather frequent experiences in developing countries in which apparently strong and persistent trends of economic expansion are abruptly derailed, leading to an acute foreign exchange or financial crisis with dramatic implications for the poor population. Most important, such sudden-stop experiences have brutally shocked Mexico's economic performance in recent decades: in the early 1980s, when the oil boom abruptly burst, and in the mid-1990s, when the peso crisis plunged the economy into a deep recession and financial crisis.

To understand these abrupt shifts from "boom to bust" we find it necessary to bring into the analysis the balance of payments constraint. This notion is rooted in two different traditions. First is the Latin American structuralist school that started with Raul Prebisch's seminal work on the deterioration of the terms of trade as a fundamental obstacle to Latin America's long-term economic growth.[2] Second is Roy Harrod's trade multiplier, as further developed by Anthony Thirlwall and his colleagues, showing that key determinants of the balance of payments constraint are the evolution of the terms of trade as well as the ratio of the income elasticity of imports relative to that of exports. The fundamental insight of this view is that the balance of payments, or more specifically the availability of foreign exchange, can act as a binding, long-term constraint on the rate of expansion of an economy. In other words, to be in a long-term growth path the economy must ensure that it is not accumulating external debt (by the public or the private sector) at an unsustainable pace, reaching ratios that are seen as too high by the international financial community.

Throughout this book we have followed these old traditions by trying to identify the obstacles to economic development (the binding constraints on economic growth) in different periods of Mexico's economic history. This is

2. See Prebisch (1950). For an in-depth historical analysis of Prebisch's thesis on the declining terms of trade, see Mallorquín (2005).

precisely what has led us to emphasize the role of perceptions and consensus in economic policy among policymakers and key economic actors. For it is because the binding constraints change over time that perceptions of those in positions of power about the nature of these constraints matter so much. The existence of a consensus in economic policy also matters to the extent that its absence can impede the implementation of policies designed to remove the constraints on growth.[3]

What have been the main binding constraints on growth and how have they changed throughout Mexico's economic history? During the lost half century after independence, the main problem was probably a low expected private return to investment more than the availability or high cost of finance, even though, as discussed in chapter 2, the persistence of financial back-wardness until very late in the 19th century is striking compared not only to advanced economies in the United States and Europe, but also to other Latin American countries such as Argentina, Brazil, and Chile. In turn, low invest-ment profitability resulted from low social returns and problems of private appropriability. The low social returns were determined by the lack of ade-quate transport infrastructure which generated extremely high transport costs in the context of geographical disadvantages such as the lack of a river system suitable for transportation, the mountainous landscape, and the long distances between urban centers and the coast. A low level of human cap-ital, associated with the high degree of inequality prevailing since colonial times, also probably contributed to low social returns, although the acceler-ation of growth during the *Porfiriato* suggests that this was probably not the most binding constraint during the period. The low private appropriability resulted from institutional disadvantages, such as the *alcabalas* that contrib-uted to the high costs of domestic trade, and political instability, with its con-comitant increase in expropriation risk.

The success of the *Porfiriato* in launching a long period of economic growth should be attributed to the fact that it consistently addressed the most binding constraints that had prevented growth in the past. First, the arrival of the railways and the sharp decline in transport costs lifted the social returns to investment from the low levels that poor geography had previously deter-mined. Second, private returns were further increased by the establishment

---

3. Of course, the existence of a consensus is not a sufficient condition for the removal of the binding constraints on growth. Sometimes there may be a consensus based on wrong interpretations of the determinants of and obstacles to economic growth, in which case such consensus has unfavorable consequences on development.

of political stability and the attendant increase in the private appropriability of social returns. The removal of these obstacles to economic development was sufficient to launch an acceleration of the growth process. If growth was sustained over a period of more than 30 years, this should also be attributed to the efforts at institutional modernization, including elimination of the *alcabalas*. Particularly favorable to Mexico's growth process was the *Porfiriato*'s success in relaxing the financial constraints on fiscal expenditures via the creation of mechanisms through which private banks would channel funds to the government. This institutional reform, plus the creation of a modern banking system, prevented the availability and cost of finance from becoming an obstacle to sustained development.

During the revolution and immediate postrevolutionary period, problems of private appropriability reappeared, not only because of the reemergence of political instability, but also as a result of the hyperinflation during the revolution. But it was probably the lack of finance for investment that constrained economic growth in this period, especially with the collapse of the Porfirian banking system and the sharp decline after 1926 in the purchasing power of exports. Both the internal and external constraints on investment thus contributed to the poor performance of investment and growth.

Following the recovery of the economy from the Great Depression, the increase in the returns to investment inaugurated a new era of sustained capital accumulation and rapid economic growth starting with the war boom of the early 1940s. Social returns were kept high by the bottleneck-breaking nature of public capital formation in both physical and social infrastructure. Industrial policy, through the activity of public development banks, trade protection, and fiscal incentives, reduced the gap between the private and social returns of industrial investment by successfully addressing information and coordination failures. Private appropriability was also enhanced by the long period of political stability that was made possible by the Cardenista agrarian reform and the corporatist organization of the political system. Later in the process, reconstruction of the financial system, especially during the stabilizing development period, contributed to a reduction in the cost of finance and an increase in its availability, which further enhanced the growth process.

With the 1982 debt crisis, the availability of finance for investment became the dominant problem, and the severity of the balance of payments constraint produced a collapse of capital accumulation during the lost decade of the 1980s. Eventually access to international capital markets was restored and the presence of slow public capital formation and low private returns to investment became the main sources of persistently low investment rates. The low levels of public investment were a legacy of the policy adjustment process to the external shocks of the 1980s. From the early 1990s onward, low private profitability had its origin in low social returns resulting from a lagging infrastructure and a recurrent appreciation of the peso, as well as in problems of private appropriability resulting from the watering down of industrial policy that generated unassisted market failures (information and coordination externalities). With the collapse of the banking system in 1995, the high cost and availability of domestic finance also became a constraint on potentially profitable investment projects.

This brief summary of the changing constraints on the process of capital accumulation through Mexico's economic history yields lessons for the current debates on development economics. Consider, for example, the controversy over the relative roles of geography and institutions (see Acemoglu et al., 2002; Sachs, 2001). The analysis of the constraints on growth during the immediate postindependence era clearly suggests that both geography and backward institutions had a role in the relative decline of the Mexican economy during that period. Geographical disadvantages determined high transport costs that depressed the social returns to capital accumulation, but so did the lack of institutional development that preserved colonial institutions and produced a large gap between the social and private returns to investment. There seems to be little doubt that both geography and institutions had a role to play in explaining why economic development was so slow to occur in Mexico and thus accounting for the origins of the present backwardness of the Mexican economy. Geography mattered in subsequent periods in other ways. The challenges posed by a 2000-mile border with an economic, political, and military superpower had a role in the rapid process of economic growth and modernization starting in the early 1940s. Today, by inducing international migration to the United States, geography continues to play a role in keeping unemployment and poverty at lower levels than otherwise. But the role of institutions continues to be no less important. In particular, the lack of industrial policy institutions in recent decades has inhibited growth by leaving unassisted a number of market failures.

Consider now the role of trade and trade openness in development (for a critical survey of the literature on the subject, see Rodríguez and Rodrik, 2001). Is trade liberalization a necessary and sufficient condition for rapid export-led growth? While the Mexican experience during the period of state-led industrialization suggests that trade protection acted as a brake on the expansion of exports, and thus a more liberal trade regime would have promoted a more rapid growth of exports (although not necessarily a more rapid growth of total output), the experience with trade liberalization and the North American Free Trade Agreement (NAFTA) over the past two decades indicates that trade openness is hardly a sufficient condition for rapid export-led growth. More precisely, the effects on growth of a greater degree of trade openness appear to be contingent on the pattern of trade specialization that the greater trade openness promotes. Mexico's pattern of trade, caught between the competition from high technology products exported by more developed economies and that of labor intensive goods from low wage competitors has not proven to be very dynamic, even despite an outstanding manufacturing export growth performance.

The Mexican experience also confirms the adverse effects of income inequality on growth that have been emphasized by the recent literature on this subject (see Bénabou, 1996, and Ros, 2000a, chap. 10, for reviews of this literature). As we saw in chapter 2, the high degree of inequality inherited from the colonial era inhibited growth in the postindependence period by preventing the emergence of a middle-class market, reducing the productivity of the labor force (through disease and malnutrition), and contributing to political instability. However, Mexico's history does not provide support for all the links between inequality and development postulated in the literature. For example, in the fiscal policy approach, inequality creates a pressure for redistributive and excessively high taxes (as the middle class allies itself with the poor to press for redistribution) which ends up inhibiting investment and growth. In contrast, Mexico is an example of the ability of the wealthy classes to prevent taxation on capital either through the political influence that wealth provides or through the threat of capital flight. Similarly, as shown in the recent literature, inequality inhibits growth largely by inhibiting the accumulation of human capital. While this may apply to the first decades of the postindependence period, it is clear that this high inequality did not prevent a rapid process of human capital accumulation during the golden age of industrialization starting in the early 1940s. One thing that inequality seems to do, in the Mexican case, is to eventually destroy the ability to reach a broadly based consensus on economic policy; under conditions of social polarization, collective decision making is very difficult to achieve. The result is that inequality reduces the stability and predictability of government decisions, with an adverse effect on investment and growth. Policy instability is aggravated when inequality also leads to political instability.

Finally, consider the role of state and market reforms in development. During the two periods of rapid economic development—the *Porfiriato* and the postwar period up to the early 1980s—the state played an active role in the economy. This went well beyond providing a reasonable degree of macroeconomic stability (except for the decade preceding the debt crisis). Despite its laissez-faire rhetoric, the state during the *Porfiriato* strictly regulated banking, used trade policy to stimulate selected activities, and intervened to promote investment in the railway network. In particular, the developmentalist nature of the *Porfiriato's* trade and industrial policies has been amply documented, as discussed in chapter 3. The focus on growth and industrialization through an array of government interventions was even more marked during the golden age of industrialization after 1940.

In contrast with the periods of rapid economic development, the past two and a half decades have witnessed a radical shift in the state-market balance. The market reforms implemented this time have had mixed results. On the positive side, the fiscal deficit and inflation were drastically reduced and have remained at low levels for years. Foreign direct investment (FDI) inflows increased and, together with trade liberalization and NAFTA, helped trigger an export boom in manufactures that transformed Mexico in the world economy. On the negative side, underemployment and outmigration have greatly increased, poverty and inequality persist, and overall productivity performance has lagged behind, as the economy has not been able to grow fast enough. Recurrent real exchange rate appreciation has had a negative effect on competitiveness and investment. Fiscal reform has failed, as it has done repeatedly in the past, or remains insufficient, leaving the state heavily dependent on oil revenues. Despite the modernization of the banking system, credit is severely rationed for productive activities. The economy's growth path has been marked by sharp, short-lived upswings that exert excessive pressure on the trade balance and are followed by slowdowns or foreign exchange crises that prevent the consolidation of a sustained and robust economic expansion. The explanation for this failure lies in the fact that, as we saw in chapter 10, an overall upturn in investment simply did not accompany the liberalizing reforms and the new macroeconomic environment.

All this leads us to a final and most important aspect of the recent overall reform process, on which we can only raise the relevant questions. Is the shift in the market-state balance a sign that, after having reduced economic backwardness by state-sponsored industrialization, use of a different set of ideas becomes more suitable in the new stage, a shift that is the natural companion of the transition from Gerschenkronian to Schumpeterian entrepreneurship? Or is it still the case that "to break through the barriers of stagnation in a backward country, to ignite the imaginations of men, and to place their energies in the service of economic development, a stronger medicine is needed than the promise of better allocation of resources" (Gerschenkron, 1952)?

A complete answer to these questions falls outside the scope of this book. What we can say, however, is that the origin of the adjustment problems and the new problems created by the reform process are not being adequately perceived in current development policy. First, the notion that the debt crisis was brought about by the exhaustion of past development strategies should not be taken for granted, even though we do not defend every single aspect of past development strategies. Second, the solution to the new obstacles may require more and better, rather than less, state participation in the economy. As we have tried to show, the source of these new problems can be found in part in the retreat of the state in areas such as public investment in infrastructure. However, as a result of the shift in ideological climate, very little attention is being given to these problems and to what government policy can do about them, while at the same time, too much is expected from the efficiency gains of market reforms.

APPENDIX

Historical Series of Economic and Social Indicators

Table A.1 Mexico: GDP, per capita GDP, and population growth

	1820	1870	1910	1940	1970	1981	2003
Per capita GDP[a]	759	674	1694	1852	4320	6717	7137
As a percentage of U.S. level	60.4	27.6	34.1	26.4	28.7	35.6	24.6
Growth rates[b]		1820–1870	1870–1910	1910–1940	1940–1970	1970–1981	1981–2003
GDP		0.4	3.6	1.3	6.2	6.8	2.1
Per capita GDP		−0.2	2.3	0.3	2.9	4.1	0.3
Population		0.7	1.2	1.0	3.2	2.6	1.8

Source: Maddison (2003, 2006).

[a] 1990 international Geary-Khamis dollars.

[b] Average annual rates of growth.

Table A.2 Mexico's per capita GDP as a percentage of per capita GDP

	1820	1870	1913	1940	1970	1981	2003	2006
United States	60.4	27.6	32.7	26.4	28.7	35.6	24.6	25.0
Western Europe	63.2	34.4	50.1	40.7	42.4	50.9	35.8	37.2
Eastern Europe	111.1	72.0	102.2	94.1	100.1	118.2	110.2	105.7
Latin America	109.8	99.7	115.9	95.8	108.3	125.4	123.4	118.9
Asia	130.7	121.2	248.6	206.5	282.2	322.3	161.0	137.8
Africa	180.8	134.8	271.6	227.7	318.8	444.9	460.7	456.8
World average	113.9	77.2	113.5	94.4	115.6	148.1	109.5	110.4

Source: Data for 1820–2003 based on Maddison (2006), data for 2006 estimated by the authors based on World Bank, World Development Indicators (per capita GDP at constant US$).

Per capita GDP in 1990 Geary-Khamis dollars.

Table A.3 Population and social indicators

Year	Population (millions)	Dependency ratio	Rural population (percent)	Life expectancy at birth (years)	Infant mortality (per thousand)	Literacy[a]	Average years of schooling[b]
1895	12.6	77.6	71.7[c]	29.5[d]	n.a.	17.9[e]	n.a.
1910	15.2	80.0	71.3	n.a.	n.a.	22.3	n.a.
1930	16.6	72.9	66.5	33.0–34.7	156.3	38.5	n.a.
1940	19.7	79.2	64.9	37.7–39.8	138.6	41.8	2.6
1970	48.2	107.6	42.2	58.8–63.0	76.8	76.3	3.4
1980	66.8	89.0	33.7	63.2–69.4	53.1	83.0[b]	4.6
1990	81.2	81.0	28.7	67.7–74.0	36.2	87.4	6.6
2000	97.5	64.3	25.4	71.6–76.5	24.9	90.5[b]	7.3
2005	103.3	66.1	23.5	74.5	24.0[f]	n.a.	8.1

Source: INEGI (1999a), INEGI, Banco de Información Económica.

Life expectancy refers to men and women (except for 1985 and 2005).

n.a. = not available.

[a] Population age 10 and older.

[b] Age 15 and older.

[e] Age 6 and older.

[c] 1900.

[d] 1895–1910.

[f] 2004.

Table A.4 Mexico: Structure of GDP (percent)

	1895[a]	1910[a]	1926[a]	1940[a]	1970[a]	1970[b]	1981[b]	1981[c]	2007[c]
Agriculture[d]	29.1	24.0	19.7	19.4	11.6	11.2	8.0	7.0	5.4
Mining	3.0	4.9	9.3	6.4	4.8	2.6	3.4	1.5	1.3
Industry[e]	9.0	12.3	14.7	18.7	29.7	30.0	29.4	26.2	25.2
Manufacturing	7.9	10.7	11.6	15.4	23.3	23.0	21.6	18.9	19.1
Services	58.9	58.7	56.3	55.5	53.9	56.2	59.2	65.3	68.1
Total	100.0	100.0	100.0	100.0	100.0	100.0	100.0	100.0	100.0

Source: INEGI (1985, 1999a), Banco de Información Económica.

[a] Based on 1960 prices.
[b] Based on 1980 prices.
[c] Based on 1993 prices (percentages of gross value added at basic prices).
[d] Includes livestock, forestry, and fishing.
[e] Includes manufacturing, construction, and electricity, gas, and water.

Table A.5 Mexico: Composition of the economically active population (percent of total)

	Primary sector	Secondary sector	Tertiary sector
1895	67.0	15.6	17.4
1910	68.0	15.2	16.8
1940	67.3	13.1	19.6
1970	41.8	24.4	33.8
1980	36.5	29.2	34.3
2000	16.3	28.7	55.0
2007	13.6	25.7	60.7[a]

Source: INEGI (1999a), INEGI, Banco de Información Económica.
[a] Includes unspecified activities.

Table A.6 Mexico: Sources of industrial growth (percent)

	Domestic demand	Export expansion	Import substitution
1929–1939	56.4	4.3	36.9
1940–1945	29.6	78.9	−8.5
1945–1950	130.2	−54.0	25.5
1950–1958	92.5	2.9	1.7
1960–1970	87.4	2.3	10.3
1970–1974	102.2	2.5	−4.7
1974–1980	105.0	2.2	−7.2
1980–1989	−54.9	154.1	0.8

Source: Cárdenas (1987), table 5.1; Cárdenas (1994), tables IV.8 and V.3; Ros (1994c), table 6.4.
The sum of the three sources of growth may not equal 100 due to changes in the structure of demand.

Table A.7 Mexico: Poverty and inequality

Year	Number of poor (millions)	Poverty rate (percent)	Gini coefficient
1950	16.7	61.8	0.52
1956	20.7	64.3	0.52
1958	20.9	61.0	0.53
1963	18.5	45.6	0.57
1968	11.6	24.3	0.54
1977	15.7	25.0	0.49
1984	16.9	22.5	0.43
1989	19.0	22.7	0.47
1992	20.0	21.4	0.48
1994	19.4	21.2	0.48
1996	35.3	37.4	0.45
1998	33.2	33.3	0.48
2000	24.3	24.1	0.48
2002	20.9	20.0	0.45
2004	18.3	17.4	0.46

Source: CONEVAL (2005).
Poverty is estimated using a nutrition-based poverty line.

Table A.8 GDP in eight Latin American countries (index 1926 = 100)

	Venezuela	Colombia	Peru	Brazil	Chile	Argentina	Uruguay	Mexico
1926	100.0	100.0	100.0	100.0	100.0	100.0	100.0	100.0
1927	112.2	109.0	101.8	107.3	98.2	107.1	114.4	95.6
1928	125.6	117.0	108.3	119.6	120.3	114.1	120.4	96.2
1929	142.5	121.2	119.7	119.9	126.6	119.0	121.4	92.5
1930	145.0	120.2	105.9	112.7	106.3	114.1	138.0	86.7
1931	117.2	119.4	97.4	110.2	83.7	106.1	114.2	89.6
1932	112.3	126.1	93.6	114.1	70.8	102.7	106.0	76.2
1933	122.8	133.2	104.2	123.0	87.2	107.4	92.7	84.8
1934	131.1	130.4	118.3	133.2	105.3	116.0	110.4	90.5
1935	140.6	145.0	129.4	136.9	111.3	121.1	116.9	97.3
1936	154.4	152.7	135.6	150.0	116.8	121.9	122.4	105.0
1937	177.2	155.1	137.4	154.9	132.8	130.8	124.6	108.5
1938	191.5	165.2	139.6	161.4	134.3	131.4	134.4	110.3
1939	203.2	175.3	140.3	163.0	137.1	136.3	134.5	116.2
1940	195.3	179.1	143.0	164.6	142.6	138.6	134.8	117.8

Source: Based on Maddison (2006).

GDP levels in 1990 international Geary-Khamis dollars were converted into an index (1926 = 100).

Table A.9 Mexico: Macroeconomic performance

	1941	1942	1943	1944	1945
GDP growth rate	9.7	5.6	3.7	7.4	3.1
Inflation[a]	7.3	9.1	20.8	22.4	12.7
Nominal exchange rate[b]	4.9	4.9	4.9	4.9	4.9
Real exchange rate[c]	93.4	96.4	83.6	68.6	62.1
Balance of payments					
Exports (% of GDP)[d]	6.9	6.5	7.3	5.5	5.7
Imports (% of GDP)[d]	9.2	6.7	7.2	9.5	11.0
Terms of trade[c]	78.9	79.8	86.0	86.4	93.5
Change in int. reserves[e]	−1.1	46.0	134.2	37.0	93.2
Public finance (% of GDP)					
Expenditure[f]	7.4	7.8	8.3	7.7	7.6
Income[f]	7.2	7.0	8.4	6.9	6.8
Budget surplus[f]	−0.2	−0.9	0.1	−0.8	−0.8

Source: INEGI (1999a), Oxford Latin American Economics History Database (OxLAD) (for terms of trade), and Fernández Hurtado (1976) (for change in international reserves). Real exchange rate based on U.S. wholesale prices (U.S. Census Bureau, Statistical Abstract of the United States, 1971) and wholesale prices in Mexico City (INEGI, 1999a).

[a] Yearly average increase in the wholesale price index in Mexico City.

[b] Pesos per U.S. dollar.

[c] Index 1940 = 100.

[d] Exports, imports, and GDP are measured at 1970 constant prices.

[e] Millions of dollars.

[f] Federal government.

Table A.10 Mexico: Macroeconomic performance

	1946	1947	1948	1949	1950	1951	1952	1953	1954	1955
GDP growth rate	6.6	3.4	4.1	5.5	9.9	7.7	4.0	2.7	10.0	8.5
Inflation[a]	15.0	5.4	7.2	9.6	9.6	24.0	3.2	-1.9	9.6	13.4
Nominal exchange rate[b]	4.9	4.9	5.7	8.0	8.7	8.7	8.7	8.7	11.3	12.5
Real exchange rate[c]	99.2	115.6	138.1	167.1	171.0	153.6	144.7	145.5	174.5	170.0
Balance of payments										
Exports (% of GDP)[d]	5.5	5.5	5.0	5.4	5.7	5.5	5.5	4.9	5.4	6.3
Imports (% of GDP)[d]	13.8	14.3	11.1	9.4	10.1	12.2	11.4	11.1	10.0	9.8
Terms of trade[c]	98.0	100.1	112.3	102.0	105.3	108.5	107.2	104.8	95.5	88.0
Capital inflows[e]	—	—	—	—	53.1	55.1	35.4	35.2	28.9	163.2
Public finance (% of GDP)										
Expenditure[f]	6.3	6.9	8.4	10.3	8.2	8.6	10.6	9.0	10.7	9.9
Income[f]	7.2	6.6	6.9	10.7	8.6	9.0	10.4	8.3	10.4	10.0
Budget surplus[f]	0.9	-0.3	-1.5	0.4	0.4	0.4	-0.2	-0.8	-0.3	0.2

Source: INEGI (1999a) and Oxford Latin American Economics History Database (OxLAD) (for terms of trade). Real exchange rate based on U.S. wholesale prices (U.S. Census Bureau, Statistical Abstract of the United States, 1971) and wholesale prices in Mexico City (INEGI, 1999a).

[a] Yearly average increase in the wholesale price index in Mexico City.

[b] Pesos per U.S. dollar.

[c] Index 1945 = 100.

[d] Exports, imports, and GDP are measured at 1970 constant prices.

[e] Millions of dollars.

[f] Federal government.

Table A.11 Mexico: Macroeconomic performance

	1956	1957	1958	1959	1960	1961	1962	1963	1964	1965	1966	1967	1968	1969	1970
GDP growth rate	6.8	7.6	5.3	3.0	8.1	4.9	4.7	8.0	11.7	6.5	6.9	6.3	8.1	6.3	6.9
Inflation[a]	5.1	3.9	4.7	0.9	4.9	1.3	1.7	0.4	4.5	2.0	1.2	2.7	2.2	2.5	6.0
Nominal exchange rate[b]	12.5	12.5	12.5	12.5	12.5	12.5	12.5	12.5	12.5	12.5	12.5	12.5	12.5	12.5	12.5
Real exchange rate[c]	98.3	97.3	94.3	93.6	89.4	87.9	86.7	86.1	82.5	82.6	84.3	82.3	82.5	83.6	81.8
Balance of payments															
Exports (% of GDP)[d]	5.8	5.1	5.4	5.6	5.1	5.0	5.4	5.0	4.6	4.7	4.6	4.1	4.0	4.2	3.6
Imports (% of GDP)[d]	10.9	10.6	9.6	8.6	8.4	7.4	6.5	6.6	6.6	6.5	6.1	6.1	6.4	6.3	7.0
Terms of trade[c]	101.2	93.9	84.0	82.8	75.4	74.4	69.7	73.5	70.0	68.9	71.8	70.6	74.8	73.4	80.1
Public finance (% of GDP)															
Expenditure[e]	10.0	9.6	9.1	10.1	12.6	11.8	10.8	9.8	11.5	23.9	22.2	24.4	23.2	24.6	24.6
Income[e]	9.9	9.2	10.0	10.1	12.2	11.5	10.9	9.5	11.7	24.0	22.4	24.4	23.7	24.5	24.6
Budget surplus[e]	-0.1	-0.4	0.9	0.0	-0.4	-0.2	0.1	-0.3	0.2	0.1	0.2	0.0	0.5	-0.1	0.0

Source: INEGI (1999a) and Oxford Latin American Economics History Database (OxLAD) (for terms of trade). Real exchange rate based on U.S. wholesale prices (U.S. Census Bureau, Statistical Abstract of the United States, 1971) and wholesale prices in Mexico City (INEGI, 1999a).

[a] Yearly average increase in the wholesale price index in Mexico City.
[b] Pesos per U.S. dollar.
[c] Index 1955 = 100.
[d] Exports, imports, and GDP are measured at 1970 constant prices.
[e] Data from 1965 onward are not comparable to the previous period.

Table A.12 Mexico: Macroeconomic performance

	1971	1972	1973	1974	1975	1976	1977	1978	1979	1980	1981	1982	1983
GDP growth rate	4.2	8.5	8.4	6.1	5.6	4.2	3.4	8.2	9.2	8.3	7.9	−0.5	−5.3
Inflation[a]	5.3	5.0	12.0	23.8	15.2	15.8	28.9	17.5	18.2	26.2	28.1	58.9	101.9
Nominal exchange rate[b]	12.5	12.5	12.5	12.5	12.5	15.7	22.7	22.8	22.8	23.0	24.5	57.2	150.3
Real exchange rate[c]	99.2	97.5	92.4	82.9	78.6	90.1	107.6	98.8	93.3	84.4	77.6	121.0	162.7
Terms of trade[d]	98.6	98.3	101.1	98.2	106.6	136.9	222.5	214.4	239.0	296.9	288.6	262.3	236.4
Real wage[e]	100.7	111.8	112.5	119.5	126.0	141.0	136.4	137.9	145.2	144.2	150.2	146.6	107.8
Wage share in GDP (%)	35.5	36.9	35.9	36.7	38.1	40.3	38.9	37.9	37.7	36.1	37.4	35.8	28.8
Composition of GDP (%)													
Private consumption	72.6	71.5	70.3	69.7	69.7	69.9	69.0	68.9	68.7	68.2	67.9	69.0	67.3
Public consumption	7.7	8.1	8.2	8.2	8.9	9.0	8.6	8.8	8.8	8.9	9.1	9.3	9.7
Fixed private investment	14.0	13.2	12.5	13.2	12.7	12.9	11.7	11.3	12.7	13.4	14.1	11.7	9.4
Fixed public investment	4.9	6.3	8.1	7.8	9.0	8.0	7.2	8.7	9.4	10.1	10.8	9.3	6.6
Change in inventories	1.9	1.7	1.9	3.9	3.0	2.3	3.5	3.0	2.8	4.6	5.1	0.5	1.0
Exports	7.7	8.3	8.7	8.2	7.1	7.9	8.8	9.1	9.3	9.1	9.0	10.2	12.1
Imports	8.8	9.0	9.7	11.0	10.4	10.1	8.8	9.9	11.7	14.3	15.9	10.1	6.2

Source: INEGI, Cuentas Nacionales de México; INEGI (1999a); Oxford Latin American Economics History Database (OxLAD) (for terms of trade); Council of Economic Advisors, Economic Report of the President (for U.S. consumer prices).

GDP and its components are at 1970 prices (INEGI, Cuentas Nacionales de México).

[a] Consumer price index (yearly average).

[b] Pesos per U.S. dollar.

[c] Using consumer price index in United States and Mexico. Index 1970 = 100.

[d] Index 1970 = 100.

[e] Yearly average wage (whole economy) reduced by consumer price index (INEGI, Cuentas Nacionales de México and INEGI, 1999a). Index 1970 = 100.

Table A.13 Mexico: Public finance (percent of GDP), consolidated public sector

	1971	1972	1973	1974	1975	1976	1977	1978	1979	1980	1981	1982	1983
Revenues	18.4	18.7	20.2	21.1	23.2	23.8	24.6	25.9	26.7	26.9	26.7	28.9	32.9
Oil revenues	3.0	2.8	2.6	3.4	3.3	3.3	3.8	4.5	5.6	7.3	7.3	9.9	14.2
Non oil revenues	15.4	15.9	17.6	17.7	19.9	20.5	20.8	21.4	21.1	19.6	19.4	19.0	18.7
Expenditures	20.5	22.9	25.8	27.0	31.9	32.0	30.0	31.4	33.0	33.5	39.7	44.5	41.0
Current[a]	14.6	15.4	17.0	17.9	21.0	20.7	19.3	19.5	19.5	19.8	21.4	25.1	20.7
Capital	4.3	5.7	7.0	7.2	8.6	8.0	7.6	8.7	9.8	9.6	12.9	10.2	7.5
Interest	1.6	1.8	1.8	1.9	2.3	3.3	3.1	3.2	3.7	4.1	5.4	9.2	12.8
Primary deficit	0.5	2.4	3.8	4.0	6.4	4.9	2.3	2.3	2.6	2.5	7.6	6.4	−4.7
Financial deficit[b]	2.5	4.9	6.9	7.2	10.0	9.9	6.7	6.7	7.6	7.5	14.1	16.9	8.6

Source: Bazdresch and Levy (1991), based on Dirección General de Planeación Hacendaria, SHCP (for 1971–1976) and Indicadores Económicos, Banco de México (for 1977–1983).

[a] Excluding interest payments.

[b] Includes financial intermediation expenditures so that it is not equal to the difference between total expenditures and total revenues.

Table A.14 Mexico: Trade and the balance of payments (billions of dollars)

	1971	1972	1973	1974	1975	1976	1977	1978	1979	1980	1981	1982	1983
Exports (goods and services)	3.4	4.2	5.2	6.5	6.8	8.0	8.7	11.2	15.3	23.6	29.1	27.2	27.2
Goods	1.4	1.7	2.1	2.9	3.1	3.7	4.6	6.1	8.8	15.1	19.4	21.2	22.3
Services[a]	2.0	2.5	3.1	3.6	3.7	4.3	4.1	5.1	6.5	8.5	9.7	6.0	4.9
Imports (goods and services)	3.9	4.7	6.1	8.8	9.9	9.9	8.6	11.5	17.1	26.2	34.3	21.8	12.8
Goods	2.3	2.8	3.9	6.1	6.7	6.3	5.7	7.9	12.0	18.8	23.9	14.4	8.6
Services[b]	1.6	1.9	2.2	2.7	3.2	3.6	2.9	3.6	5.1	7.4	10.4	7.4	4.2
Trade balance	-0.5	-0.5	-0.9	-2.3	-3.1	-1.9	0.1	-0.3	-1.8	-2.6	-5.2	5.4	14.4
Income from abroad	-0.5	-0.5	-0.6	-0.8	-1.3	-1.7	-1.8	-2.2	-3.1	-4.6	-7.3	-10.3	-9.1
Current account balance	-0.9	-1.0	-1.5	-3.2	-4.4	-3.7	-1.6	-2.7	-4.9	-7.2	-12.5	-4.9	5.3
Long-term capital balance	0.7	0.8	1.9	2.8	4.4	4.7	4.3	4.7	4.6	6.8	11.7	10.4	7.3
Short-term capital balance	0.2	-0.4	0.2	1.0	1.1	0.4	-2.0	-1.4	-0.1	5.1	10.2	-1.8	-8.4
Errors and omissions	0.2	0.8	-0.4	-0.6	-0.9	-2.4	0.0	-0.1	0.7	-3.6	-8.4	-8.4	-0.9
Bank of Mexico[c]	0.2	0.3	0.1	0.0	0.2	-1.0	0.6	0.4	0.5	1.3	1.1	-4.7	3.3

Source: INEGI (1999a).

[a] Includes nonmonetary gold and silver.
[b] Includes nonmonetary gold.
[c] Includes special drawing rights (SDRs).

Table A.15 Mexico: Composition of fixed investment

	Public	Private	Residential construction	Nonresidential construction	Machinery and equipment
1980	43.0	57.0	17.9	38.2	43.9
1981	45.4	54.6	16.7	38.2	45.1
1982	44.2	55.8	20.3	41.5	38.2
1983	39.5	60.5	26.7	40.1	33.2
1984	38.6	61.4	26.3	38.9	34.8
1985	36.1	63.9	26.4	36.2	37.4
1986	35.1	64.9	29.4	34.5	36.1
1987	30.8	69.2	30.8	34.4	34.8
1988	25.0	75.0	25.0	27.5	47.5
1989	25.3	74.7	25.2	25.7	49.1
1990	24.9	75.1	24.2	26.0	49.8
1991	22.6	77.4	24.3	24.9	50.8
1992	19.7	80.3	23.6	25.3	51.1
1993	20.3	79.7	26.7	27.0	46.3
1994	25.7	74.3	26.2	27.9	45.9
1995	24.8	75.2	29.6	23.0	47.4
1996	18.2	81.8	26.0	24.2	49.8
1997	16.5	83.5	23.4	25.4	51.2
1998	13.9	86.1	22.2	24.8	53.0
1999	14.3	85.7	22.2	25.6	52.2
2000	16.1	83.9	22.3	27.0	50.7
2001	16.3	83.7	23.7	27.8	48.5
2002	19.2	80.8	24.2	29.4	46.4
2003	20.7	79.3	24.3	30.8	44.9
2004	19.8	80.2	23.9	31.7	44.4
2005	18.3	81.7	n.a.	n.a.	n.a.
2006	17.1	82.9	n.a.	n.a.	n.a.
2007	17.2	82.8	n.a.	n.a.	n.a.

Source: For public/private composition, based on INEGI, Banco de Información Económica, at constant prices of 1993. For residential/nonresidential composition: Hofman (2000) for 1980–1987 (based on 1980 constant pesos); INEGI, Banco de Información Económica, for 1988–2004 (based on current prices).

Percentages of total fixed investment.

n.a. = not available.

Table A.16 Mexico: Macroeconomic performance, 1990–2000

	1990	1991	1992	1993	1994	1995	1996	1997	1998	1999	2000
GDP growth rate	5.1	4.2	3.6	2.0	4.5	-6.2	5.1	6.8	4.9	3.9	6.6
Inflation[a]	29.9	18.8	11.9	8.0	7.1	52.0	27.7	15.7	18.6	12.3	9.0
Nominal exchange rate[b]	2.8	3.0	3.1	3.1	3.4	6.4	7.6	7.9	9.1	9.6	9.5
Real exchange rate[c]	127.0	115.8	105.9	100.0	103.9	150.5	136.5	120.6	121.9	111.8	104.4
Terms of trade[c]	115.7	105.9	105.0	100.0	105.3	105.5	106.8	105.1	99.6	104.2	109.0
Real wage[d]	111.7	105.0	101.2	100.0	99.7	85.6	77.8	77.2	77.7	75.0	75.6
Wage share in GDP (%)	29.7	31.0	32.9	34.7	35.3	31.0	28.8	29.6	30.6	31.2	31.3
Composition of GDP (%)[e]											
Private consumption	71.2	71.5	72.2	71.9	72.0	69.5	67.5	67.3	67.7	67.9	68.9
Public consumption	11.0	11.2	11.0	11.0	10.9	11.4	10.8	10.4	10.1	10.2	9.8
Fixed private investment	12.8	14.1	15.6	14.8	14.3	11.0	13.2	15.3	16.6	17.1	17.5
Fixed public investment	4.2	4.1	3.8	3.8	4.9	3.6	2.9	3.0	2.7	2.8	3.3
Change in inventories	1.7	1.6	2.2	2.4	3.0	0.8	2.3	3.2	3.3	2.8	3.0
Exports (goods and services)	14.1	14.2	14.4	15.2	17.2	23.9	26.8	27.8	29.8	32.2	35.1
Imports (goods and services)	15.0	16.6	19.2	19.2	22.3	20.2	23.6	27.1	30.1	33.1	37.7

Source: INEGI, Banco de Información Económica; Banco de México, Estadísticas.

[a] Consumer price index (Dec–Dec).
[b] Pesos per U.S. dollar (year average).
[c] Index 1993 = 100. The real exchange rate refers to the multilateral exchange rate.
[d] Average wage (whole economy) deflated by consumer price index. Index 1993 = 100.
[e] GDP and its components are at 1993 prices.

Table A.17 Public finance (% of GDP) 1990–2000

	1990	1991	1992	1993	1994	1995	1996	1997	1998	1999	2000
Income	25.3	26.6	26.3	23.1	23.1	22.8	23.0	23.0	20.3	20.8	21.6
Oil revenues	7.7	6.7	6.4	6.1	6.0	7.6	8.2	7.8	6.1	6.2	7.2
Nonoil revenues	17.6	20.0	19.9	17.1	17.1	15.2	14.8	15.2	14.3	14.6	14.5
Expenditure	27.5	23.8	22.2	22.5	23.1	22.9	23.1	23.6	21.6	21.9	22.7
Current	11.6	11.5	11.6	13.0	13.5	12.1	12.0	12.8	12.4	12.5	13.0
Capital	3.7	3.7	3.7	3.1	3.7	3.2	3.7	3.5	3.1	2.8	2.7
Interest	9.1	5.1	3.6	2.7	2.3	4.6	4.4	4.1	2.9	3.6	3.7
Other	3.2	3.6	3.3	3.7	3.6	3.0	3.1	3.3	3.2	3.1	3.4
Fiscal Balance	−2.2	2.8	4.1	0.7	0.0	−0.2	−0.1	−0.6	−1.2	−1.1	−1.1
Primary balance	7.2	8.0	7.8	3.3	2.4	4.7	4.3	3.5	1.7	2.5	3.6

Source: Secretaría de Hacienda y Crédito Público (SHCP) (http://www.shcp.gob.mx).

Table A.18 Mexico: Macroeconomic performance, 2001–2007

	2001	2002	2003	2004	2005	2006	2007
GDP growth rate	−0.2	0.8	1.4	4.2	2.8	4.8	3.3
Inflation[a]	4.4	5.7	4.0	5.2	3.3	4.1	3.8
Nominal exchange rate[b]	9.3	9.7	10.8	11.3	10.9	10.9	10.9
Real exchange rate[c]	99.8	99.7	109.0	111.8	107.4	107.0	106.1
Terms of trade[c]	106.0	108.9	111.6	118.1	121.7	125.2	124.7
Real waged[d]	76.0	76.9	77.5	76.4	76.4	76.3	75.8
Wage share in GDP (%)	32.5	32.5	31.7	30.4	32.6	32.2	32.3
Composition of GDP (%)[e]							
Private consumption	70.8	71.3	71.9	71.8	73.5	73.6	74.2
Public consumption	9.6	9.5	9.5	9.1	8.8	8.9	8.7
Fixed private investment	16.5	15.7	15.2	15.9	17.0	18.1	18.6
Fixed public investment	3.2	3.7	4.0	3.9	3.8	3.7	3.9
Change in inventories	3.1	3.0	1.9	2.0	0.3	−0.3	−0.2
Exports (goods and services)	33.9	34.1	34.6	37.0	38.6	40.9	41.8
Imports (goods and services)	37.1	37.3	37.1	39.8	42.0	44.8	47.0

Source: INEGI, Banco de Información Económica; Banco de México, Estadísticas.

[a] Consumer price index (Dec–Dec).

[b] Pesos per U.S. dollar (year average).

[c] Index 1993 = 100. The real exchange rate refers to the multilateral exchange rate.

[d] Average wage (whole economy) deflated by consumer price index. Index 1993 = 100.

[e] GDP and its components are at 1993 prices.

Table A.19   Public finance (% of GDP) 2001–2007

	2001	2002	2003	2004	2005	2006	2007
Income	21.9	22.1	23.2	23.0	23.3	24.7	25.5
Oil revenues	6.7	6.5	7.7	8.3	8.7	9.4	9.0
Nonoil revenues	15.2	15.6	15.5	14.7	14.6	15.3	16.4
Expenditure	22.6	23.3	23.9	23.2	23.4	24.6	25.4
Current	13.3	13.8	14.6	13.5	14.0	14.4	15.3
Capital	2.6	3.2	3.0	3.5	3.4	3.7	4.1
Interest	3.2	2.8	2.8	2.7	2.5	2.7	2.4
Other	3.4	3.5	3.5	3.5	3.5	3.8	3.6
Fiscal balance	−0.7	−1.2	−0.7	−0.3	−0.1	0.1	0.0
Primary balance	2.6	1.7	2.1	2.5	2.4	2.8	2.5

Source: Secretaría de Hacienda y Crédito Público (SHCP) (http://www.shcp.gob.mx).

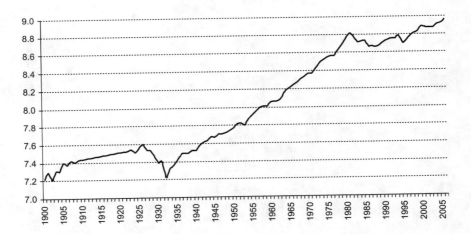

Figure A.1 Mexico's per capita GDP, 1900–2006 (Natural logarithm of per capita GDP in 1990 Geary-Khamis dollars)
Source: Based on Maddison (2006).

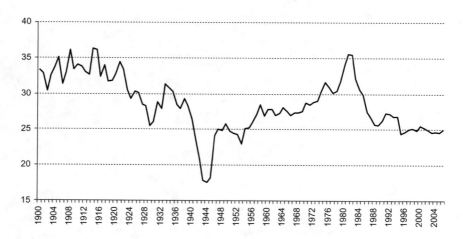

Figure A.2 Mexico's per capita GDP as percent of U.S. per capita GDP, 1900–2006
Source: Based on Maddison (2006).

References

Acemoglu, D., S. Johnson, and J. Robinson. 2002. Reversal of fortune: Geography and institutions in the making of the modern world income distribution. *Quarterly Journal of Economics* 107(4):1231–1294.

Aghion, P., R. Barro, and I. Marinescu. 2006. Cyclical budgetary policies: Their determinants and effects on growth. Mimeo, Harvard University.

Aghion, P., and I. Marinescu. 2006. Cyclical budgetary policy and economic growth: What do we learn from OECD panel data? Mimeo, Harvard University.

Aguilar, G. 1947. *Los Presupuestos Mexicanos desde los Tiempos de la Colonia hasta Nuestros Días*, 2nd ed. Mexico City: Secretaría de Hacienda.

Alberro, J. L., and D. Ibarra., eds. 1987. Programas heterodoxos de estabilización, en *Estudios Económicos*. ITAM, núm. extraordinario, Oct. 1987.

Allen, R., J. Bassino, D. Ma, C. Moll-Murata, and J. Zanden. 2005. Wages, prices, and living standards in China, Japan and Europe, 1738–1925. http://www.iisg.nl/reasearch/jvz-wages-prices.pdf.

Aschauer, D. 2000. Public capital and economic growth: Issues in quantity, finance and efficiency. *Economic Development and Cultural Change* 48:391–406.

Asociación Mexicana de Historia Económica. http://www.amhe.org.mx.

Aspe, P., and J. Beristain. 1984. The evolution of income distribution policies during the post-revolutionary period in Mexico. In P. Aspe and P. Sigmund, eds., *The Political Economy of Income Distribution in Mexico*. New York: Holmes and Meir.

Avalos, M. 2006. Condiciones generales de competencia: el caso de México. Serie estudios y perspectivas, No 48. Mexico City: CEPAL.

Aw, B., S. Chang, and M. Roberts. 2000. Productivity and turnover in the export market: Micro-level evidence from the Republic of Korea and Taiwan (China). *World Bank Economic Review* 14(1):65–90.

Bacha, E. 1984. Growth with limited supplies of foreign exchange: A reappraisal of the two-gap model. In M. Syrquin, L. Taylor, and L. Westphal, eds., *Economic Structure and Performance: Essays in Honor of Hollis B. Chenery*. New York: Academic Press.

Bacha, E. 1990. A three-gap model of foreign transfers and the GDP growth rate in developing countries. *Journal of Development Economics* 32(2):279–296.

Balassa, B., et al. 1971. *The Structure of Protection in Developing Countries*. Baltimore: Johns Hopkins University Press.

Balassa, B. 1985. Trade policy in Mexico. In R. Dávila and A. Violante, eds., *México, una Economía en Transición*. Mexico City: Limusa.

Banco de México. Estadísticas. http://www.banxico.org.mx.

Banco de México (several issues). *Informe Anual*. Mexico City: Banco de México.

Banco de México. 1988. *Informe Anual 1987*. Mexico City: Banco de México.

Barker, T., and V. Brailovsky, eds. 1982. *Oil or Industry?* New York: Academic Press.

Batiz, J. A., and E. Canudas. 1980. Aspectos financieros y monetarios (1880–1910). In Ciro Cardoso, ed., *México en el Siglo XIX (1821–1910). Historia Económica y de la Estructura Social*. Mexico City: Editorial Nueva Imagen.

Bazant, J. 1968. *Historia de la Deuda Exterior de México (1823–1946)*. Mexico City: El Colegio de México.

Bazant, J. 1977. *Los bienes de la iglesia en México 1856–1875: Aspectos Económicos y Sociales de la Revolución Liberal*. Mexico City: El Colegio de México, Centro de Estudios Historicos.

Bazdresch, C., and S. Levy. 1991. Populism and economic policy in Mexico, 1970–1982. In R. Dornbusch and S. Edwards, eds., *The Macroeconomics of Populism in Latin America*. Chicago: University of Chicago Press.

Bazdresch, C., and D. Mayer. 2006. Hacia un consenso para el crecimiento económico de México. *Economia UNAM* 3(8):39–56.

Beato, G. 2004. De la independencia a la revolución. In *Historia Económica de México*. Mexico City: Universidad Nacional Autónoma de México and Editorial Océano.

Beatty, E. 2000. The impact of foreign trade on the Mexican economy: Terms of trade and the rise of industry, 1880–1923. *Journal of Latin American Studies* 32(2):399–433.

Beatty, E. 2001. *Institutions and Investment: The Political Basis of Industrialization in México before 1911*. Stanford, CA: Stanford University Press.

Beatty, E. 2002. Commercial policy in Porfirian Mexico: the structure of protection. In J. L. Bortz and S. Haber, eds., *The Mexican Economy, 1870–1930: Essays on the Economic History of Institutions, Revolution, and Growth*. Stanford, CA: Stanford University Press.

Behrman, J., P. Sengupta, and P. Todd. 2002. Progressing through PROGRESA: An impact assessment of a school subsidy experiment. Presented at the first meeting of the Social Policy Monitoring Network, "Conditional Cash Transfers Programs," Research Department, Inter-American Development Bank.

Bénabou, R. 1996. Inequality and growth. In B. S. Bernanke and J. Rotemberg, eds., *NBER Macroeconomics Annual*. Cambridge, MA: MIT Press.

Bensusán, G. 2006. Diseño legal y desempeño real: México. In G. Bensusán (coord.), *Diseño legal y desempeño real: instituciones laborales en América Latina*. México City: UAM-X and Miguel Angel Porrúa.

Bergoeing, R., P. Kehoe, T. Kehoe, and R. Soto. 2002. A decade lost and found: Mexico and Chile in the 1980s. *Review of Economic Dynamics* 5(1):166–205.

Bergsman, J. 1974. Commercial policy, allocative efficiency and X-efficiency. *Quarterly Journal of Economics* 88(3):409–433.

Bernard, A., and J. Jensen. 1995. Exporters, jobs, and wages in US manufacturing, 1976–1987. *Brookings Papers on Economic Activity: Microeconomics* 1995:67–112.

Bernard, A., and J. Jensen. 1998. Exporting and productivity. Paper presented at the 1998 Summer Institute, NBER, Cambridge, MA, August 1998.

Birdsall, N., D. Ross, and R. Sabot. 1995. Inequality and growth reconsidered: Lessons from East Asia. *World Bank Economic Review* 9:477–508.

Blanco, M., and M. E. Romero Sotelo. 2000. *Tres Siglos de Economía Novohispana*. Mexico City: Universidad Nacional Autónoma de México Editorial JUS.

Blanco, M., and M. E. Romero Sotelo. 2004. La Colonia. In E. Semo, ed., *Historia Económica de México*, vol. 2. Mexico City: Universidad Nacional Autónoma de México and Editorial Océano.

Blecker, R. 2003. The North American economies after NAFTA: A critical appraisal, *International Journal of Political Economy* 33(3):5–27.

Blejer, M., and A. Cheasty. 1991. The measurement of fiscal deficits: Analytical and methodological issues. *Journal of Economic Literature* 29(4):1644–1678.

Boltvinik, J., and E. Hernández Laos. 1981. Origen de la crisis industrial: El agotamiento del modelo de sustitución de importaciones. Un análisis preliminar. In R. Cordera, ed., *Desarrollo y Crisis de la Economía Mexicana: Ensayos de Interpretación Histórica*. Mexico City: Fondo de Cultura Económica.

Bortz, J. 2000. The revolution, the labour regime and conditions of work in the cotton textile industry in Mexico, 1910–1927. *Journal of Latin American Studies* 32:671–703.

Bortz, J., and S. Haber, eds. 2002. *The Mexican Economy, 1870–1930: Essays on the Economic History of Institutions, Revolution, and Growth*. Stanford, CA: Stanford University Press.

Bosworth, B. 1998. Productivity growth in Mexico. Background paper prepared for a World Bank project on productivity growth in Mexico, "Mexico: Enhancing Factor Productivity growth," Report no. 17392-ME, Country Economic Memorandum, August 1998.

Brading, D. 1971. *Miners and Merchants in Bourbon Mexico, 1763–1810*. Cambridge: Cambridge University Press.

Brading, D. 1978. *Haciendas and Ranchos in the Mexican Bajío*. Cambridge: Cambridge University Press.

Brothers, D., and L. Solís. 1966. *Mexican Financial Development*. Austin: University of Texas Press.

Brown, J. 1993. *Oil and Revolution in Mexico*. Berkeley: University of California Press.

Bueno, G. 1971. The structure of protection in Mexico. In B. Balassa et al., eds., *The Structure of Protection in Developing Countries*. Baltimore: Johns Hopkins University Press.

Buffie, E. 1989. Mexico, 1958–86: From stabilizing development to the debt crisis. In J. Sachs, ed., *Developing Country Debt and the World Economy*. Chicago: University of Chicago Press.

Bulmer-Thomas, V. 2003. *The Economic History of Latin America since Independence*. Cambridge: Cambridge University Press.

Bulnes, F. 1952. *El Verdadero Díaz y la Revolución*. Mexico City: Editorial Nacional S.A.

Cabrera, C. J. 2007. Pobreza y Desigualdad. *Economía Informa*, No. 343, Nov.–Dec., Facultad de Economía, Universidad Nacional Autónoma de México.

Calderón, C., and L. Servén. 2004. Trends in infrastructure in Latin America, 1980–2001. World Bank Policy Research Working Paper 3401, World Bank, Washington, DC.

Calderón, F. 1965. Los ferrocarriles. In D. Cosío Villegas, ed., *Historia Moderna de México. El Porfiriato. Vida Económica. Primera parte*. Mexico City: Hermes.

Camacho, M. 1977. Los nudos históricos del sistema político mexicano. In L. Meyer et al., eds., *Las Crisis en el Sistema Político Mexicano*. Mexico City: El Colegio de México.

Cañonero, G., and A. Werner. 2002. Salarios relativos y liberación del comercio en México. *El Trimestre Económico* 69273, 123–142.

Cárdenas, E. 1982. Mexico's industrialization during the great depression: Public policy and private response. Ph.D. dissertation, Yale University.

Cárdenas, E. 1984. The Great Depression and industrialization: The case of Mexico. In R. Thorp, ed., *Latin America in the 1930s: The Role of the Periphery in World Crisis*. New York: St. Martin's Press.

Cárdenas, E. 1985. Algunas Cuestiones Sobre la Depresión Mexicana del Siglo XIX. *Revista Latinoamericana de Historia Económica y Social* (3):3–22.

Cárdenas, E. 1987. La industrialización mexicana durante la gran depresión. Mexico City: El Colegio de México.

Cárdenas, E. 1990. Contemporary economic problems in historical perspective. In D. S. Brothers and A. Wick, eds., *Mexico's Search for a New Development Strategy*. Boulder, CO: Westview Press.

Cárdenas, E. 1993. La política económica en la época de Cárdenas. *Trimestre Económico* 60(3):675–697.

Cárdenas, E. 1994. *La hacienda pública y la política económica, 1929–1958*. Mexico City: Fondo de Cultura Económica.

Cárdenas, E. 1996. *La política económica en México, 1950–1994*. Mexico City: Fondo de Cultura Económica.

Cárdenas, E. 1997. A macroeconomic interpretation of nineteenth century Mexico. In S. Haber, ed., *How Latin America Fell Behind*. Stanford, CA: Stanford University Press.

Cárdenas, E. 2000. The process of accelerated industrialization in Mexico, 1929–1982. In E. Cárdenas, J. A. Ocampo, and R. Thorp, eds., *An Economic History of Twentieth-Century Latin America*, vol. 3. New York: Palgrave.

Cárdenas, E. 2003. *Cuando se originó el atraso económico de México. La economía mexicana en el largo siglo XIX, 1780–1920*. Madrid: Editorial Biblioteca Nueva.

Cárdenas, E., and C. Manns. 1987. Inflation and monetary stabilization in Mexico during the revolution. *Journal of Development Economics* 27:375–394.

Cárdenas, E., J. A. Ocampo, and R. Thorp, eds. 2000. *An Economic History of Twentieth-Century Latin America*, vol. 3. New York: Palgrave.

Carmagnani, M. 1983.Finanzas y Estado en México, 1820–1880. *Ibero Amerikanisches Archiv*, NE 19, H3/4.

Carmagnani, M. 1994. *Estado y Mercado: La Política Pública del Liberalismo Mexicano, 1850–1911*. Fideicomiso Historia de las Américas, Fondo de Cultura Económica, and Colegio de México.

Carreras de Velasco, M. 1974. *Los mexicanos que devolvió la crisis, 1929–1932*. Mexico City: Secretaría de Relaciones Exteriores.

Casar, J., and J. Ros. 2004, ¿Porqué no crecemos?, *Nexos*, October (322):57–64.

Catao, L. 1991. The international transmission of long cycles between "core" and "periphery" economies: A case study of Brazil and Mexico, c. 1870–1940. Ph.D. dissertation, University of Cambridge.

Catao, L. 1998. Mexico and export-led growth: The Porfirian period revisited. *Cambridge Journal of Economics* 22(1):59–78.

Cavazos, M. 1976. Cincuenta años de política monetaria. In E. Fernández Hurtado, *Cincuenta Años de Banca Central*, Lecturas del Trimestre Económico, Fondo de Cultura Económica.

CELADE. 1998. Boletín Demográfico n. 69. América Latina y el Caribe: Estimaciones y Proyecciones de Población. 1950–2050. Available at eclac.org.

CEPAL. 1979. *Principales Rasgos del Proceso de Industrialización y de la Política Industrial de México en la Década de los Setenta*, CEPAL/MEX/1011/Rev. 1.

CEPAL. Anuario Estadístico 2004. Santiago de Chile: CEPAL.

CEPAL-NAFINSA. 1971. *La Política Industrial en el Desarrollo Económico de México*. Mexico City: Nacional Financiera, S.A.

Chavez Orozco, L. 1938. *Historia Económica y Social de México. Ensayo de interpretación*. Mexico City: Ediciones Botas.

Chenery, H. 1960. Patterns of industrial growth. *American Economic Review* 50(4):624–654.

Chenery, H., S. Robinson, and M. Syrquin. 1986. *Industrialization and Growth: A Comparative Study*. London: Oxford University Press.

Chiquiar, D. 2005. Why Mexico's regional income convergence broke down. *Journal of Development Economics* 77(1):257–275.

Chiquiar, D. 2008. Globalization, regional wage differentials and the Stolper-Samuelson theorem: Evidence from Mexico, *Journal of International Economics* 74(1):70–93.

Chong, A., and F. Lopéz de Silanes. 1994a. Privatization in Latin America. *Economia* 4(2):37–111.

Chong, A., and F. Lopéz de Silanes. 1994b. Privatization in Mexico. In A. Chong and F. Lopéz de Silanes, eds., *The Truth about Privatization in Latin America*. Stanford, CA: Stanford University Press and IABD.

Chong, A., and F. López de Silanes. 2005. Privatization in Mexico. In A. Chong and F. López de Silanes, eds., *Privatization in Latin America: Myths and Reality*. Stanford, CA: Stanford University Press.

Chor, D., and R. Freeman. 2005. The 2004 Global Labor Survey: Workplace institutions and practices around the world, NBER Working Paper No. 11598, National Bureau for Economic Research, Cambridge, MA.

Christensen, L., D. Cummings, and D. Jorgenson. 1980. Economic growth, 1947–73: An international comparison. *Studies in Income and Wealth* 44:595–698.

Clavijo, F. 1980. Reflexiones en torno a la Inflación Mexicana. *El Trimestre Económico* 47(188): 1023–1054.

Clavijo, F., and J. Boltvinik. 2000. La reforma financiera, el crédito y el ahorro. In F. Clavijo, ed., *Reformas Económicas en México 1982–1999*. Lecturas del Trimestre Económico 92. Mexico City: CEPAL, Estrategia y Análisis Económico, Consultores, S.C., Fondo de Cultura Económica.

Clavijo, F., and S. Valdivieso. 1983. La creación de empleos mediante el comercio exterior: el caso de México. *El Trimestre Económico* 50:873–916.

Clerides, S., S. Lach, and J. Tybout. 1998. Is learning by exporting important? Microdynamic evidence from Colombia, Mexico, and Morocco. *Quarterly Journal of Economics* 113(3):903–947.

Cline, H. 1962. *Mexico. Revolution to Evolution, 1940–1960*. London: Oxford University Press.

Coatsworth, J. 1978. Obstacles to economic growth in nineteenth-century Mexico. *American Historical Review* 83(1):80–100.

Coatsworth, J. 1979. Indispensable railroads in a backward economy: The case of Mexico, *Journal of Economic History* 39(4):939–960.

Coatsworth, J. 1982. The limits of colonial absolutism: The state in eighteenth-century Mexico. In K. Spalding, ed., *Essays in the Political, Economic and Social History of Colonial Latin America*. Occasional Papers and Monographs 3. Newark, DE: University of Delaware Latin American Studies Program.

Coatsworth, J. 1985. El Estado y el sector externo en México: 1800–1910. Secuencia No. 2, May–August. Mexico City: Instituto Mora.

Coatsworth, J. 1986. The Mexican mining industry in the eighteenth century. In N. Jacobsen and H. Puhle, eds., *The Economies of Mexico and Peru during the Late Colonial Period, 1760–1810*. Berlin: Colloquium Verlag.

Coatsworth, J. 1989. The decline of the Mexican economy, 1800–1860. In R. Liehr, ed., *América Latina en la Epoca de Simón Bolivar*. Berlin: Colloquium Verlag.

Coatsworth, J. 1990. *Los Orígenes del Atraso. Nueve Ensayos de Historia Económica de México en los Siglos XVIII y XIX*. Mexico City: Alianza Editorial Mexicana.

Coatsworth, J. 1993. Notes on the comparative economic history of Latin America and the United States. In W. L. Bernecker and H. W. Tobler, eds., *Development and Underdevelopment in America: Contrasts in Economic Growth in North America and Latin America in Historical Perspective*. Berlin: Walter de Gruyter.

Coatsworth, J. 1998. Economic and institutional trajectories in nineteenth century Latin America. In J. Coatsworth and A. Taylor, eds., *Latin America and the World Economy since 1800*. Cambridge, MA: Harvard University Press.

Coatsworth, J. H., and G. Tortella. 2002. Institutions and long-run economic performance in Mexico and Spain, 1800–2000, Working Papers on Latin America Series, No. 02/03–1, David Rockefeller Center for Latin American Studies, Harvard University, Cambridge, MA.

Collver, A. 1965. *Birth Rates in Latin America: New Estimates of Historical Trends and Fluctuations*. Berkeley, CA: Institute of International Studies.

Consejo Nacional de Evaluación de la Política de Desarrollo Social (CONEVAL). 2007. *Informe de Pobreza México 2007*. México: CONEVAL.

Cordera, R., and C. Cabrera. 2007a. *El papel de las ideas y las políticas en el cambio estructural en México*. Lecturas No. 99. El Trimestre Económico, Fondo de Cultura Económica.

Cordera, R., and C. Cabrera, ed. 2007b. *La política social en México: tendencias y perspectivas*. Facultad de Economia, Universidad Nacional Autónoma de México.

Cordera, R., and C. Tello. 1981. *La Disputa por la Nacion*. Mexico City: Siglo XXI.

Córdova, A. 1972. *La formación del poder político en México*. Mexico City: Ediciones Era.

Córdova, A. 1973. *La Ideología de la Revolución Mexicana: la formación del nuevo régimen*. Mexico City: Ediciones Era.

Cosío Villegas, D., ed. 1965. *Historia Moderna de México. El Porfiriato*. Mexico City: Editorial Hermes.

Council of Economic Advisors, Economic Report of the President. 2007. Washington, DC: United States Government Printing Office.

Crafts, N. 1994. The industrial revolution. In R. Floud and D. N. McCloskey, eds., *The Economic History of Britain since 1700*. Cambridge: Cambridge University Press.

Cragg, M., and M. Epelbaum. 1996. Why has wage dispersion grown in Mexico? Is it the incidence of reforms or the growing demand for skills? *Journal of Development Economics* 51:99–116.

Cripps, F., and R. Tarling. 1973. *Growth in Advanced Capitalist Economies, 1950–1970*. Cambridge: Cambridge University Press.

Cruz, C., R. de la Torre, and C. Velázquez. 2006. Informe compilatorio. Evaluación externa de impacto del Programa Oportunidades 2001–2006. Cuernavaca, Mexico: Instituto Nacional de Salud Pública.

Dávila, E., G. Kessel, and S. Levy. 2002. El Sur también existe: Un ensayo sobre el desarrollo regional de México. *Economía Mexicana* vol. 11, 202–260.

Davis, B. 2000. The adjustment strategies of Mexican ejidatarios in the face of neoliberal reforms. *CEPAL Review* 72 (December):99–119.

Deans-Smith, S. 1992. *Bureaucrats, Planters and Workers: The Making of the Tobacco Monopoly in Bourbon Mexico*. Austin: University of Texas Press.

de Gregorio, J. 2005. Economic growth in Latin America: From the failure of the 20th century to the hopes of the 21st. Paper prepared for the conference "Democratic Governability in Latin America," University of Notre Dame, October 6–7, 2005.

de Janvry, A., and E. Sadoulet. 2002. Targeting and calibrating educational grants: Focus on poverty or on risk? Presented at the first meeting of the Social Policy Monitoring Network, "Conditional Cash Transfers Programs," Research Department, Inter-American Development Bank.

de Janvry, A., and E. Sadoulet. 2006. Making conditional cash transfer programs more efficient: Designing for maximum effect of the conditionality. *World Bank Economic Review* 20(1):1–29.

de la Peña, S., and T. Aguirre. 2006. De la revolución a la industrialización. In E. Semo, ed., *Historia Económica de México*, vol. 6. Mexico City: Universidad Nacional Autónoma de México and Editorial Oceano.

de Long, B., and L. Summers. 1991. Equipment investment and economic growth. *Quarterly Journal of Economics* 106(2):445–502.

de Mateo, F. 1988. La política comercial de México y el GATT. *El Trimestre Económico* 55(217):175–216.

de Vries, M. 1987. *Balance of Payments Adjustment, 1945 to 1986. The IMF Experience.* Washington, DC: International Monetary Fund.

del Ángel-Mobarak, G., C. Bazdresch, and F. Suárez Dávila. 2005. *Cuando el Estado se hizo banquero. Consecuencias de la Nacionalización Bancaria en México.* Mexico City: Fondo de Cultura Económica, Colección El Trimestre Económico.

Díaz-Alejandro, C. 1984. Latin America in the 1930s. In R. Thorp, ed., *Latin America in the 1930s: The Role of the Periphery in World Crisis.* New York: St. Martin's Press.

Díaz-Alejandro, C. 1988. No less than one hundred years of Argentine economic history plus some comparisons. In A. Velasco, ed., *Trade, Development and the World Economy. Selected Essays of Carlos F. Diaz-Alejandro.* Oxford: Blackwell.

Dobado, R., and G. Marrero. 2006. Mining-led growth in Bourbon Mexico, the role of the state, and the economic cost of independence. Working Papers on Latin America, No. 06/07–1, David Rockefeller Center for Latin American Studies, Harvard University, Cambridge, MA.

Dornbusch, R., and S. Edwards. 1991. *The Macroeconomics of Populism in Latin America.* Chicago: University of Chicago Press.

Dussel, E. 2000a. *Polarizing Mexico. The Impact of Liberalization Strategy.* Boulder, CO: Lynne Rienner.

Dussel, E. 2000b. *El Tratado de Libre Comercio de Norteamerica y el Desempeño de la Economía en México.* LC//MEX/L.431. Mexico City: CEPAL.

Dussel, E. 2003. Ser o no ser maquila, ¿es ésa la pregunta? *Revista de Comercio Exterior* 53(4): 328–336.

Easterly, W., and R. Levine. 2001. It's not factor accumulation: Stylized facts and growth models. *World Bank Economic Review* 15:177–219.

Eatwell, J., and A. Singh. 1981. ¿Está sobrecalentada la economía mexicana? *Economía Mexicana* no. 3, 253–258. Mexico City: Centro de Investigación y Docencia Económicas.

Eckstein, S. 1966. *El Ejido Colectivo en México.* Mexico City: Fondo de Cultura Económica.

ECLAC. 2005. *CAN: análisis de la competitividad de los países, programa computacional para evaluar y describir el medio competitivo internacional.* Santiago, Chile: ECLAC.

ECLAC. 2006a. *Economic Survey of Latin America and the Caribbean 2005–06.* Santiago, Chile: ECLAC.

ECLAC. 2006b. *Competitive Analysis of Nations TradeCAN 2006.* Santiago, Chile: ECLAC.

Edwards, S. 1993. Openness, trade liberalization, and growth in developing countries. *Journal of Economic Literature* 31(3):1358–1393.

Edwards, S. 1995. *Crisis and Reform in Latin America: From Despair to Hope.* Oxford: Oxford University Press.

El Colegio de México. 1960a. *Comercio Exterior de México, 1877–1911.* Mexico City: El Colegio de México.

El Colegio de México. 1960b. *Estadísticas Económicas del Porfiriato.* Mexico City: El Colegio de México.

Elías, V. J. 1978. Sources of economic growth in Latin American countries. *Review of Economics and Statistics* 60(3):362–370.

Engerman, S., and K. Sokoloff. 2002. Factor endowments, inequality, and paths of development among New World economies. *Economia* 3(1):41–88.

Escaith, H. 2006. Can Latin America fly? Revising its engines of growth. Serie Estudios Estadísticos y Prospectivos, No. 45. Santiago, Chile: ECLAC.

Espinosa, A., and E. Cárdenas, eds. 2008. *La Nacionalización Bancaria, 25 Años Después.* Mexico City: Centro de Estudios Espinosa Yglesias.

Esquivel, G. 1999. Convergencia regional en México, 1940–1995. *El Trimestre Económico* 66(264):725–761.

Esquivel, G. 2008. Piloto automático procíclico: El diseño y conducción de la política macroeconómica en México. Paper prepared for the seminar "La Economía Mexicana en el 2010," El Colegio de México, Mexico City.

Esquivel, G., and M. Messmacher. 2002. Sources of regional (non) convergence in Mexico. Office of the Chief Economist for Latin America and the Caribbean, World Bank, Washington, DC.

Esquivel, G., and J. A. Rodríguez-López. 2003. Technology, trade, and wage inequality in Mexico before and after NAFTA. *Journal of Development Economics* 72:543–565.

Estadísticas sociales del Porfiriato. 1877–1910. Secretaría de Economía, Dirección General de Estadística, México, 1956. http://www.inegi.gob.mx/prod_serv/contenidos/espanol/bvinegi/productos/integracion/pais/historicas/porfi/ESPI.pdf.

Faal, E. 2005. GDP growth, potential output, and output gaps in Mexico. IMF Working Paper WP/05/93, International Monetary Fund, Washington, DC.

Feenstra, R. 1990. Trade and uneven growth. NBER Working Paper No. 3276, National Bureau for Economic Research, Cambridge, MA.

Feenstra, R., and G. Hanson. 1997. Foreign direct investment and relative wages: Evidence from Mexico's maquiladoras. *Journal of International Economics* 42(3–4):371–393.

Felipe, J., and J. McCombie. 2006. The tyranny of the identity: growth accounting revisited. *International Review of Applied Economics* 20(3):283–299.

Feliciano, Z. 2001. Workers and trade liberalization: The impact of trade reforms in Mexico on wages and employment. *Industrial and Labor Relations Review* 55(1):95–115.

Fernández Hurtado, E. 1976. *Cincuenta Años de Banca Central.* Lecturas del Trimestre Económico No. 17, Fondo de Cultura Económica.

Fitzgerald, V. 1984. Restructuring through depression: The state and capital accumulation in Mexico: 1925–40. In R. Thorp, ed., *Latin America in the 1930s: The Role of the Periphery in World Crisis*. New York: St. Martin's Press.

Florescano, E., and I. Gil Sánchez. 1976. La época de las reformas Borbónicas y el crecimiento económico. In D. C. Villegas, ed., *Historia General de México*. Mexico City: El Colegio de México, tomo 1.

Fondo de Cultura Económica. 1963. *México: 50 Años de Revolución. La economía, la vida social, la politica, la cultura*. Mexico City: Fondo de Cultura Económica.

Frenkel, R., and M. Rapetti. 2004. Políticas macroeconómicas para el crecimiento y el empleo. Paper prepared for the International Labour Organization, Geneva, Switzerland.

Frenkel, R., and J. Ros. 2004. Desempleo, políticas macroeconómicas y flexibilidad del mercado laboral. Argentina y México en los noventa. *Desarrollo Económico* 44 (173):33–56.

Frieden, J. 1984. Endeudamiento y fuga de capital. Los flujos financieros internacionales en la crisis de México, 1981–83. *Investigación Económica* 170.

Fujigaki, E. 2006. Monometalismo y bimetalismo en la revolución mexicana. La estabilización monetaria a debate. In M. E. Romero and L. Ludlow, eds., *Temas a Debate. Moneda y Banca en México 1884–1954*. Mexico City: Universidad Nacional Autónoma de México.

Furtado, C. 1970. *Economic Development of Latin America. Historical Background and Contemporary Problems*. Cambridge: Cambridge University Press.

Galindo, L. M., and J. Ros. 2008. Alternatives to inflation targeting. *International Review of Applied Economics* 22(2):201–214.

Garay, F. 2003. *PNR, PRM, PRI: Esbozo histórico*. Mexico City: PRI.

Garcia Alba, P. 1974. Los liberales y los bienes del clero. Manuscript, El Colegio de México.

García de León A., R. Gamboa, and E. Semo. 1988. *Historía de la Cuestión Agraria Mexicana 1: El siglo de la hacienda 1800–1900*. Mexico City: Siglo Veintiuno Editores.

Garner, R. L., and S. E. Stefanou. 1993. *Economic Growth and Change in Bourbon Mexico*. Gainesville: University Press of Florida.

Gasca Zamora, J. 1989. Fuentes para el estudio de las empresas paraestatales de México. *Comercio Exterior*, February, 39(2):151–175.

Gavin, M. 1996. The Mexican oil boom: 1977–1985. Working Paper Series 314, Inter-American Development Bank, Washington, DC.

Gerschenkron, A. 1952. Economic backwardness in historical perspective. In B. Hoselitz, ed., *The Progress of Underdeveloped Countries*. Chicago: University of Chicago Press.

Gil Diaz, F. 1984. Mexico's path from stability to inflation. In A. Harberger, ed., *World Economic Growth*. San Francisco: Institute for Contemporary Studies.

Gil Diaz, F. 1987. Some lessons from Mexico's tax reform. In D. Newberry and N. Stern, eds., *The Theory of Taxation for Developing Countries*. Oxford: Oxford University Press.

Giugale, M., O. Lafourcade, and V. H. Nguyen, eds. 2001. *Mexico. A Comprehensive Development Agenda for the New Era*. Washington, DC: World Bank.

Godínez, V. 2000. La economía de las regiones y el cambio estructural. In F. Clavijo, ed., *Reformas Económicas en México, 1982–1999*. Lecturas del Trimestre Económico 92. Mexico City: Fondo de Cultura Económica.

Golub, S. 1991. The political economy of the Latin American debt crisis. *Latin American Research Review* 26(1):175–215.

Gómez-Galvarriato, A. 1998. The evolution of prices and real wages from the Porfiriato to the revolution. In J. Coatsworth and A. Taylor, eds., *Latin America and the World Economy Since 1800*. Cambridge, MA: Harvard University Press.

Gómez-Galvarriato, A. 2002. Measuring the impact of institutional change in capital-labor relations in the Mexican textile industry, 1900–1930. In J. L. Bortz and S. Haber, *The Mexican Economy, 1870–1930: Essays on the Economic History of Institutions, Revolution, and Growth*. Stanford, CA: Stanford University Press.

Gómez-Galvarriato, A., and A. Mussachio. 2000. Un nuevo índice de precios para México, 1886–1929. *El Trimestre Económico* 67(265):47–91.

González Navarro, M. 1957. *El Porfiriato. La Vida Social* (tomo IV de la Historia Moderna de México). Mexico City: Hermes.

Gregory, P. 1986. *The Myth of Market Failure. Employment and the Labor Market in Mexico*. Baltimore: Johns Hopkins University Press.

Groningen Growth and Development Center. Total Economy Database. University of Groningen. http://www.ggdc.net.

Grossman, G., and E. Helpman. 1991. *Innovation and Growth in the Global Economy*. Cambridge, MA: MIT Press.

Grunstein, A. 1999. De la competencia al monopolio: la formación de los ferrocarriles de México. In S. Kuntz Ficker, ed., *Ferrocarriles y Obras Públicas*. Mexico City: Instituto Mora, El Colegio de Michoacán y el Colmex, el Instituto de Investigaciones Históricas de la Universidad Nacional Autónoma de México.

Guerrero de Lizardi, C. 2006. Thirlwall's law with an emphasis on the ratio of export/import income elasticities in Latin American economies during the twentieth century. *Estudios económicos* 21(1).

Haber, S. 1989. *Industry and Underdevelopment: The Industrialization of Mexico, 1890–1940*. Stanford, CA: Stanford University Press.

Haber, S. 1991. Industrial concentration and the capital markets: A comparative study of Brazil, Mexico, and the United States, 1830–1930. *Journal of Economic History* 51(3):559–580.

Haber, S. 1992. La revolución y la industria manufacturera Mexicana, 1910–1925. In E. Cárdenas, ed., *Historia Económica de México*, vol. III. Lecturas de El Trimestre Económico, No. 64. Mexico City: Fondo de Cultura Económica.

Haber, S. 1997. Financial markets and industrial development: A comparative study of governmental regulation, financial innovation, and industrial structure in Brazil and Mexico, 1840–1930. In S. Haber, ed., *How Latin America Fell Behind: Essays on the Economic Histories of Brazil and Mexico, 1800–1914*. Stanford, CA: Stanford University Press.

Haber, S. 2005. Mexico's experiments with bank privatization and liberalization, 1991–2003. *Journal of Banking and Finance* 29(8–9):2325–2353.

Haber, S. 2006. ¿Por qué importan las instituciones: la banca y el crecimiento económico en México? *El Trimestre Económico* 73(3):429–478.

Haber, S., H. Klein, N. Maurer, and K. Middlebrook. 2008. *Mexico since 1980.* Cambridge: Cambridge University Press.

Haber, S., N. Maurer, and A. Razo. 2003a. When the law does not matter: The rise and decline of the Mexican oil industry. *Journal of Economic History* 63(1):1–32.

Haber, S., and A. Razo. 2000. Industrial prosperity under political instability: An analysis of revolutionary Mexico. In B. Bueno de Mesquita and H. Root, eds., *Governing for Prosperity.* New Haven, CT: Yale University Press.

Haber, S., A. Razo, and N. Maurer. 2003b. *The Politics of Property Rights: Political Instability, Credible Commitments and Economic Growth in Mexico, 1876–1929.* Cambridge: Cambridge University Press.

Hale, C. 1961. Alamán, Antuñano y la continuación del liberalismo. *Historia Mexicana* 11(2):224–245.

Hall, L. 1995. *Oil, Banks and Politics: The United States and Postrevolutionary Mexico, 1917–1924.* Austin: University of Texas Press.

Hall, R., and C. Jones. 1999. Why do some countries produce so much more output per worker than others? *Quarterly Journal of Economics* 114:83–116.

Hansen, R. 1971. *The Politics of Mexican Development.* Baltimore: John Hopkins University Press.

Hanson, G., and A. Harrison. 1999. Trade liberalization and wage inequality in Mexico. *Industrial and Labor Relations Review* 52(2):271–288.

Harrod, R. 1933. *International Economics.* Cambridge: Cambridge University Press.

Hausmann, R., J. Hwang, and D. Rodrik. 2005a. What you export matters. NBER Working Paper 11905, National Bureau for Economic Research, Cambridge, MA.

Hausmann, R., and D. Rodrik. 2006. Doomed to chose: Industrial policy as a predicament. Mimeo, John F. Kennedy School of Government, Harvard University.

Hausmann, R., A. Velasco, and D. Rodrik. 2005b. Growth diagnostics. In J. Stiglitz and N. Serra, eds., *The Washington Consensus Reconsidered: Towards a New Global Governance.* New York: Oxford University Press.

Helpman, E. 2004. *The Mystery of Economic Growth.* Cambridge, MA: Harvard University Press.

Hernandez Laos, E., and E. Velasco. 1990. Productividad y competitividad de las manufacturas Mexicanas, 1960–1985. *Comercio Exterior* 40(7):658–666.

Herrera, I. 1977. *El Comercio Exterior de México, 1821–1875.* Mexico City: El Colegio de México.

Hirschman, A. 1986. The political economy of Latin American development: seven exercises in retrospection. Notre Dame, IN: Helen Kellogg Institute for International Studies, University of Notre Dame.

Hofman, A. 2000. Standardised capital stock estimates in Latin America: A 1950–94 update. *Cambridge Journal of Economics* 24(1):45–86.

Holden, R. 1994. *Mexico and the Survey of Public Lands: The Management of Modernization*. DeKalb: Northern Illinois University Press.

Humboldt, A. 1822. *Political Essay on the Kingdom of New Spain*. Translated from the original French by John Black, 3rd ed. London: printed for Longman, Hurst, Rees, Orme and Brown.

Ibarra A. 1999. Mercado colonial, plata y moneda en el siglo XVIII novohispano: comentarios para un diálogo con Ruggiero Romano a propósito de su nuevo libro. *Historia Mexicana* 49(2):279–308.

Ibarra, A. 2000. *La organización regional del mercado interno novohispano. La economía colonial de Guadalajara 1770–1804*. Mexico City: Benemérita Universidad Autónoma de Puebla-Universidad Nacional Autónoma de México.

Ibarra, C. 2006. A slow growth paradox in Mexico? Mimeo, Department of Economics, Universidad de las Américas.

Ibarra, D. 2005. *Ensayos sobre Economía Mexicana*. Mexico City: Fondo de Cultura Económica.

Ibarra, D. 2008. El desmantelamiento de PEMEX. *Economia UNAM* 5(13):5–29.

ILPES. Estadísticas de Finanzas Públicas. http://websie.eclac.cl/sisgen/ConsultaIntegrada.asp.

INEGI. Banco de Información Económica. http://dgcnesyp.inegi.org.mx/bdiesi/bdie.html.

INEGI. Cuentas Nacionales de México (electronic resource). Aguascalientes, Ags.: INEGI.

INEGI. 1985. *Estadísticas Históricas de México*. Mexico City: Instituto Nacional de Estadística, Geografía e Informática.

INEGI. 1999a. *Estadísticas Históricas de México*. Mexico City: Instituto Nacional de Estadística, Geografía e Informática.

INEGI. 1999b. *Encuesta Nacional de Ingresos y Gastos de los Hogares 1998*. Mexico City: INEGI.

INEGI. 2003. *Encuesta Nacional de Ingresos y Gastos de los Hogares 2002*. Mexico City: INEGI.

INEGI. 2006. *Anuario Estadistico de los Estados Unidos Mexicanos 2005*. Mexico City: INEGI.

Inter-American Development Bank. 2006. El sector rural en México: desafíos y oportunidades. Inter-American Development Bank, Washington, DC, September.

ITAM. 2008. Estadísticas históricas de México, electronic data bank. http://biblioteca.itam.mx/docs/ehm/.

Ize, A., and G. Ortiz. 1987. Fiscal rigidities, public debt, and capital flight. *International Monetary Fund Staff Papers* 34(2):311–332.

Izquierdo, R. 1964. Protectionism in Mexico. In R. Vernon, ed., *Public Policy and Private Enterprise in Mexico*. Cambridge, MA: Harvard University Press.

Izquierdo, R. 1995. *Política hacendaria del desarrollo estabilizador, 1958–1970*. Mexico City: Fondo de Cultura Económica and El Colegio de México.

Jáuregui, L. 2005. Los ingresos y los gastos públicos de México, 1821–1855. In L. Aboites and L. Jauregui, eds., *Penuria sin fin*. Mexico City: Instituto de Investigaciones Dr. José María Luis Mora.

Johnson, N. 2001. "Tierra y Libertad": Will tenure reform improve productivity in Mexico's "Ejido" agriculture. *Economic Development and Cultural Change* 49(2):291–309.

Kaldor, N. 1966. *Causes of the Slow Rate of Economic Growth of the United Kingdom.* Cambridge: Cambridge University Press.

Katz, F. 1980. *La servidumbre agraria en México en la época porfiriana*. Mexico City: Ediciones ERA.

Katz, F. 2004. *De Díaz a Madero: Origenes y estallido de la revolución Mexicana*. Mexico City: Ediciones Era.

Kaufman, R. 1979. Industrial change and authoritarian rule in Latin America: A concrete review of the bureaucratic-authoritarian model. In D. Collier, ed., *The New Authoritarianism in Latin America*. Princeton, NJ: Princeton University Press.

Keesing, D. 1969. Structural change early in development: Mexico's changing industrial and occupational structure from 1895 to 1950. *Journal of Economic History* 29(4):716–738.

Kemmerer, E. W. 1940. *Inflation and Revolution: Mexico's Experience of 1912–1917*. Princeton, NJ: Princeton University Press.

King, T. 1970. *Mexico: Industrialization and Trade Policies since 1940*. Oxford: Oxford University Press.

Klenow, P., and A. Rodriguez-Clare. 1997. The neoclassical revival in growth economics: Has it gone too far? *NBER Macroeconomics Annual* 1997(12):73–103.

Knight, A. 1986. *The Mexican Revolution*, vol. 1. Cambridge: Cambridge University Press.

Knight, A. 1992. The peculiarities of Mexican history: Mexico compared to Latin America, 1821–1992. *Journal of Latin American Studies* 24:99–144.

Knight, A. 2002. *Mexico. The Colonial Era*. Cambridge: Cambridge University Press.

Knowlton, R. 1985. *Los bienes del clero y la reforma Mexicana, 1856–1919*. Mexico City: Fondo de Cultura Económica.

Kose, M. A., G. M. Meredith, and C. M. Towe. 2004. How has NAFTA affected the Mexican economy? Review and evidence. IMF Working Paper WP/04/59, International Monetary Fund, Washington, DC, 2004.

Krueger, A., and B. Tuncer. 1980. Estimates of total factor productivity growth for the Turkish economy. World Bank Staff Working Paper 422, World Bank, Washington, DC, October.

Krugman, P., and L. Taylor. 1978. Contractionary effects of devaluation. *Journal of International Economics* 8(3):445–456.

Kuntz Ficker, S. 1999. Ferrocarriles y la formación del espacio económico en México. In S. Kuntz Ficker and P. Connelly, eds., *Ferrocarriles y Obras Públicas*. Mexico City: Instituto Investigaciones Dr. Jose Maria Luis Mora/ColMich/ClMex/ Instituto de Investigaciones Históricas, Universidad Nacional Autónoma de México.

Kuntz Ficker, S. 2002. Institutional change and foreign trade in Mexico, 1870–1911. In J. L. Bortz and S. Haber, eds., *The Mexican Economy, 1870–1930: Essays on the Economic History of Institutions, Revolution, and Growth*. Stanford, CA: Stanford University Press.

Kuntz Ficker, S. 2004. The export boom of the Mexican Revolution: Characteristics and contributing factors. *Journal of Latin American Studies* 36:267–296.

Kuntz Ficker, S. 2007. *El Comercio Exterior de Mexico en la Era del Capitalismo Liberal 1870–1929*. Mexico City: El Colegio de México.

Kuntz Ficker, S., and P. Connelly, eds. 1999. *Ferrocarriles y Obras Públicas*. Mexico City: Instituto Investigaciones Dr. Jose Maria Luis Mora/ColMich/ClMex/Instituto de Investigaciones Históricas, Universidad Nacional Autónoma de México.

Lachler, U., and D. Aschauer. 1998. Public investment and economic growth in Mexico. Policy Research Working Paper WPS1964, World Bank, Washington, DC, August.

Lal, D., and H. Myint. 1996. *The Political Economy of Poverty, Equity and Growth*. Oxford: Clarendon Press.

Larudee, M. 1998. Integration and income distribution under the North American Free Trade Agreement: The experience of Mexico. In D. Baker, G. Epstein, and R. Pollin, eds., *Globalization and Progressive Economic Policy*. Cambridge: Cambridge University Press.

Lavoie, M. 1992. *Foundations of Post-Keynesian Economic Analysis*. Aldershot, UK: Edward Elgar.

Lederman, D., W. Maloney, and L. Serven. 2003. *Lessons from NAFTA for Latin America and the Caribbean Countries: A Summary of Research Findings*. World Bank: Washington, DC.

Leff, N. 1972. Economic retardation in nineteenth-century Brazil. *Economic History Review* 25(3):489–507.

Lerdo de Tejada, M. 1853. *Comercio exterior de México*. Mexico City: Rafael Rafael.

Levine, R., and D. Renelt. 1992. A sensitivity analysis of cross-country growth regressions. *American Economic Review* 82:942–963.

Levy, S. 2000. Observaciones sobre la nueva legislación de competencia económica en México. In R. Tovar, ed., *Lecturas en Regulación Económica y Política de Competencia*. Mexico City: ITAM, Grupo Editorial Porrúa.

Little, I., T. Scitovsky, and M. Scott. 1970. *Industry and Trade in Some Developing Countries*. Oxford: Oxford University Press.

Londoño, J. L., and M. Székely. 1997. Distributional surprises after a decade of reform: Latin America in the nineties. Research Department, Inter-American Development Bank, Washington, DC.

López Cámara, F. 1967. *La estructura económica y social de México en la época de la Reforma*. Mexico City: Siglo XXI.

López Rosado, D., and J. Noyola. 1951. Los salarios reales en México, 1939–1950. *El Trimestre Económico* 18(April–June):201–209.

López, J. 1998. *La macroeconomía de México: el pasado reciente y el futuro posible*. Mexico City: UNAM y Miguel Angel Porrúa.

López, J., and A. Cruz. 2000. Thirlwall's law and beyond: The Latin American experience. *Journal of Post Keynesian Economics* 22(3):477–495.

Lopez de Acevedo, G. 2007. More Good Jobs for a Growing Labor Market. Paper presented at Foro Internacional Sobre Políticas Públicas para El Desarrollo de México, México City. http://www.foropoliticaspublicas.org.mx/docs/Empleo_Gladys%20López-Acevedo_Banco%20Mundial.pdf.

Loría, E., and G. Fujii. 1997. The balance of payment constraint to Mexico's economic growth, 1950–1996. *Canadian Journal of Development Studies* 18(1):119–137.

Lustig, N. 1992. *Mexico: The Remaking of an Economy*. Washington, DC: Brookings Institution.

Lustig, N. 2002. *México. Hacia la Reconstrucción de una Economía*. Mexico City: El Colegio de México and Fondo de Cultura Económica.

Lustig, N. 2008. México: El impacto de 25 años de reformas sobre la pobreza y la desigualdad. Unpublished manuscript prepared for the economics volume of the project "México 2010" of El Colegio de México.

Lustig, N., and J. Ros. 1987. *Stabilization and Adjustment Policies and Programmes. Country Study 7. Mexico*. Helsinki: WIDER.

MacLachlan, C., and J. Rodríguez. 1980. *The Forging of the Cosmic Race: A Reinterpretation of Colonial Mexico*. Berkeley: University of California Press.

Maddison, A. 1989. *The World Economy in the 20th Century*. Paris: Development Center, Organization for Economic Cooperation and Development.

Maddison, A. 1995. The historical roots of modern Mexico, 1500–1940. In A. Maddison, *Explaining the Economic Performance of Nations: Essays in Time and Space*. Aldershot, UK: Edward Elgar.

Maddison, A. 2003. *The World Economy: Historical Statistics*. Paris: Development Center, Organization for Economic Cooperation and Development.

Maddison, A. 2006. *Historical Statistics*. www.ggdc.net/maddison.

Mallorquin, C. 2005. Raul Prebisch y la tesis del deterioro de los términos de intercambio, *Revista Mexicana de Sociología*, Año 67, No. 2. Instituto de Sociologia: UNAM.

Manzanilla Schaffer, Y. 1963. Reforma agraria en México. In Fondo de Cultura Económica, *México: 50 Años de Revolución. La economía, la vida social, la politica, la cultura*. Mexico City: Fondo de Cultura Económica.

Marichal, C. 1989. *A Century of Debt Crises in Latin America*. Princeton, NJ: Princeton University Press.

Marichal, C. 1997. Obstacles to the development of capital markets in nineteenth-century Mexico. In S. Haber, ed., *How Latin America Fell Behind: Essays on the Economic Histories of Brazil and Mexico, 1800–1914*. Stanford, CA: Stanford University Press.

Marichal, C. 1998. La deuda externa y las políticas de desarrollo económico durante el Porfiriato: algunas hipótesis de trabajo. In L.Ludlow and C.Marichal (coord.), *Un Siglo de Deuda Pública en México*. Mexico City: Instituto de Investigaciones Dr. José María Luis Mora.

Marichal, C. 2007. *Bankruptcy of Empire: Mexican Silver and the Wars between Spain, Britain, and France, 1760–1810*. New York: Cambridge University Press.

Marichal, C., and S. Topik. 2003. The state and economic growth in Latin America: Brazil and Mexico, nineteenth and early twentieth centuries. In A. Teichova and H. Matis, eds., *Nation, State and the Economy in History*. Cambridge: Cambridge University Press.

Márquez, G. 2002. The political economy of Mexican protectionism, 1868–1911. PhD dissertation, Harvard University, Cambridge, MA.

Matsuyama, K. 1992. Agricultural productivity, comparative advantage, and economic growth. *Journal of Economic Theory* 58(2):317–334.

Máttar, J., J. C. Moreno-Brid, and W. Peres. 2003. Foreign investment in Mexico after economic reform. In K. J. Middlebrook and E. Zepeda, eds., *Confronting Development: Assessing Mexico's Economic and Social Policy Challenges*. Stanford, CA: Stanford University Press.

Matute, A., E. Trejo, and B. Connaughton, eds. 1995. *Estado, iglesia y sociedad en Mexico: siglo XIX*. Mexico City: Universidad Nacional Autónoma de México and M. A. Porrua.

Maurer, N. 2002. *The Power and the Money. The Mexican Financial System, 1876–1932*. Stanford, CA: Stanford University Press.

Maurer, N., and S. Haber. 2007. Related lending: manifest looting or good governance. In S. Edwards, G. Esquivel, and G. Márquez, eds., *The Decline of Latin American Economies: Growth, Institutions, and Crisis*. Chicago: University of Chicago Press.

McCaa, R. 2003. Missing millions: The demographic costs of the Mexican Revolution. *Mexican Studies/Estudios Mexicanos* 19(2):367–400.

McCombie, J. S. L., and A. P. Thirlwall. 1994. *Economic Growth and the Balance of Payments Constraint*. New York: St Martin's Press.

Meyer, J. 1991. Revolution and reconstruction in the 1920s. In L. Bethell, ed., *Mexico since Independence*. Cambridge: Cambridge University Press.

Meyer, J. 2004. *La Revolución Mexicana*. Mexico City: Tusquets Editores.

Meyer, L. 1968. *México y Estados Unidos en el Conflicto Petrolero (1917–1942)*. Mexico City: El Colegio de México.

Moguillansky, G., and R. Bielschowsky. 2001. *Inversión y Reformas Económicas en América Latina*. Santiago, Chile: ECLAC/Fondo de Cultura Económica.

Morales, H. 1999. Estevan de Antuñano y la república de la industria. Su influencia en México a lo largo del siglo XIX. In W. Fowler and H. Morales, eds., *El Conservadurismo en el Siglo XIX*. Puebla, Mexico: Benemérita Universidad Autónoma de Puebla.

Moreno-Brid, J. C. 1999. Reformas macroeconómicas e inversión manufacturera en México, Serie Reformas Macroeconómicas No. 47, ECLAC, Santiago, Chile.

Moreno-Brid, J. C. 2001. Essays on economic growth and the balance of payments constraint with special reference to the case of Mexico. PhD dissertation, Faculty of Economics and Politics, University of Cambridge.

Moreno-Brid, J. C., and J. Pardinas. 2007. Social development and policies in modern Mexico. Paper presented at the Conference on Social Policy, Economic Development and Income Inequality, University of London, May 31–June 1, 2007.

Moreno-Brid J.C., J. C. Rivas, and J. Santamaría. 2007. Industrial development in Mexico post-NAFTA: Policy and performance. Document prepared for the Institute for Economic and Social Planning and CEPAL.

Moreno-Brid, J. C., and J. Ros. 1994. Market reform and the changing role of the state in Mexico: a historical perspective. In A. Dutt, K. Kim, and A. Singh, eds., *The State, Markets, and Development*. Aldershot, UK: Edward Elgar.

Moreno-Brid, J. C., and J. Ros. 2004. Mexico's market reforms in historical perspective. *CEPAL Review* 84(December):35–56.

Moreno-Brid, J. C., J. Santamaría, and J. C. Rivas. 2005. Industrialization and economic growth in Mexico after NAFTA: The road traveled. *Development and Change* 36(6):1095–1119.

Mosk, S. 1950. *Industrial Revolution in Mexico*. Berkeley: University of California Press.

Murillo, J. A. 2005. La banca después de la privatización: Auge, crisis y reordenamiento. In C. Bazdresh, G. del Angel, and F. Suárez-Dávila, eds., *Cuando el Estado se Hizo Banquero*. Mexico City: Fondo de Cultura Económica.

NAFINSA-ONUDI. 1985. *Mexico: Los Bienes de Capital en la Situación Económica Presente*. Mexico City: Nacional Financiera, S.A.

Navarrete, A. 1963. *Instrumentos de Política Financiera Mexicana*. Mexico City: Publicaciones Especializadas, S.A.

Navarrete, M. I. 1960. *La Distribución del Ingreso y el Desarrollo Económico de México*. Mexico City: Instituto de Investigaciones Económicas.

Newell, R., and L. Rubio. 1984. *Mexico's Dilemma: The Political Origins of the Economic Crisis*. Boulder, CO: Westview Press.

Nugent, J. 1973. Exchange rate movements and economic development in the late nineteenth century. *Journal of Political Economy* 81:1110–1135.

Ocegueda, J. 2000. La Hipótesis de Crecimiento Restringido por Balanza de Pagos. Una Evaluación de la Economía Mexicana 1960–1997. *Investigación Económica* 60(232):91–122.

OECD. 1992. *Mexico: Economic Studies of the OECD*. Paris: Organization for Economic Cooperation and Development.

OECD. 2002. *OECD Economic Surveys: Mexico*. Paris: Organization for Economic Cooperation and Development.

OECD. 2003. *OECD Economic Surveys: Mexico*. Paris: Organization for Economic Cooperation and Development.

OECD. 2004a. *OECD Economic Surveys: Mexico*, vol. 2003, supplement 1. Paris: Organization for Economic Cooperation and Development.

OECD. 2004b. *Recent Tax Policy Trends and Reforms in OECD Countries*. OECD Tax Policy Studies No. 9. Paris: Organization for Economic Cooperation and Development.

OECD. 2007. *Getting It Right: OECD Perspectives on Policy Challenges in Mexico*. Paris: Organization for Economic Cooperation and Development.

Orozco y Berra, M. 1857. *Informe sobre la Acuñación en las Casas de Moneda de la República*, Anexo a la *Memoria* de la Secretaría de Fomento.

Ortiz Mena, R., et al. 1953. *El Desarrollo Económico de México y su Capacidad para Absorber Capital del Exterior*. Mexico City: Nacional Financiera.

Oxford Latin American Economic History Database (OxLAD). Latin American Centre, Oxford University. http://oxlad.qeh.ox.ac.uk/.

Pacheco-López, P. 2003. Trade liberalisation in Mexico and its impact on exports, imports and the balance of payments. PhD dissertation, University of Kent, Kent.

Pacheco-López, P. 2005. The impact of trade liberalisation on exports, imports, the balance of payments and growth: The case of Mexico. *Journal of Post Keynesian Economics* 27(4):595–619.

Pack, H., and K. Saggi. 2006. Is there a case for industrial policy? A critical survey. *World Bank Research Observer* 21(2):267–297.

Palma, G. 2005. The seven main "stylized facts" of the Mexican economy since trade liberalization and NAFTA. *Industrial and Corporate Change* 14(6):941–991.

Parlee, L. 1981. *Porfirio Díaz, Railroads and Development In Northern Mexico: A Study of Government Policy toward the Central and Nacional Railroads, 1876–1910*. San Diego: University of California.

Paz, O. 1985. *One Earth, Four or Five Worlds: Reflections on Contemporary History*, Helen Lane, trans. New York: Harcourt Brace Jovanovich.

Paz Sánchez, F. 2000. *La Política Económica del Porfiriato*. Mexico City: Instituto Nacional de Estudios de la Revolución Mexicana.

Paz Sánchez, F. 2006. *La Política Económica de la Revolución Mexicana, 1911–1924*. Mexico City: Universidad Nacional Autónoma de México and Fondo Editorial FCA.

Pedrero, F. 2007. En riesgo, viabilidad del programa de empleo. *El Universal* April 30.

Peres, W. 1990. *Foreign Direct Investment and Industrial Development in Mexico*. Paris: Organization for Economic Cooperation and Development.

Pletcher, D. 1958. The fall of silver in Mexico, 1870–1910, and its effect on American investments. *Journal of Economic History* 18(1):33–55.

Ponzio, C. 1998. Interpretación económica del último período colonial mexicano. *El Trimestre Económico* 65(1):99–125.

Ponzio, C. 2005. Looking at the dark side of things: Political instability and economic growth in post-independence Mexico. Mimeo, Universidad Autónoma de Nuevo León and Secretaría de Desarrollo Económico.

Ponzio, C. 2006. Export boom and rising prices in late colonial Mexico: A Dutch disease? Mexico City: Centro de Investigación y Docencia Económicas and Servicio de Administración Tributaria.

Potash, R. A. 1953. The Banco de Avío of Mexico. Unpublished dissertation, Harvard University.

Prados de la Escosura, L. 2004. Colonial independence and economic backwardness in Latin America. Working Paper 04–65, Economic History and Institutions Series 3, Departmento de Historia Económica e Instituciones, Universidad Carlos III de Madrid, December.

Prados de la Escosura, L. 2007. When did Latin America fall behind? In S. Edwards, G. Esquivel, and G. Márquez, eds., *The Decline of Latin American Economies: Growth, Institutions, and Crisis*. Chicago: University of Chicago Press.

PREALC. 1982. *El Mercado de Trabajo en Cifras*. Lima Peru: Oficina Internacional del Trabajo.

Prebisch, R. 1950. *The Economic Development of Latin America and Its Principal Problems*. New York: United Nations.

Presidencia de la República. 2006. Anexo al Sexto Informe de Gobierno del Presidente de los Estados Unidos Mexicanos. Mexico City: Gobierno de México.

Presidencia de la República. 2008. Anexo al Segundo Informe de Gobierno del Presidente de los Estados Unidos Mexicanos. Mexico City: Gobierno de México

Puyana, A., and J. Romero. 2005. *Diez Años con el TLCAN. Las Experiencias del Sector Agropecuario Mexicano*. Mexico City: Colmex-Flacso.

Ramirez, M. 2004. Is public infrastructure investment productive in the Mexican case? A vector error correction analysis. *Journal of International Trade and Economic Development* 13(2):159–178.

Razo, A., and S. Haber. 1998. The rate of growth of productivity in Mexico, 1850–1933: Evidence from the cotton textile industry. *Journal of Latin American Studies* 30(3):481–517.

Rea, D. 2007. Graduan 20,000 en Oportunidades, *Reforma*, Sección Nacional, May 18, p. 8.

Reimers, F. 2006. Education and social progress. In V. Bulmer-Thomas, J. Coatsworth, and R. Cortés Conde, eds., *The Cambridge Economic History of Latin America*. Cambridge: Cambridge University Press.

Reisen, H., and A. van Trotsenburg. 1988. *Developing Country Debt: The Budgetary and Transfer Problem*. Paris: Development Center, Organization for Economic Cooperation and Development.

Revenga, A. 1997. Employment and wage effects of trade liberalization: The case of Mexican manufacturing. *Journal of Labor Economics* 15(3):S20–S43.

Reynolds, C. 1970. *The Mexican Economy: Twentieth-Century Structure and Growth*. New Haven, CT: Yale University Press.

Reynolds, C. 1980. *A Shift-Share Analysis of Regional and Sectoral Productivity Growth in Contemporary Mexico*. Laxenburg, Austria: International Institute for Applied Systems Analysis.

Reynoso, A. 1989. Essays on the macroeconomic effects of monetary reforms, price controls and financial repression. Ph.D. dissertation, MIT.

Riguzzi, P. 1996. Los caminos del atraso: Tecnología, instituciones e inversion en los ferrocarriles mexicanos, 1850–1900. In S. Kuntz Ficker and P. Riguzzi, eds., *Ferrocarriiles y Vida Económica en México (1850–1950)*. Mexico City: El Colegio

Mexiquense, Ferrocarriles Nacionales de México, Universidad Autónoma Metropolitana-Azcapotzalco.

Robles, G. 1960. El desarrollo industrial. In Fondo de Cultura Económica, *México: 50 Años de Revolución. La economía, la vida social, la politica, la cultura*. Mexico City: Fondo de Cultura Económica.

Rodríguez, F., and D. Rodrik. 2001. Trade policy and economic growth: A skeptic's guide to the cross-national evidence. In B. Bernanke and K. Rogoff, eds., *NBER Macroeconomics Annual 2000*. Cambridge, MA: National Bureau of Economic Research.

Rodrik, D. 1999. *The New Global Economy and Developing Countries. Making Openness Work*. Baltimore: John Hopkins University Press.

Rodrik, D. 2004. Rethinking growth policies in the developing world. Mimeo, Harvard University.

Rogozinsky, J. 1996. *La Privatización de Empresas Paraestatales: Una Visión de la Modernización*. Mexico City: Fondo de Cultura Económica.

Rogozinsky, J., and R. Tovar. 1998. Private infrastructure concessions: The 1989–1994 national highway program in Mexico. In *High Price for Change: Privatization in Mexico*. Washington, DC: Inter-American Development Bank.

Romano, R. 1998. *Moneda, Seudomonedas y Circulación Monetaria en las Economías de México*. Mexico City: Fondo de Cultura Económica and El Colegio de México.

Romero, J. 1999. El holocausto y su secuela: La revolución Mexicana de 1910. *El Trimestre Económico* 66(2):145–174.

Romero Sotelo, M. E. 1997. *Minería y Guerra. La Economía de Nueva España, 1810–1821*. Mexico City: El Colegio de México/Universidad Nacional Autónoma de México.

Romero Sotelo, M. E., and L. Jáuregui. 2003. *Las Contingencias de una Larga Recuperación: La Economía Mexicana, 1821–1867*. Mexico City: Universidad Nacional Autónoma de México.

Ros, J. 1987. Mexico from the oil boom to the debt crisis: An analysis of policy responses to external shocks. In R. Thorp and L. Whitehead, eds., *Latin American Debt and the Adjustment Crisis*. New York: MacMillan.

Ros, J. 1991a. The effects of government policies on the incentives to invest, enterprise behavior and employment: A study of Mexico's economic reform in the eighties. Working Paper No.53, World Employment Programme Research, International Labour Organization, Geneva, Switzerland.

Ros, J. 1991b. La movilidad del capital y la eficacia de la política con una corrida del crédito. *El Trimestre Económico* 58(3):561–587.

Ros, J. 1992. Ajuste macroeconómico, reformas estructurales y crecimiento en México. Mimeo, University of Notre Dame.

Ros, J. 1993. *La Reforma del Régimen Comercial en México Durante los Años Ochenta: sus efectos económicos y dimensiones políticas*. Serie Reformas de Política Pública No.4. Santiago, Chile: ECLAC and government of The Netherlands, April.

Ros, J. 1994a. Financial markets and capital flows in Mexico. In J. A. Ocampo and R. Steiner, eds., *Foreign Capital in Latin America*. Washington, DC.: Inter-American Development Bank.

Ros, J. 1994b. Foreign exchange and fiscal constraints on growth: a reconsideration of structuralist and macroeconomic approaches. In A. Dutt, ed., *New Directions in Analytical Political Economy*. Aldershot, UK: Edward Elgar.

Ros, J. 1994c. Mexico's trade and industrialization experience since 1960: A reconsideration of past policies and assessment of current reforms. In G. Helleiner, ed., *Trade Policy and Industrialization in Turbulent Times*. London: Routledge.

Ros, J. 1995. Trade liberalization with real appreciation and slow growth: Sustainability issues in Mexico's trade policy reform. In G. Helleiner, ed., *Manufacturing for Export in the Developing World*. London: Routledge.

Ros, J. 2000a. *Development Theory and the Economics of Growth*. Ann Arbor: University of Michigan Press.

Ros, J. 2000b. Employment, structural adjustment and sustainable growth in Mexico. *Journal of Development Studies* 36(4):100–119.

Ros, J. 2001a. Del auge de capitales a la crisis financiera y más allá: México en los noventa. In R. Ffrench-Davis, ed., *Crisis Financieras en Países "Exitosos."* New York: CEPAL and McGraw-Hill.

Ros, J. 2001b. Política industrial, ventajas comparativas y crecimiento. *CEPAL Review* (73) April:129–148.

Ros, J. 2008. Poverty reduction in Latin America: the role of growth, income distribution, social spending and demographic change. Mimeo, University of Notre Dame.

Rosenzweig, A. 2005. El debate sobre el sector agropecuario en el TLCAN. Serie Estudios y Perspectivas No. 30, ECLAC, Mexico City, Mexico.

Rosenzweig, F. 1965. El desarrollo económico de México de 1877 a 1911. *El Trimestre Económico* 32(5):405–454.

Sachs, J. 2001. Tropical underdevelopment. NBER Working Paper No. 8119, National Bureau for Economic Research, Cambridge, MA.

Salvucci, R. 1987. *Textiles and Capitalism in México*. Princeton, NJ: Princeton University Press.

Salvucci, R. 1997. Mexican national income in the era of independence, 1800–40. In S. Haber, ed., *How Latin America Fell Behind*. Stanford, CA: Stanford University Press.

Samaniego, R. 1984. The evolution of total factor productivity in the manufacturing sector in Mexico, 1963–1981. Serie Documentos de Trabajo. Mexico City: El Colegio de México.

Sánchez-Reaza, J., and A. Rodríguez-Pose. 2002. The impact of trade liberalization on regional disparities in Mexico. *Growth and Change* 33(Winter):72–90.

Sandoval, R. 1976. Industria textil mexicana: Siglo XIX. *Estadísticas Económicas del Siglo XIX*, Mexico City.

Santaella, J. 1998. Economic growth in Mexico. Manuscript, Inter-American Development Bank.

Santamaría, H. 1985. La evolución de la inversión en México. Paper presented at the Conference on the Investment Process in Mexico and the USA, Stanford University.

Schaeffer, W. 1949. National administration in Mexico: Its development and present status. Unpublished dissertation, University of California.

Schatán, C. 1981. Los efectos de la liberalización de importaciones. *Economía Mexicana*, no. 3. Mexico City: Centro de Investigación y Docencia Económicas.

Schlefer, J. 2008. *Palace Politics: How the Ruling Party Brought Crisis to Mexico*. Austin: University of Texas Press.

Schmitz, C. 1979. *World Non-Ferrous Metal Production and Prices, 1700–1976*. London: Frank Cass and Co.

SECOFI. 1993. Evolución de la inversión extranjera en México durante 1992. El Mercado de Valores, México, no. 9, May 1.

Secretaría de Patrimonio y Fomento Industrial. 1979. *Plan Nacional de Desarrollo Industrial, 1979–1982*. Mexico City: Secretaría de Patrimonio y Fomento Industrial.

Shapiro, H. 2008. The industrial policy debate: Back to the future? In A. K. Dutt and J. Ros, eds., *International Handbook of Development Economics*. Aldershot, UK: Edward Elgar.

SHCP. 1993. *El Proceso de Enajenación de Entidades Paraestatales*, Mexico City: Secretaria de Hacienda y Crédito Público.

Solís, L. 1977. *A Monetary Will-O'-the-Wisp: Pursuit of Equity through Deficit Spending*. Geneva: International Labour Organization.

Solís, L. 1980. Prioridades industriales en México. In *Prioridades Industriales en Países en Desarrollo*. New York: ONUDI.

Solís, L. 1981. *Economic Policy Reform in Mexico: A Case Study for Developing Countries*. New York: Pergamon Press.

Solís, L. 2000. *La Realidad Económica Mexicana: Retrovisión y Perspectivas*, 3rd ed. Mexico City: Fondo de Cultura Económica.

Staples, A. 1976. *La Iglesia en la Primera República Federal Mexicana, 1824–1835*. Mexico City: Sepsetentas.

Sterret, J. E., and J. S. Davis. 1928. The fiscal and economic condition of Mexico. Report submitted to the International Committee of Bankers on Mexico.

Suárez Dávila, F. 2005. Dos visiones de la política económica en México: Un debate en la historia (1946 a 1970). In M. E. Romero, ed., *Historia del Pensamiento Económico en México: Problemas y Tendencias (1821–2000)*. Mexico City: Editorial Trillas.

Syrquin, M. 1986. Productivity growth and factor reallocation. In H. Chenery, S. Robinson, and M. Syrquin, eds., *Industrialization and Growth: A Comparative Study*. London: Oxford University Press.

Székely, G. 1983. *La Economía Política del Petróleo en México, 1976–82*. Mexico City: El Colegio de México.

Székely, M. 2005. Pobreza y desigualdad en México entre 1950 y 2004. *El Trimestre Económico* 72(288): 913–931.

Tanzi, V. 1977. Inflation, lags in tax collection and the real value of tax revenues. *IMF Staff Papers* 24(March):164–167.

Taylor, L. 1994. Gap models. *Journal of Development Economics* 45(1):17–34.

Tello, C. 1984. *La Nacionalización de la Banca*. Mexico City: Siglo XXI.

Tello, C. 2007. *Estado y Desarrollo Económico: México 1920–2006*. Mexico City: Facultad de Economía, Universidad Nacional Autónoma de México.

Ten Kate, A., and G. Niels. 1996. Apertura Comercial, Privatización, Desregulación y Políticas de Competencia en México. Documento presentado en el seminario México y la Integración frente al Siglo XXI, Universidad Nacional Autónoma de México, September 17–18, Mexico City.

Ten Kate, A., and B. Wallace. 1980. *Protection and Economic Development in Mexico*. New York: St. Martin's Press.

Tenenbaum, B. 1986. *The Politics of Penury: Debts and Taxes in Mexico, 1821–1856*. Albuquerque: University of New Mexico Press.

Tenorio, M., and A. Gómez-Galvarriato. 2006. *El Porfiriato*. Mexico City: Centro de Investigación y Docencia Económicas and Fondo de Cultura Económica.

Thirlwall, A. P. 1979. The balance of payments constraint as an explanation of international growth rates differences. *Banca Nazionale del Lavoro Quarterly Review*, 45–53.

Thomas, R. 1965. A quantitative approach to the study of the effects of British imperial policy upon colonial welfare. *Journal of Economic History* 25:615–638.

Thomson, G. 1985. Protectionism and industrialization in Mexico, 1821–1854: The case of Puebla. In C. Abel and C. M. Lewis, eds., *Latin America, Economic Imperialism, and the State: The Political Economy of the External Connection from Independence to the Present*. London: Athlone Press.

Thomson, G. 1986. The cotton textile industry in Puebla during the eighteenth and early nineteenth centuries. In N. Jacobsen and H. J. Puhle, eds., *The Economies of Mexico and Peru During the Late Colonial Period, 1760–1810*. Berlin: Colloquium Yerlag.

Timmer, M., and G. de Vries. 2007. A Cross-Country Database for Sectoral Employment and Productivity in Asia and Latin America, 1950–2005. Groningen Growth and Development Centre, University of Groningen. http://www.ggdc.net/dseries/10-sector.html.

Tornell, A., and G. Esquivel. 1997. The political economy of Mexico's entry into NAFTA. In T. Ito and A. O. Krueger, eds., *Regionalism Versus Multilateral Trade Arrangements*, NBER-East Asia Seminar on Economics, vol. 6. Chicago: University of Chicago Press.

Tornell, A., F. Westermann, and L. Martínez. 2003. Liberalization, Growth, and Financial Crises: Lessons from Mexico and the Developing World, *Brookings Papers on Economic Activity* 2, 1–88.

Trigueros, I. 1998. Flujos de capital y desempeño de la inversion: México. In R. Ffrench-Davis and H. Reisen, eds., *Flujos de Capital e Inversión Productiva: Lecciones para América Latina*. Santiago, Chile: CEPAL/OCDE.

Tybout, J., and D. Westbrook. 1995. Trade liberalization and the structure of production in Mexican manufacturing industries. *Journal of International Economics* 39:53–78.

UNCTAD. 2002. *Trade and Development Report*. New York: United Nations Conference on Trade and Development.

UNDP. 2004. *Informe sobre Desarrollo Humano México 2004*, Oficina Nacional de Desarrollo Humano, PNUD-Mexico.

UNIDO. 1998. *Industrial Development: Global Report 1997*. New York: Oxford University Press.

U.S. Census Bureau. Statistical Abstract of the United States. http://www.census.gov/compendia/statab/2008edition.html.

U.S. International Trade Commission. 1990. *Review of Trade and Investment Liberalization Measures by Mexico and Prospects for Future United States–Mexican Relations, Phase I*. Washington, DC: U.S. International Trade Commission.

Uthoff, A. 2007. Reducción de la pobreza e inequidad. Unpublished document presented at the Foro de Políticas Públicas, Mexico City, February.

Valenzuela, S. 2006. Caudillismo, democracia, y la excepcionalidad chilena en América Hispana. *Revista de Occidente* 305(October):11–28.

Van Ginneken, W. 1980. *Socio-Economic Groups and Income Distribution in Mexico*. New York: St. Martin's Press.

Van Young, E. 1981. *Hacienda and Market in Eighteenth Century Mexico: The Rural Economy of the Guadalajara Region, 1675–1820*. Berkeley: University of California Press.

Vázquez, J. Z. (coord.) 1997. *Interpretaciones de la Independencia de México*. Mexico City: Nueva Imagen.

Velasco, C. 1989. Los trabajadores mineros en la Nueva España, 1750–1810. In E. Cárdenas, ed., *Historia Económica de México*. Mexico City: Fondo de Cultura Económica.

Velasco, E. 1985. El ciclo de la productividad de la gran industria en México (1950–1982). Paper presented to the Conference on Cycles and Crisis in the Mexican Economy, La Jolla, California.

Vernon, R. 1963. *The Dilemma of Mexico's Development: The Role of the Private and Public Sectors*. Cambridge, MA: Harvard University Press.

Villarreal, R. 1976. *El Desequilibrio Externo en la Industrialización de México (1929–1975): Un Enfoque Estructuralista*. Mexico City: Fondo de Cultura Económica.

Villarreal, R. 1977. The policy of import substituting industrialization, 1929–1975. In J. L. Reyna and R. S. Weinert, eds., *Authoritarianism in Mexico*. Philadelphia: Institute for the Study of Human Issues.

Villarreal, R. 1983. Perspectivas de la economía Mexicana. *El Trimestre Económico* 50:377–401.

Werner, A., R. Barros, and J. Ursúa. 2006. The Mexican economy: Transformation and challenges. In L. Randall, ed., *Changing Structure of Mexico: Political, Social, and Economic Prospects*, 2nd ed. London: M. E. Sharpe.

Wilkie, J. W. 1970. *The Mexican Revolution: Federal Expenditure and Social Change since 1910*, 2nd rev. ed. Berkeley: University of California Press.

Williamson, J., ed. 1990. *Latin American Adjustment: How Much Has Happened?* Washington, DC: Institute for International Economics.

Womack, J. 1978. The Mexican economy during the revolution, 1910–1920: Historiography and analysis. *Marxist Perspectives* 1(4):80–123.

World Bank. Education Statistics. http://www.worldbank.org/education/edstats.

World Bank. World Development Indicators (available on line to subscribers).

World Bank. 1986. *Mexico: Trade Policy, Industrial Performance and Adjustment*. Washington, DC: World Bank.

World Bank. 1995. Privatization and deregulation in Mexico. *E-Precis*, No. 97, November, Operation Evaluation Department, Washington, DC.

World Bank. 2000. Enhancing factor productivity growth. Country Economic Memorandum. Report No. 17392-ME, World Bank, Washington, DC.

World Bank. 2003. *Private Solutions for Infrastructure in Mexico*. Washington, DC: World Bank.

World Economic Forum. 2008. *The Global Competitiveness Report 2008–09*. Geneva, Switzerland: World Economic Forum.

Yates, P. 1981. *Mexico's Agricultural Dilemma*. Tucson: University of Arizona Press.

Yunez, A. 2002. Lessons from NAFTA: The case of Mexico's agricultural sector. Final report to the World Bank, revised version, December.

Yunez, A., and F. Barceinas. 2003. The agriculture of Mexico after ten years of NAFTA implementation. Unpublished paper prepared for the Carnegie Endowment for International Peace.

Yunez, A., and J. Taylor. 2006. The effects of NAFTA and domestic reforms in the agriculture of Mexico: Predictions and facts. *Région et Développement* 23–2006:161–186.

Zabludovsky, J. 1984. Money, foreign indebtedness and export performance in Porfirist Mexico. Ph.D. dissertation, Yale University.

Zabludovsky, J. 1990. Trade liberalization and macroeconomic adjustment. In D. S. Brothers and A. E. Wick, eds., *Mexico's Search for a New Development Strategy*. Boulder, CO: Westview Press.

Zedillo, E. 1986. Mexico's recent balance of payments experience and prospects for growth. *World Development* 14(8):963–991.

Index